Richard Tregaskis

RICHARD TREGASKIS

To Bill:
Hope you enjoy
the book! *Best wishes,*

REPORTING UNDER FIRE
FROM GUADALCANAL
TO VIETNAM *Ray E. Boomhower*

High Road Books   Albuquerque

*High Road Books is an imprint
of the University of New Mexico Press*

© 2021 by Ray E. Boomhower
All rights reserved. Published 2021
Printed in the United States of America

ISBN 978-0-8263-6288-9 (cloth)
ISBN 978-0-8263-6289-6 (electronic)

Library of Congress Control Number: 2021939812

Founded in 1889, the University of New Mexico sits on the traditional homelands
of the Pueblo of Sandia. The original peoples of New Mexico—Pueblo, Navajo,
and Apache—since time immemorial have deep connections to the land and have
made significant contributions to the broader community statewide. We honor
the land itself and those who remain stewards of this land throughout the
generations and also acknowledge our committed relationship to Indigenous
peoples. We gratefully recognize our history.

Cover illustration: Richard Tregaskis Collection, COLL/566,
Marine Corps History Division, Quantico, VA
Frontispiece: Richard Tregaskis Collection, American Heritage Center,
University of Wyoming, Laramie, WY
Designed by Mindy Basinger Hill
Composed in Garamond Premier Pro and Cg Alpin Gothic

As always, for Megan.

The lure of the front is like an opiate. After abstinence and the tedium of workaday life, its attraction becomes more and more insistent. Perhaps the hazards of battle, perhaps the danger itself, stir the imagination and give transcendent meanings to things ordinarily taken for granted.

RICHARD TREGASKIS | *Invasion Diary* (1944)

CONTENTS

PROLOGUE

Walking down from the mountain, the man in the American uniform could hear the scream of something sinister headed his way. Months of previous combat experience caused him to instinctively dive to the rocky ground for safety. It was too late. He felt a "smothering explosion" engulf him. In the fraction of the second before unconsciousness came, he knew he had been hit by a German shell. He sensed a "curtain of fire" rise, hesitate, and hover for "an infinite second." An orange mist, like a tropical sunrise, arose and quickly set, leaving him, with the curtain descending, gently, in the dark.

Unconsciousness came and went in seconds. When he awoke, he knew he had been badly wounded. In that moment he realized something he had long suspected: there was no sensation of pain, only a "movie without sound." Still stretched out on the rocky ground of Mount Corno in the Italian countryside, he could see, a couple of feet from him, his helmet, which had been gouged in two places, one hole at the front and the second ripped through the side. Catastrophe. How could he manage to make it to safety, nearly a mile away down the trail, where, he hoped, the officers that had accompanied him earlier on the mountain, Col. Bill Yarborough and Capt. Edmund Tomasik, were waiting? It was eerily quiet, as if time stood still. He could still move a bit. He sat up and saw figures of crouched men he did not recognize running up the trail. He tried to yell at them but found that his voice produced only unintelligible noise instead of words. Although rattled at first, he became calmer when he realized he could still think; he had lost his power of speech but not his power to "understand or generate thought."

Another shell came screaming down. He hugged the ground and braced for the imminent explosion. When it came, he found it was a "tinny echo" of what had before been powerful and terrifying. A frightened soldier skidded into his position to escape the danger, and he tried to talk to the man, seeking his help, but only produced the strangled question: "Can help?" As another shell burst farther down the mountain slope, the soldier, with terror etched across his face, could only say, before he ran away, "I can't help you, I'm too scared."

In a haze, he barely remembered the medic who flopped beside him, bandaged his wounded head, and jammed a shot of morphine into his arm. Almost as soon as he had appeared, the medic was gone, and again he was alone. He realized that if he wanted to ever get off that mountain, he had to get up and walk. Almost miraculously, he found his glasses, unbroken, lying on the rocks a few inches away. He tried to pick them up with his right hand, and realized his entire right arm was stiff and useless. Using his left hand, he picked up his glasses, put them on, and, almost absentmindedly, placed his helmet on his bandaged head, where it sat, a fine, if precariously balanced, souvenir.

As he staggered down the mountain, he kept dropping and picking up his helmet, and he came under fire from a procession of shells. Once a shell burst so close to him that he could have touched it. He was not frightened, but only startled at its nearness. Finally, he wedged his tall, lanky frame into a small cave to wait out the barrage. He remembered being unconcerned about his plight; nothing seemed to disturb him. In fact, it seemed somehow that after escaping so many close calls during the war, his luck would finally run out. Only his instinct for self-preservation told him what to do. Despite the blood running copiously down his face, blurring his vision, he got up and staggered down the mountain like a robot, unsteady on his feet but under some directional control.

Rounding a bend in the trail, he saw Yarborough and Tomasik trying to help a wounded enlisted man. A surge of pleasure surged through him as he realized he would be saved. The colonel started to wave to him, then stopped, noticing his bloody glasses and blood-soaked shirt. With Yarborough's help, he made it to a house to await transportation for medical assistance. The wounded man, Richard Tregaskis, a correspondent with the International News Service, looked across the room and saw a line of soldiers, with "fascinated, awed looks on their faces as they stared at me, the badly wounded man." Those spectators, he noted, imagined more pain than he actually felt. "Such is the friendly power of shock," Tregaskis remembered, "and the stubborn will for preservation." Reflecting on his experience, he felt almost a sense of relief that at last it had happened: he had been hit. He felt sure he was supposed to die, but he did not.

Finally transported to the Thirty-Eighth Evacuation Hospital, Tregaskis underwent several hours of brain surgery performed by Maj. William R. Pitts. A shell fragment had driven ten to twelve bone fragments into Tregaskis's brain, and part of his skull had been blown away, with the brain, said Pitts, "oozing out through the scalp wound." Recuperating, Tregaskis received a visit from one of the biggest stars of journalism in World War II, Ernie Pyle, columnist for the Scripps-Howard newspaper chain. After chatting with his colleague, Pyle wrote in his popular column that if he had been injured as Tregaskis had been, he would have "gone home and rested on my laurels forever."

Tregaskis did go back to the United States, to the U.S. Army's Walter Reed Hospital in Washington, DC, where doctors put in an inert metal (tantalum) plate to cover the hole in his skull. It seemed an end to what had been a brilliant wartime career that included witnessing the Doolittle Raiders take off from the pitching deck of an aircraft carrier to bomb Japan, being in the thick of the action during the Battle of Midway, surviving seven nerve-wracking weeks with U.S. Marines on Guadalcanal, writing a bestselling book about his experiences (*Guadalcanal Diary*), and accompanying American and British troops for the invasions of Sicily and Italy.

Despite his brush with death and several months of painstaking effort on his part to regain his power of speech and the feeling in his right hand, Tregaskis did not decide to remain safely at home; he returned to the war. He traveled to Europe for the Normandy beachhead, then followed the First Infantry Division ("The Big Red One") across France, Belgium, Holland, and into Germany. Asked by the editors of a national magazine to return to the Pacific to follow the crew of a B-29 Superfortress as it prepared for bombing missions against Japanese cities, Tregaskis was asked by an editor, "Do you really want to go?" Without hesitating, Tregaskis gave an answer that any reporter who covered World War II would understand: "I don't want to go, but I think I ought to go." He went.

INTRODUCTION
"A Living Nightmare"

Sprawled alone in the broken shell of what once had been a house in Aachen, Germany, in the fall of 1944, Richard Tregaskis, an accredited war correspondent for the International News Service, could hear from his temporary sanctuary the "ripping sounds" of an enemy machine gun firing at advancing American troops in a nearby rubble-filled street. Tregaskis was no stranger to combat at this point in his career and had always been eager to be close to where American forces were fighting, serving as an embedded reporter long before the term came into use. He watched from the deck of a U.S. Navy cruiser as Lt. Col. James Doolittle's B-25B Mitchell bombers took off from the carrier USS *Hornet* to bomb Tokyo. Later, he was on the *Hornet* to witness its dive-bombers and torpedo planes, several of which did not return, hurtle off the ship's flight deck on their way to attack the Japanese fleet during the critical Battle of Midway.[1]

For nearly seven weeks in the summer of 1942, Tregaskis had a front-row seat to one of the turning points of the war in the Pacific, the Battle of Guadalcanal. It was by no means a certainty that the operation, code named Watchtower, would be successful. "We had no proper maps, we did not know if the beaches were defended nor how many enemy to expect," recalled Gen. Alexander A. Vandegrift, commander of the First Marine Division, responsible for taking the island. Tregaskis was one of two civilian reporters (the other was Bob Miller of United Press) who landed with the marines and stayed to cover their attempt to capture and hold the island against fierce attacks from the land, air, and sea by the Japanese. Some of the young Americans assigned to the island were not completely trained, Tregaskis observed, "but they were Marines, and being Marines they were ready to fight and eager to be the first to fight for us—God Bless them!" In his dispatches to INS client newspapers across the United States, Tregaskis captured what it was like to live and fight on a "pesthole that reeked of death, struggle, and disease." He later turned the jottings from his battered notebooks into the bestselling 1943 book *Guadalcanal Diary*, a work that awakened those on the American home front to the long struggle ahead to achieve victory.[2]

Tregaskis related his sometimes terrifying experiences to his readers simply and poignantly, using a day-by-day diary format to report what he had observed and the often matter-of-fact stories of combat told to him by enlisted men and officers. The correspondent had a remarkable journey to publication. His manuscript, heavily scrutinized by military censors, was received by his INS editors on November 6, 1942, submitted to the New York publishing firm Random House on November 11, and accepted for publication the next day. *Life* magazine contracted with Random House for a condensed version of the book, the Book of the Month Club selected it for its thousands of members, and a Honolulu bookstore preordered 5,300 copies. By the late 1960s, *Guadalcanal Diary* had sold more than three million copies and had been translated into twelve languages, including Japanese, Chinese, Spanish, French, and Danish. The Harvard-educated reporter from Elizabeth, New Jersey, had accomplished all this while dealing with what once had been a fatal illness—diabetes—a condition he kept secret from everyone but his doctor and family. For his first combat assignment in the Pacific, Tregaskis carried with him a case (one hundred tins) of sardines because he could not handle the high-carbohydrate fare served by navy cooks on his ship, as well as a handbook (*Diabetic Manual—for the Doctor and Patient*) about the disease from an early pioneer in the field. Afraid at being found out, Tregaskis even forged an inscription in camouflaged handwriting in the handbook that read, "To my friend Richard Tregaskis, best wishes from Doctor Elliott P. Joslin." If his owning the book had been questioned by anyone, Tregaskis believed he could "demonstrate that Dr. Joslin was a friend and I carried his book only for sentimental reasons."[3]

Standing approximately six feet five inches tall, Tregaskis had been warned by many friends before going into action that the Japanese, if they did not kill him, would capture him and use him as an observation post, but he left Guadalcanal relatively unscathed physically except for bouts with gastroenteritis and malaria. Tregaskis considered himself an unlikely type to be a war correspondent, due to his height, thin frame, and poor eyesight, but he risked his life out of a double sense of duty, duty to his country and to the men who fought on its behalf. He was also driven by an insatiable curiosity to uncover the stories of those who experienced combat. After his adventures in the Pacific, Tregaskis moved to the European theater, flying on a photo-reconnaissance mission with Col. Elliott Roosevelt (President Franklin D. Roosevelt's son) over Palermo, Sicily; watching from the nose of a B-17 Flying Fortress on the first bombing mission against Rome; and accompanying American and British forces during the invasion of Sicily, staying on the Mediterranean island until it was secured. His willingness to go where the action was impressed one soldier, who told the correspondent, "How you guys go ahead and stick out your necks when you don't have to—well, it just beats hell out of me!" Tregaskis had a simple answer: "But we certainly do have to—that's our job." When American troops were in trouble, he even put his notebook and pencil aside to pitch in and help, delivering much-needed medical supplies, including blood plasma, to a unit in the Italian mountains.[4]

Tregaskis's luck ran out during his next assignment, accompanying Allied forces on the invasion of Italy. On November 22, 1943, after observing U.S. Rangers battling Germans on Mount Corno near Cassino, Italy, Tregaskis was returning to headquarters to write his story when a German shell landed near him. Shrapnel struck and pierced his helmet, lodging in his brain and causing partial paralysis that robbed him for a time of his power to speak, read, and write. "They carried me out with a hole in my skull the size of a soup spoon and bone and steel fragments embedded two inches deep in my brain," he recalled. "I worked my way toward the States through six Army and Navy hospitals. Finally, a tantalum [metal] plate was put in my head at Walter Reed Hospital in Washington [DC]—and I went back to the fighting front." Before doing so, Tregaskis, who received a Purple Heart from the military, produced a second book, *Invasion Diary*, detailing his time covering the invasions of Sicily and Italy, his near-death experience on Mount Corno, and his tortuous recovery. Throughout all his difficulties, he kept his sense of humor. When a friend visited him at Walter Reed, Tregaskis asked him to do him a favor. "Sure, anything," the friend responded. "Before they put the [metal] plate on,"

Tregaskis asked, "take a look inside my head and see if my brain is still there." The friend obliged and confirmed that the brain remained where it should be. "Fine," said a relieved Tregaskis. "I might have to use it some day."[5]

A recovered Tregaskis caught up with Americans forces in the summer of 1944 after their successful breakout from the Normandy beachhead, taking time to fly on a mission in a modified P-38 fighter, becoming, he proclaimed, the first correspondent to be involved in a dogfight with an enemy aircraft (by the war's end, Tregaskis boasted that he had flown on thirty-two combat missions in a variety of aircraft). He did notice a change in his attitude after almost being killed. "I was aware of a new and dreadful sensitivity to the dangers of war—an acute, nervous state that made the sounds of incoming shells or enemy machine-gun fire crushing and unbearable." His nerves continued to be "shaky" as he made his way across France, Belgium, Holland, and into Nazi Germany. Tregaskis decided to put himself to the test by participating in the battle for Aachen alongside a frontline unit, F Company, Twenty-Sixth Infantry Regiment (known as the Blue Spaders), First Infantry Division (the "Big Red One"). If he survived he knew he would be equipped with a new set of nerves. He immersed himself into a perilous form of warfare, street fighting, a task Tregaskis described in an article for the *Saturday Evening Post* as "the bitter, exasperating block-by-block and house-by-house struggle which develops when war sweeps through thickly settled communities and the enemy is determined to make a fight of it." The fundamental doctrine for such fighting, Tregaskis quickly learned, boiled down to firepower, "the spending of millions of rounds of rifle and machine-gun bullets, thousands of tank and self-propelled gun shells, most of them, incidentally, at point-blank range." An American officer had confided to Tregaskis that he was glad such a destructive type of warfare was occurring in an enemy nation, Germany, as opposed to such friendly countries as France, Belgium, or the Netherlands. "If you're held up by one sniper in a block of houses," the officer pointed out, "you can blow them all down, without thinking of hurting anyone's feelings."[6]

As Tregaskis cautiously made his way through Aachen's rubble-filled streets to join the second squad of the first platoon with whom he would be staying, he felt "waves of terrible apprehension" washing over his body. He was now more aware than ever that the "worst could happen to *me*, that I could be a statistic in the casualty list and not someone else." Because of what he had suffered on Mount Corno, he knew what being wounded meant: the "long sessions of jolting pain, the horrible hours of not knowing whether you would ever recover, the contemplation of ways to kill yourself if you became no more than a vegetable." Tregaskis hooked up with the second squad, huddled in a cellar that served as an air-raid shelter in roofless Aachen, a city of approximately 150,000 people whose history as the birthplace of Charlemagne, the king of the Franks, had served as an inspiration for Adolf Hitler's orders to hold it "at all costs," with every man expected to "stand fast or die at his post." Talking with a corporal, Tregaskis learned that the eleven-man unit he joined had suffered three casualties in the past few days. The events of the next day failed to calm Tregaskis's nerves. The squad had been ordered to clear the city blocks ahead of them with the support of some 90 mm tank destroyers. Although the "haughty coughing" of the tank's guns, the shattering impacts of their shells beyond them, and the shaking of the earth as they hit were merely the "usual sounds before an attack," he discovered that his nerves had already reached their breaking point.[7]

Before participating in any military operation, Tregaskis always took the time to prepare himself for the coming ordeal, including calculating his odds for survival. He usually remained confident that the "worst could not happen to me; that chance would stay on my side." What he witnessed, however, almost overwhelmed him. He remembered Aachen as

> a blur of terror, a living nightmare: running down streets; faces full of dirt as shells screamed in and you hit the rubble which was the earth; the shock of the cracking bullets that were coming too close (close ones don't whine as they do on TV—if they're dangerous, they crack); the knowing that an unseen enemy rifleman or machine gunner is trying to kill you; the breathless hunt for him among the ruins; the silencing of him, usually with grenades or artillery; the horror on men's faces at the moment you know well—when you have been hit; and the dreadful ignorance of whether or not you are going to die.[8]

The fury and madness of combat might have broken Tregaskis if it had not been for one man, Capt. Ozell Smoot, F Company's commander. The officer from Oklahoma City, Oklahoma, magically seemed to appear whenever his soldiers needed a steadying hand. Darting into the street "while the firing was still going on all around," said Tregaskis, Smoot would stop to talk to his platoon leaders "as calmly as if we were on maneuvers. He would make sure our wounded were carried out and reached ambulances. And he would spot snipers and Kraut artillery and observation posts with a cool eye and call artillery or mortars down on them." When one of his officers was hit by a sniper's bullet and seriously wounded, Smoot raced up to his comrade to mumble "the tender unprintable things that one brave man will say to another," Tregaskis reported. Smoot cut the wounded man's clothes away from his gaping wound, fed him sulfa pills, and shouted to bring up a medic and a stretcher team to take the fallen soldier to the rear. At the same time, Smoot never let his attention waver from his duties. "He'd say, with great tenderness, that the wounded man would be all right; that the jeep would be coming any minute now," Tregaskis wrote. "And then he'd wheel and bark an order, and lard that order with hair-curling cuss words." The reporter remembered his astonishment at Smoot's coolness and effectiveness when matters were at their worst. "He never seemed concerned that he would be killed or wounded," he said of Smoot. "He was just what a company commander should be: a prime mover, a leader, an example of courage."[9]

In addition to serving as an example for his men, Smoot helped steady the anxious reporter's shaken spirits, as Tregaskis suffered from what he described as "Purple Heart syndrome." Almost every soldier, he noted, naturally assumed that he would be safe while under fire and that "the wounds will happen to anybody else but him, that he is not a statistic, and that somehow some unquestioned magic will keep him safe, no matter how bad the casualties get or how scared he is." When the nearly worst happened, and a soldier was wounded, shock and pain soon followed. "And very often," said Tregaskis, "if he is not given to powerful flights of imagination, if he is not the imaginative type, more a man of deeds than thought, the shock can get very profound. The idea is burned in letters of fire in his brain: *I can get hurt too*."[10]

Tregaskis, while huddled in a hole in the ground in Aachen, suffered from his own brand of the syndrome. He could hear a fusillade of small-arms fire coming at him like a cascade: "It seemed closer; it seemed to be moving in *my* direction." The sound stopped for a moment and, at that instant, Smoot skidded into the broken bricks that formed Tregaskis's sanctuary. The commander grinned at Tregaskis and mentioned in an offhand manner that it had been a "rough day." Reading Tregaskis's face, or perhaps having heard from members of his platoon that the correspondent had "been running much too scared," Smoot quietly related, "I got it myself a couple of times. I came in with the Division at North Africa." In another lull in the fighting, Smoot added, without looking at Tregaskis as he talked, "It took me a while to figure it out.

Your chances aren't any worse after you've been hit once. It just seems like it. It takes more guts because you know what can happen."[11]

Just seconds after he finished his conversation with the reporter, Smoot left Tregaskis behind, running down the street toward his men. His words, however, had made a difference. Tregaskis recalled that the "fighting seemed less dreadful, and I knew I had gained a new grip on myself." The captain had restored to Tregaskis the toughness he needed, a "new kind of toughness, the seasoned kind of inner strength that comes after battle scars." Both Tregaskis and Smoot emerged from Aachen physically unscathed. The reporter was lucky enough to be able to return to the United States for some needed rest before an assignment for the *Saturday Evening Post* to follow the crew of a B-29 Superfortress bomber making its way overseas for service in the Pacific against targets in Japan.[12]

Tregaskis could not, however, get Aachen out of his mind. Seized with what he called "a fever" to write something about that battle, in a couple of months of "frenzied work," he produced a novel, titled *Stronger Than Fear*, which he dedicated "[t]o the valor of the infantry, the soldiers without armor who are the vanguard of every attack." The book detailed the experiences of a captain named Paul Kreider, "not unlike Ozell Smoot," who fought his own battle with fear during intense fighting in a city Tregaskis named Unterbach, a stand-in for Aachen. "The writing of the book was a hard struggle," he recalled, "but when it was over, I felt I had distilled a central truth of life at war, and perhaps even of life in general. The truth was that when you are faced with a mortal fear which demands the deepest kind of courage, and you can find that courage, you have won life's most important battle, the battle for self-respect."[13]

As he prepared to report onslaught against the Japanese in the Pacific, Tregaskis lost touch with Smoot. Not until the war was over did he learn the officer's fate. Smoot had been killed in combat on November 17, 1944, about a month after he and Tregaskis had parted company in Aachen. The officer had been one of the approximately thirty-three thousand American casualties of the tough winter fighting in the Hürtgen Forest. "He died a soldier's death," Tregaskis noted of Smoot, "leading his troops in battle, taking the chances he had to with his usual calm competence. He died facing the ultimate danger, respected and loved by his men."[14]

Tregaskis's interaction with Smoot typified his time as one of the approximately 1,800 men and women who worked as combat reporters (a job Tregaskis once described as "an outsider with special privileges") during World War II.

"He never in his career as a correspondent sent home a rewrite of a head-quarters communiqué," Robert Considine said of his fellow INS employee. "He didn't believe in communiqués. He had to see for himself." Tregaskis knew from personal experience which of his colleagues would not be content with merely taking information from military headquarters safe behind the lines. To make their dispatches as accurate as possible, they would make the fatiguing journeys, he pointed out, "up to the various division headquarters, even the progressively smaller units—to regiments and battalions, and even companies—each stop grown increasingly dangerous, yet more productive of the real facts—as the distance from the enemy diminished." Such reporters as Don Whitehead of the Associated Press, Russell Hill of the *New York Herald Tribune*, and George Hicks of radio's Blue Network all possessed the "courage to go up and get the material," Tregaskis said, as well as having the guts to write about what they uncovered honestly, even with the constant demand from their editors for sensational headlines from the front. The best correspondents, he added, stuck to the facts, "even when it hurt," when a less principled rival "might twist a story into a fake, to make it a 'better' story."[15]

As an example, Tregaskis remembered an unnamed correspondent who visited Guadalcanal for a few days during the height of the fighting on the island. The reporter fled when the situation appeared grim, but he did find the time to file one of the most astounding articles Tregaskis had ever read. A high-ranking Marine Corps officer told him about the story, which had been stopped by the censor. "This man is amazing," the officer told Tregaskis. "He's written everything that happened since we landed on Guadalcanal as if he'd seen it all in the couple of days he was here—and he's added blonde amazons flying Japanese planes, for good measure." Other examples Tregaskis cited included reporters datelining their articles as written from Sicily during the early days of the invasion when they were really crafted while the authors were far behind the lines in Algiers; a correspondent who described the "glint of the sun on the windows of the Vatican during the first [air] raid on Rome," all from the vantage point of more than five miles high; and those he accompanied while covering the fighting in northern Europe who "reported things which did not happen at all, except in some mysterious fourth dimension invisible to my human eye."[16]

Other reporters, civilian and military, admired Tregaskis's "profuse" note taking and his willingness to "stick his neck out when the value of the story is proportional to the risks involved in getting it." Ernie Pyle, arguably the best-known chronicler of fighting men in World War II, in a column he wrote after visiting Tregaskis following his wounding in Italy, noted that the INS reporter was "no adventurer, but a deeply sincere and conscientious man who did what he did because he felt he should." Dedication to his chosen profession had been part of Tregaskis's character from his early days in journalism. In seeking his job with the INS in early January 1941, Tregaskis, who had worked for a variety of Boston newspapers owned by William Randolph Heart, wrote Barry Faris, the news service's editor in chief, that he was in "excellent health, unmarried, unattached" and stood ready to "go anywhere."[17]

The places the INS sent Tregaskis were dangerous, but he had the luxury of being an officially accredited correspondent, wearing a green armband with the letter "C" to indicate his status (the armband was later replaced by a patch worn on the sleeve). He and his colleagues wore uniforms so they would not be shot as spies if they were captured, were given honorary officer status, and could count on the military providing them food, housing, and transportation. There were times, however, when Tregaskis strayed from the War Department's strict regulations, especially one stating that correspondents could not "exercise command, be placed in positions of authority over military personnel, nor will they be armed." While with the marines on Guadalcanal, Tregaskis had learned early that the war between the Japanese and Americans would be waged with little, or no, mercy. Both sides did everything they could to dehumanize the other. The Japanese military viewed surrendering as dishonorable, and its soldiers fought to the death, viewing becoming prisoners of war as shameful to their family's honor. They sometimes even pretended to be dead or injured before rising to kill as many of the Americans as possible. Taking no chances, marines on Guadalcanal, Tregaskis reported, pumped round after round into Japanese bodies with rifles and pistols just to make sure they were really dead. "War takes on a very personal flavor when other men are shooting at you, and you feel little sympathy at seeing them killed," Tregaskis said. These atrocities, combined with outrage over the sneak attack on Pearl Harbor and racial hatred, fueled a take-no-prisoners approach by American ground forces in the Pacific. Ghastly acts were committed by both sides. Japanese soldiers mutilated the bodies of marines and soldiers, leaving them for their comrades to find on patrols. They also regularly shot at army medics and navy corpsmen attempting to aid wounded men on the battlefield. Although it was prohibited under military law, a few Americans pried gold teeth from the mouths of enemy corpses and passed along instructions about the "cooking and scraping of the heads of Japanese," preparing to keep the skulls as souvenirs for themselves and even for loved ones back home.[18]

For soldiers and noncombatants alike, danger lurked everywhere in the Pacific. Following a major action on the island—the Battle of Bloody Ridge—Tregaskis had been sitting on the side of a ridge that looked over the valley where American tents were located. "A throng of Zeroes were dogfighting with our Grummans in the clouds and I was trying to spot the planes," he recalled. "Suddenly I saw the foliage move in a tree across the valley. I looked again and was astonished to see the figure of a man in the crotch of the tree. He seemed to be moving his arms and upper body." Tregaskis had spotted a Japanese sniper, who fired at the American several times, but missed his target. Retreating behind a tent to seek cover, Tregaskis, as he related in *Guadalcanal Diary*, had been angered at being shot at and wanted "to get a rifle and fire at the sniper." What Tregaskis failed to relate in his book, however, was that both he and Miller, while on the island, were armed with Colt 1911A1 pistols. "We knew and the Marines knew that if we ran up against Jap[anese] snipers, they weren't going to ask for our credentials," Tregaskis reminisced after the war. Upon leaving Guadalcanal on a B-17 bomber, the correspondent helped man one of the plane's .50-caliber machine guns during a reconnaissance mission over Bougainville and fired upon an attacking Japanese Zero fighter. "The Zero was far out and I could see my tracers, like golden balls on a string, curving aft of the enemy plane," Tregaskis wrote a friend. "I corrected a little, saw the tracers going into the fuselage. The Jap keeled over and came straight toward me. . . . I hung onto the gun grips and kept on firing, and the Jap, in a three-quarter frontal pass, curved along our flank. . . . One of us hit him in the engine and he went down. Naturally, I think it was my shooting that did it."[19]

A less lethal problem Tregaskis encountered during the war involved dealing with censorship, one imposed by military authorities and the other self-motivated. Dispatches were carefully checked by public relations officers, many of them former civilian journalists, who reviewed them to ensure that no information was included that could possibly aid the enemy. The officers who censored articles had to contend with the possibility that material they had cleared as safe could come back to haunt them. Fletcher Pratt, the military correspondent for *Harper's* magazine, remembered that a new PRO for the navy, which had a reputation as the strictest service when it came to censorship, had been told before taking up his duties that he would be judged not on "what you get into the papers but on what you keep out of them." An oft-repeated anecdote had it that during an unguarded moment at a party in Washington, DC, a top navy official had expressed the view that he would not tell the press anything until the war was over, and then he would tell them who had won. Such strictness was unnecessary, if John Steinbeck is to be believed. The bestselling novelist had risked his life covering the war in Europe for the *New York Herald Tribune* and noted that he and other Allied reporters "edited ourselves much more than we were edited. We felt responsible to what was called the home front." Correspondents had to walk a fine line in their articles. The best of them attempted to present to their readers a true picture of the sacrifice being made by those on the front lines and the inevitable errors and miscalculations of combat, as seen in the work of such journalists as Pyle, Tregaskis, Keith Wheeler of the *Chicago Times*, A. J. Liebling of *The New Yorker*, Robert L. Sherrod and John Hersey of *Time* magazine, and Martha Gelhorn of *Collier's*. Sherrod even pressed President Franklin D. Roosevelt to release to the public the grim photographs and moving pictures that captured the bloody fighting on Betio Island during the Battle of Tarawa to awaken them to the long road to victory in the Pacific. But reporters also worried, as Steinbeck noted, that unless the home front was "carefully protected from the whole account of what war was like, it might panic."[20]

At its worst, censorship, according to Tregaskis, obscured facts to such a degree that the public might begin to believe its side was winning when it was really losing. At best, he added, censorship offered a check against giving the enemy information that could impede Allied military operations or cost lives. While covering the war, the finest censor setup he encountered occurred during the Battle of Northern Europe following the Normandy breakout, a time "where one could write almost freely," while the worst came from U.S. Navy censors in the Pacific in the early days of the war. He also discovered that censors were more liberal during times when the front lines were static and tightest when an attack was imminent. Usually, censorship could be, and was, relaxed as time passed (it took a year for Tregaskis's reports about the Doolittle Raid to be published). Although Tregaskis made his living delivering regular dispatches from the front lines for publication in newspapers across the United States, he came to believe that Americans might instead obtain a better understanding about a battle from a magazine article or a book than by scanning day-to-day stories. By the time a book appeared, he noted, it was too late for the enemy to make "military use of the specific facts in the book."[21]

One aspect of his profession that saddened Tregaskis involved his belief that editors on the home front were certain that the public would accept only good news and could not take or be engrossed in news about reverses in American fortunes on the battlefield. "There is, of course," he noted, "as much variation as there is in reputations, but may times I have heard editors of different publications say in effect: 'The public isn't interested in bad news; you can't sell it.'" For his part, Tregaskis thought that anyone who possessed that opinion had to be "laboring under the delusion that the American public has a child mind; and furthermore, the mind of a *spoiled* child, which is probably as false and low-grade a conclusion as the presumption that Americans cannot and will not learn to read the war news intelligently."[22]

Tregaskis had often pondered why he and others risked their lives to report on the war. Good correspondents, like other people of action, were generally unwilling to make themselves heroes, he said, but most "will admit that they take chances in war zones for the same reason the mountain climber gave when asked why he wanted to scale [Mount] Everest: 'Because it is there.'" Although Associated Press reporter Hal Boyle joked that all one needed to be a war correspondent was "a strong stomach, a weak mind, and plenty of endurance," he and his colleagues were aware of the dangers they faced. Casualty rates for reporters during the war matched that of the American military, with 2.2 percent of reporters killed and 6.8 percent wounded, while the figures for the armed forces were 2.5 percent killed and 4.5 percent wounded. Reporters even joked about the risks they took in order to get their stories. Tregaskis noted that one of the first American correspondents to die in World War II was Robert Post of the *New York Times*, who was killed when the B-24 Liberator bomber he in was shot down during a mission over Wilhelmshaven, Germany, on February 26, 1943. "For a long time after that a correspondent who was killed doing his duty in a frontline area was said to have taken 'the Post road,'" Tregaskis said. Despite the deaths and disabilities that went hand in hand with war, he said there was another facet that drew people "whatever their personal persuasion or sex: the instant elimination of personal ambition in favor of unselfish sacrifice to a great cause. Never mind that the fact that the cause is the destruction of an enemy and the expenditure of resources—including life and health—to destroy something the foe considers highly valuable." Still, he acknowledged, "War can be as exciting as anything in life."[23]

Tregaskis had discussed his role as a war correspondent during a September 1943 bull session with Robert Capa, the Hungarian combat photographer later made famous by his grainy images of the D-Day landings. The journalists were waiting in a small Sicilian town called Licata with the men of the 504th Parachute Infantry Regiment, Eighty-Second Airborne Division. While Capa relaxed by playing poker, Tregaskis, the photographer noted, "typed glowing preinvasion stories which never passed the censor." Just before the planned Allied landing at Salerno and the invasion of Italy, the paratroopers were "expecting to be dropped in Rome, and Capa and I were going with them," remembered Tregaskis, who had participated in a practice parachute jump while in the Pacific and had also flown in a practice glider flight in North Africa. Capa had been thrilled to be a part of one of the "big scoops of the war," noting that while other photographers were taking pictures of "a dreary beach and maybe a few local mayors," he would be "firmly established in the best hotel in Italy, calling the bartender by his first name." The top-secret plan called for an airborne mission on Rome the day before the Salerno operation, with Italian military authorities cooperating by lighting the way to the Ciampino airport, keeping German fighters on the ground, and providing trucks for use by American troops. "Fortunately, the mission was aborted at the last minute—fortunately, because it was discovered that five German divisions surrounded the airfield," said Tregaskis.[24]

On the night before the mission was scheduled to happen, Tregaskis and Capa were sitting on the edge of the Licata airfield, trying to fill the time by talking about the war. Tregaskis mentioned to the photographer that he had flown from North Africa to Sicily in a Douglas C-47 transport aircraft with one of the ranking officers of the Eighty-Second and had said to him that he believed war to be "tragic waste and such bloody double destruction." The officer, who had already been tested in battle, merely smiled at the reporter and said frankly, "I like it." Relating the conversation to Capa, Tregaskis theorized that there was a distinctive philosophy about a frontline area. "I vouchsafed the idea that when you were at the front you didn't expect to live long," Tregaskis recalled. "Thus you tended to be free of the petty selfishness that governs us in times of absolute safety and assumed longevity. At the front if someone wants your shirt you'll give it to him. Men are unselfish and self-sacrificing as never elsewhere. While they're trying to kill people on the other side they'll die for people on their own." Capa's usual attitude was "sardonic and cynical," and his upbringing in central Europe often led him to poke fun at many of Tregaskis's ideas as "over American. We were good friends, but he violently opposed some of my theses as too idealistic and unrealistic; at such times he would address me as 'Tregasgoose.'" On this occasion, Capa called his friend Tregasgoose but endorsed his ideas, "which was quite a concession for him." According to Tregaskis, Capa told him, "I agree with you Tregasgoose; fighting is exciting."[25]

AUTHOR'S NOTE   World War II in the Pacific Theater was a conflict with little or no mercy shown by either side. The hatred engendered by Japan's devastating surprise attack on the American fleet at Pearl Harbor without a formal declaration of war, mixed with racial animosity, produced such harsh epithets for the enemy as "Japs," a term Tregaskis used in his dispatches from the Pacific. Although such a term is anathema today, I have retained it when quoting Tregaskis's work.

1

A CRUSADE FOR IDEALS AND SURVIVAL

The manuscript came into the offices of the International News Service, 235 East Forty-Fifth Street, New York, without fanfare in early November 1942. It had made quite a journey. The pages had been transported from Fleet Head-quarters in Pearl Harbor, Hawaii, via airmail from a young INS reporter, Richard Tregaskis. For the previous two months, Tregaskis had been in the Southwest Pacific on a little-known island in the Solomons named Guadalca-nal, accompanying the approximately eleven thousand men of the First Ma-rine Division who stormed the beaches there on August 7, 1942. The landing marked America's first use of ground troops in a major offensive against the Japanese Empire. Tregaskis's dedication to his job during his time on Gua-dalcanal, however, had impressed the marines' commander, Gen. Alexander Vandegrift. The general recalled that Tregaskis seemed to be everywhere, and the information he acquired was "factual and not a canned hand-out." Van-degrift especially remembered that during the height of the fighting for what came to be known as Edson's Ridge, he could hear through the darkness the sound of a typewriter clacking away. "I asked who could be writing at this time when he could not possibly see the paper," noted Vandegrift. "Dick spoke up, 'It's me, General, I want to get this down while I am still able. Don't worry about my seeing, I am using the touch system.'"[1]

On November 6, Barry Faris, INS editor-in-chief, wrote Tregaskis that his manuscript—with information so secret that military censors in the U.S. Navy offices at Pearl Harbor had locked away the reporter's notebooks and big, black diary in a safe every night after he had finished working on his story during the day—had arrived that morning. Faris turned the pages over to Ward Greene, executive editor of King Features, owned and operated, as was INS, by newspaper publisher William Randolph Hearst. Faris wrote that Greene would make every attempt to get Tregaskis's manuscript accepted by a book publisher and subsequently serialized in magazines. "I did not have a chance to read it thoroughly as I would have liked," Faris informed Tregaskis, who would be splitting the revenue from the book fifty-fifty with his employer, "but from what I did see I think you did a magnificent job on it."[2]

One person who did take the time to read Tregaskis's writing from beginning to end was Bennett Cerf, cofounder with his friend Donald Klopfer of the New York publishing firm Random House. Greene had distributed copies of the manuscript to nine publishers and asked them to bid for the opportunity to publish the book, a method "that had never been done before," Cerf noted. Just the day before he received Tregaskis's text, Cerf had been talking with his colleagues that the first book that came out about Guadalcanal would "be a knockout because Guadalcanal marked the turning of the tide" in the war in the Pacific, which had been going badly for the Allies since the Japanese had bombed the American fleet at Pearl Harbor in the Hawaiian Islands on December 7, 1941. As the publisher noted, "the dictators were ready and the liberty-loving people were caught unprepared."[3]

Cerf received the manuscript from King Features on November 11, took it home with him, read it that night, called Greene at nine the next morning, and told him, "I've got to have this book." A pleased Cerf related years later that Random House had signed up to publish the young reporter's work before "any of the other eight publishers had even started reading it." His premonition that the American public would be interested in learning more about the marines and their pitched battles with the enemy on a remote island thousands of miles away turned out to be accurate. Rushed into print on January 18, 1943, *Guadalcanal Diary* became a bestseller and the first Random House book to sell more than a hundred thousand copies. Critic John Chamberlain of the *New York Times* wrote that Tregaskis's book served as "a tonic for the war-weary on the homefront," showing to the Japanese and those who doubted America's resolve that a country "doesn't necessarily have to love war in order to fight it."[4]

Although an unknown in the publishing world, Tregaskis had already made a name for himself with his employers at INS and the other correspondents who had followed American forces into battle during the early desperate days of the fighting in the Pacific. Before he landed with the marines on Guadalca-nal, Tregaskis had been on the scene and had written dispatches for INS mem-ber newspapers about some of the main turning points for the American navy, including witnessing from a nearby cruiser Lt. Col. James Doolittle leading his force of army B-25 bombers off the deck of the aircraft carrier USS *Hornet* (CV-8) to bomb Tokyo on April 18, 1942. Confronted by reporters three days later about sketchy information they had received about the U.S. mission, President Franklin D. Roosevelt had blithely said that it had originated from a secret airplane base in the Himalayas at Shangri-La, the fictional Tibetan utopia of James Hilton's 1933 novel *Lost Horizon*. Asked to confirm Japanese reports that enemy aircraft had bombed Tokyo, Roosevelt, pleased with the results of the raid, refused to elaborate, saying only that he was "depending on Japanese reports very largely." Because of wartime censorship, Tregaskis's dispatches about the daring mission—called by a navy admiral "one of the most courageous deeds in all military history"—were not published in American newspapers until a year later.[5]

After the Doolittle Raid, Tregaskis had boarded the *Hornet* and remained with the carrier's officers and enlisted men as they attempted but missed out on joining the other American carriers at the Battle of the Coral Sea in early May 1942. He remained on the *Hornet* for its next foray into the Pacific and saw the carrier's pilots (airedales in naval parlance) take off from its wooden flight deck to seek further revenge for Pearl Harbor against Japanese carriers at the Battle of Midway, a smashing victory for the U.S. Pacific Fleet. While on the *Hornet* before the crucial battle, Tregaskis shared with an engineering officer "an ironic ditty" he had written celebrating that during action, an engineer would be "more or less imprisoned deep within the intestines of a ship," because all hatches had to be securely shut to ensure watertight integrity. Tregaskis's creation read, "The engineer need have no fear / He has no cause for frowning; / He's locked in a well, / Far from bomber and shell, / And his only worry, is drowning." The engineer read the verse, looked at the correspondent seriously, and added, "Or being burned to death by steam." Tregaskis noted that the crewman had offered the extra verse in "such a matter of fact way that it brought home a striking point: that to him such hazards as being drowned or burned to death were simple matters of course."[6]

In his daily interactions with the ship's crew during routine operations and under fire, Tregaskis came to learn more about their attitudes about war and death, which he discovered were "very sane" and matter of fact, as each man might have his life ended any day at sea, either by the enemy's doing or by routine accidents. "I had seen some of our fliers virtually drunk with excitement immediately after their first experience in the maelstrom of actual combat," Tregaskis recalled. "But I was to find that such oft-repeated matters as being locked below decks while there was action above, or sailing through waters thick with submarines, or witnessing accidents, or losing one's best friend in battle, can become routine when repeated often enough." After Midway, in which a number of *Hornet* pilots had been killed, including every member of Torpedo Squadron 8 (VT-8) except for one man, Ens. George Gay, Tregaskis had been startled when gathered for dinner that nobody mentioned the empty chairs at the table. Instead, the conversation "revolved around the usual unimportant matters. But when I reflected on the matter, I could see that silence was the sensible approach."[7]

Covering the Doolittle Raid and Midway represented an impressive achievement for an inexperienced war correspondent hired by the INS shortly before the Japanese attack on Pearl Harbor. Tregaskis had also just learned from his doctor that he suffered from diabetes (a family illness) and had been turned down for service in the war for being nearsighted and a hair too tall for the military's height limit of six feet five inches. Working on the late shift on the rewrite desk at INS's New York office, Tregaskis had grown so despondent about his failed contribution to the war effort that he even contemplated taking his own life. He rallied, however, and excitedly took to his assignment as an INS war correspondent covering Pacific Fleet operations. After all, Tregaskis reflected, the closer he came to "getting killed in this career, the better my story would be, if I survived."[8]

From the Pacific to Sicily, Italy, France, Belgium, Germany, and back to the Pacific, Tregaskis followed the troops, paying the penalty many others paid in the war. "I gave that effort a lot of my own blood and I didn't hold back when it came to risking my neck to do what I was supposed to do," he recalled. In doing so, Tregaskis discovered that he possessed an innate affinity for covering combat, writing his sister Madeline shortly after he had finished his Guadalcanal book that it was funny the way "this war business hits you, after you've been meddling around with it for a while. Action, and particularly some new variety of action, gets to be like a drug. You feel let down without it and with it you feel a sort of unhealthy excitement. And frightening—shooting at people and that sort of thing—comes to have a compelling interest, although you're fully aware of the unpleasantness of it." He even began to look forward to the next assignment, hating to miss any upcoming big battle, even if he had an opportunity to return to his wife, Marian, and his family.[9]

Journalism and adventure had been a big part of Tregaskis's life growing up in Elizabeth, New Jersey. Born on November 28, 1916, he was the second child and first son of Archibald and Maude M. Osterman Tregaskis. Maude, whose family came from Germany and included a long line of scholars and teachers, said that her children were both "excellent students and stood at the head of their classes each month with very few exceptions. They were invited to all the important social functions in our town, and were popular with their classmates and friends." Tregaskis's father had been born in Falmouth in the county of Cornwall in England but had numerous relatives in and around New York City and became a U.S. citizen on September 13, 1906; he married Maude on November 24, 1910. He made his living as head of the editorial department for the Singer Manufacturing Company, which produced Singer sewing machines in a factory on Elizabeth's outskirts. The senior Tregaskis earned a salary high enough to join the local country club. After just one visit, however, the gregarious Archibald resigned because of "what he considered excessive formality," Maude remembered. "I imagine it was from him that Dick inherited his dislike for the overly-formal." She, however, retained her membership so that her children could use the club's tennis courts, "which were excellent," and she enrolled them in the club's dancing class taught by a Miss Florence. While Madeline loved attending the classes, Richard, perhaps put off by the formality of wearing white gloves and bowing to his teacher before each class began, balked at attending and refused to return after just six sessions. Maude took advantage of being so close to New York City, just twenty miles away, and took her children on trips to the city's many cultural institutions, including the Bronx Zoo, the Metropolitan Museum of Art, and the Museum of Natural History. "They became quite well oriented in the latter building, and finally I would wait for them to explore at will whatever they wished to see, while I sat comfortable and waited," Maude recounted. "By that time I am sure I knew every exhibit in the place, starting with the tremendous war canoe on the main floor. It was really a wonderful education for children."[10]

As a boy, the young Tregaskis had been a keen reader, drawn, he remembered, to "many warlike sagas of the past," including King Arthur and his Knights of the Round Table; Spain's legendary El Cid; the Chevalier de Bayard, who came to be known as "the knight without fear and beyond reproach"; and the Scandinavian hero Beowulf and his battle against the monster Grendel.

All these characters, Tregaskis noted, were "brave men at war for ideals in the past. As a schoolboy, always bigger than the others of my age, I had resented and done battle with the bullies who picked on smaller boys." As he grew older, Tregaskis turned his attention to stories from what was then known as the Great War, including a book that might have influenced his future work using the diary format for his war writings. He read *War Birds: Diary of an Unknown Aviator*, the day-to-day journal of a then unnamed American fighter pilot serving with the Royal Air Force (Tregaskis later learned the pilot's name, John MacGavock Grider). Another favorite of his was *Count Luckner the Sea Devil*, published in 1927 and written by famed world traveler Lowell Thomas. The book examined the escapades of Count Felix von Luckner, who prowled the Pacific during the war in an armed sailing ship, the *Seeadler* ("Sea Eagle"), surprising and capturing Allied merchant craft. Tregaskis's literary tastes matured, and he perused such classics as the Greek epic poems of Homer (the *Iliad* and the *Odyssey*), Herodotus's *Histories*, and Arrian's work on the campaigns of Alexander the Great. He also found time for a few hobbies, including hunting, fishing, and rock collecting. Maude noted that her son's bedroom "abounded with samples of rocks, some donated by friends, and others obtained the hard way—by scouting and searching." While these pursuits may have faded from his interest over the years, one remained a lifelong passion: swimming. "We bought a small cottage at the shore when he was about seven," Maude recalled, "and every summer he and his sister practically lived in the water, and both became excellent swimmers."[11]

Tregaskis's interest in journalism started at the age of fifteen. He attended two private preparatory institutions in the area, the Peddie and Pingry schools. Tregaskis helped his parents, strapped for cash due to the Great Depression and Archibald's poor health due to his diabetes, by paying for his education through winning academic scholarships, working as a student waiter, and writing short articles about sports and other school events for newspapers in New York City; Newark and Trenton, New Jersey; and Philadelphia. He got more of his articles into print, and made extra money, by using aliases, including "Coppy Wright." Receiving scholarships from such groups as the Harvard Club of New Jersey, in 1934 Tregaskis was able to accept admission to the freshman class at Harvard University in Cambridge, Massachusetts. Recommending Tregaskis for the club's $300 scholarship, a former neighbor and friend of his father's, John Heine, described the young man as possessing "a high order of intelligence and exceptional qualifications. He is thoroughly reliable and honorable, industrious, perseverant and physically sound. He has a likable, clean-cut and pleasant personality, is well balanced and possessed of a driving force to get ahead."[12]

Tregaskis needed that "driving force" during his years at Harvard. It was a time in America, reflected another member of the class of 1938, historian and political insider Arthur M. Schlesinger Jr., when if students wanted a sandwich, they had to use a knife to cut a slice of bread from a loaf, as presliced bread had not yet appeared; men wore hats, "gray felt in winter, soft panama in summer"; and those wishing to write a letter had to fill their fountain pens from ink-wells, as ballpoint pens were not yet widely available. Haircuts cost fifty cents, newspapers were two cents, attending an afternoon movie set a student back a quarter, and five-and-ten-cent stores, Schlesinger pointed out, "sold things for five and ten cents." Socks were held up by garters, and suits came with a jacket, vest, and two pairs of trousers. The pants were equipped with buttons, not zippers, recalled Schlesinger. Zippers did not become standard issue until the late 1930s and did not always function as they should, said Schlesinger, "thereby sometimes causing acute embarrassment on dates."[13]

The class of 1938 included names familiar to anyone interested in twenti-eth-century American history: Roosevelt (John and Kermit), Kennedy (Jo-seph Jr.), and Rockefeller (David) among them. Theodore H. White, who later achieved fame as a political journalist and author of *The Making of the President* series, entered Harvard the same year as Tregaskis as a scholarship student from Boston. White remembered squatting on the floor of the Fresh-man Union with the rest of his classmates to hear James B. Conant, the rela-tively new university president, tell them, "If you call everyone to the right of you a Bourbon [a reactionary] and everyone to the left of you a Communist, you'll get nothing out of Harvard." White also noted that while he attended Harvard, students organized "a neat system of classification," which broke down into three groups. He belonged to the "meatballs," day or scholarship students, usually Irish, Jewish, and Italian young men from Greater Boston, attending Harvard "not to enjoy the games, the girls, the burlesque shows of the Old Howard," but to get the vaunted badge of a Harvard degree that would lead to a job "in some bureaucracy, in some institution, in some school, laboratory, university or law firm." Those in the "white men" classification included students who possessed the "great names" of distinction. They owned automobiles, went to the football games, and belonged to the elite clubs, the "preppies" of their times. Between the "white men" above and the "meatballs" below, White reflected, were the "gray men," mostly "public-high-school boys, sturdy sons of America's middle class," who went out for the sports teams and manned the staffs of the *Harvard Crimson* and *Harvard Lampoon*. "They came neither of the aristocracy nor of the deserving poor, as did most meatballs and scholarship boys," White noted.[14]

Tregaskis, with his middle-class upbringing, prep-school education, and dependence on scholarship money, fell outside of White's rigid hierarchy during his four years at Harvard. He studied English literature, history, government, and economics. With an eye toward a career in journalism after graduation, Tregaskis believed that possessing a "broad sweep of information" was important to a writer, more so than in any other profession. A nonfiction writer, especially, he noted, should "know something about almost every subject: because his article assignments may carry him into many highly specialized fields, and without a basic knowledge he is apt to be sorely handicapped in his research." To cover the cost of his tuition ($400 a year), he took a variety of odd jobs, including working in the university's library and zoological museum cataloging manuscripts, books, and drawings. During his summer breaks Tregaskis, no doubt through his father's connections, peddled Singer sewing machines door to door in several cities and worked in the Singer factory. His struggle to remain at Harvard influenced his studies, something he realized only later in life. "I was so eager to get my degree—and maintain a high average so I could hang onto my scholarships—that I spent more time learning *about* books than in learning the books themselves. I enjoyed reading novels; but to save time, I was apt to skim over the reading of *Great Expectations*, and devote more effort to learning the proper critical judgments about it so that I could pass my examination," he noted. Tregaskis usually received A and B grades, with a C mark scattered here and there.[15]

For both his junior and senior years, Tregaskis was lucky enough to earn a spot, barely, on the university's excellent swimming team, which finished undefeated both in 1937 and 1938 (beating its hated rival, Yale, both years) and was lauded as "one of the most powerful teams ever produced in the East." As a senior, Tregaskis had won a place on the team as its second backstroker over the brother of his classmate Joseph Kennedy Jr.: John Fitzgerald Kennedy, called Jack by his family and friends. "It was a dubious distinction," Tregaskis said, "since we were both far slower than the first backstroker, Graham Cummin, who was the national [Amateur Athletic Union] champion." Coach Hal Ulen set up a 150-yard race between Tregaskis and Kennedy to determine who would be selected as the second backstroker. "Torby Macdonald, Jack's roommate (later a Congressman from Massachusetts), said later that Jack had been ill with the grippe in Stillman Infirmary, and that his strength was below par," Tregaskis noted. "Macdonald said that Jack had sneaked out of Stillman to swim laps so that he would be in shape for the contest." It did not work out for the young Kennedy. Tregaskis remembered that he was far inferior to Cummin, and "Kennedy lagged a long distance behind me." Tregaskis was in no way a "star" of the team, remembering that during the swimming meet with Yale his senior year he finished fourth (last) in the backstroke. "Jack could have done at least that well, maybe better," he said, because Kennedy had a way of bearing down with "utter determination" on the things he really wanted. In his report on the swimming team's 1938 season, George P. Byrne Jr., the varsity squad's manager, praised Tregaskis and another team member, Robert C. Murphy Jr., for "continually pressing the supposedly better men. Without these men the team would have lost the indispensable asset of internal competition."[16]

While swimming remained a part of Tregaskis's life as an enduring avocation, he continued an activity while in school that became his vocation: journalism. During his junior year, Tregaskis heard there was an opening as the university correspondent for the city's three newspapers owned by publishing magnate William Randolph Hearst, and went to meet with John Noonan, the city editor for the afternoon newspaper, the *Boston American*. The job seemed like a golden opportunity for Tregaskis to finance the remainder of his college education. He later discovered that Noonan, a "big, jug-eared Irishman," habitually bristled at the mere mention of the name Harvard. "And he was bristling this day as I sought him out at the newspaper 'slot,' the hard-edged, ink-stained section of the copy desk where the city editor parked his straight wooden chair," Tregaskis remembered. "It was stained with cigarette burns, the rings of paper coffee cups, and piled up as usual with ill-assorted manuscripts jammed onto steel copy spikes."[17]

Noonan did nothing to make Tregaskis feel welcome. The city editor took a sip of his coffee, glared at the interloper, and asked, "So, you wanna be the Harvard correspondent?" Tregaskis thought he would be quizzed about his previous newspaper experience, which had been extensive, and that that might sway Noonan into giving him the chance to cover Harvard news at "space rates," twenty-five cents per printed inch. Instead of delving into his writing background, however, Noonan took a different approach, quizzing him about what he was studying while in college. When Tregaskis responded with "English," Noonan focused his blue eyes on him and asked, "What for? You gonna go to England?" The question floored Tregaskis, who stammered and failed to come up with an answer, but still got the job. He later decided that Noonan's question must have been serious. As a self-made newspaperman, Noonan understood that in those days "journalists don't learn their trade at Harvard or any other educational institution, but in the painful jungleland of Hard Knocks and demonstrable value for value received—at 25 cents an inch or whatever the going rate for beginners."[18]

Tregaskis provided plenty of value during his time as the Harvard correspondent. His articles, most printed without a byline, examined everything from a blind student's adventures climbing a mountain in Switzerland with his guide dog, aptly named Lucky, who celebrated the duo's success by attacking the Mer De Glace glacier and biting off a piece of the ice to eat; efforts by nineteen-year-old F. Behn Riggs to create super-slow-motion pictures by making a homespun "relaxation oscillator" and "cam-communicator"; to tracking down President Franklin D. Roosevelt's son, Elliott, at his brother's wedding reception to get his comments about his opposition to the Roosevelt administration's plans for New Deal power projects on the Colorado River. Tregaskis also proved he could cover hard news as well as features by reporting on an automobile accident in Woonsocket, Rhode Island, that killed five men, one of them a police officer with seven children.[19]

Jack Malloy, managing editor of the Hearst newspapers in Boston, was impressed by Tregaskis's contributions. After Tregaskis graduated from Harvard in June 1938 (cum laude with special honors in English), Malloy hired him as a feature writer for the *Boston Advertiser*. Tregaskis's schedule at the *Advertiser* included four days of writing feature articles and a double day of news reporting and rewrite. "I covered all the beats, including waterfront, State House, Federal Building, police headquarters, and courthouse," he recalled. The *Advertiser* also assigned him to report on some of the biggest news stories of the day, including the visit of Crown Prince Olaf of Norway; a case of poisoning and murder in Ashuelot, New Hampshire; the sinking of the submarine *Squalus* during test dives off the coast of Portsmouth, New Hampshire, on May 23, 1939; and a tour of area defense factories by President Roosevelt. One of the most valuable mentors Tregaskis had while working in Boston was Freddy Perkins, a whiz rewrite man, who every so often would "go off on a bender, to be dragged back to the re-write desk when the booze had worked its way to the bottom of his current income and beyond." Although unstable, Perkins was probably the best feature writer in Hearst's Boston office and he patiently taught Tregaskis the mechanics of putting together a workable feature article or magazine piece, advising him, "First you tell 'em what you're gonna tell 'em, then you tell 'em you told 'em."[20]

During a relaxed moment in the office one day, as they reviewed one of Tregaskis's articles, Perkins, who had served as a soldier in World War I, talked about his time in France and said something that resonated with Tregaskis during his subsequent time as a war correspondent. "In everybody's life," Perkins told the young journalist, "there are maybe a few days or weeks—or even months, if you're lucky—when you really feel as if you're alive. And that's the way it was with me in World War I. Everything's that happened since has only been a bore in greater or less degrees." Tregaskis ran across many more men such as Perkins in the years to come, those who "thought that life amid the dangerous winds of the front was something special. In the front lines of a war, despite the discomforts and suffering and ever-present dangers of being crippled or killed at the merest flick of hostile wind of chance, they really believed that fighting was good living."[21]

At the age of twenty-three, Tregaskis became the *Advertiser*'s top contributor to its Sunday magazine section. His articles sometimes appeared, he boasted, "under two or three aliases," as well as his own name, in a single issue. He also started contributing feature stories to King Features Syndicate, which distributed the pieces to its client newspapers across the country. In what little spare time he had, Tregaskis took up boxing and continued swimming, becoming known in the Boston area for stroking for long distances in the cold waters of Massachusetts Bay.[22]

Working as a reporter was something Tregaskis enjoyed, describing it years later as "the most exciting and satisfying of jobs (except in salary)." He looked forward to being outdoors "or at least on the move, shifting locale and meeting different people all the time," as well as the "relative freedom" from a boss's direct supervision. It certainly compared favorably to those newspapermen who were stuck inside on the rewrite desk, he recalled, "working all night sitting on their butts in the big stuffy room—right under the noses of the managing editor and even the publisher." After a few years writing for the Hearst newspapers in Boston, in early 1941 Tregaskis sought a position with the firm's newswire operation, the International News Service. It was not American journalism's preferred wire service, running a poor third to the top two, the Associated Press and the United Press. Although "scorned and often bad-mouthed by both," noted longtime INS reporter and syndicated columnist Bob Considine, "we were some of the proudest people in the news business." They were proud, said Considine, despite being outmanned by the other wire services when covering a story. During World War II the INS had only one correspondent assigned to report on what was happening in India, and Considine recalled that for one big story he was the lone INS representative on hand, while the UP sent seven reporters and the AP twelve. These difficulties did not sway Tregaskis, who wrote in his application letter to Faris that he would like "very much" to work for the news service. He also told Faris that he had started studying Portuguese at a Berlitz language school "in the hopes of someday getting a [reporting] job in Brazil."[23]

The next few months were busy ones for Tregaskis. He married Marian Holmes of Boston on August 30, 1941; began a new job at the INS; and learned, with a shock and horror shared by the rest of America, about the Japanese bombing of the American fleet at Pearl Harbor on December 7. Although caught by surprise, American forces did shoot down twenty-nine Japanese aircraft, but two battleships (the *Arizona* and *Oklahoma*) were put out of action for good and another six battleships suffered severe damage. Approximately two hundred aircraft were destroyed on the ground, and some 3,600 servicemen were either killed or wounded. Although the American public was kept in the dark about the extent of the losses, a stunned President Roosevelt shared details of the devastation with newsman Edward R. Murrow at a White House dinner late in the evening of December 7. "Our planes were destroyed *on the ground*!" Roosevelt exclaimed. "On the *ground*!" The next day, Congress, with only one dissenting vote (Congresswoman Jeannette Rankin of Montana, who had also voted against the country's entry into World War I), formally declared war against the Empire of Japan. Three days later, Germany and Italy declared war on the United States.[24]

The American public was soon gripped by an epidemic of panic, fueled in part by the rapid advance of Japanese forces in the Pacific against possessions controlled by the British, Americans, and Dutch. United States forces on Guam and Wake Island (after a spirited defense by U.S. Marines) were overwhelmed, effectively isolating the Philippines, and, on January 2, 1942, Manila, the Filipino capital, fell to the enemy. Gen. Douglas MacArthur made his famous escape from the Philippines, vowing to return and liberate the islands. Officials in Washington came to realize, noted one historian, that the Japanese had faster ships, larger guns, better torpedoes, and air power "matchless in number and quality." Although confident that the United States would eventually prevail, Secretary of War Henry L. Stimson warned Americans that Japanese soldiers were veterans and well-equipped, and that their fighting men were wiry, tough, and disciplined. Those living on the West Coast feared a possible Japanese invasion. Gen. John L. DeWitt, in charge of the Western Defense Command, failed to calm fears when he warned the citizens of San Francisco that "death and destruction are likely to come to this city at any moment." Afraid that American citizens of Japanese ancestry living on the West Coast might prove to be disloyal, the U.S. government, under Executive Order 9066 signed by Roosevelt, forced them from their longtime homes and moved more than a hundred thousand of them to isolated internment camps in Idaho, Nevada, Utah, Wyoming, Colorado, and Arkansas. Gen. Joseph "Vinegar Joe" Stilwell could not believe what he saw, commenting on the hysteria: "Common sense is thrown to the winds and any absurdity is believed."[25]

While attending Harvard Tregaskis had seen "protest meetings galore against the imminent war," with young men "swearing they would never go to war for any reason, and even the No. 1 politician, FDR, pledging to the mothers of America that their sons would never be buried in foreign soil in a foreign war." The fact remained, Tregaskis believed, that the war America found itself engaged in "*was* a war of survival. And it was a war against aggressive dictatorship bent on subverting the principles of self-determination and self-government." He possessed firsthand knowledge of just how difficult survival would be while working in the INS's New York office in early 1942 as its assistant night foreign editor, trying to make sense of the rash of bad news flooding in from the battlefronts in the Pacific and Europe. "My job was to be on top of all the developments in all the war fronts and convert the abbreviated cables into news stories and get them on the International News Service wire to papers all over the country before the competition, Associated Press and United Press, should do so," he recalled. Tregaskis worked as an understudy to Bill Lee, the senior man on the rewrite desk. "Lee demanded nothing short of perfection in my job," Tregaskis noted, "but he was fair and he helped where he could: all you would want from a newspaper superior." Getting to his new job proved challenging for Tregaskis, who commuted daily from his family's home in Elizabeth, New Jersey (his salary was too low to bring along Marian, who had a job, from Boston). On freezing winter nights, Tregaskis took the Jersey Central train from Elizabeth to Bayonne, New Jersey, where he took the ferry across the Hudson River. He then had to walk across downtown Manhattan to Dey Street to catch a subway train going uptown, changing to the local at Grand Central Station, and walking "in the black winds" to his office.[26]

Once at INS, Tregaskis faced a far greater challenge: keeping secret from his colleagues and superiors that he had been recently diagnosed with diabetes, a debilitating and sometimes fatal disease in which the body cannot properly burn the nutrients it needs to survive. "I did not want them to know about it, because if they did, they probably wouldn't give me the chance to go overseas as a correspondent," he explained. Although in 1921 researchers in Toronto had isolated a pancreatic extract, insulin, that could be used to fight and control the disease, and the Indianapolis pharmaceutical firm Eli Lilly and Company had begun distribution of the life-saving medication in 1923, the doctor that had diagnosed Tregaskis's illness steadfastly recommended a different treatment. Instead of daily shots of insulin with a hypodermic needle, the physician told him that he should eat nothing but meat, as lean as possible, and "five-per-cent-carbohydrate vegetables: which later meant, I rapidly found out as I became a war correspondent, that the only allowable vegetable while with the Armed Services in the field, was tomato juice, when, as, and if it could be found." Tregaskis's doctor, a hard taskmaster, lectured him: "You'll never be able to eat any bread, or potatoes, or eat any sweets, as long you live. And if you get fresh with your diet, you'll pay with losing a foot, or a leg, or go blind."[27]

Tregaskis, who after the war switched to an insulin regimen to control his diabetes, went to work each night at INS carrying a paper bag containing his lunch, consisting of a half-pound of baloney, "no bread and nothing else. And I knew that I would be hungry, ravenously hungry, that night as every night, as I fought the diabetes demon, as well as the demons of the job." Of course, Tregaskis admitted, his suffering in no way compared to the discomforts being experienced by those directly involved "in our many-front war." But there were many times when the pressure got to be too much for the young reporter, and, when a subway train "would come clattering and banging and roaring into the station," he thought seriously of jumping in front of one and ending his misery. "Life didn't seem worth this hard a struggle," Tregaskis said, "and the diabetes, despite the starvation diet, didn't seem to be improving." He even fantasized about taking a one-man submarine, penetrating the enemy's defenses, and destroying a Japanese warship so his death would have some meaning. "It never occurred to me that this was just about impossible," he recalled. "There would have to be months of training, and some way to put the sub where it was supposed to do its work, and most important, somebody in authority would have to be convinced that the project was worth trying. It was a vainglorious Walter Mitty dream, though with an unhappy ending."[28]

In early March 1942 Tregaskis got his opportunity to do something for the war effort. On a rainy night at the INS office, Lee told his fellow rewrite man that Faris wanted to see him the next morning. Tregaskis was elated, believing it meant he would be given the foreign assignment he had desired. "Round faced with round dark glasses, medium sized, Faris was physically undistinguished, but as an editor he was great," said Tregaskis. "He was a working, shirt-sleeve editor, who would pitch in to do the work himself if there was a slow-up, and he could do all the jobs as well as anyone." Tregaskis admired the INS editor for his liking for "direct action—the shortest way to a point." It marked a characteristic of all the good newsmen he knew, and a quality "in common with the great military leaders I came to know, the leaders among the brave men."[29]

By this time, Tregaskis was ready to go wherever INS wanted to send him. His diabetes seemed to be under control and he had even been able to gain weight while maintaining his low blood sugar. He had also saved enough money to have his wife leave Boston to join him and his family in New Jersey. Before their marriage, Tregaskis had warned Marian that his work came first and "that was the way it was, like it or not. And I remember saying that she would respect me more because my mind was clear on that issue." What stuck in his mind, however, was a caution issued by his mother, who had told him, "When you want to travel, you have to expect to collect scars." Tregaskis translated her "prescient foreboding" into a belief that while engaged in action the "bitter pill wasn't the risk of death, so much as being badly hurt or crippled." Later, he felt "pangs of conscience" about the "willfulness with which I bulled ahead to get to that war" and the sufferings his single-mindedness had caused his wife, mother, and sister. At his meeting with Faris, Tregaskis remembered his editor being polite and to the point: he had his choice between two assignments, London or Australia. "I knew he characteristically didn't brook a 'think it over' kind of answer," Tregaskis said of Faris. "I knew my chance was now and that he was assuming I had already thought it over and made up my mind. 'Australia,' I said, simply." Tregaskis was on his way to combat, pleased that "out there in the void of the future was a shape I had dreamed of: men at war in a crusade for ideals, and for survival."[30]

2 WARTIME IN PARADISE

Upon his arrival in Hawaii as a new war correspondent for the International News Service, Richard Tregaskis discovered a place quite unlike what he had been used to seeing in tourist brochures before the war. Shortly after the disaster at Pearl Harbor, the U.S. territory had been placed under martial law. Military courts, presided over by an armed officer, replaced civilian tribunals; a strict curfew and blackout (lights out at 6:00 p.m.) had been established; and tight censorship existed on newspaper articles, radio broadcasts, mail, and long-distance telephone calls. Everyone had their fingerprints taken—even First Lady Eleanor Roosevelt when she visited in 1943—and Japanese alien residents had to hand over to authorities their firearms, radios, and cameras, among other items. "No white or red flashlights were permitted—even in the hands of those privileged to go out of doors in the blackout. You weren't allowed to smoke cigarettes in the street," noted Robert J. Casey of the *Chicago Daily News*, who had arrived in Hawaii a few weeks after the Japanese attack. Casey heard a story about a guard who delivered a stern warning one evening to a passerby for wearing a wristwatch with a luminous dial. A photographer confided to Casey: "This town is sitting right on the edge of its chair all ready to get up and run somewhere."[1]

Tregaskis's journey to war began in San Francisco, California, where he waited at the end of March 1942 for about two weeks before he sailed to the Hawaiian Islands on a former luxury ocean liner of the Matson Line, the SS

Lurline, which had been requisitioned by the U.S. Navy for use as a troopship. "I have a fine uniform, which is like the regular officer's outfit except there is no insignia," he wrote his parents. "Since the company is paying for it, I can enjoy it all the more." As he prepared to be shipped out, Tregaskis had the opportunity to tour the city and meet its people, who had been "extremely hospitable." A few aspects of the city had particularly impressed him, especially its hills. "They're the steepest I've ever seen—far steeper than in Boston—and yet the roads run over them in straight lines and the biggest and most sumptuous buildings, in fact the whole downtown section is strewn over them without any apparent concern for altitude or grade," Tregaskis wrote. "Some of the trolley cars run on cables which move continuously under the street surfacing. You hook your streetcar onto the cable through a slit in the street. It's very novel." There were also more taverns in San Francisco than he had ever seen anywhere else. "They're as plentiful as phones or taxicabs in New York," he noted, no doubt due to the large numbers of sailors and soldiers who crowded into the city looking for diversions. Turning to more serious matters, Tregaskis warned his parents that the letter they were reading would probably be the last they would receive from him for about a month. He told them not to waste their time worrying about his safety. "If anything should happen, which is unlikely, you will hear about it immediately," Tregaskis wrote. "No news is good, etc., these days."[2]

It seemed to take forever for Tregaskis to get to his Pacific destination. The *Lurline* had started its engines and left the dock only to suddenly stop and drop anchor in the middle of San Francisco Bay. A frustrated Tregaskis had been warned by one of the sailors aboard that if he intended to be part of naval operations in the future, he had better get used to waiting. Barges came alongside the troopship and began to transfer ammunition, tons of it, Tregaskis recalled. The passengers were not supposed to know about what is being loaded onto the ship, but one of Tregaskis's companions, Astley Hawkins, a correspondent for Reuters, the international news agency, had found out. "A pleasant ship to be torpedoed on," said Hawkins, who had previously worked as a reporter for newspapers in New Zealand and Tasmania and had traveled on the *Lurline* during its days as a luxury liner. "I envied Hawkins his superior knowledge and experience," Tregaskis recalled. "His manner, I was aware, was easier than mine, and quite naturally so; and even his equipment seemed to be more right than mine. I had a huge old suitcase in which to carry my gear, and a battered, ancient Corona [typewriter] I had bought second hand. Hawkins had a very military looking duffle bag and a proper bedding roll." In spite of their differences, Tregaskis found Hawkins to be a charming companion, pleasantly calm, and possessed with a "constantly good natured smile on his lips, and mild but steady eyes behind large, steel-rimmed glasses."[3]

Other passengers on the *Lurline* included army, navy, and marine officers; a rear admiral; a group of approximately twenty-five nurses; a handful of Hawaiian residents caught on the mainland following the December 7 attack and returning home; and throngs of civilian war workers on their way to Honolulu and Midway Island to construct military facilities. To accommodate all these people, the ship's lounge had been renovated to hold bunks four tiers high, and meals were served cafeteria style. At least the food was good, said Tregaskis, as the mess caterer who had been employed by the ship in its civilian days, and his crew, still worked in the kitchen. The one discomfort of being aboard he could not get used to was the lack of fresh water. "One always felt sticky after washing with the brine [saltwater] which ran in the bathroom pipes," Tregaskis recalled. His assigned cabin, which once had contained only two beds, was now filled with two triple-decked bunks. "The distance between bunks, horizontally, was about two feet, and one had to be an athlete at least to sandwich himself into bed," Tregaskis noted. The cabin had no chairs, except for one folding stool with a canvas top. One lucky person could sit on the chair while the others had to perch on their baggage or "jackknife their bodies into a sort of sitting position between the second and third levels of bunks." One stuffy lounge—blacked out day and night—did still have some chairs scattered about. "Here the air was always thick with smoke," Tregaskis said of the lounge, "but one could at least relax on cushions, if the chairs were not all filled."[4]

One of Tregaskis's cabinmates provided respite from the journey's monotony. Jack Baich was a retired director of the Hawaiian Telephone Company, and he could be counted on to tell "wonderful stories" about his pioneer grandfather, who had overcome numerous obstacles while living in the American West to become a ship's master, a gold miner, and a ranch owner. Baich also brooked no nonsense from those passengers who dared disturb his nightly rest. Tregaskis recalled that in the cabin next to his resided some young girls whose exact status was "indeterminate." One evening, the women began to "giggle excessively," so loudly that Tregaskis and the other men in his cabin could hear them through the thin partition. "Finally they began to beat significant tattoos on the wall. Perhaps they had found some liquor aboard in some obscure corner and had come to feel playful," observed Tregaskis. Stirring out of his slumber, Baich roared at the miscreants, "Stop that knocking! We're trying to sleep in here!" Silence followed for the rest of the evening.[5]

As the *Lurline* started on its way with other members of its convoy, including some navy destroyers serving as escorts, the seas eventually grew rough and the ship began to roll heavily. Many on board, Tregaskis reported, had never been on a ship before and they soon became seasick. "Some made the rails and a few let go [vomited] in the corridors," he said. "The ship was so crowded and busy that some of the slop remained underfoot, and one occasionally slipped on it." The ship's canteen had to deal with a run on lemon drops, which a sailor confided to Tregaskis were supposed to be a remedy for seasickness. At least the *Lurline* faced no threats from Japanese submarines, although Tregaskis did learn that when the ship had sailed from San Francisco a submarine had been reported far to the south off San Diego. "This fellow had not bothered us or even put in an appearance," he said. Tregaskis did have the opportunity to see guns fired for the first time when the ships in the convoy took target practice. "I noticed particularly the bright gold color of the tracer bullets, and the fact that when the other transport was firing, we saw the dashed lines of her tracers leaning into the sky long before we heard the popping of her firing," he said. "When she fired all her 50 calibers at once, the sound was an interesting combination of rattles and pops, and the sheet of orange flame which came from her larger guns when they fired, seemed amazingly large and long." When the *Lurline*'s guns fired, the noise "rattled our eardrums," he recalled. "I was awed by the ease and precision with which our 50 caliber gunners swung their mounts by their broad, bicycle type handlebars, and sent streams of bullets lancing out at the target." He tried to piece all these new sights and sounds and observations into "imagined pictures of an actual engagement; and finally gave it up, deciding I could not be sure until I had seen the reality."[6]

The *Lurline* made good time on its passage. One of the first things Tregaskis saw as the ship neared the Hawaiian Islands was Molokai, the famous leper colony, "a blue, hazy, sprawling mass on the horizon." The ship reached Oahu and "slowed to a walk," said Tregaskis, as it entered Honolulu's harbor. Forced by the packed crowds on deck to watch their arrival from a doorway, Hawkins and Tregaskis could see the tents and shacks of encampments on the shore, and even could make out small figures of men in khaki. "These soldiers stood still, silently watching our convoy come into the harbor," Tregaskis noted.

"And some of our Marines, standing on deck, shout out, 'Hello, suckers!' We moved close enough to shore to hear a bell ringing, apparently somewhere in the Army camp. 'Answer the phone!' one of our wits yelled." Tregaskis knew something had changed from peacetime days when he saw that the large warehouses along the waterfront had been painted with "zig-zag, crazy camouflage in many shades." Even the famous Aloha Tower, which he had remembered as a beautiful white spire in the tourist booklets he read, had been camouflaged with "streaks of brown and bilious green." At least Tregaskis could see palm trees, which grew in great numbers.[7]

Trudging down the gangplank from the *Lurline* to the dock, Tregaskis and Hawkins found a telephone to call a taxi for a ride to a hotel. Tregaskis called at least a dozen taxi companies listed in the classified section of the phone book, and in every case a "surly voice" informed him that no taxis would be available. "Almost every time, the party at the other end of the wire hung up before I could say another word," said Tregaskis. "Once I managed, by speaking quickly, to ask why there were no taxis; the voice answered 'No More tickets' and the receiver clicked sharply. (I found out later that the reference was to gasoline rationing tickets.)" The newsmen decided to walk into town, but first tried to make reservations at a hotel. "We called three hotels and all told us that they had no rooms available," said Tregaskis. He had his first taste of how difficult life could be in wartime Hawaii.[8]

Tregaskis and Hawkins finally found a room, sharing one at Honolulu's Moana Hotel. Checking out their surroundings, they discovered that the streets were crowded with men in uniform—clad either in army khaki or navy white—as well as numerous "disheveled civilian workers, usually traveling in groups." Stores displayed only limited stocks of food, and many counters stood bare of any goods. Trying to buy a can opener, Tregaskis visited eight stores, including drug, department, hardware, and grocery establishments, and in all of them he found that the "shopkeeper fixed a hopeless gaze on you the moment you entered. No one seemed in a hurry to sell anything, because amounts of goods available were so small, and profits, in any case, were limited by fixed prices. The shopkeeper would have no trouble in selling everything he had, so why rush, why hurry?"

There were some positive aspects to price fixing. At their hotel Tregaskis and Hawkins stayed in a "marvelously located room, labeled $16 a day, for $6," with the price including breakfast, lunch, and dinner. Overall, however, Tregaskis was disappointed with what he had seen of Honolulu. "I had expected to find a clean white city, under palms, with broad sandy beaches and clear tropical water nearby," he explained. Instead, he encountered a dusty and crowded metropolis similar to a typical American city of medium size. His first dinner on the hotel's enclosed terrace overlooking Waikiki Beach and Diamond Head was more to his liking. "The evening air touched one's cheek softly, like a kiss, and sitting on the open terrace, looking over the banyan court and beyond it the lines of phosphorescent surf rolling in to shore, was an experience more like the Hawaii we expected," Tregaskis remembered.[9]

The perils of living under martial law quickly snapped Tregaskis back to reality. Upon returning to his room after dinner, he noticed on his door a sign that warned guests to be sure that their windows were closed during the mandatory blackout. He glanced at the windows, the panes of which he had noticed earlier were all painted black, and thought he could see nothing but darkness, indicating to him that the windows were closed. Five minutes later, a policeman knocked on Tregaskis's door and said, "Your windows are wide open." Although he protested to the officer that his windows were shut, upon checking them Tregaskis found they were open and he had "seen only the completely blacked out Hawaiian night instead of the proper panes of black glass." The next day, the correspondent had to appear before "a stern judge in [a] major's uniform," who disposed of the numerous cases that came before him in a manner Tregaskis described as a "mass production fashion, as if he were applying one bolt at a Ford assembly line" and was anxious to get through his daily quota. Before his case was heard, Tregaskis witnessed a person accused of his second offense for being drunk and disorderly fined $250 and given six months of hard labor. "The clerk called my name, and I stood before the judge, looking up at the shiny bald head couched behind the desk of authority," Tregaskis said. A clerk read out the police officer's report—"two windows wide open . . . light visible a great distance"—and the judge asked him how he pled. "'Guilty,' I said, and attempted to add that I had thought the windows were shut, that this was my first experience with blackout," he noted. The judge was unmoved by Tregaskis's explanation and fined him ten dollars. "I felt relieved to escape with a ten dollar fine; having watched other sentences being passed, I had imagined myself paying $50 and going to jail for a month," said a relieved Tregaskis. "Remarkable how quickly one can become conditioned to a new environment."[10]

Although initially tasked by his INS employers to report from Australia, Tregaskis had received instructions from his office to remain in Hawaii to accompany, when he could, U.S. Navy task forces sailing for missions from Pearl Harbor against the Japanese. The ships were under the authority of Adm. Chester W. Nimitz, commander in chief of the Pacific Fleet (usually designated as CINCPAC), who had the reputation, needed during this time, as one historian noted, of doing "much with little." Since March 30, 1942, the Pacific theater had been split into two commands. Gen. Douglas MacArthur had been named commander in chief of what came to be known as the Southwest Pacific Area, a vast region that included Australia, New Guinea, the Philippines, the Solomon Islands, the Bismarck Archipelago, and the Dutch East Indies (except for Sumatra). The U.S. Navy had been entrusted with the rest, called the Pacific Ocean Areas, and was commanded by Nimitz. To report on the navy's actions, Tregaskis had to navigate a mass of red tape, including obtaining an official identification card, required of everyone who resided in Hawaii, and a police pass, required if he wanted to venture out on the streets after the nine o'clock curfew. Reporters also had to go to the Navy Yard to obtain Pacific Fleet credentials and to Fort Shafter for U.S. Army papers. "Then, to round out the assortment," said Tregaskis, "one might also acquire a waterfront pass and a Navy yard pass. Several days at least would be required for this rigmarole."[11]

Tregaskis also had to make an important trip to the Pacific Fleet public relations office to have his name listed as ready for the next naval operation against the enemy. Before Tregaskis's arrival in Hawaii, American carriers had made hit-and-run raids on Japanese installations in the northern and southern Marshall Islands and also against Wake Island. Because the U.S. government had decided that defeating Nazi Germany was its first priority, Tregaskis likened the American forces fighting in the Pacific to a "boxer with an injured right hand, jabbing the opponent with his light left jab until the hurt hand grows strong enough to hit." Dick Haller, the "plump, jovial" INS bureau chief in Honolulu, took Tregaskis and Hawkins to meet Lt. Cdr. Waldo Drake, the chief of the Pacific Fleet's public relations office, who often seemed to be "vexed by the correspondents in general," and his assistant, Lt. Jim Bassett, whom Tregaskis regarded as bright and responsive and who peppered his conversations with jokes. Both navy men had worked for newspapers in Los Angeles before coming to Honolulu. "Drake, a gray-haired, extremely worried looking man with a hoarse voice, said confidentially that he thought there might be 'something going out pretty soon,'" Tregaskis recalled, and advised the newcomers that they should be prepared to move quickly when called, as the operation might be "a good one." To Tregaskis, those words had a "sinister sound to us whom warfare was utterly novel."[12]

The fleet public relations office occupied a "mad little corner of a larger Naval office," Tregaskis noted. Navy yeomen were clacking away on typewriters as he and Hawkins talked to Drake, and the room was also filled with correspondents wearing clean, light-khaki uniforms equipped with green armbands bearing the letter "C." Tregaskis and Hawkins met the other members of their profession, including Al Brick, the newsreel cameraman for Fox Movietone News, who had captured dramatic film of Pearl Harbor under attack (the navy had confiscated Brick's work, and his scenes of the devastation and recovery were was not released into movie theaters in the United States until a year later); Foster Hailey of the *New York Times*; Jack Rice, an Associated Press photographer; Walter Claussen, AP bureau manager who had been on the SS *Lurline* with Tregaskis and Hawkins; and Frank Tremaine, the United Press bureau manager.[13]

Correspondents had to follow strict rules to report on the navy's actions in the Pacific. They were prohibited from talking about the strength or composition of naval forces, where they were located, and ship losses and sailor casualties. All copy had to be reviewed by navy censors before being released for publication. Just how strict the grip Drake and his public relations office had on news articles coming out of fleet headquarters was brought home to Tregaskis when he tried to gain official approval for stories he had written about his convoy trip. An item in one of his stories caught the eye of navy authorities. Tregaskis had mentioned that lemon drops were a popular item on board the troopship because they were supposed to be a remedy for seasickness and most of the sailors had not been at sea before. After being told his story could not be sent, Tregaskis asked for a reason why, and Drake told him it was because he has used the sailors' names, which was prohibited (officers could be, and were, identified by name). "Why should one not use the names of common sailors in stories, I asked," Tregaskis remembered. "Because there was a rule that said one could not, was the answer." The INS reporter kept harping on the matter for the next several weeks and was given several reasons for the restriction. The most common was that if a sailor's name was used, the enemy might identify his ship, and then know when that ship was in the Pacific. The restriction remained in place even when Tregaskis pointed out that if the Japanese were familiar enough with a ship to have a full list of its crew, "they probably also knew which ocean it was sailing in."[14]

While awaiting word about his first task-force assignment, Tregaskis made an impromptu tour of downtown Honolulu with Jim Kilgallen, the veteran INS reporter he was relieving on the Pacific Fleet assignment. As they walked they passed several sidewalk soda pop stands clogged with soldiers and sailors and a bordello with an irate woman yelling out the door at would-be customers that they were closed for the day. "Everywhere, garish neon lights glowed and nickelodeons blared," said Tregaskis. "This was like Coney Island on a Sunday. There were souvenir shops featuring cheap paper leis, necklaces of coral dyed sickly colors, grass skirts stained red or green, shiny pillow covers bearing sentimental inscriptions." Tregaskis could not believe how many jewelry stores there were: several in every block they traversed, each packed with displays of wristwatches and bright, cheap women's trinkets serving as bait for the wads of cash sailors accumulated during their long stretches at sea. Later he learned that those who ran the jewelry establishments made large profits on the wristwatches, known in the trade as "Reamers," poor, inexpensive versions of "shock proof" service watches that cost them $8.50 wholesale and which they sold for $30 to $35. One of the "genial rogues" who ran one of the stores confided to Tregaskis that he had even learned a new profession after a sailor who had bought one of the more expensive "Reamers" asked if it could be engraved with "a touching" sentiment. The store owner noted, "I go into conference with myself, and then I come back and say, 'Sure, our engraver can do it.' So I do it myself. It takes me a couple of hours to learn it, but I get thirty bucks for the job."[15]

Dropping into a tavern for a drink, the two newsmen sat down on two of the tall, wooden stools and tried to order. The bartender seemed annoyed and informed his customers that it was closing time, pointing to a group of sailors shuffling out the door as proof of his statement. Tregaskis and Kilgallen looked at their watches and noticed the time: four o'clock. "If they catch you open a minute after closing hour, they take your license away," the bartender explained, starting to become more agreeable. "We reasoned with him that the closing hour, legally, was five o'clock; but he said he was closing at four anyway, but finally, after considerable argument, weakened and set up a couple of drinks for us on the sticky bar," Tregaskis recalled. The bartender went on to complain that he had more business than he could handle and also had to spend considerable time making sure nobody, especially servicemen, had too much to drink, as that was another reason authorities used to take away liquor licenses. In addition to drinking, Kilgallen told Tregaskis that another popular form of entertainment for servicemen involved visiting amusement parlors in which Hawaiian girls dressed in "grass skirts and brassieres would pose with interested males for snapshots." The backdrop for the pictures, said Tregaskis, presented a "palmy tropical landscape, the charge was a quarter, and the vast majority of customers were sailors, anxious to send some supposedly authentic memento of Honolulu to the folks back home."[16]

In early April 1942 Tregaskis and Hawkins finally received the call they had been waiting for when Bassett telephoned and told them to report to the Navy Yard, ready to sail at noon for duty with a new naval task force. Although tight-lipped as usual on where they would be going, Bassett did let slip that the mission promised to be a "really big one," said Tregaskis. He and Hawkins "wrote what we thought might be our last letters home, rushed about cleaning up odds and ends of business, and reported to Comdr. Drake, ready for the great adventure." Several correspondents, including Casey, joined Tregaskis and Hawkins on the captain's gig transporting them to their respective ships. All the reporters, except for Tregaskis and Hawkins, had been part of earlier combat sorties into the Pacific. "The knowing air of the veterans made me feel more than ever the newcomer," said Tregaskis. As the ship made its way through the harbor, Tregaskis could see the hulks of the battleships *Oklahoma* and *Arizona* and, sitting on the harbor's shallow bottom, the battleships *West Virginia* and *Nevada*. It was the first time Tregaskis was aware that more than two battleships had been sunk on December 7. To lighten the mood, Casey quoted a dispatch he had written trying to irk the censors: "The Navy has completed plans for raising three of the two battleships sunk at Pearl Harbor."[17]

By ones and twos the correspondents were dropped off at their assigned vessels: John Field of *Life* magazine and his photographer, Ralph Morse, to a carrier, the USS *Enterprise*; Keith Wheeler of the *Chicago Times* to a destroyer, the USS *Balch*; Casey to a cruiser, the USS *Salt Lake City*, on which he had made two previous voyages; and Hawkins, Rice, and Tregaskis to the other cruiser in the task force, the USS *Northampton*, which had been at sea since being commissioned in 1930 and was named for the city in Massachusetts, the home of former president Calvin Coolidge. The *Northampton* and *Salt Lake City* had worked together before, bombarding the Japanese-held Wotje Atoll and Wake Island in February. "Bassett came aboard with us to conduct the formalities—for these were the formal days of the war; we were introduced to the officer of the deck, a young lieutenant in spotless whites; he in turn presented us to the executive officer, and we were promised that we would shortly be presented to the captain," Tregaskis said. (As the war went on, these formal introductions were scrapped, and each correspondent, he noted, was simply "handed his orders and told where to go; one introduced himself and presented his own orders as he moved about.")[18]

Hawkins, Rice, and Tregaskis were shown to their room, which turned out to be the cabin of the ship's captain, William D. Chandler. Tregaskis described the cabin as a "palatial suite with rugs and bridge lamps and overstuffed furniture in the sitting room, and a separate bedroom and private bath and shower." For this trip, Chandler would sleep in his emergency cabin in the mast. "This was going to war in luxury!" Tregaskis recalled. The *Northampton* stayed in port the first afternoon and night, and after dinner the correspondents learned they would be leaving Pearl Harbor the next morning, Wednesday, April 8.[19]

Tregaskis and Hawkins awoke early the next day and climbed up the mast, seventy-five feet above the water, for a bird's-eye view of the flotilla's departure. Tregaskis was astonished by just how quiet it was as the ship moved away from its berth; he could hear neither shouts of excitement nor any ripples of conversation from the deck below. "The faces of the seamen moving about their jobs were inexpressive, of any emotion," he recalled. A young ensign told Tregaskis that the *Northampton* had battled the Japanese already and the crew had no illusions about what might lay ahead. As the task force headed out to sea, Tregaskis said the huge, dark shapes of the cruisers and the carrier "formed in a sort of funeral procession." It was not at all the beginning he had imagined for a task force setting out to accomplish great deeds. There was no visible action on the other ships, except the rapid hoisting and lowering of bright-colored signal flags, and an occasional thin cloud of smoke rising from a stack. "I wouldn't be surprised no matter where went or what we did," the ensign told Tregaskis. "I've gotten over being surprised by anything, on these task forces."[20]

3 REPORTING FROM SHANGRI-LA

Richard Tregaskis had been eager to test his courage in warfare, but he and the other Americans on board the USS *Northampton* did not know that they were on their way to be a part of an audacious attempt to strike back at the Japanese and gain a measure of revenge for the attack at Pearl Harbor. They were part of Task Force 16, which included ships led by Vice Adm. William F. "Bull" Halsey Jr., sailing for a midocean rendezvous with Task Force 18, which included a newly commissioned carrier, the $32 million, approximately twenty-thousand-ton USS *Hornet*. The *Hornet* and its escorting ships sailed from San Francisco Bay on April 2. Once the two task forces rendezvoused and became Task Force 16 under Halsey's command, the ships set course on a secret assignment to bomb Japan. Instead of its usual complement of Douglas SBD Dauntless dive-bombers, Douglas TBD Devastator torpedo aircraft, and Grumman F4F Wildcat fighters, the *Hornet* had crammed on its narrow flight deck sixteen twin-engine B-25B Mitchell army bombers of the Seventeenth Bombardment Group, joined by aircrews of the Eighty-Ninth Reconnaissance Squadron, commanded by Lt. Col. James H. Doolittle.

The Seventeenth had been the first group to receive the new bombers, named for military aviation pioneer Maj. Gen. William "Billy" Mitchell and designed and built by North American Aviation, the firm responsible for the development of such successful aircraft as the T-6 Texan trainer and the P-51 Mustang fighter. The bombers and their small, five-man crews (pilot, copilot, bombardier, navigator, and engineer/gunner) had been ordered to hit industrial and military installations—steel factories, gas and chemical plants, and power stations—in Tokyo, Yokohama, Osaka, Kobe, and Nagoya. If they survived their bombing runs, the crews were supposed to land at airfields hurriedly being prepared for them in China.

Since the destruction at Pearl Harbor, President Franklin D. Roosevelt had been seeking a mission against Japan that would bolster morale in the United States and in other Allied countries. According to Lt. Gen. Henry "Hap" Arnold, the head of the U.S. Army Air Forces, the president had insisted that his military commanders "find ways and means of carrying home to Japan proper, in the form of a bombing raid, the real meaning of war." To meet Roosevelt's goal, Capt. Francis Low, an officer on the staff of Adm. Ernest King, commander in chief of the U.S. Fleet, came up with the idea to use the *Hornet* as the launching platform for army bombers to raid the Japanese mainland. Low worked with Capt. Donald Duncan, King's air officer, to develop a plan for the mission, which received approval from both King and Arnold in early 1942. Arnold tasked the mission to Doolittle, who titled the assignment "Special Aviation Project No. 1" and selected the B-25B bomber, with a cruising range of 2,400 miles, as the aircraft best suited to meet the demands of the mission. The plane's 67-foot wingspan was almost too wide to take off safely from the carrier's narrow, 114-foot-wide deck. Although Doolittle realized the Mitchell's two-thousand-pound bombload could do "only a fraction of the damage the Japanese had inflicted on us at Pearl Harbor," its main purpose would be psychological, both boosting American morale and causing "confusion in the minds of the Japanese people and sow doubt about the reliability of their leaders." He also hoped that the shock might nudge the Japanese military to "divert aircraft and equipment from offensive operations to the defense of the home islands."[1]

With two trial flights off Norfolk, Virginia, in early February, the *Hornet*, commanded by Capt. Marc Mitscher, proved that a Mitchell bomber could take off safely from a carrier. The carrier set out in early March for the West Coast to await delivery of the sixteen modified B-25Bs and their crews at the Alameda Naval Air Station on San Francisco Bay. The planes were loaded by a crane onto the carrier on April 1. Mitscher noted that when all the army bombers had been arranged on the *Hornet*, the last plane in line "hung far out over the stern ramp in a precarious position. The leading plane [to be flown by Doolittle] had 467 feet of clear deck for take-off" from the 824-foot-long flight deck. The bombers had been modified to better accomplish their mission, but the airmen knew they faced perilous odds as the *Hornet* sailed off on April 2 to join Halsey's task force. 2nd Lt. Chase J. Nielsen, navigator on the bomber nicknamed the "Green Hornet," figured that his crew had a 50-50 chance of taking off from the carrier without crashing. "If we got off, there was a 50-50 chance we'd get shot down over Japan," Nielsen recalled. "And, if we got that far, there was a 50-50 chance we'd make it to China. And, if we got to China, there was a 50-50 chance we'd be captured. We figured the odds were really stacked against us."[2]

Having the 134 army pilots and crewmen sharing cabin space engendered plenty of questions about their purpose, with some navy men believing the bombers were meant for delivery to Hawaii or an isolated American base somewhere in the Pacific. The *Hornet* crew only learned about their destination after the ship had passed beneath the Golden Gate Bridge and was well out to sea. Lt. Cdr. Oscar Dodson, the *Hornet*'s communications officer responsible for all confidential messages, met daily with Mitscher. On April 3 Dodson remembered going to Mitscher's cabin and seeing the captain seated at his desk holding a document and smiling. "Without a word he passed the papers to me," Dodson said. "It was a CNO [chief of naval operations] order for HORNET to launch the B-25s for an attack on Tokyo and other nearby cities. He said quietly: 'As soon as we are well clear of the shore line, I will announce our mission to the ship.'" Mitscher spoke to the crew over the ship's public-address system, announcing the details about their mission. "In the ship there was a moment of stunned silence," Dodson noted, "followed by wild cheers which rang throughout the ship." Still thinking of secrecy, Mitscher, Dodson added, cautioned his men to avoid throwing overboard any "identifying material," including magazines, letters, daily schedules, or the ship's newspaper.[3]

Tregaskis remained blissfully unaware of the *Northampton*'s destination during the early days of the voyage. He found the ship's wardroom a comfortable place to relax after they had reached the open sea, as it had leather-upholstered chairs, some dog-eared magazines, and a continuous supply of hot coffee. "It can be had at almost any time of night or day—replacing old-fashioned (and banned) spirits to warm up cold stomachs," noted Tregaskis. An officer told the correspondent that an average of four and a half cups of coffee was consumed every day by each person on board. At dinner, Tregaskis tried to get some of his tablemates to conjecture about where they might be headed. There were plenty of guesses, including Australia and the Indian Ocean to relieve the British fleet. Some sailors anticipated a repeat of former raids on the Marshall and Gilbert Islands. "We're going on a polar expedition to engage the icebergs," one sailor joked. When questioned by Tregaskis, Captain Chandler would only say, "You know, when you're on a ship, there's no use worrying about where you're going. It just makes the trip seem longer. How good are you at relaxing?"[4]

Accepting the captain's mild rebuke, Tregaskis decided to spend part of his time looking for the best spot to be during any action to "watch the fireworks," as well as investigating the pastimes of the more than one thousand men on board the *Northampton*. One place he investigated as a possible perch was on the bridge, which gave him a good view of the ship. A crew member, however, warned Tregaskis that he had to watch out for the number two turret, as during the raid on Wotje it had caught him unawares and knocked him "ass over teakettle." An officer pointed out that a newsreel cameraman who had accompanied the cruiser on its previous raids had set up his camera on the derrick forward of the ship's aftermast, which gave him the opportunity to take cover in a nearby room if the going got too tough. "The only disadvantage of this spot, said my informant, was that when the guns went off, great clouds of soot were knocked loose from the stack and covered the area," Tregaskis remembered. Discouraged, he climbed two levels higher to a fairly open, if precarious, platform upon which, at least, he would be clear of the concussion blasts from the big guns and the resulting showers of soot. "Here I consulted a seaman who laughed and said that he thought this would be as good a place as any. 'But,' he pointed to the yard arm, 'you have to watch out for strafing [aircraft]. On the Wotje trip, we had a bullet in there.'"[5]

For amusement on their off hours, *Northampton* crewmen spent much of their time playing cribbage, acey-deucy (a variant of backgammon that had been played on navy ships since the 1900s), chess, and checkers. While the officers preferred cribbage, most of the enlisted men spent their leisure time at acey-deucy. "Yeah, right now you'll see more of 'em playing acey-deucy," a seaman engaged in a game explained to Tregaskis, "but sometimes, all of a sudden, everybody starts to play cribbage. Then they all play cribbage for a while, and pretty soon they start playin' acey-deucy again. It goes in sorta fads." One thing both ranks shared was a love for ice cream. Long lines of men stood at the modern soda shop on the ship. Behind the chrome-plated faucets, Tregaskis watched as two men busily stuffed ice cream into containers. "Vanilla, chocolate, and cherry flavors were available with or without syrup," he noted. "Hawkins and I talked to the soda jerkers—one of them had been a soda jerker in civilian life—and gathered some facts and figures on the daily consumption of ice cream. We divided the figure by the ship's complement, and found that one quart of ice cream was sold each day for every four men aboard."[6]

Stopping by the ship's library, Tregaskis asked the sailor in charge about the literary tastes of the crew. He discovered that they preferred westerns "with plenty of action." An assistant librarian told the correspondent that the next most popular books were "blood-curdling mysteries." Favorite authors included Clarence Mulford, creator of the Hopalong Cassidy character, and Zane Grey, who had penned the popular western *Riders of the Purple Sage* (1912). "It seemed almost ironic," Tregaskis observed, "that these men, who had been through a lot of dangerous action . . . should want to spend their spare time reading stories about gun-play and murder; however, I could see already that there must be long periods on any naval strike, when boredom reached an absolute maximum." Later, Tregaskis talked about the matter with Adm. Raymond Spruance, who at that time commanded Cruiser Division Five from the *Northampton*, his flagship. (As a correspondent, Tregaskis discovered he was able to "talk as an equal . . . with the highest officers on board as well as the lowliest of Swabbies.") Spruance pointed out that on any mission the men spent the greatest part of their time "going and coming back, and only a very small part of the time in action," due to the vast distances involved in getting anywhere in the Pacific, which, after all, covered seventy million square miles. Spruance's remark matched Tregaskis's observation. Each day the reporter had marked the ship's progress on a map and, on the vast scale of the Pacific, it looked to be infinitesimal. "We were moving fraction of an inch by fraction of an inch," he noted. "I had never realized that one can travel for thousands and thousands of miles in the Pacific in a straight line, without ever seeing any land or any living thing."[7]

The crew's pragmatic attitude about their situation gnawed at Tregaskis's mind when he sat amidst a crowd in the stuffy mess hall to watch the movie *The Wizard of Oz*, starring Judy Garland. He recalled, "I thought that this was another curious irony: that men outward bound on a trip which might bring them face to face with death and grisly bloodshed, should sit so calmly and watch a pleasant, luxurious fairy tale about wizards and witches. However, they did not appear to enjoy it greatly; remained as impassive as they had been at their other activities. They had certainly developed a magnificently calm attitude towards this war business." If the crew of the *Northampton* did not seem worried, the correspondents aboard were certainly apprehensive about the likely dangers to come. Tregaskis and Rice believed that whatever their mission might be, it probably involved striking deep into Japanese-held territory, and they expected to face fierce opposition. Rice had previously been aboard another cruiser when it hit the Japanese on Jaluit Atoll in the Marshall Islands. His ship endured a heavy air attack and had been hit on its quarterdeck by a bomb that resulted in several casualties. "I don't like that stuff," said Rice to Tregaskis. When the two men predicted to Hawkins that they would be lucky to return to Pearl Harbor unharmed, Hawkins met their gloom with his usual cheeriness and imperturbability. "Don't be silly old boy," Tregaskis remembered Hawkins telling him. "Probably nothing will happen at all." Tregaskis's nerves were already rattled a bit by the morning routine of being awakened by the sounds of the "thudding of feet, a ghostly clanking of chains and creaking of machinery" as a loading drill was carried out in one of the ship's turrets near his cabin. "These sounds depress me," Tregaskis said, "but Hawkins joked about it, saying the ship must be haunted."[8]

The men and ships of Task Force 16 had the answer they were waiting for on April 12, when, northwest of Midway Island, aircrews from the *Enterprise* were sighted by the approaching *Hornet*. Soon thereafter, Tregaskis heard the "electrifying news" that the now combined group, designated as Task Force 16, had as its mission a bombing strike against Japan. "We're four months late, but we'll give it to 'em now," Tregaskis heard a gunner exclaim as the news reached the *Northampton*'s crew. There was another wave of excitement when he trained his binoculars on the *Hornet* as it moved closer to the cruiser. He could see a high, irregular mass on the carrier's deck, which marked the presence of "much larger aircraft than the usual carrier planes. As the ship drew nearer, we could make out the double tails, wide wings, and tricycle landing gears of B-25 army bombers." Tregaskis believed there must have been "exhaustive" tests done in secret to prove the feasibility of launching such a large plane from a carrier. "Our force was told they will approach to a point about 400 miles from Tokyo. There the bombers will take [to] the air, and we will hightail our way home," Tregaskis said. Obviously, he noted, the bombers could not return to the carrier deck to land, as there was not enough room nor did the aircraft have the necessary arrester hooks that carrier planes possessed to catch the wires stretched across the flight deck. Spruance suggested to Tregaskis the possibility of the planes landing in China after their mission. "The admiral was not over-optimistic about our chances of getting away unscathed from the expedition," the correspondent reported. "He spoke of the long range of the

Jap patrol aircraft which might spot us; also of the hundreds of small patrol vessels known to operate along the Jap coast. He spoke of the need for lightning withdrawal after we had made our thrust." At dinner that evening, a marine captain, crossing the fingers on both of his hands, spoke for many of the crew when he exclaimed: "Oh, oh, oh, God, may they [the bombers] get there."[9]

On April 17, after refueling, the *Enterprise*, *Hornet*, and their supporting cruisers, including the *Northampton*, sped away from the slower destroyers and oilers to make their final dash to the launching point east of Japan for the Doolittle Raid. The bombers, each of which had been equipped with four five-hundred-pound bombs, were set to take off on the afternoon of April 18. The afternoon before the scheduled launch, Tregaskis noted that the skies had darkened and the seas were rougher. "The other ships were following in close, but they were barely distinguishable in the heavy, driving mist," he remembered. "It was perfect weather for our raid—for no Japanese 'eyes' could be flying on such a day as this. And so we hurried on to make the most of the weather, rising up over the high combers, rolling and pitching, and shivering from one end to the other, but always crowding on full steam." That evening on the cruiser, Tregaskis observed no more "nerves" than usual. Officers read books and played cribbage to pass the time, and one aviation officer entertained others by speaking "earnestly on the subject of airplane armament." Below decks, the sailors and marines, except for those on watch, had turned in for the night. Tregaskis came upon a veteran petty officer standing alone near the edge of the mess hall and asked him where everyone was. "They're all squared away for the night," the man told the correspondent, shrugging his shoulders toward the sailors' sleeping quarters. "These days when they're not on watch, they're so tired they turn in." On deck Tregaskis could see only a few men, well bundled up against the cold, passing each other in the dark. "There was a stern, rolling sea and a shrieking wind," he reported. "Spray flew over the railing and smashed against the catapult towers. The ship's air compressor was chugging, making a loud, unpleasant sound between a throb and a rattle. This was a fitting night before the day."[10]

Tregaskis awoke at 4:00 a.m. on April 18 not wanting to miss anything, as there was the possibility the army bombers might take off at dawn, but they did not, remaining firmly tied down. He did uncover a rumor—"scuttlebutt" in navy jargon—that at about 3:00 a.m. the *Northampton* had detected an unknown ship approximately twelve miles away. When the cruiser turned off course, the mystery vessel turned in the same direction and followed until the

Northampton's superior speed dropped the other ship astern. At about 7:00 a.m., as he was sitting down to breakfast, Tregaskis heard that a scouting plane had spotted an unidentified ship but had quickly avoided it. Later that morning came a report that the cruiser running behind them had sighted a Japanese patrol boat, the *No. 23 Nitto Maru*, a modified fishing trawler. These small vessels, dubbed "spitkits" by American sailors, were part of Japan's early warning system. The *Nitto Maru* had identified the approaching ships as hostile and radioed a warning home: "enemy carriers sighted. Position 650 nautical miles east of Inubo Saki." Fighters and dive-bombers from the *Enterprise* attempted to sink the Japanese boat but were unsuccessful, so the cruiser *Nashville* was sent by Halsey to destroy the vessel. "We could see her streaking towards the horizon, where the Japanese ship was only a faint smudge of gray on the horizon," Tregaskis recalled. "At last, we had met the enemy."[11]

Although the *Nashville* was about four miles away from the *Northampton* when it opened fire, Tregaskis could plainly see the "brilliant flashes" from the cruiser's six-inch guns. "Clouds of dirty smoke, with a yellowish hue, were rising over the cruiser. And near the horizon we could see tall narrow geysers like a line of white columns, springing into existence," he observed. "Then the small popping sound of the gunfire came to us from the distance. Sound is slow to travel in such vast spaces. Almost immediately, the bright flashes of a second salvo burst along the cruiser's deck. And then the bright little sunbursts of color came in rotation, rolling up and down the length of the ship." Later, Tregaskis, who called the action an "impersonal introduction to the art of war," learned that before the *Nitto Maru* went under, it had charged at the much larger ship, firing its "three-inch deck gun, until it was blown apart." Mitscher had briefed Doolittle on the encounter with the Japanese picket boat, telling him, "It looks like you're going to have to be on your way soon. They know we're here." With secrecy compromised and other enemy patrol craft dotting the sea, Halsey decided to proceed with the mission twelve hours ahead of schedule and 150 nautical miles farther away than planned. The admiral sent a message to the *Hornet* that read, "Launch Planes. To Col. Doolittle and Gallant Crew: Good Luck and God Bless You." At 8:03 a.m. the crew on the *Hornet* heard the announcement: "Now hear this! Now hear this! Army pilots, man your planes."[12]

Because the *Northampton* had moved into a position to protect the *Hornet*, Tregaskis had a "marvelous view of the activity on her flight deck. If the demonstration had been arranged for our benefit, we could not have had better 'seats.'" Sailors and marines busy on the cruiser's deck snatched seconds from their duties, despite the constant danger of an enemy air raid, to watch what was happening on the carrier, entering into the action "as wholeheartedly as a great football audience," Tregaskis reported. The correspondent could see small figures hurrying around on the *Hornet*'s deck starting the B-25B's engines. At about 8:20 a.m. the first of the bombers, piloted by the mission's commander, Doolittle, with 2nd Lt. Richard Cole as his copilot, "waddled forward" to begin its takeoff. At that moment Tregaskis noticed that the wind had increased to "almost gale force" and he could see the *Hornet* varying its speed to find a moment at which the least pitching would occur in the raging seas. "I could hear the motors now as the bomber inched forward gaining speed," he remembered. "Soon the craft was airborne, lifting gradually from the deck of the carrier as a great shout rang out on our deck from the sailors and marines who were awaiting this sight for many days." Doolittle's plane staggered into the wind, leveled off, "moving steadily but low, over the waves and gaining speed," Tregaskis observed. The B-25B eventually swung over the ships in a slow circle, accompanied by "great cheers" from the crew of the *Northampton*. "Nobody spoke of the great dangers facing this intrepid crew," Tregaskis recalled.

All the remaining army bombers took off successfully from the *Hornet*, but some just barely. The fourth bomber in line appeared to almost stall, Tregaskis recalled, and "it hung sluggishly over the sea its nose pointed upward, but the plane fell forward toward the high waves." The concerned crew on the *Northampton* groaned in anticipation of a crash and cried "Up, up" as the bomber staggered down a few feet more to almost hit the waves, gained altitude for a moment, and bogged down again. "The plane was sinking, but finally gained speed, power and height, and streaked off into the stormy sky," Tregaskis reported, adding that a nearby marine commented, "That makes me feel good all over."[13]

As the army bombers continued to streak off the *Hornet*, the weather worsened and the seas grew even rougher, breaking over the carrier's bow. "It's the first time in my life I ever saw that happen; I probably will never see it again," one of the *Northampton*'s officers said to Tregaskis. "Waves breaking over the flight deck of a carrier." Green water also crashed over the cruiser's bow, with the water reaching as high as the ship's navigation bridge. "Steel uprights on our midship deck were bent like bows," Tregaskis noted. "The captain's coat was soaking wet and our stacks were dripping with salt water." During all this, lookouts on the *Northampton* received a report that Japanese aircraft had been spotted at a range of thirty thousand yards, but they later learned what they had seen was an American plane. Tregaskis continued to watch as the final B-25B prepared for its takeoff. "The last plane wobbled down the deck and paused, waiting for a giant swell to pass by," he noted. "While the bomber paused, a second gigantic wave rolled into the carrier and crashed high over the flight deck. With field glass[es], I could see the spray sweeping through the propellers of the plane." The aircraft's motors, however, did not stall, and after a few seconds the bomber moved slowly into the wind, steadied itself, and rose abruptly into the sky. Picking up speed after it was airborne, the B-25, nicknamed "Bat Out of Hell," made a slow turn over the *Northampton*, and its crew could see the star insignia on its fuselage and the large words "U.S. Army" on the underside of its wings. "I could make out the black silhouetted figure of a gunner in one of the plane's transparent 'bubbles' or turrets," Tregaskis reported. "I wondered then if this one man—the [only] one whom I had seen as an individual since the planes began to take off—would survive." As he pondered the army crewman's fate, the *Northampton* and the *Hornet* made sharp U-turns and, with the *Enterprise* and other escorting cruisers, headed for home "at our greatest possible speed," twenty-five knots, approximately twenty-nine miles per hour. On the *Hornet*, a relieved ensign, Robert Noone, reflected that after the last bomber had left the carrier there was "a physical let down all over the ship. Everyone was exhausted from the nervous tension of watching them take off. We mentally pushed every plane off the deck."[14]

Although the Japanese military had intercepted radio traffic that hinted at a possible U.S. fleet attack, they expected any such mission to be launched from closer to land, approximately two hundred miles, the expected range of a carrier plane. They had no expectation of being attacked by long-range army bombers. Doolittle's raiders used their high-explosive and incendiary bombs to hit their targets, receiving scattered opposition from antiaircraft batteries and Japanese fighters. With their fuel exhausted, the bombers, fifteen in all, had to either bail out or crash land in China. The sixteenth, flown by Capt. Edward J. York, went off course and had to land near Vladivostok in the Soviet Union. Although treated well, its crew was interned by military authorities, but managed to escape from the country in May 1943. Doolittle, looking at the thousands of pieces of shattered metal that had once been his plane, sat down on a wing at his crash site in China and felt as "dejected as a frog's posterior. This was my first combat mission. I had planned it from the beginning and led it. I was sure it was my last." As he sat there, Doolittle saw his gunner/ flight engineer, Staff Sgt. Paul J. Leonard, snap his picture. Trying to cheer up his pilot, Leonard asked him what would happen when they got back to the United States. A dejected Doolittle predicted he would be court-martialed and sent to prison at Fort Leavenworth. Leonard had a different fate in mind for his commander, telling Doolittle he would be promoted to general and given the Medal of Honor. Leonard's prediction came true, but what brought tears to Doolittle's eyes was his staff sergeant's comment that when Doolittle was given charge of another airplane, he wanted to serve as his crew chief. "It was the supreme compliment that a mechanic could give a pilot," Doolittle said. "It meant he was so sure of the skills of the pilot that he would fly anywhere with him under any circumstances."[15]

The weather remained overcast and windy as Task Force 16 sped away from Japan's home waters. An officer confided to Tregaskis that they would probably not have to worry about the Japanese fleet but still faced danger from patrolling submarines on the lookout for the Americans. One morning the cruiser tested its guns and the sudden "blasting and banging, without notice, set jittery nerves to jumping," Tregaskis recalled. Because the ship's course had changed sharply during the night and seemed to be heading directly for a hostile island base, Tregaskis and others wondered if the task force might be headed for another attack on the enemy. "It was obvious many of the officers wanted to do that," Tregaskis remembered. One officer told him, "Wild Bill Halsey's going to hit 'em again before he hauls out of here." The correspondent, however, could uncover no confirmation for such a plan. He talked to an officer higher up the chain of command, who admitted they knew nothing official but were willing to bet him that the task force was headed "straight home." Later that day the matter was settled when the ship's course reverted to its former direction. "And thus more scuttlebutt was laid to rest—as it usually is," wrote Tregaskis. One of the final scares came when the lookouts "jumped a mile" when they spotted what appeared to be a two-man submarine directly in the cruiser's path. "It was the carcass of a dead whale," the correspondent learned. "We passed quite close by the moldy old beast; and, I must say, his resemblance to a submarine was amazing."[16]

During its high-speed run to Pearl Harbor, the *Northampton* picked up a news report from Los Angeles that quoted Japanese shortwave broadcasts indicating that Tokyo had been bombed by American aircraft. One of the cruiser's lieutenants reported that the Japanese had claimed they had shot down one of the U.S. planes and gave a purported interview with one of the pilots in which he had confessed that he had been forced to make the flight against his will. "Which gave a good laugh to all of us who had witnessed the unfaltering bravery with which the bombers took off," Tregaskis wrote. "A good laugh, and a twinge of sadness when we thought some had not come through." At lunch, a marine officer had cut through the table chatter with something that was on the minds of several of the crew: "I can't believe it," Tregaskis remembered him saying. "Can't believe what?" he was asked. The marine responded, "I can't believe that we got over there and back, and sent out our planes, without even a bomb falling on us. It's impossible." One of the *Northampton*'s top officers talked freely with the correspondent about the strain involved with a modern war at sea. "The reason we seem to take it so calmly is that you can either take it or you can't," he explained to Tregaskis. "Some people are just not fitted temperamentally to take it. And trying to resist the strain only makes it worse for them." The officer added that it was hard to judge how a person would react under such extreme pressure. "We had a man who I thought would be splendid. He was the careful, thoughtful, methodical type," the officer recalled. "But he went to pieces and had to be hospitalized after only two months out. I guess he tried too hard and thought too much."[17]

After a few days without any enemy contacts, the *Northampton* crew began to relax a bit and turned their attention to routine maintenance. Tregaskis awoke one morning to the sounds of hammering and scraping, as sailors chipped away rust from the edges of hatches and scrubbed the inside of one of their small boats. Below decks, officers were busy censoring the crew's mail, which would be sent out when they returned to port. Tregaskis offered his help and discovered that the old adage "about a soft heart under a hard shell applies to our fighting men at sea." One machinist's mate peppered his letters to his wife with how much he loved and missed her, as well as his "protestations of faith and absolute trust in her fidelity—but at the same time," Tregaskis noted, "in the same mailing, there would always be a letter to the sailor-boy-lover's mother or a friend, asking that he or she keep an eye on the bride, because he had heard that she was playing around." He recalled another crewmen who set up his letters to his wife, Martha, in the following fashion: At the top of the first page he drew three contiguous boxes, in which he lettered the words "Me," "Martha," and "God." Then the sailor would tell his wife what dreadful combat he had been through, but that he was unable, because of censorship, to "write about these horrors and besides it was all too horrible to talk about."

As he gained more experience as a war correspondent, Tregaskis developed an instant suspicion whenever someone involved in a campaign or a battle parried his questions about it with the "I can't talk about it, it's too secret—or horrible" routine. He found that the men who had been through the goriest parts of the fighting were glad to share their stories, in detail, with a reporter, provided that "you listened with an understanding ear and weren't trying to exercise your own ego in some way or other when you asked the questions."[18]

On the return voyage the *Northampton* ran out of refrigerated food, forcing the crew to dine on rice and curry, with ice cream for dessert. That might have been "thoroughly acceptable if not always delightful for normal stomachs," noted Tregaskis, but, because of his diabetes, it would have meant a starvation diet for him if he had not had the foresight to bring along with him a case of tinned sardines. "So after lunch or dinner, when the other men had filled themselves with rice, curry, rolls, and ice cream, and I had tried to make do with a small stain of curry on my otherwise empty plate," he remembered, "I would go back to the cabin and open a can of oily sardines. Same for breakfast, when the shortage of refrigerated stores had reduced the menu to items which were very-much taboo for me: hot cakes, French toast and cereal." The greasy sardines, sloshing around in their "copious linseed-oil juices," seemed as good a treat to Tregaskis as steak or chicken. "After all, I was hungry; or more exactly, I was <u>starving</u>," he said. Luckily for Tregaskis, who was trying to keep his diabetes a secret, his roommates never pressed him for an explanation about his "weird and illogical tastes in food."[19]

The ships that had launched and protected the Doolittle Raid had their homecoming at Pearl Harbor on the morning of April 25, cruising into port on calm seas. It was good, said Tregaskis, to be able to walk on deck without "unintentionally zig-zagging: good to eat breakfast without chasing plates about the table." Because their arrival was unexpected, there was no "public rejoicing" at their safe return. All hands, including the correspondents who accompanied the task force, received orders from naval authorities to observe "absolute secrecy" about what they had been through. "They did not even fly the victory flag from the mast, as the ship slid in to her anchorage," Tregaskis wrote.[20]

Although prevented, for now, from sharing his adventures with the American public, Tregaskis by chance discovered some fascinating information about where U.S. forces in the Pacific might soon strike. He received this hint from an unlikely source: Spruance, whom he described as the man "with the eyes and look of the eagle and a mind to go with them." One evening on their return from the Doolittle Raid, the two men had been talking on the *Northampton* about the war. Tregaskis, a self-described "brash new correspondent," asked Spruance where he would next hit the enemy if he were the supreme commander: "He rose and moved quickly to a colored world map on the bulkhead of his living room. 'If I were doing it,' he said, 'I'd hit them right about here.' And he made a sweeping motion in the vicinity of the Solomon Islands—Guadalcanal being one of the southernmost of the group. It seemed to me that his hand hesitated over the island marked Guadalcanal." For the next few months, Tregaskis was on the alert for the campaign that, "like Valley Forge and Gettysburg, was going to change all our lives—mine especially." That was still to come. For his next mission, Tregaskis graduated from life on a cruiser to life on a carrier, joining the crew of the *Hornet* as it looked for its first tangle with the Japanese fleet.[21]

4 THE CORRESPONDENT AND THE "FIGHTING LADY"

The great bulk of the vessel berthed off Ford Island at Pearl Harbor towered over the dock as Richard Tregaskis, overloaded with the paraphernalia of his profession—a portable typewriter, notebooks, pens and pencils, and binoculars—prepared to climb the gangway. Ever since Task Force 16 had completed its daring mission, the Doolittle Raid, the correspondent had used all the influence he could muster with the Pacific Fleet's public relations office to gain a berth on this ship, a *Yorktown*-class carrier, the USS *Hornet* (CV-8), known throughout its service under the fitting nickname "The Fighting Lady." It seemed to Tregaskis that the *Hornet*'s next engagement would certainly expose its crew of approximately three thousand to "the full fury of combat," and he wanted to be there to write about what they endured.[1]

On April 29, 1942, Tregaskis joined the *Hornet*, commanded by Capt. Marc "Pete" Mitscher, described by one of his officers as a "man who could inspire a shipload of men or a task force of men, and he never used five words where one would do. Sincerity just oozed out of him." Later, after meeting Mitscher, Tregaskis came away with the impression of having been introduced to a "genial old hawk" who possessed "deep humorous twinkles around his aquamarine-colored eyes—which gave him the effect of always being a-twinkle." From his first steps aboard, Tregaskis knew that an aircraft carrier was far different from other U.S. Navy ships, about as different as New York City was from Newton Upper Falls, Massachusetts. He had believed that the cruiser he had been on for his last assignment, the USS *Northampton*, was a "massive piece of machinery—with its 10,000 tons of bulk, its heavy guns, its more than 600-foot length." He realized that in comparison to the behemoth now under his feet, the cruiser was just "a dwarf. I had heard carriers called passenger liners by slightly contemptuous salts. Now I could see what they meant." The lofty ceiling of the carrier's hangar deck stood in stark contrast to the "unending low bridge I had encountered on the cruiser," said Tregaskis, who had quarters in the *Hornet's* bow. That evening, when movie call was sounded and hundreds filled a block of chairs at the center of the hangar deck, he noticed that even this large group of men seemed "lost in the great space of the deck; and their whistling and cheers—sailors are responsive to movies—echoed only faintly in the far corners."[2]

Oscar Dodson, the *Hornet's* communications officer, led Tregaskis on a tour of the ship as it moved out to sea the next day, April 30, heading for parts yet unknown. "Prepare for some exercise," Dodson warned the reporter as they started out. It proved to be no overstatement, as it took the duo about forty minutes to traverse the length of the carrier, taking time only for quick glimpses into each department: paint shop, metal-working shop, electrical rooms, machine shop, sick bay, bunkrooms, kitchens, and numerous offices. "This was certainly a city within itself," Tregaskis noted. Dodson explained that the carrier's function was to carry and launch planes, a "floating airport," in contrast to a cruiser or battleship, which "might be called a floating fort or gun platform," Tregaskis said. A carrier had to be large enough to support the flight deck and hangar deck, Dodson pointed out, and, incidentally, to provide accommodations for pilots, mechanics, machinists, gunners, radio operators, and, the officer slyly added, "the people who merely ran the ship."[3]

Climbing up three flights of stairs ("ladders" in navy nomenclature) to reach the flight deck, Tregaskis, once on top, saw stretched before him a "wide, open plain of gray," which he described as looking more like an overgrown board-walk by the sea than the mere deck of a ship. Once back below, he peered into officers' quarters, which he noted compared well in terms of size and comfort with staterooms on a passenger liner. The cabins, equipped with one or two spring beds in each, were nearly twice the height of a man, leaving plenty of air space and headroom. Standard equipment included a built-in reading lamp at bedside, an electric fan, an air-conditioning blower, a compact desk with indirect lighting, and a washbasin with running hot water. "That last item," Tregaskis recalled, "startled me after my days on a cruiser. I knew the officers who had been my shipmates would have growled at the luxury of it." In the next few days, as the *Hornet* and the other ships of Task Force 16, including the carrier USS *Enterprise* (CV-6), moved south in the warm Pacific, Tregaskis learned another striking truth about a carrier. Even when no action with an enemy was expected, he noted, "life aboard this type of ship is a constant rush of activity, and a constant awareness of danger."[4]

The first day at sea, the *Hornet* turned into the wind preparing to welcome the planes of its air group back aboard from their stay at Ewa Field, a U.S. Marine Corps facility on Oahu (those in Air Group 8 lived in barracks on the base when the carrier was in port). Watching the action from about midway down the side of the island, the "great smokestack and bridge structure at one side of the deck," Tregaskis was approached by an officer who "politely" warned him that he should leave such an exposed position and go forward or aft, where he could run for cover if an aircraft went off course when attempting to land. "He pointed out several reddish creases in the steel side of the island, and ploughed-up streaks of raw wood in the deck, where, he said, a plane had recently cracked up," Tregaskis remembered. "It had scraped a wing on the island, sheered off the tip, struck the deck and then pinwheeled into the island side."[5]

That afternoon Tregaskis witnessed one of the ship's Grumman Wildcat fighters run into trouble on its approach. "The warning signal began to squeal like a donkey in pain," he reported, "and in the slow fractions of seconds that passed, when all the action seemed slowed to a walk, we knew that the plane was going to crash." He saw one of the fighter's wings strike the island near where he had stood earlier in the day, and he watched as a rescue crew pulled the pilot's limp body from his plane. Fortunately, Lt. Bruce Harwood, although knocked out, had suffered only a few bumps and bruises from his crackup. "I thought of the escape as miraculous; but as time passed and I saw many more such crashes on land and at sea," said Tregaskis, "I learned that such good luck is quite commonplace amongst aviators." During the carrier's first three days at sea, the *Hornet* lost two of its Wildcat fighters into the sea. The correspondent also observed a Dauntless dive-bomber swing low to land and then, suddenly, dip and slide into the water far astern. "Plumes of spray shot over her wings, then her tail stuck straight up into the air," he recalled, "and we could see the figures of two men clinging to her. In a few seconds the tail disappeared under the water. But pilot and radioman were rescued, unharmed, by a destroyer," which always trailed behind the carrier for just such emergencies. "Such were attrition losses: The seepage of material which goes on in the best of Navies and

Armies and Air Forces; and as I acquired more experience I came to see that our losses in such manner were slight, compared to the tremendous number of hours of operations," Tregaskis noted.[6]

The twin elements of danger and excitement were part of Tregaskis's daily existence while on the *Hornet*. As Dodson told him, "It's a great, continuous show." Launching missions from an aircraft carrier involved a swarm of activity on and below the flight deck. In addition to a fighter squadron, a *Yorktown*-class carrier such as the *Hornet* included two dive-bomber squadrons, one designated as a scouting squadron and the other as a bombing squadron, but usually interchangeable, as they flew the same planes, the workhouse of the fleet, the Douglas SBD Dauntless. "Each day at dawn and every afternoon the dive bombers whine up the deck and leave the ship to scout miles ahead of and around the [task] force, searching for any evidence of a hostile presence," remembered Lt. Frederick Mears, a navy pilot briefly assigned to the *Hornet* and who later died in a training accident. "They are the 'eyes' of the ship, and it is upon their radioed reports that the strategy of attack is based." Because they were so essential to their ship's survival, the pilots had the best of everything, including, one officer pointed out, access to "refrigerators with cold cuts, the makings of sandwiches, and warm loaves of bread . . . and all kinds of fruit drinks."[7]

Once called to duty, pilots pulled on their khaki flying suits and cotton helmets with leather earphone covers and clear goggles, buckled on their inflatable Mae West life vests (named in honor of the buxom Hollywood actress), strapped on their parachutes, stowed their survival knives in their proper position, and placed in their shoulder holsters a .38-caliber revolver or .45-caliber pistol in case they had to bail out and defend themselves against the enemy. While the pilots got ready for their mission, out on the wooden flight deck sailors performed an intricate dance to get the planes ready for takeoff: fighters in front, the dive-bombers behind the fighters, and the torpedo bombers on the stern. Officers on the bridge barked out orders to steer the ship into the wind to aid in launching the planes. Given the signal to launch, the pilot "revs his engine up to full power with the brakes still applied, gives thumbs up to indicate plan okay, then lets go of the brakes and lumbers up the deck," noted Mears. "The next plane is in the spot with wings spread ready to go as the first is rising off the bow."[8]

Each crewman wore a color-coded uniform and helmet to distinguish one from another on the crowded flight deck. "They look like monkeys or men from a different world," Mears recalled. "They are all over the deck and move quickly." Ordnance men in red shirts loaded ammunition and bombs on the aircraft, while yellow-shirted plane directors made sure crews placed the planes in the proper position for launch. Tregaskis had been impressed by the plane-handling crews, who, after spending all day running up and down the deck, "pushing, tugging, rolling planes about and busily folding and unfolding wings," had enough energy left for horseplay when their work was done. "Such was the vitality of the American fighting man," he noted. Watching over all this frenzied activity, ready to jump in when emergencies happened, were the firefighters, nicknamed "Hot Pappas," clad in silver fireproof clothing. The landing signal officer (LSO), standing on the ship's stern in front of a canvas screen that helped make him more visible, became the most important person for a pilot to watch upon his return to the carrier. The LSO used color-coded paddles to signal a pilot if he was on course for a safe touchdown or if he had to be waved off to try again. When that happened on the *Hornet*, Tregaskis remembered that pilots had to gun their engines and pull up for another try, coming so close to the island that those watching could make out their helmet and goggles. Sometimes, a damaged plane did not have time for another approach, and the LSO and others near him had to dive out of the way and onto a protected catwalk nearby to escape danger.[9]

When planes returned to their carrier, it once again had to steam into the wind. A pilot hoped for an easy landing by catching with the tailhook trailing from the bottom rear of his aircraft one of the first arresting wires that were stretched across the deck. If he was skilled enough to catch the first wire near the stern, his plane would be "brought to a gradual stop with plenty of slack wire unraveling to ease the jolt," according to Mears. The tension on the wires increased the closer a pilot came to running into a safety barricade made of netting and catching the last wire "jerks the plane like a dog at the end of a rope," Mears recalled. He compared crashing into the barrier to hitting a brick wall in a car traveling about forty miles per hour. The pilot, strapped into his plane by a safety belt, "usually takes only a black eye or a split lip down to the ready room with him," he added.[10]

Almost constantly throughout his time aboard the *Hornet*, Tregaskis heard the roar of engines as planes taxied or took off, the thud and bump of their landing, or the hum of engines being tested on the hangar deck. There were days, too, when the dive-bombers practiced their deadly art, and spectators on board "watched the wings of planes glint whitely in the sun as they dived straight down on the spot of spray that marked a spar target; and heard the crack of their practice bombs; and strafing practice, when the angry little fighters darted in toward the towing spar; we saw streaks of tracers darting from their wings, watched the fiery lines scoot into the target, or riffle up fences of bullet-splashes in the water." Tregaskis also witnessed two other kinds of target practice, "a simulation of the deadly reality." A plane passed over the ship towing a target sleeve for the antiaircraft gunners to shoot at. "Red and gold tracer bullets streaked into the sky as the din of firing shook the ship," reported Tregaskis. "And the gunners were amazingly accurate." When the carrier's big guns fired, the men could hear a terrific crash and bang, as if, he said, someone had "dropped a load of granite blocks on deck." He could also feel the bulkheads shake, and from a spot near the gun mounts he could see "large sheets of orange flame darting out 10 or 15 feet from the barrels."

The Douglas TBD Devastator torpedo bombers also rehearsed their war tactics. Carrying water bombs, Tregaskis reported, the Devastators, the navy's first all-metal aircraft when it joined the carrier fleet in 1937, dove out of the clouds and skimmed in toward the *Hornet*'s beam low over the water. "Their bombs splashed, marking the spots where the torpedoes would have hit the water," he said. "That would have got us," one sailor said to the reporter, pointing at the last splash the pseudo attacker's bomb had made. "If he had ever got in that far. But he never would have got that close." Tregaskis asked a gunnery officer his opinion, and he agreed with the sailor's view. "That's right," the officer said to Tregaskis. "We can throw up a pretty solid curtain of 'flak.' I'd hate to have to fly through it."[11]

Always on a carrier there was the chance of unforeseen accidents, medical emergencies unrelated to shipboard activities, and death. Tregaskis talked to one of the ship's doctors who had to perform an emergency appendectomy; the patient survived. Talking about the procedure with the reporter, the doctor related that one of the ship's officers had been keen on an earlier occasion to witness an operation and had been allowed to do so. But when the procedure began, the officer had suddenly rushed out of the room. "I couldn't stand that chloroform," the officer explained. "It would make a tough seaman sick." The doctor told Tregaskis he had a good laugh, as there was no chloroform on board; an odorless spinal anesthesia had been used for the operation. Also during Tregaskis's time on the *Hornet*, one of its crew, SiC S. I. McGowan, suffered a fatal accident involving a fighter's propeller blades and was chopped up "into a raw hamburger," Tregaskis reported. He watched the burial services when the man's body, sewn in canvas, slid down a wooden chute and "belly-flopped with an uncouth splash in the water." The American flag that had draped the body during the service was folded and put away for another day, another casualty of war.[12]

The *Hornet*'s fighter, dive-bomber, and torpedo pilots spent some of their time waiting for action in their specially appointed ready rooms, studying models and silhouettes of Japanese aircraft carriers, battleships, cruisers, and destroyers. Tregaskis noted that down the center of the rectangular-shaped room were rows of high-back soft chairs bound in black leather and looking like passenger seats in a transport plane. "The effect, in fact," he noted, "was like that of a large plane's cabin." On one visit, he noticed several aviators in slacks and shirts lounging in the chairs and thumbing through popular magazines. "It seemed incongruous that on such a mission as this, leading the adventurous daily lives they led, they should find a measure of reality in fiction," he marveled. "But apparently they did." One pilot read an adventure story packed with vivid illustrations showing an "outdoorsy gentleman" in a lumberjack shirt shielding a glamorous female from the elements on a narrow mountain ledge. Another pilot flipped through the pages of an adventure novel while a third perused a twenty-five-cent mystery. At the end of the room the seats faced a blackboard full of symbols beyond Tregaskis's comprehension and "a moving picture screen," which, the correspondent learned, flashed vital information to the waiting pilots before a mission. "There are no mystery stories on board that I haven't read," a lieutenant told Tregaskis at breakfast one day. "I know them all by heart." Sailors lounging on deck in their off-duty moments could also be seen carrying magazines and books with them. The correspondent noticed a pre-eminence of pulp westerns and sports magazines. "Many sprawled on deck," Tregaskis said, "reading much-thumbed periodicals. I saw the worn magazines and books being exchanged, in a sort of impromptu chain-library system."[13]

As Task Force 16 steamed ahead, Tregaskis tried to, but could not, pry any details about the mission from the *Hornet*'s top officers, who remained tight-lipped about the ship's ultimate destination. One impatient pilot complained to the reporter: "Either I'm going to get my rear end shot off or I'm not. But I'd like to get it OVER WITH." While visiting the bridge, Tregaskis questioned one of the officers about what might lay ahead. The officer shrugged, pointed in the distance toward the *Enterprise*, the flagship of the task force's commander, Vice Adm. William "Bull" Halsey, and said, "He's the only one that knows.

I wish I could read his mind." Off the record, Tregaskis had been informed that a number of Japanese warships and transports had gathered in the harbor at Rabaul on the island of New Britain in the southwest Pacific. Intelligence reports indicated that the enemy ships might be preparing to hit Nauru and Ocean (Banaba) islands in the Gilberts, northeast of the Solomon Islands. "Our task force, I am told, may thwart this project by raiding the Japanese force in Rabaul Harbor; or engage the Japs when they put out to sea," Tregaskis recalled. "If so, we will probably be in for some trouble. Because Rabaul is well supplied with land-based aircraft and these are poison to a carrier." He also heard a rumor that the *Hornet* might well shift its course and hit other targets in the Gilberts. Although many on the carrier were eager for any kind of action, the long hours at sea caused many to long for home. Tregaskis fell into a conversation with a member of the crew from New York City, who reminisced about the restaurants he had frequented, the special meals he had enjoyed, and the dancers who entertained customers in Greenwich Village cafes. "Yes, New York is a fine city," Tregaskis commented. "'Wasn't it,' he corrected me."[14]

At dinner on May 4, Tregaskis and the *Hornet* crew heard sketchy reports that dive-bombers and torpedo bombers from Task Force 17, which included the carriers USS *Yorktown* (CV-5) and USS *Lexington* (CV-2), had caught and surprised Japanese ships in the harbor at Tulagi in the Solomons. "Since these are the waters for which we are headed, we all listened with added interest," he noted. According to the announcement, aircrews from the *Yorktown* had sunk a Japanese light cruiser, two destroyers, four "tugs or gunboats," and a cargo vessel. A nine-thousand-ton seaplane tender had been listed as "probably sunk" and a cruiser and a transport had been badly damaged. *Yorktown* pilots, however, had overstated their success, as only one destroyer, the *Kikuzuki*, as well as three minesweepers and four landing barges, were put out of action. Adm. Chester Nimitz described the results as a disappointment regarding "ammunition expended to results obtained." The initial positive report resulted in a "burst of handclapping" sweeping the wardroom on the *Hornet*. "This was the kind of medicine the officers liked to see fed to the Japs—and would enjoy dishing out themselves," Tregaskis wrote.[15]

The news particularly pleased the skipper of the *Hornet*'s Torpedo Squadron 8, Lt. Cdr. John C. Waldron, a navy veteran from Fort Pierre, South Dakota, with more than two decades of experience. Tregaskis remembered Waldron's eyes sparkling with glee when he said, "I tell you, Mr. Correspondent, when my boys hit 'em, some Jap ship is gonna get sunk. They may get some of us, but the way we go after 'em, we'll get 'em. They won't get away from us . . . got it all figured out . . . doesn't matter which way they turn." In his early forties, Waldron was much older than the men under his command, who noted that he never let them, or anyone else, forget that he possessed Native American ancestry (his mother had Sioux relatives). "Whenever he solved a problem ahead of others by what seemed to be uncanny intuition, he always credited it to 'the Indian in me,'" remembered Ens. George H. Gay Jr., a member of Torpedo 8 from Waco, Texas. Many members of Waldron's squadron believed their skipper had been "born with a six-shooter in each hand," added Gay.[16]

During stateside training, Waldron had often yelled at his men, "Don't sit there fat, dumb and happy—do something." He ran his squadron with a firm hand, teaching them things about their planes most pilots never learned, said Mears, including how to change an engine, how to load a torpedo, and the inner workings of the aircraft's hydraulic system. "He gave lecture after lecture on torpedo plane tactics and explained to his pilots how a well-planned and firmly executed attack could not fail to drive home several fish," said Mears. Waldron also had a sixth sense about when he had driven his men too hard. Sensing the tension, he would drop everything and host a party for his men at his home, offering them plenty to eat and drink. "It was almost like New Year's Eve every time this happened," said Mears. The young members of his team found they had a hard time keeping up with Waldron. "Boy, he was a party man," remembered Gay. "But he had his parties when he had his parties, and when he got aboard ship it was business." Even in the middle of the revelry, Waldron never forgot his goal, gathering his men around him to talk about his plans for combat and shouting out the squadron's motto, "Attack!"[17]

Waldron made quite an impression on Tregaskis. The correspondent particularly recalled the officer's "bright little eyes that flashed with sincerity when he spoke about something close to his heart—like torpedo bombing." The one distinguishing characteristic Tregaskis noticed most about Waldron was the "sharp jagged jut of his jaw. His jaw seemed to be his whole face, and it seemed to be leaning out towards you, when he spoke." The skipper could not be mistaken for a "subtle type," the reporter noted. Waldron's squadron reflected its commander's intrepid spirit, with Tregaskis describing them as the "death or glory boys," men who would take the greatest chances when attacking the Japanese. As *Life* photographer Ralph Morse observed about those serving in torpedo squadrons: "They don't stand any watches. They don't have to go out and do patrol jobs. They don't have any dogfights to worry about. They may sit around playing poker for a month before they have to go out. . . . . Then they go out and they don't come back."[18]

One day Waldron invited the correspondent to attend a regular class he held for members of Torpedo 8. During these sessions, he expounded on "the Waldron Method," going over again and again his catalogue of approaches and attacks. Tregaskis eagerly accepted the offer and sat in on the class, held the next morning in one of the pilot's ready rooms. The correspondent remembered that a lieutenant wrote on a blackboard the crude shape of a ship viewed from above. "Other lines indicated the direction and distance of the approach of our torpedo planes," he noted. "John had formulized this type of attack and applied a number to it, just as he had analyzed and catalogued all of the approaches and conditions: the scientific mind, bringing order and system to a helter-skelter collection of action and reaction." As the explanation of the attack went on, Tregaskis could see Waldron swivel around in his chair, point a finger at one of his squadron, and quiz him on the correct target angle for the release of his weapon, which the commander invariably referred to as the "pickle." When asked a question, Waldron would bounce up to the chalkboard and begin a lengthy response. Tregaskis described the officer as "sparkling with enthusiasm for his subject" and able to snap to attention what had been a sleepy audience with his sheer eagerness for the subject. Waldron's determination to succeed, whatever the cost, could be quickly deduced from his squadron's symbol, a closed fist. Talking with some of the "students" after the class, Tregaskis began to understand why they had appeared to be so nonchalant about what appeared to be a deadly serious business. "We've been through this stuff a million times," one of the squadron members told the correspondent. "I could tell it to you in my sleep. But Waldron keeps hammering at it. He lives the stuff."[19]

To an outsider such as Tregaskis, Waldron's fervor was exciting, so much so that the reporter asked if it might be possible to accompany Torpedo Squadron 8 on one of its missions. Waldron said that the Devastator's load on any initial attack would be too heavy to add the weight of a passenger, but he might be able to accompany a subsequent flight if he received permission from the ship's executive officer. G. M. "Scotty" Campbell, one of the squadron's pilots, showed Tregaskis where he could find, if he needed them, a parachute, a pair of goggles, and a helmet, all of which were stashed in the ready room. "If I don't come back from this one, you'll know where to find the stuff," Campbell said, with no hint of concern about his ominous forecast. Talking to other Torpedo 8 members, Tregaskis found that Campbell's calm acceptance of the "probability of death" was a common trait. One member even nicknamed the group the "Coffin Squadron." The pilots knew that their cumbersome, slow Devastator aircraft, equipped with an unreliable Mark 13 torpedo that could not be released at speeds above 115 miles per hour, would probably make them "sitting targets" for the enemy's antiaircraft and fighter opposition, unless their attack was "perfectly timed and luck was good," noted Tregaskis. Even if they discovered the enemy fleet, the pilots in Torpedo 8 could never be sure that their one-ton Mark 13s, once dropped, would find their way to their targets, as they had a habit of running deeper than their established setting and often failed to explode even when they successfully hit a ship.[20]

The *Yorktown* strike on Tulagi had been the opening salvo in what became known as the Battle of the Coral Sea, the first time in history that carriers from opposing sides engaged one another and in which the ships involved neither sighted or fired directly upon the other. From May 7 to May 8, Japanese Imperial Fleet and American carriers launched air strikes against one another off the northeast coast of Australia. Tregaskis said he and others on the *Hornet* had learned on the evening of May 6 that a large Japanese task force seemed to be heading into the Coral Sea from the north. A senior officer said the key to the battle would be to knock out the enemy's carriers. With that accomplished, the U.S. Navy could "hit them whenever we pleased. We'd have air superiority and they wouldn't dare put to sea with their surface units." The U.S. task force did sink a Japanese carrier, the *Shoho*, and heavily damaged a second, the *Shokaku*, putting it out of action for some time. An excited pilot from the *Lexington*, Lt. Cdr. R. E. Dixon, radioed a message after the *Shoho* went down: "Scratch one flattop! Dixon to Carrier, Scratch one Flattop!" Unfortunately, the *Lexington* became a prime target for Japanese planes and suffered severe damage. Wracked by internal explosions ignited by gasoline vapors, the "Lady Lex" had to be abandoned. A destroyer, the USS *Phelps*, finished off what the Japanese started by putting a swarm of torpedoes into the carrier's side, keeping it out of the enemy's hands. Japanese dive-bombers also hit the *Yorktown*, but it survived the onslaught and was able to safely retire from the scene. With heavy losses in aircraft, the Japanese had to abandon their planned invasion of Port Moresby in New Guinea. "It was a tactical victory for the Japanese but a strategic victory for the United States," according to naval historian Samuel Eliot Morison.[21]

Before they could hope to engage the Japanese, the *Hornet* had to rid itself of some visitors, U.S. Marine Corps pilots assigned to ferry a dozen F4F-3

Wildcat fighter planes to an American base on Efate Island in the New Hebrides. "The Marines joked about the fact that they had never before taken off from a carrier," Tregaskis reported. "What would it be like? 'I'll carry off the port gun gallery,' said one red-haired lieutenant." On May 11 the marines left the *Hornet* but not for their original destination, Efate. Instead they were to head to the island of New Caledonia in the southwest Pacific, a long flight. "Unless they pulled their wheels up and conserved fuel," Tregaskis noted, "they might not be able to make it." He watched as a plane handler held up a message changing the destination as the squadron leader's plane "revved up at the starting line on deck. The checkered starting flag jerked. The first plane roared forward and rose from the deck. One good!" The rest followed without major incident, except for the red-haired lieutenant, who skimmed close over the port gun gallery. "The black dots marking the heads of the crew standing watch there dropped abruptly from sight as the banking plane's wing nearly scraped the deck," recalled Tregaskis. Rid of its cargo, the *Hornet* headed north. The correspondent wondered if the carrier would swing around and come into the Coral Sea to join the fight.[22]

Tregaskis could not secure a definitive answer on just where the ship was going, as it headed north one day, making progress toward Tulagi, then shifted to a course northeast of the harbor, "now swinging around, heading straight towards it; our course, roughly southeast. Were we going to make a raid on the place?" The distance between the carrier and Tulagi continued to shorten, causing some pilots to be keyed up to a fever pitch, while others, "utterly crushed by previous disappointments," swore that there would be no action. "Notice we are within easy range of Nip seaplanes based at Tulagi," Tregaskis recalled the teletypes in the ready rooms spelling out on the morning of May 15. "Eyes open." At about 11:00 a.m. he learned that the ship's radar had spotted an unidentified aircraft many miles ahead at an altitude of twenty-five thousand feet. Wildcat fighters roared off the flight deck to intercept the "snooper," probably a Japanese flying boat, said Tregaskis, who joined others on the flight deck to see if they could identify the plane. "It was an eerie feeling, standing there knowing you were being watched without being able to see the other fellow," he wrote. "Like sitting behind one way glass with the other party, invisible, examining every inch of you, making detailed observations, writing them down, reporting them by radio, maybe making pictures too." Tregaskis came upon the *Hornet*'s captain, Mitscher, who was also squinting up into the sun trying to track the intruder. "It's practically impossible to see them if they fly high enough and keep the sun behind them," Mitscher confided to the correspondent. Later that afternoon, Tregaskis learned from a radioman that the carrier had intercepted a Japanese transmission that broadcast the strength of the American task force, as well as its position. At about sunset, the crew spotted another Japanese plane, and after dark the carrier swung sharply around and headed back where it had come from, Tregaskis reported.[23]

The sudden course change caused some discontent among the crew. "I thought we were going to attack," Tregaskis heard one sailor complain, "but it just looks like more puddling around." The correspondent found the move mysterious, but after some thinking, he said the stratagem became clear to him. Tregaskis already knew that the Japanese were planning to attack Nauru and Ocean islands, and the Americans wanted to thwart such a move, but at a minimum cost to their ships. "Now we had done it, by simply poking our nose within patrol range of Tulagi and allowing ourselves to be spotted," he noted. Also, he went on, the enemy knew their opponent possessed a strong force and would have to halt their planned operation. "This war game is like a game of chess," Mitscher told Tregaskis when he visited the captain on the bridge. "You spend an eternity of time getting the other fellow where you want him, bluffing and feinting. And when you have him, you hit him hard." Task Force 16 set course for Pearl Harbor. If there had not been the usual busy routine of carrier operations to worry about, Tregaskis said that the "sinking of morale would probably have become oppressive. Under the circumstances, it was at least noticeable."[24]

Although they had missed the Coral Sea engagement, the *Hornet* and the other ships in the task force did not let down their guard. At breakfast on the morning of May 16 Tregaskis heard a low-toned "boom" on the carrier's port side. "What's that?" a squadron leader sitting next to him asked. "Sounds like a depth charge." The pilot hurried on deck, followed closely by Tregaskis. Once there, they saw two destroyers prowling off the carrier's beam, several miles distant. "They were covering the water thoroughly, nosing in towards each other, then away, then at angles, then back together—like two cats with a mouse between them," the reported recalled. As he watched the destroyers through his binoculars, Tregaskis saw a low mushroom of white water rise behind one of the vessels, then another. From far away the destroyers seemed to be moving slowly, and Tregaskis described it as an "unexciting performance." He tried to track down word about what had happened, but he only learned that the destroyers could not confirm a definite hit. "And I had not seen the black nose of a submarine rising to the surface—the usual definite indication of victory," he noted. Later, he learned that one of the destroyers had received a "very good" sound contact on its listening device as it steamed alongside the *Hornet*. Because the distance between the two ships was only a thousand yards—excellent torpedo range—the destroyer's officers decided to take no chances and let loose with its depth charges. Another destroyer had joined in the search for the underwater enemy.[25]

Task Force 16 arrived at Pearl Harbor on May 26. At that time, the *Hornet* and the *Enterprise* were the only two fully operational American carriers available for action in the Pacific. Both carriers and other ships in the task force immediately began taking on fuel and provisions. Tregaskis barely had enough time to leave the *Hornet* to meet two reinforcements sent by the International News Service to assist in covering the Pacific war: Jack Singer, a former sportswriter for the *New York Herald*, later mortally wounded while aboard the aircraft carrier USS *Wasp*, and Frank Neal, a young reporter who had worked for the INS's Washington, DC, bureau. "Then it was back to the ship for me, and we were off again; and again, no one seemed to know where we were heading," Tregaskis said. The correspondent could not have known it at the time, but he and the *Hornet*'s men were headed to an atoll in the North Pacific—Midway—to finally meet the enemy in combat.[26]

5 "THE DANGER OF SUDDEN DEATH"

From his perch on the second level of the bridge on the USS *Hornet*, Richard Tregaskis could see below him the carrier's Air Group 8—Wildcat fighters, Dauntless dive-bombers, and Devastator torpedo bombers—warming up on the flight deck. The "shimmering arcs of their propellers mingled amidst a disorderly pile of wings and fuselages, punctuated by the blue flame and spitting smokes of exhausts," he recalled. With the roar of the engines reaching their peak, a deck operations officer, clutching a "ridiculously small checkered flag in his hand," staggered out against the multiple gales of propeller slipstreams to send the aircraft hurtling off the flight deck into their first clash against the *Kido Butai*, Japan's combined carrier battle group.[1]

As the first plane—its motor roaring full force—began to waddle forward, Tregaskis tried to detect the expression on the pilot's face as he swept by, gaining momentum. Even equipped with field glasses, however, the reporter could make out only the pilot's goggles "trained fixedly forward, his drawn, intense cheek, his hands aptly busy with the controls. The roar of his motor reached a peak of sound as he swept by, an unpleasant rough-throated gargle rising to a shout—and then he was near the end of the deck, his wheels lifting a thin distance off the boards, then sweeping off over the blue water." Tregaskis kept trying to pick out the faces of the men he had come to know while on the ship as they roared by, but they appeared to him merely as parts of their machines, "indistinguishable faceless men, one like the other, going out on a job of death."[2]

Tregaskis could imagine the "thoughts passing through their minds at this time of stress: the forward straining of their nerves as they swept down the deck knowing they were heading for combat; the quick imaginings of the action that might wait for them; the reality of the presence of death, the first straight look into the eyes of death; and superimposed against this thought-landscape, the hand and foot motions, the habited reactions, the intricate worry of simply flying—of the oft-repeated technique of simply getting a plane into the air." Reflecting on his impressions of that morning launch, Tregaskis said it represented to him the modern beginning of a modern conflict, one far different than the "ponderous maneuvering" of past naval battles, a reversion, perhaps, to the "old style of knights rattling out to meet the foe in a tourney." The *Hornet* airmen were on their way to make their mark on one of the turning points in the war in the Pacific: the Battle of Midway.[3]

Returning for another trip on the *Hornet*, Tregaskis had been unsure where it was headed as they left Pearl Harbor on May 28 with Task Force 16. Watching the *Hornet*'s posted position and bearing, as he had learned how to do, Tregaskis realized they were going to cruise by the U.S.-occupied French Frigate Shoals northwest of Hawaii and head toward Midway. Some of the correspondent's pilot friends, disillusioned by weeks of waiting and days of false suspense, swore that "this time as last time, we were simply cruising about," Tregaskis recalled, "that there would be no action for us. But here again, the hell of being at sea with a task force was that one could not relax; that one must at least continue day after day and hour after hour to expect action and the danger of sudden death."[4]

Danger was certain. Under the direction of Cdr. Joseph Rochefort, American cryptanalysts in Hawaii had intercepted and partially decoded messages from the Japanese Combined Fleet indicating an elaborate plan to seize the American-occupied Midway Atoll, consisting of two islands (Eastern and Sand) approximately 1,300 miles northwest of Hawaii. The Japanese also planned to capture the islands of Attu and Kiska in the Aleutian Island chain in the Territory of Alaska. Once U.S. forces on the two-thousand-acre Midway had been neutralized, Adm. Yamamoto Isoroku, the hero of the surprise attack on Pearl Harbor and commander of the Japanese Combined Fleet, expected to trap and annihilate the remaining U.S. carriers rushing to the scene to confront his forces. A ruse by American codebreakers helped to confirm the enemy's target. Japanese messages had often referred to U.S. installations with the code letters "AO" and "AF." Rochefort and his men were convinced that "AF" was the intended target of the Japanese and those letters represented Midway. Taking a suggestion from Wilfred J. "Jasper" Holmes, Midway transmitted a fake, urgent message in plain language telling of a problem with its fresh water system. Nimitz approved the plan, and the Japanese obliged the Americans by taking the bait. The cryptanalysts decoded a message from naval intelligence in Tokyo indicating that an air unit stationed on AF had reported a problem with its fresh water supply. "You can imagine Admiral Nimitz's delight when I showed him . . . the decrypted translated message proving beyond a doubt that AF was in fact Midway and allowed him to prepare his warm reception for those visitors in early June," noted Lt. Cdr. Edwin Layton, Nimitz's intelligence officer.[5]

To meet the threat to Midway, Nimitz assigned Task Force 16, built around two carriers, the *Enterprise* and *Hornet*. Nimitz also wanted to have the *Yorktown*, damaged in the Coral Sea action, available. Approximately a thousand workers had swarmed over the carrier when it slipped into its dry dock at Pearl Harbor. Told by his technical advisers that the needed repairs would take at least ninety days, Nimitz replied, "We must have this ship back in three days." The admiral planned to have the carrier as part of Task Force 17, commanded by Rear Adm. Frank "Jack" Fletcher. The *Hornet* and *Enterprise*, leading Task Force 16 with their accompanying cruisers, destroyers, and oilers, left Pearl Harbor on May 28 under the command of Vice Adm. Raymond Spruance (Rear Adm. William "Bull" Halsey Jr. had been hospitalized with a serious skin condition). The *Yorktown*, with workers still aboard frantically making repairs, moved out of the dry dock on May 29; it headed out to sea the next day. Fletcher would have overall command when the two carrier groups rendezvoused at "Point Luck," a spot in the Pacific approximately three hundred miles northeast of Midway. Both Fletcher and Spruance were cautioned by Nimitz to "be governed by the principle of calculated risk which you shall interpret to mean the avoidance of exposure of your forces to attack by superior enemy forces without good prospect of inflicting, as a result of such exposure, a greater damage to the enemy." Nimitz was willing to sacrifice Midway to the Japanese invasion force in favor of safeguarding America's precious carriers. The admiral did act to reinforce the American forces at Midway, sending additional troops and equipment. Nimitz counted on the 110 aircraft stationed on the atoll—his "unsinkable" aircraft carrier—to shadow and report on the enemy fleet's movements, as well as attack Japanese ships whenever possible.[6]

Shortly after the *Hornet* left Pearl Harbor, its crew heard from its commander,

Marc Mitscher, that the Japanese were approaching "for an attempt to seize the island of Midway. We are going to prevent them from taking Midway if possible. Be ready and keep on the alert." With a battle imminent, the pilots tried as best they could to deal with the news. Some of them had to fulfill rigorous schedules for patrol flights seeking enemy air and surface craft. In the evenings, however, instead of going straight to bed, they relaxed by engaging in numerous "bull sessions" that were full of talk usually involving either their families or the women they knew in civilian life, Tregaskis noted. Lt. William J. "Gus" Widhelm, executive officer for one of the scouting squadrons, provided plenty of diversion from the strain of waiting by playing records on a phonograph he had brought on board. Pilots with idle moments drifted in, night or day, to Widhelm's cabin in the ship's forecastle, to pick out their favorite popular music from his "ample collection," said Tregaskis, adding that Widhelm, "one of the lustiest recounters of personal experiences of all sorts, entertained in intervals." A frequent visitor to Widhelm's quarters was Lt. Cdr. Samuel G. "Pat" Mitchell, who commanded Fighter Squadron 8. Mitchell particularly enjoyed the song "(There'll Be Bluebirds Over) The White Cliffs of Dover," playing it again and again, as its singer crooned the tune's haunting lyrics, "I'll never forget the people I met braving those angry skies / I remember well as the shadows fell, the light of hope in their eyes." Tregaskis found something touching in Mitchell's fondness for the tune, "with its nostalgic longing for days of peace." The correspondent tried to get the pilots to talk about the dangers they seemed sure to face, but most did not want to discuss the subject. "Some of them, I believe," he noted, "never considered the possibility of dying and had thus resolved no particular attitude towards the subject. This was for them a job and the risks were only incidental fixtures in their everyday lives."[7]

On the morning of June 3 Tregaskis reported that the ship's radios had picked up a plain-language message from a navy operator in Dutch Harbor in the Aleutian Islands that the naval and army bases there were under attack by Japanese aircraft. He and others wondered if the American fleet had been outsmarted by the enemy, "if they were going to slam a wedge of landing forces into Alaska and menace our coast, now that the bulk of our Pacific naval strength hovered near Midway." Later that day came another dispatch indicating that the Midway Defense Forces had sent a squadron of B-17 Flying Fortress bombers to hit enemy warships and transports. Tregaskis slept "only intermittently through the night," thinking he was about to witness his first great sea battle, but also suspecting that it might be another of "those imminent battles which faded like mirages; making the mental reservation, to ward off possible disappointment, that after all it might never happen and might be instead only another near miss like our venture into the Coral Sea. In the flashes of anxiety which come and go often, like swift shadows in such times, the thought that the anticipated battle might not develop into a fight was comforting." He said his predominant feeling was "anxiousness that the excitement should begin."[8]

That evening, gathered in Ready Room Number 4, the members of Torpedo 8 were handed a mimeographed message from their commander, John C. Waldron. The message read:

> Just a word to let you know I feel we are all ready. We have had a very short time to train, and we have worked under the most severe difficulties. But we have truly done the best humanly possible. I actually believe that under these conditions, we are the best in the world. My greatest hope is that we encounter a favorable tactical situation, but if we don't and worst comes to worst, I want each of us to do his utmost to destroy our enemies. If there is only one plane left to make final run-in, I want that man to go in and get a hit. May God be with us all. Good luck, happy landings, and give 'em hell!

As his squadron read his words, Waldron spoke, warning them that the approaching battle promised to be the biggest of the war and could also be a turning point for the American cause in the Pacific. "It will be an historical and, I hope, a glorious event," Waldron told them. Lt. Frederick Mears, who had joined the *Hornet* just as it left for Midway and was assigned to Torpedo 8, knew he probably would not be part of the first mission, as Waldron did not want a pilot along who had never landed a Devastator on a carrier. Mears did get to participate in the mission briefing. He remembered that Waldron wanted not only to make a couple of strikes during the day, but also planned a surprise attack after dark. "His theory is that the enemy will be in one hell of a mess after the day attacks, with their morale low and confusion rampant," Mears said. Waldron knew, however, that some of his men might not return. Mears said the commander urged his squadron to make sure their personal affairs were in order and, above, all, "to write letters to their families, 'just in case some of us don't get back.'"[9]

Ens. George H. Gay Jr.'s logbook for the day indicated that he had checked his plane until he knew "every bolt on it. It's in the pink, . . . Things are oiled and ready." He remained nervous, however, because the Midway mission would mark the first time he "had ever carried a torpedo on an aircraft and was the first time I had ever taken a torpedo off a ship, had never even seen it done. None of the other Ensigns in the squadron had either." Of course, Gay noted, he and the others had a few months earlier watched as Lt. Col. James H. Doolittle and his army pilots, who had never seen a carrier before, all took off safely in their B-25B Mitchell bombers from the *Hornet*, so "we figured if they could do it, well we could do it too." Although nervous, not unlike the feeling one had before a big football game, Gay said, the squadron had full confidence in its commander. "We could almost look at the back of Comdr. Waldron's head and know what he was thinking," Gay recalled, "because he had told us so many times over and over just what we should do under all conditions." The torpedo plane pilots knew they were at a disadvantage in combat because of their outdated Devastators. Their aircraft could not climb to the same altitude as the fighters and dive-bombers, so they expected to be on their own. "We didn't expect to run into the trouble that we found of course," Gay said, "but we knew that if we had any trouble we'd probably have to fight our way out of it ourselves."[10]

Tregaskis joined the other *Hornet* pilots as they gathered in their ready rooms on the morning of June 4. In one room he found the men draped as usual in relaxed postures in their overstuffed chairs, responding quickly to any message that came in over the teletype. Their eyes remained fixed on the growing lines of letters until the words made sense. The early messages were innocuous: "wind 18," "weather fair," or identification signals. Then came a radio message from Midway that Japanese bombers were swarming on them in large numbers. "The black letters of type popped onto the teletype screens to spell out the position, distance, course and composition of the Japanese forces, which included four carriers. This was not going to be easy," Tregaskis realized. Finally, the *Hornet* flyers, who had never before flown in combat, were ordered, "Pilots, man your planes." Tregaskis watched them as they pulled open the heavy, watertight hatch and ran out to their aircraft. "I heard the shout, 'Stand clear of propellers' relayed along the deck by hoarse, excited voices," he said. "Then, 'Stand by to start all engines.' And after that, the hiss and sputter of the start, the rough raucous sound of the engine catching and shouting out the rowdy, disordered sound of its horsepower. The mounting of the sound of engine upon engine left the deck shaking with the power of it."[11]

The *Hornet* sent out fifty-nine aircraft for its first mission—ten Wildcat fighters, thirty-four Dauntless dive-bombers, and fifteen Devastator torpedo bombers—to find the four large carriers of the Japanese striking force, the *Kaga, Akagi, Soryu,* and *Hiryu*. Before leaving the *Hornet*, Waldron, according to Mitscher, has stressed to his captain that Torpedo 8 was "well trained and ready and that he would strike his blow at the enemy regardless of consequences." When the last plane was gone, the carrier became strangely quiet. Gun crews stood at alert, scanning the skies for any Japanese planes that might "fleck the blue horizon at any moment, and in a few seconds grow into diving animals pregnant with bombs and torpedoes," remembered Tregaskis. A ship's photographer dashed by to snap a picture of those at battle stations in sky control, all dressed in the "regalia of battle," including grotesquely large helmets that fit over earphones, shiny black goggles designed for peering into the sun, and bulky flash clothing, preventive measures against "the flame-sheets of bursting bombs," he noted. One of the men in the group told the reporter after the photographer had left that they had asked him to take the picture as a worthwhile memento to send to their wives or sweethearts. Stopping in at the air-plot office, Tregaskis noticed a group of officers sitting on a leather-upholstered couch and standing between the map boards and bank of radio equipment awaiting word from the *Hornet* squadrons. "No one spoke, and the radio speaker, except for a few cackles of static, made no sound," he recalled.[12]

Checking in again later at the air-plot office, Tregaskis discovered the listeners gathered there in a state of tense excitement; they had finally received word of the first contact with the Japanese fleet. They had heard Waldron's voice shouting something about "Zeros," the dangerous Japanese fighters, and asking "Stanhope," Cdr. Stanhope Ring, commander of the *Hornet*'s air group, for help as the enemy latched on to his aircraft. Also heard over the communication gear was Waldron's sharp order to his squadron to immediately attack. The messages, however, were garbled by distance and distorted by the crackle of static, which only served to confuse those listening in on the *Hornet*. Tregaskis had plenty of questions: "What had happened? Had our attack been pressed home successfully? Had our people all been shot down? Why didn't they come back? They were overdue, for it was past noon. What had happened to John Waldron and the Zeros? Where was our dive-bomber force? Most important, where were our fighters, whose gasoline should be running out at just about this time?" Finally, he wondered, "where were the Japanese?"[13]

Early that afternoon Tregaskis had some of the answers to his questions when a few dive-bombers returned to the *Hornet*. Climbing down from their planes, Ring and Walter Rodee, who led the scouting squadron of Dauntless aircraft, wore "forlorn faces," said Tregaskis. They had missed the enemy fleet and, with their fuel exhausted, had barely managed to make it back to the carrier. Tregaskis also learned that the Wildcat fighters could not find their way back, had run out of gas, and crashed into the sea (eight of the ten pilots were eventually found and rescued by Consolidated PBY Catalina patrol planes from Midway). "What about John Waldron's TBD's?" the reporter asked. One of the radioman/gunner on a returned Dauntless indicated that his group had lost track of them, but he believed the torpedo squadron had found its way to the Japanese fleet. "He [Waldron] said he was being jumped by Zeros and asked for fighter protection," the crewman told Tregaskis. The grim news was received "with a noticeable deflation among all present," remembered the correspondent. "One could see our morale sinking." Down in one of the ready rooms Tregaskis came across a fighter pilot who always seemed to complain the most among the crew. The young officer was not happy, saying, with his voice rising and quivering: "Same old snafu business. Everything all f—— up. Why don't they get rid of the old fuds running this war? They won't win anything until they do."[14]

The officer's mood would not have improved if he had known the full story of what came to be known as the *Hornet* aircrew's "flight to nowhere" that morning. Air Group 8 had set its course for due west, 265 degrees, with the forty-four fighters and dive-bombers flying at an altitude of 20,000 feet, while the fifteen torpedo planes were far below at 1,500 feet. Although they were supposed to observe radio silence, Waldron, believing they were taking the wrong course, could no longer contain himself, yelling at Ring that he was leading the air group the wrong way if he wanted to find the Japanese carriers. "I'm leading this flight," Ring responded. "You fly with us right here." Frustrated, Waldron, disobeying his superior's orders, radioed, "I know where the damned Jap fleet is" and led his squadron to the southwest. Before leaving the carrier, Waldron had told his squadron not to worry about their navigation, but to follow him, "as he knew where he was going," said Gay, who also noted that his commander had been able to fly straight to the Japanese fleet "as if he'd had a string tied to them." A short while later, the Wildcat pilots, with their fuel beginning to run low, also abandoned Ring and attempted a return to the *Hornet*. Radiomen on the dive-bombers eventually heard snatches of messages from Waldron, trying to reach Ring, as well as the warning, "Watch those fighters!" and the order, "Attack immediately!"[15]

Waldron had found the enemy, but, with no fighter protection, his squadron, flying low and slow in order to launch their white-nosed torpedoes, proved easy prey for the Zeros protecting their carriers. "Zeros were coming in from all angles and from both sides at once," said Gay. "They would come in from abeam, pass each other just over our heads, and turn around to make another attack, . . . The planes of Torpedo Eight were falling at irregular intervals. Some were on fire, and some did a half-roll and crashed on their backs, completely out of control." Waldron had been shot down early on during the attack. Gay saw his commander's Devastator burst into flame and watched as Waldron tried to stand up out of the fire, putting his right leg outside of his cockpit before his plane hit the water and disappeared. Gay heard his radioman/gunner, Bob Huntington, call out that he had been hit and then heard no more from him. With his gunner out of action, Gay no longer had to fly straight and level to provide him a solid firing platform from which to shoot, so he could dodge the incoming Zeros. With his plane "pitching like a bronco," Gay believed he had been able to drop his torpedo, aiming it to strike the *Soryu*, but could not tell for sure, as he had never done it before. His electrical release system had been knocked out by enemy fire, so he had to release his torpedo manually, flying right at the carrier, "balls to the wall," as he described it, trying to present the smallest target possible. He never knew what happened to his torpedo, if it ran true and hit the Japanese carrier, dived down and hit the bottom of the ocean, or if it turned around and headed for Pearl Harbor. "What I know for sure is I tried," Gay said. Flying over the carrier, he could see action on its bridge, including an officer "waving his arms. I could even see a pair of binoculars in one hand and a Samurai sword in the other. He was pointing at me like they couldn't see me." With his Devastator shot to pieces, the ensign had to ditch it in the Pacific. Gay survived, but the other twenty-nine members of his squadron had been annihilated. Mitsuo Fuchida, an officer on the *Akagi*, observed the slaughter and noted that nearly fifty Zeros had intercepted the "unprotected enemy formation! Small wonder that it did not get through."[16]

On the *Hornet*, the spirits of Tregaskis and others had been cheered somewhat as they could see the *Enterprise* recovering its fighters, dive-bombers, and even a "few straggling torpedo planes" it had launched earlier. The correspondent learned that the *Enterprise* planes had found and hit the Japanese carriers. "No further details for the moment, but the critical ensign must have been gratified," said Tregaskis. The forty-one torpedo planes launched from the *Hornet*, *Enterprise*, and *Yorktown* had been badly mauled, with only four surviving to return home and none scoring any hits. American dive-bombers had far better luck, delivering fatal blows to the *Kaga, Akagi,* and *Soryu.* Lt. Cdr. John S. "Jimmy" Thach, who commanded the *Yorktown's* fighter planes, had a tough time with the Zeros, remembering that the air "was like a bee hive, and I wasn't sure at that moment that anything would work" to counteract the enemy's attacks. "I was utterly convinced then that we weren't coming back," he recalled. Suddenly, Thach saw a "glint in the sun—it looked like a beautiful silver waterfall—these were the dive bombers coming down. I could see them very well, because that's the direction the Zeros were, too. They were above me but close, not anywhere near the altitude of the dive bombers. I'd never seen such superb dive bombing. It looked to me like almost every bomb hit. Of course, there were some near misses. There weren't any wild ones."[17]

The one large Japanese carrier left undamaged, the *Hiryu,* responded, launching its dive-bombers and torpedo planes against the Americans, eventually tracking down the *Yorktown.* Tregaskis remembered that the *Hornet* had been maneuvering normally on the bright, sunlit sea, when everyone began to move and talk fast and the ship put on a sudden burst of speed and began a sharp turn, "heeling over on her beam ends, so that one had to brace against the slope." He looked around and could see the ships in Task Force 16 making full speed and turning in several different directions. "Our wakes must have looked like crazy scrawls on a blackboard, from the air," he noted. Tregaskis did not know what was happening from his position at sky control. He remembered thinking at the time that if he had been a more seasoned correspondent, he might have tried to run to the bridge or the communication office to overhear the latest information from the task force's commander. Being new to his job, however, he labored "under the delusion that a sea battle could be understood if it was merely watched. I believed I could see everything; and with some commonsense, I felt that the moment I ducked below, Jap aircraft would surely come in, attack, and be gone before I could catch a glimpse of the action." Tregaskis could see, on the *Hornet's* port side, astern, a mushroom-shaped black geyser that grew fatter and taller as he watched. "What had happened?" he wondered. "Everyone about me seemed to be too busy to be bothered. I wondered if this could be a Japanese ship, which our planes had hit. Or one of ours? How about the carrier Yorktown, which was working with us, but over the horizon somewhere[?] Could this be the Yorktown?" It was; the carrier had been hit by bombs from three Japanese Val dive-bombers, with one bomb landing forward, one amidships, and one astern. With the carrier badly damaged, Fletcher had to transfer his command to a nearby cruiser, the USS *Astoria*, and planes that had been stationed on the carrier had to look elsewhere to land.[18]

One of the *Yorktown* fighter planes, a F4F-4 Wildcat flown by Ens. Dan Sheedy, tried to find sanctuary on the *Hornet* after protecting from the deadly Zeros a squadron of torpedo planes from his carrier. The *Hornet* turned into the wind and an LSO took his place at the stern to wave Sheedy in for a landing. Tregaskis could see, however, that the stubby Wildcat did not "swing in the conventional wide landing circle. Instead, it cut a swift, ragged half circle directly towards the side of the ship, skidded sharply in with one wing low. A wounded pilot? We waited for the crash." Sheedy had been wounded in the shoulder and ankle, and his plane had suffered damage severe enough to knock out the safety mechanism for his six .50-caliber Browning machine guns that were supposed to be switched off when landing. Instead, the guns were ready to fire. "I watched one wheel and wing crumple under the impact, and then machine guns chattered and stopped and chattered again," said Tregaskis, "and I saw the wings of the crashed plane smoking. Her guns going off." At almost at the same instant, he saw a figure jump from the Wildcat's cockpit and take a few limping steps across the flight deck before being aided by deck crewmen.[19]

When the fighter's guns finally stopped firing their steel-jacketed rounds, *Hornet* emergency personnel ran to the after end of the island, as there were reports that men had been injured and killed. "I felt in the air the sickening shock that comes after a terrible accident, and hesitated about going aft," Tregaskis remembered. Finally, he went, looked into the circular shield of an antiaircraft gun position, and could see, inside the ring around the gun, four bodies "looking sodden and heavy, like rough piles of gray sandbags. Next to the ring, outside of it, sprawled a dead marine, arms stretched out, legs stretched out in the middle of a circular red sheet of gore. The gray face looked straight up. There was no top to the head, for the head became red above the eyebrows and melted into the pool of gore." An officer informed Tregaskis that five men had been killed and twenty more seriously wounded. "I gulped. Well, the accidents of war . . . bound to happen . . . lucky it hadn't happened to me . . . yesterday I had stood here to watch the planes landing . . . oh well," he thought to himself.[20]

Tregaskis visited Sheedy in one of the ready rooms, where the pilot had been taken, given a sandwich, and had his injured leg propped up awaiting medical attention. The correspondent looked at the pilot's face to see how he had reacted to the accident, but could see that the ensign was too shocked to know anything: "His words rolled over each other: 'Plane's shot up like a sieve . . . the Zeros riddled the hell out of me. . . . I shot one down. . . . I followed him down to the water and he fell off one wing and went right in . . . then they shot me up . . . through my cockpit . . . all around me . . . hit me in the ankle. . . . I just made that landing . . . plane no good for anything . . . they threw it overboard." Tregaskis asked Sheedy how he came to land on the *Hornet* instead of his own carrier, and finally received confirmation that the *Yorktown* had been hit and was on fire. "No one asked the pilot then if he had left his gun switches on when his plane crashed on our deck," Tregaskis noted. "Any anger we might have felt about those killed, was put aside . . . accidents, bound to happen, even in the best organized war."[21]

Repair crews patched the *Hornet*'s flight deck so air operations could resume and planes set off to find the surviving Japanese carrier, the *Hiryu*, which had been spotted by search planes from the *Yorktown*. About a half hour after the *Enterprise* had sent off twenty-five Dauntlesses, including some from the *Yorktown*, the *Hornet* launched sixteen dive-bombers to find the *Hiryu*. "I tried to get more specific information on what had happened, but none was available," said Tregaskis. Once again, the *Hornet* began to maneuver erratically, with the wakes of the ships in Task Force 16 crossing and crisscrossing and men scanning the skies for the enemy. On this occasion, Tregaskis could see the bump of a ship on the horizon, probably, he thought, the *Yorktown*. Suddenly, the sky above the ship became spotted with specks of black breaking out like a rash, spreading, smudging, and growing larger, with other flecks—antiaircraft fire—also visible. "The anti-aircraft fire continued to burst on the horizon, where the sky was already smudged, and now I saw a spot of light flash among the bursts," Tregaskis noted. "It seemed like a small electric bulb, rather high in the sky. It was a bright yellow color. While I watched, fascinated, knowing it was a plane falling in flames, the little bright light sank slowly to the horizon, then disappeared against the blue. 'One Jap down,' I thought, and added, 'I hope.'" A nearby crewman exclaimed, "Flamers! Three down! I saw three!" Tregaskis had seen only one plane fall, but the excitement was so great among those on the carrier that he could not be sure who was right. Six months before Midway, Tregaskis would not have believed it was normal to be confused during a battle. "Now, I knew that confusion is unavoidable," he mused.[22]

After some more wild maneuvers by the *Hornet*, Tregaskis spied the shape of a ship on the horizon with the box-like shape of a carrier. "Then everything I had seen became clearer to me," he said. "The ship was the Yorktown. She had been hit in the earlier afternoon attack, and now she had been hit again. She was dead in the water. Listing. She must be badly hit." Tregaskis could not know from such a distance, but Japanese planes had penetrated Task Force 17's defenses and slammed two torpedoes into the *Yorktown*'s side. Some of the carrier's pilots achieved a measure of revenge by working with *Enterprise* dive-bombers to hit and set afire the *Hiryu*, the fourth Japanese carrier put out of action by the Americans that day. Coming onto the scene, a pilot from the *Hornet* reported that the enemy carrier was "burning throughout its entire length."[23]

Anxious to catch up on the latest information, Tregaskis hurried to one of the fighter ready rooms, which were already filled with pilots, including several from the *Yorktown*. The shock of their first contact with the enemy affected the rookie *Hornet* fliers "as variously as alcohol intoxication," Tregaskis remembered. Ens. George Formanek had been greatly depressed by the experience of shooting down an enemy plane, with his face dark and despairing as he told the correspondent, "That was terrible! I saw him explode . . . a big ball of flames! He burned." Ens. Morrill Cook, who had downed two Japanese torpedo planes, had quite the opposite reaction. Cook, said Tregaskis, smiled happily at the memory "as he might after having tasted some pleasant dish at the table." Ens. Warren Ford also "spoke with an exaltation that was almost defiant, as he told about knocking down one of the attackers." The pilots from the *Yorktown* seemed calmer, which was natural, said Tregaskis, as they had seen action at the Battle of the Coral Sea. Lt. Arthur Brassfield, a former high school principal from Browning, Missouri, told the reporter in a matter-of-fact, humorous manner about how he had shot down four Japanese. "It's a rough game," Brassfield said with a smile. "If they don't knock it off pretty soon, somebody's going to get hurt."[24]

6 "THE MOST INTENSE EXCITEMENT IN THE WORLD"

The terrible cost of the American victory at the Battle of Midway hit correspondent Richard Tregaskis while at lunch on the USS *Hornet* on June 5, 1942. Tregaskis tried his best to ignore the empty seats at his table, where officers such as John C. Waldron and Samuel G. "Pat" Mitchell had once sat, as well as those now vacant at the next table, where many of Torpedo Squadron 8 had gathered to eat and share the latest rumors. To Tregaskis, the table near him seemed "like a graveyard, with chairs for stones." The thirty men from Squadron 8 had been given up as lost, but many on the *Hornet* hoped they might simply have been forced down in the Pacific and would eventually be found floating somewhere, safe, in rubber lifeboats. Fighter pilots from the *Yorktown* filled the places at another table where once the *Hornet*'s Wildcat pilots had sat. Tregaskis heard no mention made about the empty seats. "The usual chit-chat passed over our table," he remembered, "as if the situation was perfectly normal."[1]

After dinner, however, one of the ship's officers, in a conversation with the correspondent, said odds were that Waldron and his squadron had made out all right. The officer noted, "John always said that if one of his planes went into the water, all of them were to go in and tie their life rafts together; that was part of his doctrine. I bet they're floating around somewhere." Tregaskis hoped so as well, but the last word from Waldron, indicating his planes were under heavy attack from Zeros, "did not sound auspicious." Word finally came from Midway that Ens. George H. Gay Jr. had been rescued. He had avoided detection by the Japanese by hiding under a seat cushion he had found floating in the water. After spending thirty hours treading water and floating in a leaky life raft, Gay been seen by a PBY Catalina rescue plane, which later went back to pick him up. As the Catalina landed and drew closer to him, the exhausted pilot, his eyes encrusted with salt water, could see a sailor leaning out of the airplane's hatch and heard him yell, "Seen any Jap planes lately?" Gay called out, "I haven't seen a thing since you came by this morning." The sailor had the last word: "Good. Let's get the hell out of here!"[2]

Hornet pilots continued their run of bad luck on June 5, as twenty-six dive-bombers went after Japanese ships that had been spotted northwest of Midway. Late that day, it seemed as if the search was going to prove fruitless, Tregaskis recalled, until he heard reports that a group of the carrier's planes had found the enemy and had made an attack. Some of the group, including Cdr. Stanhope Ring, returned to the *Hornet* before sunset. "I watched Ring's face as he made his report to Capt. [Marc] Mitscher," said Tregaskis. "The commander's face was a study in disappointment. 'I think it was a light cruiser,' he said. 'It was all we found. We dived on it—but—I don't think we got any hits.' And he added as if wringing out a last desperate drop of hope, 'Might have had some close misses.'" Other pilots, upon their return, reported the ship they had attacked was a destroyer (later identified as the *Tanikaze*) and no hits had been made. "A wave of gloom spread about the ship on the heels of the news," reported the correspondent. Several of Dauntless dive-bombers were still unaccounted for, and, with the day ending, those who had enough fuel to make it to the carrier would have to negotiate a difficult night landing. Risking detection by the Japanese, the *Hornet* switched on its deck lights to help guide its pilots home. Tregaskis described what happened:

> The planes did not waste time making landing circles. The first one swung sharply in, and the red light and the green light which marked the ends of his wings grew steadily farther apart as he came in closer and his motor grew louder. Then the motor diminished in sound, and we knew he was getting ready to hit the deck in a landing; but still the red and green stars rushed in towards us and grew larger and farther apart; then the engine spat blue flame between the red and green stars, one star dipped as the other rose, and the plane careened in between the rows of the deck lights at a speed which seemed terrifyingly fast. Watching from the exposed flag bridge, we ran for cover; but the expected crash did not come. The red and green lights, the

blue torching motor of the plane, bounced and bounced again and then settled. One down, and safely!

The other planes followed close behind, and as each one arrived Tregaskis and the carrier's crew were sure, based on the alarming speed of the approaches, that crashes were inevitable, but all the aircraft landed safely. "A pilot who stood next to me on the flag bridge breathed a sigh and said, 'Well, they qualified.' He explained that most of these pilots had never before made night carrier landings, that this was their first, and qualifying run," recalled Tregaskis. With several planes still unaccounted for, the *Hornet* took a final risk, turning on its searchlights, waving the beams of light "across the sky like tall, stiff fingers," he reported. It worked; three additional aircraft made precarious, but safe, landings.[3]

The morning of June 6 brought a vast change from the "bad luck and wasted effort of the previous day," according to Tregaskis. A reconnaissance flight from the *Enterprise* reported seeing what appeared to be a Japanese battleship, heavy cruiser, and accompanying destroyers headed toward Wake Island. The ships were two heavy cruisers, the *Mikuma* and *Mogami*, which had collided earlier trying to avoid an American submarine. Facing no air opposition, strike missions by the *Hornet* and *Enterprise* left both cruisers heavily damaged; the *Mogami* escaped, but the *Mikuma*, gutted by fires and barely recognizable as a ship, eventually sank. Gus Widhelm and his fellow *Hornet* pilots were thrilled at finally hitting the enemy. Tregaskis remembered that although Widhelm's plane had been struck by heavy antiaircraft fire and had been damaged badly enough that he could see its inner workings, the pilot had climbed out, "still grinning like a good-natured ape and giving the thumbs-up sign." Widhelm ran up to the bridge to give his report to Mitscher, telling his captain, "Those thousand pound bombs are great. Load us up with those and let us go back and sock 'em again. And armor-piercing—give us all armor-piercing ammo—we can sink the cans [destroyers] with just strafing—blow 'em apart." Tregaskis noted that Widhelm had strafed enemy ships on his previous flight and "was anxious to go back and do it again."[4]

Tregaskis also came across a young lieutenant who had returned from the successful attack. The flyer's hair stood askew on his head like "a disordered pile of feathers. His eyes stared. He talked so fast his words fell over each other. He gesticulated like a marionette," Tregaskis remembered. The officer bragged about smacking the enemy and seemed eager to make a return engagement.

The reporter tried to ask him if he had left the ship afire, but the pilot did not seem to hear the question, repeating, "We'll go back and hit 'em again. What are we waiting for?" A few days later, with the battle over and the pilots having had a chance to rest and regain their usual composure, Tregaskis saw the same pilot, but this time he seemed to be "in a blue funk," with his face drawn and pockets under his eyes. "Feel bad?" the correspondent asked him. "Terrible," the pilot replied. "Like a hangover." Tregaskis agreed, describing the lieutenant's condition as a "hangover after a jag of the most intense excitement in the world."[5]

The Japanese did provide some comic relief to the *Hornet*'s crew following the battle. On the evening of June 6 the carrier intercepted a propaganda broadcast asserting that Japan's fleet had won a glorious victory in the Pacific, crushing the Americans and sinking three of their carriers: the *Hornet*, *Enterprise*, and *Yorktown*. "This gave rise amongst us to the usual run of jokes about being sunk without knowing it," Tregaskis said. The broadcast, however, did make a deep impression on the correspondent's consciousness, and he thought a lot about it that night. It was the first time he had ever been confronted with a "falsehood perpetuated on such a colossal scale—when within my grasp I had definite evidence that the falsehood was deliberate and unmitigated." Within a short time, just five minutes, Tregaskis had acquired a fundamental conviction about the fate of truth and public information under a totalitarian form of government such as Japan's, a conviction that "six months or six years of reading might never have bred." He went to bed and enjoyed a "reasonably peaceful sleep," but with his semiconsciousness ready for developments the next morning that might "send us into battle again." After all, Tregaskis noted, the Japanese might still be able to "mass another force and try to make their propaganda come true."[6]

The next morning, June 7, Tregaskis could see that the *Hornet* appeared to be headed east, and he and the carrier's crew "happily surmised" they were making for Pearl Harbor. Soon, however, Task Force 16 headed north as well, and the correspondent wondered if they might be off to seek the Japanese ships involved in the attack on the Aleutians. "Now we resigned ourselves to the fact that weeks might elapse before we reached Pearl Harbor again," Tregaskis said. "And in hours which were painfully idle, compared with the days of the Battle of Midway, time passed with playing acey-deucy and cribbage, and the spinning of bull-sessions in the ward-room." These sessions included many on board wondering about the fate of the *Yorktown* (it went down later that day after taking two torpedoes from Japanese submarine *I-168*) and hearing dispatches about specially modified Martin B-26 Marauder army bombers equipped with torpedoes sent out to attack the enemy carriers (four participated, two were shot down, and none scored any hits). "One startling piece of information arrived by secret dispatch: that an Army B-17 had scored directs hits with 1,600 pound armor-piercing bombs on an enemy cruiser," Tregaskis recalled, "and that the cruiser had sunk in 16 seconds." The crew greeted the news with "great delight and approbation," he noted, but he later discovered that the B-17 had not bombed a Japanese cruiser, but an American submarine, which had escaped without damage.[7]

The *Hornet* and *Yorktown* airmen also held intense discussions about the performance of the enemy's Mitsubishi A6M2 Zero fighter. All the American fighter pilots agreed that the Zero, Tregaskis reported, was faster, more maneuverable, and could outclimb the Wildcat, described by many as looking like a "flying beer bottle." The protective armor and self-sealing fuel tanks on the Wildcat did save many lives, especially in comparison to the Zero, which had no such protection for its pilots and burned easily when hit. But Lt. Cdr. John S. "Jimmy" Thach, who had developed the famed "Thach weave," a self-defense maneuver for Wildcat pilots under attack by Zeros, pointed out to the correspondent that even if "you took the armor and leak-proof tanks out of the Grumman, it would still be inferior in performance to the Zero." It was a tribute to the combat ability of U.S. pilots, Thach continued, that they had been able to escape with their lives and shoot down as many Japanese aircraft as they had. (In the battle, the Japanese had lost 256 aircraft to 150 for the Americans.) Tregaskis also noted that Thach expressed some strong opinions about the enemy's "much-vaunted hara-kiri courage," his alleged preference to death in battle to life in peace. After his wingman had been shot down, Thach said he had "went a little out of my head" and tried to ram three Japanese planes. "But they didn't like the idea," Thach told Tregaskis. "They pulled out each time I tried to take them in a scissor (i.e., head on)."[8]

As Task Force 16 sailed on for the Aleutians, Tregaskis worked at a frantic pace to finish several articles describing the Battle of Midway. He typed five copies of one long general story about the battle (four copies were required under navy regulations) and sent them to Pearl Harbor via a tanker headed in that direction. "Then came news that another ship was returning to Pearl—and anxious to have the story aboard the first ship which might reach port, I typed four more copies of the same long story and sent them back on the second ship," he said. The correspondent could have saved himself the trouble of both jobs. Tregaskis's story about the biggest battle so far in the Pacific war—one that Fleet Adm. Ernest King said marked the first defeat suffered by the Japanese navy in 350 years and "restored the balance of naval power in the Pacific"—did not receive its official release from the fleet censor until June 22, ten days after Task Force 16 had returned to Pearl Harbor.[9]

Stepping ashore in Hawaii, Tregaskis could feel a "listlessness in the atmosphere." In the crowded naval offices at the submarine base, where the press office was located, the usual rushing pace of activity had slowed to a walk. He soon found out the reason. With the smashing American victory at Midway, Hawaii, which had been in the throes of "great nervous tension during that fight—the natural tension of a land watching the struggle which would determine her life or death—had relaxed, almost relapsed." Everywhere the correspondent went, he had the unpleasant experience of being told just how the Battle of Midway had been won, as if it was a closed issue, with all the facts in and the event ready to take its place in history. "It seemed disconcerting to me," Tregaskis observed, "that this should be the attitude when the work of naval units which had participated in the fight had hardly been mentioned; when the men of Admiral [Raymond A.] Spruance's battle force, who had formed the backbone of our fighting force, had just reached port and not yet had a chance to tell their stories."[10]

When Tregaskis read over the previous week's newspapers, he could see how the public had come to such a misunderstanding. The papers were filled with articles extolling the high-level bombing done by the B-17s based out of Midway, which, it became clear later, had sunk no Japanese ships, as well as the gallant but unsuccessful mission of the B-26s carrying torpedoes. A front-page article by Robert Trumball in the June 12 *New York Times* under the headline "Big Bombers Won" credited army fliers with hitting three Japanese carriers, one cruiser, a large vessel that could have been a cruiser or battleship, a destroyer, and a large transport. Although the army airmen Trumball interviewed in Hawaii emphasized that their operation against the enemy was just "one phase of a well-coordinated attack involving the Army, Navy and Marines," their commanding officer, Brig. Gen. Willis H. Hale, felt confident enough in his men's success that he claimed the Battle of Midway was "primarily won in the blasting by the Flying Fortresses of a Japanese naval task force, including carriers, off the island [Midway] on the morning of June 4." Trumball did include a comment by a B-17 pilot that may have caused some readers to doubt

Hale's statement. After noting that his crewmen reported hits on the enemy ships, the pilot told the reporter that his plane "didn't stay around too long to check up. Anti-aircraft fire was making this hot and we left in a hurry." As one historian of the Pacific War later pointed out, the heavy bombers based on Midway flew forty-five sorties and dropped 184,000 pounds of bombs, so surely "they must have hit *something*." They had not.[11]

What particularly distressed the correspondents who accompanied the navy into the Battle of Midway, including Tregaskis, was that the navy's press office in Hawaii seemed to be in no hurry to release the stories that detailed the vital role played in the victory by Spruance's and Rear Adm. Frank "Jack" Fletcher's task forces. When Tregaskis's dispatch about the battle was finally published by International News Service client newspapers in the United States, datelined June 23 from Pearl Harbor, it ran under headlines crediting him as an eyewitness to the havoc caused by carrier-based planes on the Japanese. He praised the aircrews for "darting daringly through a blistering hell of Japanese anti-aircraft fire and enemy planes," engaging in the savage "in-fighting" necessary to destroy three Japanese carriers and gut a fourth, while suffering only light losses, one carrier damaged and one destroyer sunk (navy censors kept the *Yorktown*'s fate a secret). Tregaskis's article included a dramatic account of the attack by a squadron commander, but, like Trumball's piece, written when all the details had yet to be gathered, he passed along some erroneous information to the American public, including a comment by a navy flier that he saw a torpedo hit a Japanese carrier (none did), as well as hits from the dive-bombers. The pilot reported, "The carrier exploded amid flames as high as the ship was long. The fire was bright red in color with pinkish shades. It looked like a huge bonfire of kindling wood. The explosions were apparently caused by gasoline or the ship's magazines were afire. Over a second carrier I saw a great, black smoke column with red flames at the bottom. The third, or trailing carrier was burning so badly that I couldn't see the ship's outline." Tregaskis credited the American victory to "highly effective dive bombing," which was true, but his crediting of "accurate torpedoing" was off target.[12]

As America's military services jockeyed for credit for their part in the Midway triumph, Tregaskis rested in Honolulu. He attended movies "in cool theaters with comfortable seats," ate meals with fresh vegetables and fruit and milk, and enjoyed "the luxury of being able to sleep late in the morning without fear of a sharp awakening by the general quarters alarm, by a bombing or sub attack." He felt relieved to be away from the almost constant "dinning noise of aircraft engines," and savored his ability to walk on solid ground, a "pleasant novelty after days of constriction aboard ship."[13]

The correspondent's living arrangements had also improved, as Dick Haller, the INS bureau chief in Honolulu, had leased an apartment in the Waikiki section for his correspondents. Tregaskis described the apartment as "modern, light, well decorated; there were stall showers with glass doors, soft beds; luxuries much appreciated by a man who has been at sea aboard a warship (and a hundred times more, I was to find out later, by one who has been in the field, at the front, with ground troops)." A new reporter assigned to Pacific Fleet headquarters, Robert C. Miller of the United Press, introduced Tregaskis to a beach in Honolulu (Niumalu at the Niumalu Hotel) where he could partake in one of his favorite pastimes, swimming. It marked a "pleasant change after attempting to swim amongst the coral banks of Waikiki," Tregaskis noted.[14]

Tregaskis could relax—play paddle tennis with Haller at the Pacific Club— because one of the new INS men, Jack Singer, had been tabbed to accompany the next naval task force to sail from Pearl Harbor. The other rookie reporter, Frank Neal, however, became ill, and Tregaskis started to prepare himself for another foray into combat. He had not forgotten about the tip he had received from Spruance regarding a possible operation in the Solomon Islands. Tregaskis had also stumbled upon some information that pointed to such an invasion, discovering that bombardment ammunition, a type intended for use against land targets, was being loaded aboard the cruisers and destroyers remaining at Pearl Harbor. "That indicated that either a raid, like the Marshall and Gilbert and Wake [Islands] and Marcus attacks, or a landing party was in preparation," he recalled. "Checking further, I finally discovered definite information that a landing party was intended."[15]

Wanting to accompany the expedition, no matter its destination, Tregaskis sought out Waldo Drake, the Pacific Fleet's public relations officer, and told him he needed to secure a letter from Nimitz authorizing him to go aboard a transport and join the upcoming invasion. "Drake seemed startled and said he had heard nothing of such an expedition, but that he would inquire," Tregaskis remembered. "He finally returned, swore me to secrecy, and promised he would try to get me the letter I sought." A few days later, the correspondent had the necessary paperwork assigning him to a carrier, the USS *Enterprise*. He also secured authorization allowing his transfer, at the convenience of the ship and task force, to a transport to be part of the landing operation. On July

15 the *Enterprise* and its escorts left Pearl Harbor, "outward bound," noted Tregaskis, "for an unknown destination."[16]

Task Force 16, which included the *Enterprise*, the battleship *North Carolina*, the heavy cruiser *Portland*, light cruiser *Atlanta*, and several destroyers, steamed south and after several days arrived at Nuku'alofa in the Tonga Islands. "When we sailed into the harbor," the correspondent recalled, "my heart jumped into my mouth in excitement: drawn up at anchor were a fleet of transports, loaded with troops!" Tregaskis was on his way to join Operation Watchtower, America's first offensive in the Pacific against the Japanese, with the intention of capturing and holding the island of Guadalcanal in the Solomons. It would be a mission marked by risks, uncertainties, and shortages, with those involved agreeing that a better code name for it would be "Operation Shoestring." As Gen. Alexander A. Vandegrift, the commander of the U.S. Marine Corps tasked with defeating the Japanese, noted before his troops landed on August 7, 1942, "We didn't have much of anything, we didn't know what we were going to hit, but we did know enough, in my opinion, to justify what military writers like to call 'a calculated risk.'"[17]

7 OPERATION SHOESTRING

Preparing to get some rest one evening after a day spent talking to American pilots engaged in dueling with their Japanese opponents, Richard Tregaskis, one of only two reporters covering the fighting on Guadalcanal, decided to take a chance, despite rumors about a possible attack, to sleep more comfortably for once. He pulled off his pants, shirt, shoes, and socks and climbed into his cot. It turned out to be a mistake. Just after midnight, a shattering noise jolted him awake. "I could hear the heavy gunfire, in a sequence that I knew instantly was ominous: the metallic, loud brroom-brroom of the guns going off, then the whistle of the approaching shells, then the crash of the explosions, so near that one felt a blast of air from the concussion," Tregaskis said. He fumbled for his helmet but could not find it, and he finally dashed outside looking for a dugout to dive into for cover. What ensued was a bit of comic opera, as the correspondent and a U.S. Marine Corps officer, Col. LeRoy P. Hunt, also clad in his skivvies, arrived at the dugout at the same time. "We bumped into each other at the entrance and then backed away and I said, 'You go first, Colonel.' He said politely with a slight bow, 'No, after you,'" noted Tregaskis. They stood there for a few moments, arguing, as shells continued to rain down on their position, with one slamming into the earth close to Tregaskis's canvas tent.[1]

The comic aspects of the situation soon turned to horror. As the enemy barrage halted, Tregaskis could hear a "blubbering, crying sound that was more animal than human." A marine ran up to the dugout's entrance to report that several men had been badly wounded and required medical attention. The correspondent left the shelter, passed by a smashed tent, and found himself "amidst a scene of frightfulness." He saw a body with a small red hole in the middle of its chest. Another wounded man—the person who had been making the cries Tregaskis had heard—also lay nearby with a doctor and corpsman already attending to the man's shattered legs. Additional wounds to the marine's face "rained blood on the ground," Tregaskis reported, noting that the stricken man's shoulder had also been ripped apart by shrapnel. "He was crying, sobbing, into a pool of blood. The blood distorted the sound of his wailing, as water would have done, into a bubbling sound," Tregaskis remembered. "The sound still came in cycles, rising in peaks of loudness. One of the wounded man's hands moved in mechanical circles on the ground, keeping time with his cries." Corpsmen loaded the wounded into a nearby ambulance. Tregaskis long remembered the harsh squeaking of the wooden stretchers as they were loaded into the ambulance, "a sound much like that of a fingernail scratched across a blackboard." Upon his return to the shack that served as headquarters for the marine unit he stayed with, the correspondent talked to an Australian guide, who was uninjured, discussing how a blasted treetop had fallen through his tent's roof and onto his bunk. "First time I ever had a tree in bed with me," he joked to the reporter.[2]

Tregaskis's brush with death and destruction came a few weeks after he had landed on August 7, 1942, with the approximately eleven thousand men of the First Marine Division tasked with the responsibility of taking the island of Guadalcanal, code named Cactus, from the Japanese. The campaign was viewed by some U.S. military officials as foolhardy and that there was "considerable room for doubt" that the marines could hold their ground. Even the marines' commander, Gen. Alexander Vandegrift, later noted that there were a "hundred reasons why this operation should fail," and a First Marine Division report on the campaign lamented, "seldom has an operation begun under more disadvantageous circumstances." Aerial photographs and maps provided little help in planning, and the information offered by former colonial residents differed on geographical features and place names, so much so that the river called "Ilu" by the troops was actually the "Tenaru," and vice versa. Lt. Herbert Merillat, the marines' public relations officer on Guadalcanal, had a simple answer for all the campaign's logistical difficulties: "The United States was simply not ready to support a major operation for the seizure, holding, and rapid development of an air and naval base open to heavy enemy counterattack."[3]

Years later, Tregaskis uncovered a report that an army transportation officer in Townsville, Australia, had been responsible for forwarding aerial photographs of Guadalcanal to marine headquarters in Wellington, New Zealand. "Apparently the tropical climate had got to the officer, or maybe he was in love, because he stalled around for ten days before forwarding the A-1 priority shipment," said Tregaskis. By the time the delayed shipment reached Wellington, the marines were having trouble with union longshoremen, who balked at handling the needed supplies for the Guadalcanal campaign during New Zealand's rainy season. Soaked by the rain, some of the cartons split open, spilling their contents onto the dock to be ruined. "When the Marines pitched in to do the loading," Tregaskis added, "friction and confusion ensued, and somewhere in the shuffle the box of photo maps was lost." Consequently, he said, the troops responsible for the first American amphibious operation since the Spanish-American War went into battle without decent maps.[4]

Until he left the island on September 26, Tregaskis endured the same dangers faced by the marines, including bombing by Japanese aircraft during the day and shelling from their navy—dubbed the "Tokyo Express"—at night. The marines also had to deal with inadequate supplies of food and equipment and the constant fear of being overrun by a single-minded foe. These hardships were matched by the difficulties of fighting on the island itself, an often impenetrable jungle that limited vision to just a few yards, jagged mountains climbing to a height of eight thousand feet above sea level, sharp-bladed kunai grass, pesky and venomous insects, dangerous crocodiles, screaming birds, swarms of mosquitos that brought with them tropical maladies that could incapacitate a man for weeks or months, nauseating odors, and hot, humid conditions that bred all sorts of funguses and infections that were lumped under the description "jungle rot." Tregaskis and the marines longed for such simple pleasures as fresh bread and modern indoor plumbing. "One thinks of warm water, the smooth water-closet seat of civilization, and a bed with sheets as things that exist only in a world of dreams," he wrote. With no laundry facilities, Tregaskis had to do his washing by hand, using a wooden bucket and a cake of laundry soap. "After some hours of effort," he reported, "I found the clothes were at least a tattletale gray, whereas they had formerly been a darker shade." A simple matter of receiving a letter could instantly brighten downcast spirits. When the marines received their first mail shipment, Tregaskis noted that they were as happy as if someone had handed each man a hundred-dollar bill.[5]

After a time, too, Tregaskis became hardened to scenes of death and destruction, particularly those that happened to the enemy. "War takes on a very personal flavor when other men are shooting at you, and you feel little sympathy at seeing them killed," Tregaskis observed. Even seeing the horribly mangled bodies of the Japanese lying on the ground after a failed attack prompted in him no disgust. "The first one you see is the only shock," he recalled. "The rest are simple repetition." Not an unusual sentiment in a war unrestrained by mercy on both sides. Japanese soldiers feigned death so they could spring up to kill as many Americans as possible with any weapon they could get their hands on, including rifles, grenades, and knives. Japanese soldiers more often than not fought to the death, viewing surrender as dishonorable. On Guadalcanal, after turning back a frenzied Japanese assault on their lines at the Battle of the Tenaru, the marines took no chances, Tregaskis remembered, shooting the dead scattered on the ground "to make sure." He described the "re-butchery of the dead" as "brutal but necessary," and watched the men "standing in a shooting-gallery line, thumping bullets into the piles of Jap carcasses. The edge of the water grew brown and muddy. Some said the blood of the Jap carcasses was staining the ocean." Seeking revenge for Pearl Harbor, and slain friends as the war grew bloodier and bloodier, the U.S. military matched their enemy's fury on the battlefield. Adm. William Halsey spoke for many when he insisted that the "only good Jap is a Jap who's been dead six months." Halsey also promised, "When we get through with them, the Japanese language will be spoken only in hell."[6]

Tregaskis's journey to his first experience with ground combat and a Japanese army yet to be defeated in battle had not been easy. After securing the necessary paperwork from the public relations office at Pacific Fleet headquarters in Hawaii, he had been a passenger on the USS *Enterprise* as it and the escorting vessels of Task Force 16 sailed for a rendezvous with the Guadalcanal invasion force in the Tonga Islands. Although armed with the required official documents, Tregaskis had considerable difficulty making the transfer from the *Enterprise* to the troop transports. First, the carrier's executive officer sent him to the wrong ship, a navy tender, and, upon returning to the *Enterprise*, the correspondent discovered that none of the ships' boats were available to take him to the transports. He finally sought out Rear Adm. Thomas C. Kinkaid, commander of Task Force 16, who kindly gave the correspondent a letter securing him a place on one of the transports and also commandeered for him a ride to the USS *Crescent City*, a converted civilian ocean liner that had become the temporary home of the Second Marine Regiment. "Once aboard, I was able to relax with a feeling of satisfaction," Tregaskis remembered. "This was at least the right ship. It was filled with Marines, and they knew they were heading for a landing operation somewhere, though they did not yet know where; nor did even their commanding officer, Col. John M. Arthur."[7]

Colonel Arthur and his executive officer, Maj. Cornelius Van Ness, both made a calculated guess that the expedition was on its way to the Solomons, and the marines' objective would be either the island of Guadalcanal or Tulagi. "The colonel and the major spent hours poring over charts of Tulagi and the surrounding islands," Tregaskis said, "and of Guadalcanal, picking beach-heads and speculating over ways and means to land troops. Maj. Van Ness said he had drawn up tentative plans for a landing operation, just in case this particular group of Marines should win the Guadalcanal assignment; which struck me as being the height of enterprise."[8]

A push by American forces into the Solomons had been on the mind of Adm. Ernest King, commander in chief of the U.S. fleet in Washington, DC, as early as February 1942, with the eventual goal of proceeding from the Solomons into the Bismarck Archipelago to seize Rabaul. Planning for the operation intensified when reports from Australian coast watchers and decoded messages indicated that the Japanese had begun to build an airfield on Guadalcanal's northern coast, making the little-known island—ninety miles long, thirty miles wide, and just sixty miles south of the equator—a key objective. King came to an understanding with Gen. George Marshall, U.S. Army chief of staff, to adjust the boundaries previously set as the operating influences between the U.S. Navy and Gen. Douglas MacArthur in the Pacific so that the navy could handle the operations in the Solomons. Adm. Chester Nimitz selected Vice Adm. Robert Ghormley as the commander of the South Pacific Forces, and he eventually established his headquarters on Nouméa, the capital city of the French territory of New Caledonia. Rear Adm. Richmond Kelly Turner had charge of the amphibious force responsible for getting Vandegrift's approximately nineteen thousand marines ashore on Guadalcanal and its surrounding islands (Tulagi and Gavutu-Tanambogo) and supplying them. Vice Adm. Frank "Jack" Fletcher, a veteran of both the Coral Sea and Midway battles, controlled the carrier force consisting of the *Enterprise*, *Saratoga*, and *Hornet* (Task Force 61), which provided aerial protection for the operation.[9]

Vandegrift believed it was "unfortunate" that Fletcher had been given tactical command, as he was "not available during the planning phase." When he met Fletcher, Vandegrift remembered thinking that the admiral looked "nervous and tired," probably due to the strain of his recent battles against the

Japanese. "To my surprise," said Vandegrift, "he appeared to lack knowledge of or interest in the forthcoming operation. He quickly let us know he did not think it would succeed." Vandegrift's operations officer, Lt. Col. Merrill Twining, described Rear Adm. Richmond Kelly Turner as a "loud, strident, arrogant person who enjoyed settling all matters by simply raising his voice and roaring like a bull captain in the old navy." Twining added that Turner's peers understood the admiral's moods and accepted them with "amused resignation because they valued him for what he was: a good and determined leader with a fine mind—when he chose to use it." Twining's commander, Vandegrift, possessed just the right attitude to deal with Turner's bombast, as the general was a "classic Virginia gentleman. I have heard him harden his voice, but I never heard him raise it—not even at me," Twining said.[10]

Initially, Tregaskis had a pleasant voyage with the Second Marines as they sailed from the Tongas to the Fijis for a planned landing rehearsal on Kore Island. His ship, the *Crescent City*, which had carried passengers and freight between New Orleans and Buenos Aires, had been launched in 1940 and retained some of its former elegance. The correspondent had been lucky enough to find a berth in a comfortable cabin with pleasant roommates: Albert Campbell, a Red Cross volunteer; Father Francis W. Kelly, a Catholic chaplain from Philadelphia; and Dr. John Garrison, a Los Angeles dentist in civilian life but now a navy medical officer. Campbell noted that when he had first boarded the ship, he, Kelly, and Garrison had successfully steered interlopers away from the four-bunk accommodation, which included its own bathroom and shower, by a skillful arrangement of their luggage and arguments that there was no room for another person. Shortly before leaving the Tongas, Campbell said he had found in his cabin "a tall, lanky stranger in glasses, who introduced himself as Dick Tregaskis." Campbell and his cabin mates immediately took to Tregaskis, so much so that they "didn't have the heart to pull the same story about overcrowding which had kept out other invaders." Soon the correspondent's "long legs were hanging from the top bunk as he told us about the Coral Sea battle, Midway and other engagements which he had witnessed," Campbell recalled. The Red Cross worker learned that Tregaskis, like him, came from Elizabeth, New Jersey, and had also attended the Pingry School. "He was a nice guy and in a few days everyone on the ship knew and liked him," said Campbell.[11]

On its way to the Fijis, the *Crescent City* met a large fleet of transports, supply ships, cruisers, destroyers, carriers, and other warships "spread out over the whole horizon circle and beyond," Tregaskis remembered. Those on the transport made a game of trying to identify the different types of ships stretching out before them. "We were conscious of the fact that this was one of the largest and strongest groups of war vessels ever gathered," he noted, "certainly the largest and strongest of this war to date. The thought that we were going into our adventure with weight and power behind us was cheering." The next day, a boat came up alongside the transport to deliver dispatches that Tregaskis guessed included information about the fleet's destination. After lunch, Tregaskis received an invitation to Colonel Arthur's cabin "for a spot of tea." Once there with a beverage in hand, Arthur told him, "Well, it looks as if we're not going to have as much excitement as we first thought," as his men would not be part of the attack on the Japanese-held territory, but instead would serve as a reserve force. If Tregaskis wanted to accompany beachhead troops, Arthur advised him to transfer to another ship. "I had come out here for action," said the correspondent, so, after dinner, he packed his bags in his blacked-out cabin. "It took some resolution to do the job, for in the evening I had learned that the forces I would join are going to attack the Japanese strongholds on Guadalcanal and Tulagi, in the Solomon Islands," he recalled.[12]

The top officers for Operation Watchtower met on the USS *Saratoga*, Fletcher's flagship, on July 26. What occurred at the conference has been hotly debated over the years, with some involved describing it as "one long bitter argument" between Fletcher and Turner, and others remembering the conversations as "animated rather than stormy." The main issue centered on how long it would take to land the troops from the transports and their supplies from the cargo ships (Turner estimated five days), and how long Fletcher would provide air support for the operation with his carriers. At the time of the Guadalcanal campaign, Fletcher's carriers represented three-quarters of the U.S. fleet's assets for that essential vessel, with no replacements for them from American shipyards expected for many months. According to some accounts, Fletcher had said to those assembled, "Gentlemen, in view of the risks of exposure to land-based air[craft], I cannot keep the carriers in the area for more than 48 hours after the landing." Vandegrift recalled that he had to force himself to remain calm, informing Fletcher that the "days of landing a small force and leaving were over" and he could hardly be expected to "land this massive force without air cover—even the five days mentioned by Turner involved a tremendous risk." According to Vandegrift's account, although Turner backed him, Fletcher refused to budge, "curtly" announcing the *Saratoga*, *Enterprise*, and *Wasp* would only stay until the operation's third day, and ending the conference. Years later, Fletcher could remember no bitterness involved in the discussions on the *Saratoga*, instead merely noting there were a variety of opinions "vigorously expressed" as to what could or could not be done. Twining, who said Vandegrift accepted Fletcher's edict with "the best grace he could muster," did give credence to the admiral's cautious approach, noting that Fletcher had "seen U.S. carriers sunk in battle and was loath to risk our best carriers in action against a greatly superior force."[13]

A few days after the spirited conference on the *Saratoga*, Tregaskis left the *Crescent City* for Turner's flagship, the USS *McCawley*, nicknamed the "Wacky Mac" by its sailors, to secure permission for his transfer to a transport carrying troops assigned to combat. The correspondent discovered that the *McCawley's* wardroom was "clogged with Marine officers of all shapes and sizes, mulling over maps, mumbling secret advices and arguing moot points in groups at the tables. . . . Officers with intent expressions passed in steady streams up and down the corridor leading to the admiral's office." Although Turner was far too busy to see Tregaskis, the admiral's marine aide, Col. Harold Harris, took pity on him, took the reporter's credentials to Turner, and obtained the admiral's approval for Tregaskis to join one of the two transports carrying the assault troops for the landing on Guadalcanal. Tregaskis also had the opportunity to meet Vandegrift, who stopped to "exchange a polite word; he was cordial and cheerful, as I later found him to be, however desperate the situation, on Guadalcanal."[14]

Tregaskis had two shocks after leaving the *Crescent City*. He learned that the landing rehearsal on Kore Island had been a mess. The troops involved ran into problems with a coral reef that prevented many from making it to the beach; the transports drifted and came close to tangling with one another at the debarkation line; the landing boats were ponderous, experienced engine troubles, and roughed up their propellers on the reef; and the timing of the preliminary naval bombardment was off. Vandegrift, who later described the exercise as a "complete bust," consoled himself with the thought that a "poor rehearsal traditionally meant a good show." Tregaskis also discovered that his new ship, the USS *American Legion*, was an "ancient, angular horror, with a black, dirty hull and patches of rust on her flanks." When he climbed up a rope ladder and set foot on its deck, he could see that not all the Americans heading into combat were traveling on the newest ships (the transport had been plying the seas for more than twenty years). "I had certainly come from the best and newest to one of the oldest and most decrepit," he recalled.[15]

The *American Legion*'s deck was black with slime and grit because, as he later discovered, the ship had no modern equipment for pumping water. "The marines cramming the deck were just as dirty," he noted. Tregaskis met with the Fifth Marine Regiment's commanding officer, Col. Leroy P. Hunt, a World War I veteran, in the officer's cabin, which at least had a clean floor. Hunt said his men might be unkempt and looked like gypsies because there was no water available to clean up, but he believed they would fight when called upon to do so. "They got it here," Hunt told Tregaskis, tapping his chest in the region of his heart. Returning to his cabin, which he shared with Capt. William Hawkins, a former schoolteacher in Bridgeport, Connecticut, Tregaskis went to the bathroom he shared with the adjoining stateroom and tried to wash off the sweat and grime he had collected during the day. When he pressed the tap, no water came out. A neighbor informed him, "The water's only on for about ten minutes at a time, about three times a day. And the times it's on are a mystery that only the Navy and God know about."[16]

As the *American Legion* sailed south on the big sweep that would take it into Guadalcanal, Tregaskis got to know more about the marines and their commander. Hunt and his officers tried to be realistic about their chances, believing from intelligence reports that there were anywhere from five thousand to ten thousand enemy troops on the island, most of them labor troops, numbers that proved to be greatly inflated. The Japanese would probably be able to bring some large guns to bear upon the American landing craft on their way into the landing beaches five miles east of Lunga Point, as well as machine-gun fire and mortar rounds. Zealous map interpreters, Tregaskis recalled, straining their eyes over aerial photo-mosaic maps, believed they had identified evidence of intense enemy defensive preparations on the beach chosen for the landing. "The interpreters said they saw worn truck tracks, indicating movement in the vicinity of the beach," he recalled, "and conjured machine gun positions out of minute combinations of shadows in the beach area." One of Hunt's aides confided to Tregaskis that he and the other officers expected about a third of the assault boats to be destroyed and a quarter of the combat troops would be casualties during the landing. The officers were also sure that Japanese reconnaissance planes would spot the U.S. armada long before it reached its destination and would send planes to bomb and strafe the ships, and the Japanese fleet would not be far behind. "This estimate did not improve the pleasantness of the prospect of accompanying the assault troops in their attack," the correspondent noted. Hunt remained confident that whatever might happen, the marines in the fifteen ships of Transport Group X-Ray, destined for Guadalcanal, would take the beachhead and "secure the problem." When Tregaskis suggested the possibility of failure, Hunt was prompt in his reply, telling the reporter, "You mustn't ever think of it that way. We'll do the job."[17]

Although the enlisted marines were dirty and roomed in quarters no better than a dungeon, Tregaskis said they displayed a tremendous esprit de corps and supreme confidence in their ability to handle any assignment. One afternoon Tregaskis watched a group of enlisted men, most of whom came from either New York or Boston, cleaning and checking their weapons on the ship's forward deck, treating them with an almost motherly care. Some of the men were also sharpening their bayonets, which, he noted, "seemed to be a universal pastime." Others checked over their Springfield rifles and submachine guns, and a few busied themselves by fashioning homemade blackjacks, canvas sacks filled with lead balls to be used for "infighting," he reported. A large part of the marines' conversation during this time included tough talk about what they expected to do to the enemy. As marines loaded cartridges into machine-gun belts, he listened as "one of them kept time with the clink of the belter. 'One, two, three, another Jap for me,' he said." Tregaskis heard a marine brag that he intended to make a necklace from the gold teeth taken from dead Japanese, while another said, "I'm going to bring back some Jap ears. Pickled." Other marines seemed resigned about the dangers they were to soon confront. Tregaskis came across a group lounging by the starboard rail watching two of their friends throwing half-dollars over the side, trying to make them skip on the waves. A sailor coming upon the scene pointed out that he had seen a number of servicemen have a good time while on liberty with the amount of money they were throwing away. "Oh hell," said one of the marines, "money don't mean a thing out here anyhow. Even if you stay alive, you can't buy anything." Several marines were reprimanded one day by a noncommissioned officer for swimming while the transport had stopped for a short time, telling them they might be court-martialed, that is, if they were not first eaten by sharks. "What do we care?" one of the men said. "We're going in the first wave on Guadalcanal, anyhow."[18]

For entertainment, those on the *American Legion* gambled, including playing poker and craps. A large percentage of the marines preferred to escape their uncomfortable quarters below deck, sleeping instead in lifeboats, around stanchions, or on the deck. Walking on the deck of the blacked-out ship at night could be dangerous, as Tregaskis had to step carefully to avoid tripping over slumbering marines. At least he had the pleasure of hearing the men sing themselves to sleep with such favorites as "Blues in the Night" and "Old Mill Stream." Hunt entertained his officers by demonstrating a tap-dance routine he used to perform while a student at Stanford University, complete with a rendition of "I Want a Girl Just Like the Girl That Married Dear Old Dad." Tregaskis ascribed Hunt's "youthful exuberance" to his nearness to the "zone of action." Busy imaginations also filled the time by engaging in unfounded rumors, "scuttlebutt," including one in which a marine told Tregaskis that he had seen flashes of gunfire, an American cruiser attacking and sinking a Japanese submarine running on the surface. Tregaskis checked the story with the transport's executive officer, who laughed and said, "There was some heat lightning early this morning behind that cruiser."[19]

As the invasion force neared Guadalcanal, the fickle Pacific weather cooperated with misty, overcast conditions, keeping the American ships hidden from enemy aircraft based on Rabaul. "We went on our way straight up the 158th meridian, straight into Jap territory, without ever being detected," Tregaskis recalled. He attributed their success to Japanese overconfidence, as they had been so successful to date in the Pacific War they could not imagine their enemy embarking on such a bold strike. Still, he wondered if perhaps the Japanese were laying low, preparing to spring a trap on the unsuspecting Americans. On the afternoon of August 3, four days before the scheduled landing, Hunt issued a mimeographed notice to his men outlining what was expected of them. The colonel wrote that the Guadalcanal action marked the first offensive of the war against the enemy involving ground forces of the United States, and the marines had "been selected to initiate this action which will prove to be the forerunner of successive offensive actions that will end in ultimate victory for our cause. The Marine Corps is on the spot. Our Country expects nothing but victory from us and it shall have just that. The word failure shall not even be considered as being in our vocabulary." The colonel warned his troops they were about to meet a "tough and wily opponent," but that the Japanese were not "sufficiently tough or wily to overcome us because We are Marines." Urging each man to complete his assigned tasks to the utmost of his ability, with "added effort for good measure," he closed his message with the words "Good luck and God Bless you and to hell with the Japs."[20]

Tregaskis roamed throughout the *American Legion* the night before the landing. The correspondent was set to accompany Hunt on his landing craft the next day, which was to be a "free" boat, with the colonel deciding when to take it into the beachhead. "He might go in after the first landing wave," Tregaskis noted, "and, at any rate, we would not be later than the fifth wave." On his rounds he encountered marines preparing their packs and lining them up in careful rows along the ship's bulkheads. Men hurried by, carrying armfuls of hand grenades, while on deck crates were being opened to unpack artillery ammunition. Supplies were distributed, enough for two days, including canned rations of concentrated coffee and biscuits, meat and beans, vegetable stew, and chocolate bars. Officers and enlisted men crowded into the ship's armorer's shop to make a final check on their weapons. At dinner some of the officers "betrayed signs of nerves," said Tregaskis, as they mistook the noise of heavy drums moving on deck for the sound of antiaircraft machine guns being fired on the upper deck. Some of the men and sailors blew off steam by dancing a jitterbug to the sound of music from a jukebox in the mess hall. With breakfast to be served the next morning at 4:30, the men turned in early. While roaming about the ship, Tregaskis saw a group of officers playing cards in their wardroom, but when he stopped by the same room at 10:00 p.m. it was empty; so was the mess hall. "The lights were out," he remembered. "All the life was gone from both places."[21]

Everyone seemed calm at breakfast on August 7, 1942, eight months to the day after the attack on Pearl Harbor. The lack of any response by the Japanese to the invasion fleet made Tregaskis and the others on the *American Legion* feel "strangely secure, as if getting up at four o'clock in the morning and preparing to force a landing on the enemy shore were the perfectly normal things to do on an August morning in the South Seas." The Americans had achieved complete surprise. It seemed like a dream to Tregaskis: "We were slipping through the narrow neck of water between Guadalcanal and Savo Islands; we were practically inside Tulagi Bay, almost past the Jap shore batteries, and not a shot had been fired." The ship's officers were dumbfounded, with one lieutenant telling the correspondent that the enemy could not be so foolish. "Either they're very dumb," said the lieutenant, "or it's a trick." Tregaskis jotted down his impressions of the operation, including the prelanding bombardment, in the pocket-sized notebooks he carried with him during the weeks he spent on Guadalcanal. Every night he transferred the information he had gathered during the day in his notebook into a large, black, gilt-edged diary. Here is what he wrote on the morning of the invasion:

6:10 Flash on right side. Catapult? Sound of plane in mist ahead. Cruiser catapulted 2 of planes.

6:15 Plane bearing 320 [degrees]. 'Do not fire. Friendly plane bearing 320.'

6:23 Shells like red rockets on starboard bow. Cruiser—Vincennes class—begins shelling. Flashed from ship light green.

6:25 Cruiser, Vincennes class, astern to starboard begins firing.

6:27 Tracers coming towards our ships. (6:28 cruiser dead ahead firing.) A-A [antiaircraft] bursts in sky.

6:31 Firing on Tulagi opens. Two other ships—cruisers—Vincennes class—ahead firing. Five planes sighted starboard bow.

6:32 Four cruisers turning back our starboard side.

6:37 [Japanese] Ship afire dead ahead—white spot first then a red flame. . . . 2 planes got it.

6:38 Planes strafing beach.

[6:41 Admiral Turner gives the order to "land the landing force."]

6:42 Bombs starboard side.

6:55 Tracers still ricocheting. Our planes strafing Lunga. Can see bomb splashes all along shore. Some bright blue. Some yellow and sandy.

6:58 Boats swung out (our landing boats). Our ships turning in towards beach. Jap ship still burning at one end. Oil slick behind.

7:01 Boats in water from Fuller ahead. Our hoists clinking, lowering, lowering. Our boats in water. Port side. And starboard. Flags on stern waving signal flags for boats come alongside.

7:14 Two fires Lunga Point black smoke. Our guns still firing.

7:19 First men climbing down nets. Cruisers, close in, astern, shelling. Already burning Lunga.

7:55 Flock of ships Tulagi shore—firing—Australian one turns.

8:00 Left ship—passed around stern. All told duck down low. Flames Lunga cruiser lying offshore red fire flashing in blue smoke.

8:06 Fighters overhead covering op[eration]. We cruising circles.[22]

Tregaskis's boat finally headed for shore at 8:34 a.m., following not far behind the first wave of landing craft. Although he could not see the first men to reach the beach, he did see signals that the landings had been successful. Early that morning a Japanese radio operator on Tulagi had sent a message to Rabaul asking his superiors what was happening, asking, "LARGE FORCE OF SHIPS UNKNOWN NUMBER OR TYPES ENTERING SOUND WHAT CAN THEY

BE?" Later, the commander on Tulagi, under assault by the men of the First Raider Battalion led by Lt. Col. Merritt "Red Mike" Edson, radioed that the enemy forces appeared to be landing in overwhelming numbers. Despite the odds, the Japanese commander vowed to remain on the island and defend his post "to the death." At 9:50 a.m. Tregaskis finally reached the island. "I jumped carefully from the bow and got only one foot wet, and that slightly; hardly the hell-for-leather leap and dash through the surf, with accompaniment of rattle machine guns, which I had expected," he remembered.[23]

Instead of standing and fighting, the Japanese soldiers and construction troops based on Guadalcanal (many of whom were Korean) fled their camps and disappeared into the jungle. Tregaskis credited the surprise of the Americans' attack and the fury of the naval and air bombardment preceding the landing as the joint causes of the "precipitous retreat" the enemy made. Capt. Charles V. Hodges, a former owner of a coconut plantation on the island who served as a guide for the marines, joked with Tregaskis about how easy it had been to take Guadalcanal, saying, "I'm exhausted by the arduousness of landing against such heavy fire." As darkness fell, however, jittery sentries confronted any noise they heard with orders to "Halt!" that were "followed almost immediately by volleys of gunfire," said Tregaskis. Close to midnight, the correspondent awoke to the sounds of a submachine gun firing near the grove of tall coconut trees he had bedded down under with Hunt's command. Numerous rifle shots rang out afterward, with five or six guns firing at once. He could see the bright, white tracers "zipping in several different directions over the grove where we slept. Some of the slugs whined through the trees close by. And then the firing fell off, and died, and we went back to sleep again."[24]

August 8 brought more good news, as the Americans captured the airfield, which, Tregaskis learned, had its main runway already graded and about two-thirds surfaced. The marines named it Henderson Field, in honor of Maj. Lofton R. Henderson, who had been killed while leading sixteen marine dive-bombers against the Japanese carriers at the Battle of Midway. On his way to the airfield that afternoon, Tregaskis had his first encounter with the enemy when he came upon two marines herding three prisoners to the rear. These Japanese did not appear to be seasoned warriors. "None of them was more than five feet tall, and they were puny," Tregaskis noted. "Their skins were sallow. The first two in line had shaved heads and were bare from the waist downward; the marines had been diligent in their search for weapons." An interpreter told the correspondent that the prisoners were members of a navy labor battalion and had been captured in a tent camp that lay directly ahead. Reaching the former enemy facility, Tregaskis rummaged through one of the large tents and discovered serving dishes on a table still filled with meat stew, rice, and cooked prunes. Half-eaten bowls of food remained on the table, with chopsticks propped on the dishes or dropped on the floor. In other tents he found shoes, mosquito nets, toilet articles, soap, and other essentials. The Japanese at the camp had removed the ignition keys from many of the hundred-odd trucks and cars found there, but did not take the time, Tregaskis noticed, to damage the vehicles so that they could not be used by the Americans.[25]

Eventually coming upon Japanese headquarters at Kukum, Hunt's troops uncovered large stores of food left behind: boxes of sweet biscuits; tins of hardtack; cases of soda; two varieties of Japanese beer; canned pears, peaches, and pineapples; goulash; crab meat; and shredded fish and salmon, "hardly the primitive diet on which the Japanese is traditionally supposed to subsist," Tregaskis observed. He noted that the Japanese were obliging enough to also leave behind their cooking kettles. A pleased Vandegrift described the bounty the marines had captured: "A power house, an alternate one, a radio receiver station with six sets with remote control to a sending unit 3 miles away, innumerable pieces of machinery such as generators, engines, pumps, etc. 9 Road Rollers, over 100 trucks so far found of the Chev[rolet] 2 ton types, Anti-air guns, loaded and locked—can you beat that. Tons of cement, some fifty or sixty thousand gals. of gas and oil and double that much destroyed by bombs."[26]

A stirring ceremony occurred at Hunt's command post that had been established at the old Japanese headquarters. Lt. Evard J. Snell of Vineland, New Jersey, a middle-aged World War I veteran on the colonel's staff, had been brought in on a stretcher by corpsmen. Snell, accustomed to handling his commander's paperwork, had been overcome by the heat and exertion four times that day, gamely struggled on with the marching column, and now could not move. Trying to cheer up his aide, Hunt took from Snell's pocket a small American flag the lieutenant had been carrying with him during his service with the marines in China and the Philippines and had it hoisted atop a now bare Japanese flagpole. "It was touching to see the little flag, proud but pitifully small, ride up the mast, to see Snell's eyes watching it, and his mouth twisting and contorting as he tried to smile," Tregaskis remembered.[27]

As Tregaskis bedded down for the evening on August 8, sharing a poncho with Father Thomas Reardon, it looked as if the worst he could expect would be a storm. Rain started to thunder down upon him shortly after midnight, and the correspondent awoke and took shelter in one of the captured Japanese tents, which was already "fairly well filled with marines." Just as he dropped off to sleep again, he heard cannonading coming from offshore. "It had stopped raining. We stood in a quiet group under the palms, listening and watching," Tregaskis recalled. "The flashes of the gunfire were filling the sky, as bright and far spreading as heat lightning. And a few seconds after each flash, we could hear the booming of the guns that had caused it." He and the others realized they could be watching a battle that could decide their fate. If the Japanese won, it would mean a desperate fight for survival, and soon. Tregaskis felt helpless: "One had the feeling of being at the mercy of great accumulated forces far more powerful than anything human. We were only pawns in a battle of the gods, then, and we knew it." The booming of the guns continued for more than an hour, and during that time the correspondent and the marines speculated among themselves just what was happening. By about 3:00 a.m. the firing stopped and Tregaskis left the crowded tent for the comfort of an abandoned Japanese sedan that had been left by the side of the road. "The soft cushions felt good," he said. "Except for the slight disturbance of being bitten by mosquitoes, I was quite comfortable for the rest of the night."[28]

The sea battle Tregaskis witnessed from Guadalcanal had been a disaster for the U.S. Navy and the last in a chain of setbacks that left the marines' position in the Solomons extremely perilous. At about 6:00 p.m. on August 8, Fletcher had sent a message to Ghormley that read, "Fighter-plane strength reduced from 99 to 78. In view of the large number of enemy torpedo planes and bombers in this area, I recommend the immediate withdrawal of my carriers. Request tankers sent forward immediately as fuel running low." Before Ghormley could respond to his request, Fletcher took his carriers away from the danger zone. The news of Fletcher's withdrawal, and the loss of air support, stunned Turner, who believed he had been left "bare-arse." The admiral decided he had no choice but to begin withdrawing his transports and supply ships the next day, and he informed Vandegrift of his decision during a conference on the *McCawley* in which he also shared Fletcher's message. Meanwhile, an impressive Japanese task force that included five heavy cruisers, two light cruisers, and a destroyer under Vice Adm. Mikawa Gunichi was about to strike the American ships under the cover of darkness. The result—the Battle of Savo Island—was one of the worst disasters in U.S. naval history since the War of 1812. The American cruisers *Vincennes*, *Quincy*, and *Astoria* went down, and the

Australian cruiser *Canberra* had to be abandoned and sunk. The only bright spot came when Mikawa decided to disengage from the fight and return to his base without pressing on to wreak havoc on the unprotected transports.[29]

The marines on Guadalcanal had about a four-day supply of ammunition and enough food for seventeen days, plus an additional three days on C rations and ten more days if they used the captured Japanese supplies, according to U.S. officers on the scene. The Americans were without the heavy equipment needed for completing the airfield and such essential defensive supplies as sandbags, barbed wire, and long-range coastal defense guns. For weeks to come the troops, and Tregaskis, had to exist on two unappetizing meals a day. "God only knew when we could expect aircraft protection much less surface craft; with the transports gone the enemy would shift his attacks against us and we could expect surface attacks as well," Vandegrift said. They would have to fight alone, living, as Tregaskis remembered, day after day, "under the shadow of dire peril." The correspondent remembered Vandegrift putting on a brave face after the naval disaster and the transports' departure. The general did, however, caution Tregaskis that it might be a "long time before there would be another chance to make my exit," the reporter remembered. Tregaskis walked to the beach where the last load of supplies was being dropped. "I watched the last craft shoving off one by one and then heading out down the line of Admiral Turner's supply ships," he noted. "I remember cudgeling the problem of whether to stay put and get that good story written, or to hightail it to the nearest cablehead with something like a news scoop." Being the indecisive type, "and phlegmatic to boot," Tregaskis said, he hesitated until only a few transports were left on the beach, and, with his "usual Anglo-Saxon disinclination to sparkle," trudged off into the jungle to rejoin the marines.[30]

8 THE CANAL

One of the men peering over the side of the Higgins landing boat saw it first, a long, low black shape moving slowly about a mile away in the bay between the islands of Guadalcanal and Tulagi in the Solomons. The American flotilla that included two landing craft and a barge-like lighter filled with gasoline drums had several miles yet to travel before it reached its destination, Carpenter's Wharf on Tulagi. Once there, the boats were set to disgorge their passengers, which included U.S. Marine Corps officers seeking information about the fighting on Tulagi from the First Marine Raider Battalion and from Richard Tregaskis of the International News Service and Bob Miller of the United Press. They were the only two civilian reporters who had accompanied the men of the First Marine Division as they landed on Guadalcanal on August 7, 1942, and had stayed with them on the island to face the inevitable counterattacks from the Japanese.

Now, five days later, exposed on the open water, the U.S. vessels had already endured one close call when an unidentified airplane appeared overhead. "I suppose in that moment we all realized how helpless is a small boat under the attack of a well-armed aircraft," Tregaskis recalled. "One felt suddenly very much alone, out there in the middle of the bay, with at least ten miles of water on every side." Fortunately, it was an American plane, a Consolidated PBY Catalina headed to make the first landing on the recently completed airfield on Guadalcanal. "It's ours," one of the gunners on Tregaskis's boat announced, and the correspondent and his companions began to "breathe freely again."[1]

Unfortunately, the second sighting turned out to be a deadly menace to their safe passage: an enemy submarine. At the moment the Americans spotted the submarine, it saw them, swinging around on an interception course. "I thought things couldn't happen like that except in the movies," said Tregaskis. "But there we were . . . racing with a Japanese submarine, trying to reach land before he cut us off—and he was winning." Desperate to survive, the boats attempted to outrun the enemy, going so fast the occupants were "practically drowned in spray," according to Tregaskis. He could also see geysers of water rising up near them, each one closer than the last, representing shells fired at them from the submarine's deck gun. "The first water spouts, the first sharp sounds of explosions, were far short," he remembered. "But each successive shot crept closer." Confusion reigned on board at what course to take until the coxswain on Tregaskis's boat swung around sharply to the right. "There was a chance, we thought, that we could make the eastern tip of Florida Island, or at least come somewhere near it, before the submarine caught us," Tregaskis remembered. Seeing their comrades' plight, the marines on Tulagi did all they could to drive off the submarine, firing on it with their 75 mm pack-howitzer artillery. Undeterred, the submarine continued its relentless pursuit, with its shells falling closer and closer to its prey.[2]

The Americans' chances at survival seemed dim when one of their vessels suffered engine trouble. Tregaskis could see the men in the other boat waving wildly at them and a haze of smoke issuing from its motor. His boat pulled alongside the stricken one, and they bumped and banged into each other as they tried to run at top speed. "The crew of the other craft fell, slid and vaulted into our boat," Tregaskis said. A marine public relations officer, Lt. Herbert Merillat, ordinarily "quite a dignified young man," tumbled in with great haste, leaving behind his shoes in the excitement. Tregaskis found it a comical sight even at such a dangerous moment. But his relief turned to apprehension when he realized that they had lost precious time in picking up the other crew and the submarine had kept up its relentless pursuit. "I told myself that this was my last day of existence, as it seemed certain to be," Tregaskis recalled. Fortunately, the artillery fire from Tulagi had come closer to the Japanese, with several shots hitting only yards from the submarine's conning tower. Fearing for its safety, the submarine turned away, heading west for the open sea. The Americans had survived their ordeal, chugging without further incident into Tulagi's harbor. "It was distinctly a pleasure to set foot on land again," said Tregaskis.[3]

After talking to the marines who wrested the islands of Tulagi, Gavutu, and

Tanambogo from Japanese control, Tregaskis and his companions stayed the night on Tulagi. The near-fatal encounter with the submarine, however, had shaken Tregaskis. Although scheduled to make his return with his companions to Guadalcanal the next morning at 4:30, well before sunrise, Tregaskis was convinced that the Japanese submarine that had pursued them before "would be lying off the harbor entrance, waiting." Tregaskis and the others in his party took shelter for the night on the floor of a shack near the Tulagi dock so they would not have to pass a line of vigilant marine sentries in the dark. But the correspondent could not fall asleep. He lay awake for hours, fretting that instead of risking a sea voyage, they should make their return by air. "'How about the PBY which had flown into Guadalcanal this morning?' was the thought that suddenly occurred to me," he noted. The correspondent stepped over the sleeping officers in the shack, woke one of them—Capt. James C. Murray—and asked if the PBY could be called upon to ferry them back? The answer was no. The PBY had left Guadalcanal long ago, taking with it a few wounded men. "I felt better then, knowing that we had no alternative except to run for it," Tregaskis remembered. "But it seemed to me inevitable that we would be caught and sunk, for the sub had obviously decided, this morning, that we were some sort of official boat, worth chasing—and worth waiting for." For the rest of the evening, Tregaskis sat on the shack's front steps, looking up at the soft white stars overhead and thinking it would be his last night on earth. "I thought that, all in all, it had been a good life, although it seemed to be ending a little early," he recalled.[4]

Tregaskis's fears did not come to pass; he and the others had a tense but uneventful return to Guadalcanal the next morning. The submarine did not reappear. It was not the last time, however, that he came close to injury and death in the Solomons. Until he left the island on September 26 to work on a book about his experiences, he withstood almost daily attacks by enemy bombers and nightly visits by another Japanese submarine, dubbed Oscar by the Americans, which let loose with an occasional potshot with its deck gun into the marines' bivouacs. The correspondent and others also had their sleep interrupted by harassing flares and bombs from aircraft nicknamed Louie the Louse and Washing-Machine Charlie, so named by the marines for the distinctive sound made by the plane's engine. These attacks caused only minor damage, except, that is, to "the nerves of exhausted men who yearned to sleep," recalled Merillat. Maneuvering through the jungle during the day, Tregaskis and others had to be on the lookout for cleverly concealed snipers.

He admitted years after the war that while on the island both he and Miller—contrary to U.S. War Department regulations that forbade them to carry and use weapons—armed themselves with M1911 .45-caliber pistols. He knew that an enemy sniper could not possibly distinguish between a combatant marine and a noncombatant correspondent. He was right. While covering the aftermath of what became known as the Battle of Bloody Ridge, Tregaskis looked across a ravine into the thick jungle foliage and saw a sudden movement, a Japanese sniper swinging his gun toward him. He could see that the sniper wore a camouflage suit, shaggy and brown, that looked like coconut husks. "He was sitting in the crotch of a tall tree and his movement had been to bring his gun to bear on me," Tregaskis recounted. "I hit the bushes underfoot and he fired three or four times, missing me every time, and I moved away from there fast to a more sheltered spot where three or four Marines were lying."[5]

Tregaskis and Miller, through sheer repetition, honed their survival instincts, particularly when it came to Japanese air raids. They learned how long they could observe the bombers overhead before seeking shelter in a convenient foxhole or dugout, as well as how to adjust their bodies—supporting themselves slightly on the elbows—to avoid concussion in case a bomb struck nearby. "The worst time in a bombing is the short moment when you can hear the bombs coming," Tregaskis said. "Then you feel helpless, and you think very intensely of the fact that it is purely a matter of chance whether or not you will be hit." Such chances varied by location, with the airfield—Henderson Field—a favorite target. "But even in other parts of the island, where odds may be greater, say, nine out of ten that you won't be hit, you wonder if you will be the unlucky tenth case," Tregaskis noted. While under attack, his thoughts sometimes drifted to those who had been badly wounded or killed in previous bombings, and in his imagination he suffered "the shock of similar wounds." He also castigated himself for not immediately running for cover to a dugout with a sandbagged roof. Instead, the approaching bombers had transfixed him, leaving only enough time for a quick dash to leap inside an open foxhole, crouch behind a handy limestone boulder, or fling himself to lie flat on the bare ground. "When you have nothing but the earth and your lack of altitude to protect you," Tregaskis recalled, "you feel singularly naked and at the mercy of the bombs." He could feel the ground jerk with the bombs' impact, followed by dirt clods showering down on his body. Often shaken by the experience, Tregaskis would arise to see before him rows of "clean-cut, black bomb craters," and the ground everywhere around him strewn with "small, cube-shaped clods of earth." Measuring the distance once between his position and the nearest bomb crater, he discovered it "was not much more than 200 yards." As for Miller, Tregaskis noted that the UP reporter's "courage and cheerfulness never seemed to leave him, not even when the bombs were rattling down on Henderson Field, or snipers were trying running shots at us."[6]

During the early days on Guadalcanal, Tregaskis and the marines lived in constant anticipation that the Japanese would hurl a counterattack directly at their defensive positions, described by the correspondent as "a small, well dug-in ring of protecting troops set in a rough arc around the [air]field, with the beach at their backs." If the enemy had done so, Tregaskis predicted, and at the same time "squeezed the inland edges of our defense, we would have been hard pressed to hold what we had taken." Most of the fighting during his time on Guadalcanal, the correspondent remembered, was confined to a strip of land running along the island's northern edge. "South of this area, an east-west range of mountains, the great high backbone of the island, made fighting next to impossible, and travel extremely difficult," Tregaskis said. "Even on the northern coastal strip where fighting did take place, precipitous ridges interspersed with nearly impenetrable jungle made military operations extremely trying." Without their heavy coastal-defense artillery, the marines could do little except suffer when Japanese ships appeared to rain shells down upon them. Tregaskis remembered standing at Kukum and watching a "swift, modern Jap destroyer prowling up and down offshore, so close that with field glasses I could plainly see his orange flag with a red rising sun in the center. It gave one an eerie feeling to see the enemy so close, taking his leisure, choosing his time to fire."[7]

Although the U.S. naval disaster at the Battle of Savo Island had left the marines exposed, Gen. Alexander Vandegrift insisted he did not believe that his men would suffer the same tragic fate surrendering U.S. troops had endured at the hands of the enemy on Wake Island and Bataan in the Philippines. "Since 1775 Marines had found themselves in tough spots," Vandegrift said. "They had survived and we would survive—but only if every officer and man on Guadalcanal gave his all to the cause." Trying to keep spirits high, the general called together his staff and command officers at an August 11 conference to report on the progress being made to complete the vital airfield and to stress his determination to hold the island. "I ended the conference by posing with this fine group of officers, a morale device that worked because they thought if I went to the trouble of having the picture taken then I obviously planned to enjoy it in future years," Vandegrift noted.[8]

Vandegrift always tried to exude confidence when making his daily tours of the perimeter. Once, seeing a position protected by a few strands of barbed wire, he confidently predicted, "That will hold anything they can throw against us." Other officers shared their commander's determination. Col. Clifton Cates noted that he carried with him into combat a Zenith portable radio on which he could receive broadcasts during the evening from San Francisco. "We would sit there and listen to these people make a statement, well, they hoped we could hold Guadalcanal," Cates remembered. "One Army Air Force General even said it was foolish to try to hold Guadalcanal." The marines, he said, treated such pessimism with disdain: "We never had any idea that we were not going to hold it." Guadalcanal had a code name—Cactus—but Tregaskis said that servicemen preferred to simply call it "the Canal," a nickname he said had an affectionate sound about it. "Men cursed and hated Guadalcanal," said Tregaskis, "a pest-hole that reeked of death, struggle, and disease, but the Canal was like a good-for-nothing cousin or brother. When you make tremendous sacrifices for someone or something, when you give your blood or your last drop of muscular effort or sweat, you feel something like affection for that object or person."[9]

Tregaskis did all he could in inhospitable conditions to let those on the home front know of the sacrifices being made by the marines. He often went from his usual spot staying near Col. LeRoy Hunt's command post to Vandegrift's headquarters, which included some Japanese tarpaulins, a small iron safe for storing classified materials, field telephones, and a table, "an unusual luxury on Guadalcanal," Tregaskis noted. He used the table as a handy place on which to compose his typewritten articles. One day he found it difficult to do any work, as there were three air-raid alarms (sounded by a "dilapidated dinner bell") keeping him on the run seeking shelter. Fortunately, they were all false alarms; no Japanese bombers appeared. For his part, Vandegrift gave the reporters on Guadalcanal plenty of freedom, letting them "go where they wanted and write what they wanted so long as it came within logical security confines." The general refused to tie up his "meager staff" by publishing "canned communiqués" and also did not want to waste any of his valuable time by holding regular press conferences. Vandegrift did make it clear that any of the correspondents "could come to me at any time with any question." Miller's and Tregaskis's fortitude won the respect of the marines on Guadalcanal. Sgt.

James Hurlbut, a marine combat correspondent, remembered his comrades saying, "Those civilian reporters are good guys. They're good enough to be Marines," which Hurlbut described as "high praise from the 'fightingest outfit' in the world." Tregaskis even won the respect of Vandegrift's gruff mess cook, Technical Sgt. Raymond C. "Butch" Morgan, who fussed over Tregaskis like a mother hen. "If Dick came in from a patrol too late for evening chow," Hurlbut noted, "Butch always rustled up coffee for him. He growled, grumbled, and profaned the atmosphere, but Dick always got the coffee."[10]

Paradoxically, the enemy played a part in helping the correspondents do their jobs on Guadalcanal. Plans had called for the U.S. Navy to provide a radio station for the marines during the initial landings, but the early withdrawal of the supply ships had left that order unfilled. The Japanese, however, had left behind communication equipment (two one-thousand-watt continuous wave radios housed in a wooden building) when they abandoned their base. Although unable to read Japanese, a marine technician, Sgt. Felix Ferranto, worked to get the station on the air with the call sign NGK, finally giving the marines a dependable method for connecting to the outside world. For the first month, Radio Guadalcanal's one officer, Lt. Sanford "Sandy" Hunt, spent hours painstakingly enciphering and transmitting to navy censors at Pearl Harbor the reams of news reports from the civilian correspondents— Tregaskis and Miller—as well as work by Merillat and his public relations colleague, Hurlbut. "Neither we, the generators of this workload for Hunt, nor a world waiting for news of Guadalcanal, realized how much was owed to Hunt's labors," Merillat said.[11]

Preparing the early dispatches from Guadalcanal for transmission took time, as did the necessary censoring. Merillat, who also served as the First Marine Division's historian, and Col. William Capers James, Vandegrift's chief of staff, were responsible for reviewing the stories the journalists produced "to guard against release of information that might be useful to the enemy," said Merillat. James grew frustrated, as more reporters joined Tregaskis and Miller on the island, at the heavy workload. He once complained after being handed a day's stack of press stories that he was "getting damned tired of reading this crap." There was still more editing to come. After the marine officers on Guadalcanal cleared the dispatches, they still had to be sent to Pearl Harbor, where they were "somewhat paraphrased (to safeguard the cipher system), censored, and, beginning late in August, released," explained Merillat. (Vandegrift later said he was unaware that "higher echelons were drastically censoring" the correspondents' copy.) Pondering his often exasperating profession, Tregaskis said that it was funny to work as a war correspondent, to toil long hours to gather the needed material, to write the story, shepherd it through censorship and transmission, and then, "after all that, to see no palpable effect or result." As one of his colleagues at INS observed, "it's like writing to yourself."[12]

Tregaskis did not know what kind of an exclusive he and Miller had enjoyed until September 2, when they were joined by two additional correspondents, F. Tillman Durdin of the *New York Times*, who in the late 1930s had reported on the Japanese invasion of China, and Tom Yarbrough of the Associated Press, who had covered the German bombing of London and the attack on Pearl Harbor. (Carleton "Bill" Kent of the *Chicago Times* arrived a few days later.) Merillat noted that Durdin and Yarbrough came to Guadalcanal believing they were the first reporters to reach the island. "Of course, they were sick on learning that Tregaskis and Miller have been here all the time, sending out reams of copy," said Merillat. The one thing that Tregaskis recalled of his new colleagues was that they wore "glamorous fresh uniforms," making him and Miller feel like "street urchins," as their hand-washed clothes were "scarcely clean and our faces stand in need of a good scrubbing with hot water." On his first night on Guadalcanal, Yarbrough shared a hillside trench with Merillat during a Japanese raid and told the marine public relations officer that "even in London he had never been through such a bombing." Eventually, the correspondents roomed together in a tent at the foot of a ridge facing the jungle near Vandegrift's headquarters. Rumors abounded about possible Japanese infiltrators, and the reporters were told that if an attack came they were to make their way to the crest of the ridge, "where a stand would be made," said Tregaskis. One night, lying awake, worried about a possible attack, and trying to calm their nerves by conversation, the correspondents could hear something hitting the roof of their tent; macaws in the trees overhead were "bombing" them. "The plopping of their missiles was loud and frequent," Tregaskis remembered. A marine officer observed that the birds "have got the correspondents' number, all right."[13]

Although forbidden to discuss the disaster the U.S. Navy suffered at the Battle of Savo Island, Tregaskis did not lack for subjects to share with his readers on the home front. His early pieces from Guadalcanal were often featured in newspapers as the correspondent's "War Diary," a format that might have influenced the style he used for *Guadalcanal Diary*. Describing Tregaskis as the "meticulous journalist that every newspaperman thinks he ought to be and seldom is," Hurlbut remembered that Tregaskis always made sure to keep his journal up to date. "Everything that took place was faithfully recorded in that black book," Hurlbut said, including the hometowns and first names and middle initials of every officer and enlisted man that had made news. In his dispatches, Tregaskis made sure to highlight the bravery and ingenuity displayed by the marines who fought tough engagements against the Japanese on islands few Americans had ever heard of: Tulagi, Gavutu, and Tanambogo, all "honeycombed with seemingly impregnable Japanese dugouts, and hill positions which swept our force with a deadly crossfire." Impossible, he wrote, did not seem to be a word in the marines' vocabulary. "Difficult jobs they do quickly," Tregaskis said. "The impossible takes a little longer."[14]

The Japanese garrison on Tulagi numbered about 350 men of the Kure Third Special Naval Landing Force, sailors trained for land warfare, who offered stiff resistance from seemingly impregnable dugouts and caves. Led by Lt. Col. Merritt A. "Red Mike" Edson, the First Marine Raider Battalion had to methodically knock out each position on Tulagi, some of which held from thirty to thirty-five of the enemy, one by one, destroying each until no Japanese remained alive. "It was impossible to approach the dugout from one direction," Edson told Tregaskis. "One man had to crawl to the dugout and try to destroy it with dynamite grenades while continuously exposed to deadly fire. And no dugout could be considered wiped out until all the Japs inside were dead. The marines had to go clear inside and wipe them out." A raider enlisted man, Martin "Whitey" Groft, remembered that Edson led Tregaskis on a tour of the caves in which the Japanese had made their final stand. "Tregaskis's nostrils flared as they reacted to the stench of death that seeped out of the cave openings," Groft noted. "He stepped gingerly over some yet unburied Japs, their bodies bloated and turned black from the tropical sun and heat."[15]

The marines of the First Parachute Battalion encountered similar rugged Japanese defensive works on the small island of Gavutu. Capt. Harry L. Torgerson, covered by four men armed with submachine guns, blew up more than fifty caves the Japanese had used as shelters by thrusting dynamite into the entrances. For his assault, Torgerson tied together thirty sticks of dynamite, ran to the cave's entrance, lit the fuse on his homemade bomb, threw it into the cave, and ran "like hell," Tregaskis reported. In all, the marine officer used twenty cases of TNT and only stopped his rampage because he ran out of matches. On one foray against the enemy, the resourceful Torgerson attached a five-gallon can of gasoline to one of his bombs—"to make it better," he explained. "The bomb went off with a great roar, knocked Torgerson down and blasted away most of his pants—as well as blowing in the roof of the Jap dugout," reported Tregaskis. The captain's only comment on the experience: "Boy, that was a pisser, wasn't it!"[16]

Torgerson's exploits on Gavutu had impressed Tregaskis, but not as much as had the commander of the raiders on Tulagi, Edson, whom he later described as the "bravest, the most effective killing machine" he had ever encountered in his career covering combat with troops of twelve nationalities. The colonel was medium sized, wiry, with thin gray hair showing only a few traces of the reddish mahogany that had been his youthful color, the reporter recalled, and possessed a "shy, lopsided, Cheshire-cat grin which warmed the hearts of his troopers far beyond its actual candle power." Edson usually spoke in a hoarse whisper so that the person he was talking to had to lean forward to hear what he was saying. "But though he never raised his voice, his men trembled when he was displeased," said Tregaskis. "He could wither a man with a glance of his China-blue gimlet eyes—or a few flatly intoned words of criticism." When he met the forty-five-year-old marine officer on Tulagi, Tregaskis remembered that Edson's talk had been all been about praise for his men; nothing about himself. The reporter heard stories from the raiders that in the worst fighting on the island, Edson had calmly walked around amid a storm of bullets, "directing machine gun fire, moving it up and down the Japanese positions. One man told me: 'His other officers were so scared they couldn't talk. But I saw him walking around with bullet holes in his clothes and his helmet, and he just didn't bat an eye. He talked like it was a Baptist picnic.'" Edson and his aiders would go on to play a critical role on Guadalcanal, and Tregaskis, reporting on that fighting, remembered what the colonel had once told him, "I'd never knowingly enter into a fight which I didn't think I could win." Edson prepared for every possible move and countermove in advance, noted Tregaskis. "Then, when the action was joined," the correspondent added, "he faced every surprise with clear-headed daring and resourcefulness."[17]

The marines' position on Guadalcanal improved considerably on the afternoon of August 20, when the escort carrier USS *Long Island* delivered nineteen Grumman Wildcat fighters and twelve Douglass SBD Dauntless dive-bombers—part of Marine Air Group 23—to Henderson Field. "The powerful roar of their motors was reassuring," recalled Tregaskis. "It seemed almost unbelievable that we did not have to dive for shelter at the sound." He could hear cheers all over the island, and one officer told him that morale must have skyrocketed twenty points in just one day. From that day forward, noted Tregaskis, everyone on Guadalcanal "felt much more secure," believing that what came to be known as the Cactus Air Force could now seek out and destroy the Japanese ships that had been harassing them. On August 22 the marine pilots received additional support when five U.S. Army P-400 Aircobra fighters of the Sixty-Seventh Fighter Squadron joined the fight. Although the army planes were no match for the Japanese Zero, they did prove effective against ground targets, using the formidable 20 mm cannon in the plane's nose to blast the enemy. Thus, the stage was set; when not hamstrung by overcast skies, the Cactus Air Force dominated the waters around Guadalcanal in daylight, while the Japanese navy remained supreme during the night, quickly retreating to its base before the sun rose and exposed them to American airpower. The pilots and ground crews both operated under less-than-ideal circumstances. Merillat pointed out that ground crews had to hand-pump gasoline into planes from fifty-five-gallon drums and hoisted heavy bombs into position using their own muscle power. "Pilots," he noted, were "like the rest of us, living on or in the ground, exposed to nighttime shellings and bombings. Indeed, they and their planes were the prime target." As one haggard pilot, exhausted from the grind of combat, later told Tregaskis, there came a point "where you just get to be no good; you're shot to the devil—and there's nothing you can do about it."[18]

The marine aircraft had arrived just in time for the first major attempt by Japanese troops to drive the Americans off Guadalcanal. On August 19 off of Taivu Point east of the marines' perimeter, the Japanese landed approximately nine hundred men under the command of Col. Ichiki Kiyoano, who was fully confident of his ability to march his troops twenty miles west, attack under the cover of darkness, annihilate any Americans opposing him, and capture Henderson Field. Ichiki and other Japanese officers had low opinions of their opponents' fighting ability, especially under adverse conditions, describing Westerners as being "very effeminate, and very cowardly," as well as having "an intense dislike of fighting in the rain or the mist, or at night. Night, in particular . . . they cannot conceive to be a proper time for war. In this, if we seize on it, lies our great opportunity." According to Tregaskis, the Japanese were also overconfident because they expected to find only three thousand to five thousand Americans defending Guadalcanal; instead there were now approximately fifteen thousand on the island. "But even under these circumstances their arrogance was extreme," he noted. Although it came to be known as the Battle of the Tenaru, those opposing the Japanese, including members of Col.

Clifton Cates's Second Battalion, First Marine Regiment, led by Lt. Colonel Edwin A. Pollock, had set up their defenses, including barbed wire scrounged from a former British coconut plantation and a 37 mm antitank gun, along a tidal lagoon known as Alligator Creek, which was separated from the sea by a broad sandbar. The Americans had some warning that an attack might be coming. Earlier, an American patrol had ambushed Japanese soldiers near Koli Point. Investigating the enemy dead, the marines noted that their uniforms and equipment seemed relatively new, and they carried information showing they knew about their opponents' defensive positions protecting Henderson Field.[19]

The first Tregaskis heard of the fighting came at 2:30 in the morning on August 21, when he was awakened by the sound of heavy machine-gun fire coming from the east. "There were several long bursts," he recalled, "and then rifle fire joining to form a waterfall of sound." The fire slackened, however, and he brushed it off as a skirmish between a Japanese patrol and a marine listening post. At 4:30 a.m., however, Tregaskis knew something serious had occurred, as a sound came as if "hundreds of rifles and machine guns were firing at once," followed by the crash of mortars and artillery. Immediately after breakfast, Tregaskis jumped into a jeep with Col. Jerry Thomas, Vandegrift's operations chief, and headed to Cates's command post. Once there, Tregaskis listened in as Cates made plans with Col. L. B. Cresswell to send his forces, supported by five M2A4 Stuart light tanks, to flank the Japanese position, boxing them in from two sides. After Cresswell left, Tregaskis remained with Thomas and Cates, hearing the sound of what seemed to be mortar shells near the front. Thomas wondered if the shelling had come from the marines or the Japanese, and Cates, a World War I veteran, had responded, "That's the trouble with this war. You never know. In the last war we used to know where the enemy was."[20]

While Thomas returned to report to Vandegrift, Tregaskis stayed behind, joining Cates for a trip to the front lines to see how the battle was progressing. The correspondent witnessed the tanks—"those awful machines"—plunge through a grove of palm trees, flushing the hidden enemy from their foxholes and mowing them down. "It was fascinating to see them bustling amongst the trees, pivoting, turning, spitting sheets of yellow flame. It was like a comedy of toys, something unbelievable, to see them knocking over palm trees which fell slowly, flushing the running figures of men from underneath their treads, following and firing at the fugitives," Tregaskis reported. "It was unbelievable to see men falling and being killed so close, to see the explosions of Jap grenades and mortars, black fountains and showers of dirt near the tanks, and see the flashes of explosions under their treads." He saw one of the tanks flush a couple of Japanese from a foxhole. One of them ran for the beach, with the tank's machine-gun bullets ripping up the ground behind him as he sprinted for safety. The soldier made it to the beach, squatting for a second before rising and being hit by a marine sharpshooter. "Everywhere, the Japanese resisted to the last ounce of life in their bodies," Tregaskis noted. He saw some of them playing dead along the sandspit, saw them start to move and try to reach their rifles, only to be gunned down. "I saw others who pretended to be dead, who when rising tide set them afloat, tried to swim out to sea and swim ashore behind our lines. They were killed as they approached the beach or as they swam out," he reported. The marines showed no mercy. The correspondent noted that the Americans relished the job of finishing off their victory. "Whenever we could see the head of a swimming man, a small storm of little waterspouts rose around him as our bullets smacked home," he reported. Those doing the firing had probably already learned that wounded Japanese had waited until their captors bent over to check on them before flinging hand grenades into their faces. "There were two such cases reported: fortunately in both cases the thrown grenades missed their target and exploded some distance away," recalled Tregaskis.[21]

Only a handful of Ichiki's men survived the attack; the marines counted nearly eight hundred dead Japanese, while they suffered far fewer casualties; Tregaskis counted twenty-eight killed and seventy-two wounded. The fierce engagement had been the "first action for many of the marines involved," he noted, but they "had stood up to the enemy like more seasoned troops." Returning to the battlefield on August 22, Tregaskis said it was not pleasant to look upon the piles of bodies lying on the sandspit. The carnage there, however, paled in comparison to the scene of destruction where the American tanks had operated. "That was a macabre nightmare," he recalled. Vandegrift described the scene as "a slaughter," adding that the rear of the tank's treads looked "like meat grinders." Everywhere Tregaskis turned he came across piles of bodies with grotesque disfigurements caused by American firepower. The correspondent observed one body with its backbone visible from the front and the rest of its flesh and bone "peeled up over the man's head, like the leaf of an artichoke." In other places Tregaskis came across a charred head, a Japanese with a red bullet hole through his eye, and an enemy in a private's uniform lying on his back "with his chest a mess of ground meat." Ichiki managed to make his way through the jungle to Taivu Point. There he burned his regimental colors and killed himself. His superior reported to Imperial headquarters that the attack of Ichiki's detachment "was not entirely successful."[22]

Pitched engagements like the Battle of the Tenaru provided great material for Tregaskis's dispatches to the INS, but mere day-to-day existence on the island proved to be a challenge for the marines. One of Tregaskis's most effective articles involved exploring what a typical day on the island meant for an average marine—the imaginary John Marine—relayed via a letter home to his mother. The marine's day started at 12:45 a.m. with three Japanese cruisers dashing in close to the island to unleash a torrent of shells at American positions. "There was a sea battle right after the shelling—a knock-down, drag-out fight—and all hell broke loose as usual," the marine wrote. There were also two air raids, one in the morning and one in the afternoon. The Japanese turned back in the morning, and were frightened away in the afternoon. "Our own dive bombers, with some fighter planes, went out to annoy Jap troops trying to land on Santa Isabel island. We destroyed seven or eight landing boats on the beach there," the marine continued. Tregaskis goes on to quote John Marine describing the rest of the day as "pretty dull and routine," although there were rumors of an imminent large invasion force, some Japanese tried to break through the marines' line, and a slight earthquake shook his bunk at about nine in the evening. "Well, Mom," the letter concluded, "that's about all that happened today. I wish there was more news, but then you know every day can't be a red letter day. It must be nice to be back home where there are plenty of dances and night clubs, shows and all sorts of excitement."[23]

Bombs, bullets, and shells were not the only dangers lurking on Guadalcanal. Tregaskis discovered that fact on the evening of August 26, when he felt the first symptoms of a local epidemic, gastroenteritis, which was marked by a combination of nausea, vomiting, diarrhea, and a high fever. Tregaskis attempted to "sleep off" his sickness, but failed. He felt so ill that when an air-raid alert sounded, he remained huddled in his cot. "I heard the drone of planes in the sky and got my helmet and put it on," he said, "then turned face down on the cot. That way, I figured, I would have a maximum of protection." Fortunately for the correspondent, the Japanese that day, perhaps spooked by American fighters, jettisoned their bombs into the jungle away from the Americans' positions. Shortly after the aborted raid, Tregaskis had to be carried off in an ambulance to the medical tent. "I remember hearing the familiar squeak of the stretcher as I was put into the ambulance, the jouncy ride, losing my sense of direction, and reading, several times, the red letters

'USN, MC' painted on the stretcher above mine, being placed on a cot that was too short for me, as most of them are, and then suffering through four or five hours of tortured sleep and being conscious that my fever was rising and nausea increasing. I had a bad case."[24]

The other patients in his tent were in better shape than the correspondent, and Tregaskis had to endure hearing endless rumors they had heard about the Solomons campaign: of the Japanese ability to speak English, of their dead wearing American high-school rings, and of U.S.-made mementoes being discovered on their bodies. The yarns went on until somebody told what had become a classic tale about two marine jeep drivers on Guadalcanal, supposedly, Tregaskis said, a true story, "very true, anyhow, in its essential American psychology." The drivers had come upon one another, one with his headlights dimmed for the blackout, while the other had his headlights blaring brightly. The driver of the dimly lit jeep called out to the other as they passed, "Hey! Put your f—g lights out!" The other driver replied, "I can't. I got a f—g colonel with me!"[25]

Tregaskis recovered from his illness in time to accompany Edson's raiders, who had been moved to Guadalcanal from Tulagi on August 30, on two missions against the Japanese. The first occurred in early September after reports of suspicious activity regarding Savo Island, off the northern tip of Guadalcanal. Tregaskis and Miller received permission from Edson to join the two companies of raiders sent on combat patrol on the high-speed transports USS *Gregory* and the USS *Little* (both former World War I destroyers), led by Edson's executive officer, Lt. Col. Samuel B. Griffith. The correspondents arrived late in the afternoon of September 3 and saw the two transports sail away without them. Luckily, they were able to hitch a ride on a cargo ship set to rendezvous with the raiders that evening. "We were not sorry to be aboard the cargo ship. She was clean and brightly modern," said Tregaskis, who took the opportunity to enjoy a hot bath, the first he had taken in weeks. After his luxurious washing, Tregaskis went to dinner and felt like a country mouse visiting his more sophisticated city relative. "I found my values had grown so primitive on Guadalcanal that I was dazzled by the white tablecloth and shining silverware," he recalled. "I wondered if unconsciously I would put the silverware into my pocket after the meal, for on Guadalcanal, one carries his own spoon, and knows that if he loses it, he will probably have to rely on his fingers for feeding purposes."[26]

The landing the next morning near the village of Panuila went smoothly, with the raiders encountering no enemy resistance, eventually splitting into two groups to reconnoiter the eastern and western parts of the island. Tregaskis went with the marines covering the eastern end. As the Americans passed through the villages of Septatavi and Pokelo, they discovered no evidence of Japanese, but plenty of debris—life rafts, life belts, and oil drums—from the disastrous Battle of Savo Island. "The debris was washed up on the beach, and even now, nearly a month after the battle, the water's edge was still stained with oil. Stones and branches farther up the beach were still coated with oil, some of it a quarter or half inch thick," Tregaskis reported. Farther to the south, the patrol came upon more debris along the shore: an oil-soaked life raft from the USS *Quincy*, a waterlogged notebook that had been kept by an officer on the USS *Astoria*, the propeller from a catapult aircraft from the HMAS *Canberra*, and wooden crates marked "Australia." By midafternoon the two groups of raiders had come back together at the island's southern end. Neither had seen any Japanese. Although rough seas had Tregaskis worried about their ability to get back to their transports, they made it and returned to Guadalcanal. When they reached the island, there was some debate, he remembered, as to whether or not the correspondents and troops should remain on the *Little* and *Gregory*, as Edson had been planning another operation and wanted his men to remain on the ships. But by the time Edson's message reached Griffith, one group of raiders had already disembarked, so all the marines, as well as Tregaskis and Miller, came ashore. It was lucky they did.[27]

Shortly before 1:00 in the morning Tregaskis was awakened in his tent by the sounds of gunfire toward the sea and the whirr of large shells passing overhead. Taking cover in a nearby dugout, the correspondent felt as if he was "at the mercy of a great, vindictive giant whose voice was the voice of thunder; the awful colossal scale of modern war has brought the old gods to life again." Flares lit up the night, followed by a piercing white light, Tregaskis recalled, probably a searchlight illuminating a target. Three Japanese ships had sneaked in close to the shoreline to bombard, with little effect, American positions on Guadalcanal. In doing so, however, they discovered the *Little* and *Gregory*, sinking both. The next morning Tregaskis hurried to Kukum to watch as survivors from the ships were brought ashore, some barely clad in tattered clothing covered with oil, standing together in silence while stretcher bearers passed by carrying "inert, white-bandaged wounded," including burn cases. A chief bosun's mate from the *Little*, Ralph G. Andre, told Tregaskis that the Japanese had fired point-blank at the American ships at a distance of no more than a thousand yards. "We fired all our guns, probably three or four rounds, before the Japs' first salvo hit us," said Andre. "Their first shell set us afire, hit into a fuel tank. Then they turned a searchlight on us and kept firing until we were aflame all over. Then they went over and sank the Gregory, and it looked like they came back and gave it to us again after that." Andre had floated on a life raft off the coast of Guadalcanal for six hours with other sailors, all the time trying to disregard the shell fragment wound to his leg. While talking to the correspondent, Andre was urged by several other sailors to get treatment for his injury, but he refused, saying, "I'll wait till the others [those more seriously wounded] are treated." Another survivor, Lt. (jg) Heinrich Heine Jr. of San Diego, California, served on the Gregory and described the sea battle as "fifty kinds of hell, put together."[28]

Tregaskis did not have much time to ponder his good fortune at avoiding what had befallen the sailors, as he hurried from the beach to Vandegrift's command post and from there to Henderson Field headquarters to see what damage U.S. dive-bombers had dished out the last few days. At the airfield Tregaskis heard an air alert, so he and other members of the Guadalcanal Press Club—Miller, Yarbrough, and Durdin—climbed into a jeep and drove to Lunga Point, where there was a radio. Miller slipped on a pair of headphones, listened in on the interplane communications, and called them out so his colleagues could have "a blow-by-blow description of the fighting." They also heard the sound of dogfighting in the sky over them, but the planes were too high in the clouds to see. "Then one of our casualties called in, 'I'm in trouble and I don't mean maybe. I'm going down,'" Tregaskis recalled. A few moments later, the correspondents saw the damaged aircraft, streaming smoke and propeller still, attempt a dead-stick landing. (The pilot made it.) Although a rumor swept the island that afternoon about a possible attack by thirty-three Japanese ships, the report proved to be false. Still, Tregaskis did not have an easy night. At nine o'clock he awoke to find his cot shaking "as if someone had a grip on one end and was trying to jostle me," he remembered. "It was an earthquake—which they say, is a fairly common occurrence hereabouts." Later that night, Tregaskis's rest was interrupted again by sounds of rifle and machine-gun fire. "Had the Japs broken through? I wondered," he said. "But after a while one grows bored with the incessant repetition even of thoughts like these. I went back to sleep."[29]

9 THE REPORTER AND THE RAIDERS

The tip came from Lt. Col. Merritt "Red Mike" Edson to reporter Richard Tregaskis on the morning of Monday, September 7, 1942. Edson and his men, the First Raider Battalion, assisted by the First Parachute Battalion, about 850 in all, were planning a mission to investigate reports of a Japanese buildup that had grown from an initial estimate of 300 troops to anywhere from 1,000 to 3,000. Edson and marine intelligence officers on Guadalcanal had selected the small village of Tasimboko in the Taivu Point area as their target. They were to be ferried there from Kukum by two destroyer-transports (the *Manley* and *McKean*) and two smaller vessels classified by the navy as YPs (patrol craft), or "Yippies," as the raiders called them. Undeterred by the pelting rain that greeted him at the embarkation point, or the small size of the craft in which he would make the journey, Tregaskis climbed aboard, accompanying Samuel B. Griffith, Edson's executive officer, and a group of approximately one hundred high-spirited marines. One of them jokingly inquired, "This is the battleship *Oregon*, I presume?" after stepping on the deck of what had once been a California tuna boat.[1]

Those high spirits were dampened a bit as the raiders and Tregaskis attempted to find enough room on the diesel-powered boat (YP-346) to get some rest before the next day's attack. "Getting to sleep was a terrible job," Tregaskis recalled. "The ship's steaming hold, full of the noise of the engines, was crammed with marines; no room to sprawl there. Every nook about the deck seemed to be filled as well." Those sheltering in the cramped engine room kept busy by "munching canned rations, and oiling up their guns," Tregaskis reported, adding that in a marine's estimation, food, guns, and ammunition "run a close tie" for premiere importance. One of the raiders described the night as "the most miserable" he had ever spent, as rough seas caused some of his comrades to become seasick. At least the waves that cascaded over the deck helped to wash away the vomit of the men who had become ill. Although the ship's cheerful Portuguese skipper, Joaquin S. Theodore, told those aboard that they should not smoke on deck lest their lighted cigarettes alert the enemy, the marines questioned his reasoning. Griffith pointed out, "Belching showers of bright red sparks as they chugged eastward through the blackness with engines pounding, the Yippies announced their presence to all but the blind and deaf." Unable to find a decent place on deck that could shelter him from the rain and the cold, Tregaskis stumbled his way to the stuffy captain's room, collapsing on the floor and drifting off. "It was better than sleeping in the rain," he noted.[2]

Tregaskis accepted the discomforts of traveling on a ship that was little more than "a floating engine room" because he knew that wherever the hard-charging raiders went, he would be sure to encounter action intense enough to satisfy the curiosity of even the most jaded newspaper reader on the home front. Viewed as the American counterpart to the British commandos, the raiders depended upon speed and surprise for successful completion of their quick strikes deep behind enemy lines. They trained intensely to become experts in the art of combat—both armed and unarmed—and were in top physical condition after a rigorous training regimen that included punishing hikes interspersed with runs at top speed. The raiders became an elite within an elite in the all-volunteer (at the time) U.S. Marine Corps, which held to the concept that every marine was a rifleman, whatever his specialty might be. As Robert L. Sherrod, a reporter from *Time* magazine who followed the corps as its men leapfrogged their way across the Pacific, pointed out, "The Marines assumed that they were the world's best fighting men."[3]

The raiders attracted the "most dedicated, aggressive, competitive, and ambitious Marines" and so had little hesitation in considering themselves to be a superior fighting force. In covering the raiders' activities on Tulagi and Guadalcanal, Tregaskis had become fascinated with their courage and fighting skills, as well as being particularly impressed by Edson's deft leadership and bravery while under fire. "He knew his business was killing the enemy and making his men fight well," Tregaskis said of Edson. "He was a devoted, loyal, honorable 'Can-Do' Marine, a brilliant officer—and when we needed his kind to protect us, he was in there swinging with every ounce of energy and brain power in him." The officer instilled in his men the belief that they had been trained to be the best, "second to none," as a raider sergeant once told Tregaskis. No matter what kind of dangers they faced, Edson made his men believe they would prevail, which translated into a "terrific amount of confidence," the sergeant recalled. For their part, the raiders also admired Tregaskis's determination to risk his life alongside them, naming him, years after the war had ended, an honorary member of the battalion.[4]

The expedition to Tasimboko came as a result of the most determined effort made yet by the Japanese to eliminate the Americans from Guadalcanal. Approximately six thousand troops under the command of Maj. Gen. Kiyotake Kawaguchi had reached the island and were struggling through the jungle on their way to—they were confident—tear through the marines' main line of resistance and capture Henderson Field. Kawaguchi reminded the soldiers of his Thirty-Fifth Brigade that the Americans feared their massed bayonet charges. "The strong point of the enemy is superiority of fire power. But it will be able to do nothing in the night and in the jungle," Kawaguchi boasted. The general was so certain of victory that he packed his white dress uniform to wear when Japan's Rising Sun flag was raised in triumph over Henderson Field. Unfortunately for Kawaguchi, while his troops were positioning themselves for an attack on the American airfield, Edson and his raiders were on their way to hit Tasimboko, where the Japanese had left behind a large cache of supplies. Because intelligence reports indicated the enemy's defenses faced west, Edson planned to land his men east of Tasimboko near Taivu Point and attack the encampment from the east. The raiders could always tell by looking at their commander's face that he had managed to find them another dangerous assignment, noted Lt. Houston Stiff. He remembered fellow raiders exclaiming, "Oh, Christ! The Old Man's got that so-and-so grin on his face again. Now there'll be hell to pay!" Later, a few of the raiders grew disenchanted with Edson's eagerness to involve them in hazardous missions, referring to him by the unflattering nickname Mad Merritt the Morgue Master.[5]

Tregaskis and the raiders had some good fortune early in the morning of September 8 as they climbed into the Higgins boats taking them to shore. A small convoy of American cargo ships, escorted by a cruiser and four destroyers, passed close by them on their way to another part of the island, Lunga Point. With what seemed to be a large armada approaching their position, many of the Japanese—about three hundred members of Kawaguchi's rear echelon—panicked. They abandoned their positions and fled into the jungle, leaving unmanned two antitank guns that could have decimated the American force. "But we naturally had no way of knowing this as we dashed for shore in our landing boats," Tregaskis reported. "We were ready for a real struggle, and a bit puzzled when there were no shots from shore." The correspondent's colleague, Robert C. Miller of United Press, also joined the raid; he remembered the twenty minutes it took for him to make it to shore as the longest twenty minutes of his life. "I made the mistake of being in the front of the boat and got pushed ashore first—unarmed," Miller reported. "Ran like hell for the bush and found four Marines had beaten me to it." Tregaskis and the raiders were mystified again when, shortly after landing, they found not only a "serviceable 37 mm field piece" complete with ammunition, but also full packs, life preservers, entrenching tools, and shoes "strewn in disorder on the ground." There were also fresh foxholes dug in the black jungle earth and camouflaged with palm leaves. "I'm thinking they've gone up for breakfast and knocked things off," Edson said to Tregaskis. The group pushed on, hurrying through a small village with only two huts and others "in skeletal condition (having been burned)," noted the correspondent. Tregaskis could hear the sound of aircraft engines in the distance, dive-bombers and fighters from Henderson Field attacking Tasimboko from the air. As the Americans circled around a small pond, forded a stream, and struggled through the jungle's thick, tangled vines and leaves, they remained puzzled, Tregaskis noted, by the lack of any Japanese resistance, fearing they might be walking into a trap.[6]

Shortly after eight in the morning the raiders encountered their first enemy resistance. Tregaskis could see the marines running around "in numerous directions at once," and he knew immediately that something had happened. He ran to the beach and encountered a line of Japanese landing boats lying on the sand, and with them a small group of figures clad in brown uniforms. Edson quietly called out for Maj. Floyd Nickerson, who anticipated his commander's order to open fire. Soon, raider machine-gun crews hammered at the enemy, who responded in kind. "I heard the familiar flat crack of the .25 [caliber] rifle, and the repetition of the sound in long bursts of light machine-gun fire," said Tregaskis, who sought cover by burrowing deep into the wet jungle foliage as bullets whirred among the leaves behind him. "Others of our men joined in the firing and it swelled in volume. In the midst of the outburst, we heard the crash of a heavy explosion," he said. Edson, who had taken cover, told the correspondent that it sounded like mortar fire. With a lull in the firing, which Tregaskis said seemed to be a common occurrence in jungle warfare, Edson hurried ahead, and the reporter struggled to keep pace, noting that he found the colonel to be "one of the quickest human beings" he had ever known.[7]

The firing started up again, and Tregaskis heard cries calling for a corpsman to tend to a wounded raider. The Americans came under fire from what seemed to be a heavy artillery piece (they turned out to be 75 mm field guns). Tregaskis could hear the "furry whistle of a shell" passing over his head and heard it explode a couple of hundred yards to the rear. "It was so loud it made my ears ring, and the concussion shook chips of wood on my head from the trees above," he reported. As the raiders killed the crew manning one of the guns, another took its place, continuing to fire on the Americans. Tregaskis, who had taken cover among a tangle of vines and dwarf trees, could feel a blast of hot air from the gun's muzzle each time it fired. He also had to keep an eye out for Japanese riflemen, later learning that one had been no more than fifty feet away from where he had been, all this while being soaked by a sudden rainstorm. "There's nothing worse than lying in a jungle, wringing wet, with a war going on around you," joked Miller. At about 10:45 a.m. a raider reported to Edson that the second Japanese 75 mm gun had been put out of action. "It began to look as if we might have tackled a bigger Jap force than we could handle," noted a concerned Tregaskis. Edson called for naval gunfire support for his men, and the *Manley* and *McKean* responded and shelled Tasimboko. "I went out to the beach to watch the yellow flashes and the geysers of smoke and debris rising where the shells had hit," Tregaskis said. He learned later that one of the marines, Corp. Maurice Pion, had suffered a shattered left arm in the shelling. Pharmacist mates Alfred W. Cleveland and Karl B. Coleman used a penknife to amputate what remained of Pion's arm, saving his life in the process. Pvt. Andrew J. Klejnot used his skills as a marksman to shoot and kill one of the two Japanese soldiers manning one of the guns. The other tried to hide behind some boxes in a small ammunition dump, Klejnot told Tregaskis, so he "fired into the dump and set it afire."[8]

In any engagement he participated in during the war, Tregaskis noted that there came a time, always a "very pleasant one," when his doubts and fears suddenly cleared away and he could see a successful conclusion nearing. Such a time came in the raid on Tasimboko at about noon. A raider from a company led by Capt. John J. Antonelli came into Edson's command post to report that "we secured the problem and took the village." The clouds that had been unleashing torrents of rain cleared, and Nickerson indicated that his forces had also reached the village. Once they reached Tasimboko, the marines set about destroying numerous cases of Japanese food and sacks of rice (urinating on the contents or spilling it on the ground), as well as burning approximately 500,000 rounds of ammunition, Griffith estimated, and destroying radio equipment.[9]

As they neared the bamboo huts in which the ammunition was stored, Tregaskis heard Nickerson tell his men, "All right. Here you go. In here and start burning, you arson artists." Miller joined in, helping the marines torch the huts. "It was fun," he told his readers. "Especially when I remembered I would have gone to jail back home for doing the same thing. . . . . Had more fun later, towing some Japanese artillery pieces out into the ocean and leaving them there to rust." Raider Marlin "Whitey" Groft recalled that he and other members of his team picked through the pockets of the dead Japanese for whatever they could find, including documents, possible souvenirs, and even photographs and letters from the soldiers' families in Japan. Groft added that some of the more "stalwart" raiders used their knives or stilettos to cut out gold teeth from the dead men's mouths. "It's funny how in war," he remembered, "men do things they would never consider doing under normal conditions." According to Griffith, Tregaskis, whom he described as the "lanky I.N.S. [International News Service] correspondent adopted by the Raiders," also lent a hand, poking around the village and filling a Japanese blanket with papers, notebooks, maps, and charts that were later used by marine intelligence officers to gain a better understanding about the pending Japanese offensive.[10]

The raiders suffered eight casualties (two killed and six wounded), counted twenty-seven Japanese bodies, and estimated they had killed a total of fifty. A pleased Griffith described the raid as "one of the really very successful small operations of World War II." The marines left Tasimboko late in the afternoon for the return to Kukum, with officers and enlisted men, Griffith remembered, "sagging under a load of tinned crab and sliced beef packed in soy." Twenty-one cases of Japanese beer and seventeen half-gallon flasks of *sake*, he added, were also smuggled aboard. In addition, Tregaskis reported that the raiders helped themselves to large numbers of British-made cigarettes, still bearing Netherlands East Indies tax stamps, and brought back captured Japanese medical supplies. As a final insult to the enemy, the raiders liberated the dress uniform Kawaguchi had intended to wear at his expected victory ceremony at Henderson Field. Tregaskis credited Cpl. Phil A. Oldham with coming up with the classic line of the excursion when, upon seeing an enemy soldier pop up in front of his platoon, he shouted, "Don't shoot him. Let me get him. He's mine!"[11]

With the setting sun only a reddish glow in the sky, Tregaskis and the raiders had a final bit of excitement as the transports and YPs neared their homeport. A report passed among the marines that a dozen Japanese aircraft had been spotted. Fortunately for them, the enemy aircraft did not strike Guadalcanal, but selected Tulagi as their target. The correspondent could see "cup-shaped bursts of bright white light rising from the direction of the island, just over the horizon rim," as well as hearing the "distant thudding of bombs" a few seconds later. The tension and exhaustion of the operation hit Tregaskis early that morning as he tried to get some rest. He could hear others in his tent dashing outside to a nearby shelter. An officer with the Fifth Marines, Maj. Bill Phipps, shouted for him to join them, but Tregaskis was "too tired to move" and remained behind. At breakfast the next morning he heard that Japanese ships had shelled Tulagi, hitting Captain Theodore's tuna boat, setting it afire, and wounding him through the chest; the Portuguese sailor was expected to live. "This is the second time that I have left a ship in the evening and it has been attacked and lost before morning," Tregaskis observed. "This fact gives rise to the thought that my luck has been good, so far."[12]

Tregaskis would need all the luck he could muster the next few days as Kawaguchi prepared to conduct a three-pronged attack on the marines' lines, the main one against the airfield from the south. Using the documents captured on the Tasimboko operation, Edson consulted with Gen. Alexander Vandegrift and his intelligence staff to devise a strategy to blunt the Japanese offensive. The raiders and parachutists were to be sent to defend the bare slopes of ridge about two thousand yards south of the vital airfield. Griffith described the new position as "a broken, rugged, kunai-covered coral hogback which paralleled the Lunga [River] south of the airfield. Jungle lapped at its south, east, and west slopes; to the north the ground gave off gently toward battered Henderson." On September 10 Edson told his men that there had been too much bombing and shelling around their position in a grove near the abandoned Lever Brothers coconut plantation and that they would be moving to "a quiet spot." If the raiders expected a rest, they were soon jolted back to reality. Their suspicions were heightened when they saw forward artillery observers from Col. Pedro del Valle's Eleventh Marines identifying probable target areas for their guns, as well as a scattering of other officers scouting the territory. "On top of this," noted a raider sergeant, "were our own officers and NCOs [noncommissioned officers] constantly pushing us in the laying of barbed wire, digging foxholes, building machine gun emplacements and cutting fire lanes." The next morning Tregaskis looked up to see twenty-six Japanese twin-engine bombers unloading their ordnance not against their usual target—the airfield—but the marines on the ridge, who had barely managed to scratch out shelters in which to take cover.[13]

With two of his colleagues, Miller and Tillman Durdin, Tregaskis had reconnoitered the ridge and found a deep and wide pit to pile into when the enemy bombers arrived. "The bombs made a slightly different sound this time, perhaps because they were closer than before," noted Tregaskis. "Their sound was louder and more of a whistle. And the explosions were deafening." The reporters could hear bomb fragments whizzing through the air over the top of their shelter, and one of the hot metal shards whirled into the pit and embedded itself into Durdin's shoe. When the bombing ended, Tregaskis could hear shouts for corpsmen to tend to the wounded and saw several marines taken away on stretchers. Stunned by what he had undergone, a raider corporal exclaimed, "Some goddam rest area!"[14]

Preceded by a bombardment from cruisers and destroyers, Kawaguchi's forces struck the raiders' defensive line on the ridge on the evening of September 12. Tregaskis and his fellow correspondents were bivouacked in Vandegrift's command post, about a hundred yards from Edson's position. At about nine o'clock that evening a marine poked his head into their tent and told them, "Get up, fellas, we're moving up the ridge." The reporters wasted no time in grabbing their helmets and shoes and leaving. From their vantage point on the ridge top, they could see the distinctive flashes of naval gunfire coming from the direction of Kukum. "Just as we heard the boom of the gun, the shell whizzed over our heads and crashed a few hundred yards around," Tregaskis recalled. "There was a second's pause, and then more flashes followed, so continuously that the sky seemed to be flickering constantly, and shells whined overhead almost in column. They kept coming for minutes on end, fortunately hitting into the jungle several hundred yards behind us, skimming over the trees under which we were lying. We simply lay there clutching the side of the ridge and hoping the Japs would continue to fire too high." Tregaskis could also hear the sound of small-arms fire coming from the south and could not help but wonder if the Japanese were making another effort to break through the American lines. As the firing dwindled, Tregaskis and his colleagues made the decision not to return to their tent in the valley. "I slipped my poncho over my head, put on my mosquito head-net and my helmet, and lay down on top of the hard ridge to sleep," said Tregaskis.[15]

Edson told Vandegrift the next morning that he believed the enemy had been just "testing us" when they had hit his men. The raider commander expected Kawaguchi's forces to try again that night. "He [Edson] spent the day moving back his front, tying in automatic weapons, improving fields of fire and laying more communication wire," Vandegrift recalled. At Edson's request the general moved his reserve force—the Second Battalion, Fifth Marines—closer to the raiders' lines, while marine artillerymen pinpointed possible targets for their fire and the Cactus Air Force received reinforcements, including two dozen Wildcat fighters and additional dive-bombers and torpedo planes. Kawaguchi felt only frustration. He had fully intended to make his main attack against the Americans on the evening of September 12, but had been impeded by the "devilish jungle," which caused his forces to be "scattered all over and completely beyond control. In my whole life I have never felt so helpless."[16]

As the raiders prepared for another onslaught by the Japanese against the ridge, Tregaskis had the foresight, when told once again to move from his tent to the ridge top, to take along a blanket and his satchel full of notes. He spread his poncho and blanket on the ground and tried to get some sleep, but was jolted awake shortly after midnight on September 14 by the noise of action that had welled into a "cascade of sound" from the raider lines. He saw a gray mist drift in among the trees on the ridge and wondered if it might be smoke from the Eleventh Marines' howitzers (he later learned it had been smoke released by the Japanese to fool the Americans into thinking they were using gas, the dreaded weapon from World War I). Enemy snipers infiltrated Vandegrift's command post, causing Tregaskis to hug the ground to avoid ricocheting bullets that skidded among the trees. In all the commotion, with rumors that the Japanese had landed parachute troops, Tregaskis noted that Vandegrift remained calm, sitting on the ground outside the operations tent and cheerfully observing, "Well, it's only a few more hours till dawn. Then we'll see where we stand." The general even had the wit to be amused at Tregaskis's efforts to jot down some notes despite the darkness. Calls came in from Edson's command with urgent requests for more machine-gun ammunition and hand grenades, while at about midnight Vandegrift learned that one of his battalions dug in along the upper Tenaru River had been hit as well. Tregaskis reported that a marine from the outpost under attack eventually staggered into Vandegrift's headquarters, gasped out, "They got 'em all," and promptly fainted. Snipers continued to pepper the command post from all sides. "We had our hands full," Tregaskis noted.[17]

So did the marines on the ridge. The situation grew so desperate that Edson had to call in artillery fire almost directly on top of his positions. Terrified Japanese soldiers tried to escape the withering fire by jumping into their enemy's foxholes; the marines pitched them back into the maelstrom. The artillerymen fired more than two thousand rounds during the battle, and a grateful raider later acknowledged, "They saved our asses." From Vandegrift's headquarters, marine public relations officer Herbert Merillat could hear the artillery officers shouting out their orders and their shells ripping through the air directly over his head. Japanese prisoners later reported that their units caught in the barrage had been annihilated. One raider described the Japanese attack as almost constant, likening it to a "rain that subsides for a moment and then pours the harder." Wave after wave fell under the marines' concentrated rifle and machine-gun fire and exploding grenades. Firing his Springfield rifle into the mass of Japanese who screamed "Banzai!" "Death to America!" and "We drink Marine blood!" as they charged, Groft had a thought flash through his mind: "So much yelling. So much dying." Edson seemed to be everywhere on the ridge, rallying his men with harsh words when they seemed to be wavering. Groft remembered seeing his commanding officer yank his .45 automatic from his holster and threaten to shoot any man who dared flee to the rear. "The only thing they have that you don't have is guts," Groft quoted Edson as saying. "Get back in line. You'll die in your foxholes." Maj. Ken Bailey also proved to be an indomitable presence on the ridge, delivering badly needed ammunition and shoving his men back to the positions, yelling out a question made famous by another marine in World War I: "Do you want to live forever?" (Edson and Bailey both later received the Medal of Honor for their actions on the ridge.) The raiders and parachutists held their ground, strengthened by reserve forces from the Second Battalion of the Fifth Marines. When daylight finally appeared, P-400 fighter aircraft from Henderson Field swooped down upon the Japanese that remained to unleash additional carnage upon the battlefield.[18]

Although the marines had triumphed, pockets of resistance remained. Tregaskis remembered returning to Vandegrift's command post for a cup of coffee after working his way to catch a glimpse of the battlefield only to hear a loud, blubbering shout, "like a turkey gobbler's cry, followed by a burst of shooting." When the commotion had died down he walked to the spot and saw the bodies of two dead Japanese and one dead marine. Three Japanese, who had been hiding in a bush at the edge of the ridge road, decided to make a suicide charge against the Americans. According to Tregaskis's report about the attack, Master Technical Sgt. John McAdams had spotted the trio's leader, fell upon him, and shot him in the side. Another marine, Cpl. Harvey W. Skaugen, threw his rifle at another charging Japanese, knocking him to the ground, and Sgt. Maj. Shepherd Banta interrupted his dressing down of a clerk long enough to fire the shots that finished off the invaders, then returned to finish his reprimand. Tregaskis felt some relief when he saw Edson and Griffith arrive to report to Vandegrift. "The mere fact that they had come in was a good sign," he observed. "It meant the fighting was at least slackening and perhaps, ending, for they would not have left the front lines if there had been any considerable activity." The correspondent knew the fighting had been intense when Major Bailey, a hero of the raiders' fighting on Tulagi, showed him his helmet, which had been "pierced front and back" by a Japanese bullet. "The slug had grazed his scalp without injuring him," noted a relieved Tregaskis. The correspondent later noted that Edson did not mention it, but Tregaskis could see that the colonel's clothing had been ripped and marred in a couple of places by Japanese bullets.[19]

In the battle that the correspondents on Guadalcanal had agreed to call "Edson Hill" in their stories and later also came to be known as Edson's Ridge and the Battle of Bloody Ridge, the raiders suffered 135 casualties and the parachutists lost 128; of those numbers, 59 were dead. The Japanese left behind approximately 700 to 800 men killed on the ridge, with another 500 wounded, who did their best to join the other survivors struggling through the unforgiving jungle. The six-mile-long retreat to Point Cruz took the tattered remnants of Kawaguchi's command five days; some barely subsisted by eating roots and tree bark and quenching their powerful thirst by drinking from puddles or unhealthy river water. A Japanese naval officer later noted regretfully that the army "had been used to fighting the Chinese." Edson, usually guarded when it came to praising his men, felt only satisfaction about the raiders' performance. The morning after the fight, he borrowed a cigarette from one of his men, sat down beside him, and commented, "Now I know I have a real fighting outfit."[20]

Miller joined Tregaskis at the command post after a night spent at Kukum, and the two reporters went out to examine a battlefield described by one participant as "a charnel house permeated by the stench of death," which was made only worse by the brutal tropical sun. Another raider noted that he had never before seen "so many dead men in such a small area." Everywhere on the ridge Tregaskis saw empty cartons that had once held hand grenades and metal ammunition boxes ripped almost to shreds. Along the flank of a hill, there were bodies strewn about, with the marines and Japanese tangled as if they had "fallen in a death struggle," Tregaskis reported. As the reporters looked down the ridge's steep south slope, they counted about two hundred enemy bodies, many of which had been "torn and shattered by grenades or artillery bursts, some ripped, a marine told us, by the strafing planes which we had seen this morning." On another knoll there were more bodies, and Tregaskis could see the terrible effect of the battle on the landscape. "The whole top of this knoll had been burned off and wisps of smoke still rose from the smoldering grass," he noted. Danger still lurked nearby. One of the exhausted, dirty marines warned the reporters that a sniper had been observed in the nearby jungle. Miller and Tregaskis had only walked about fifty feet off the knoll when they heard a shout; a marine had been hit at the exact spot where the reporters had been standing. "He had a bad wound in the leg," recalled Tregaskis. "Our luck was holding."[21]

Although Durdin worried that the correspondents' stories about the ridge battle might well be the last they would send from Guadalcanal, his concern about being overrun by the enemy faded as patrols had no encounters with Japanese troops. Instead, rumors began to spread that the marines would soon be receiving reinforcements. Often on the island, such optimistic reports were given little credence, but on the morning of September 18, Tregaskis received a tip from an officer he trusted that he should go for a walk on the beach. The correspondent did so with Miller, and, to their great surprise, saw ships of every kind steaming into view, including cargo vessels and transports. "All along the beach our weary veterans stood and watched the process, passively," Tregaskis recalled. "We had been talking about reinforcements, and waiting for a long time." Landing that day off Lunga Point were more than four thousand members of the Seventh Marine Regiment, as well as much-needed vehicles and supplies, including rations and clothing. Tregaskis noticed that the Seventh Marines wore clean uniforms and new helmets, and they seemed confident about their ability to meet and defeat the enemy. One veteran told the correspondent he had been talking to some of the rookie forces. "Chees," the marine said to Tregaskis, "these guys want to tell *us* about the war." It would take some time with the new arrivals, the correspondent believed, as it had with others, to "get rid of that loud surface toughness and develop the cool, quiet fortitude that comes with battle experience."[22]

Tregaskis sensed over the next few days a "great upturn in confidence among the marines. The growing security of life on Guadalcanal had been demonstrated by the fact that not once during the long day the troops and supplies had been unloaded had Japanese aircraft or ships attacked the American vessels. "Food was now coming through in ample quantities, which was a welcome change," he noted, especially as the marines had consumed all the enemy food they had captured from the large enemy camp at Lunga Point. "Now we enjoyed three meals a day, and even fresh bread—a pleasant change from the C-ration hardtack—was being served," Tregaskis said. Mail was starting to come in again and even a post exchange was about to be established where marines could purchase candy ("porgy bait"), soap, toothpaste, and other necessities. The threat of a concentrated Japanese air, naval, and land attack, however, remained, and the amount of territory held by the Americans "was still the pie segment arced around Lunga Point; and it was only a thumb-nail held against the bulk of Guadalcanal, only a toe-hold, only a small area by comparison with the total area and even by comparison with that part of the island in which the Japs still roamed free," Tregaskis noted. The Seventh Marines learned how dangerous the island could be on their first night, as Japanese ships came near and shelled the coastline. According to Groft, the raiders had warned the newcomers to dig in for the night. Tired from their sea voyage, many chose to ignore the advice; three were killed and two wounded by the naval gunfire.[23]

There were other signs of civilization coming to Guadalcanal that Vandegrift pointed out to Tregaskis, including an engineer coming up to his quarters towing an electric wire behind him to hook up a light for the general. A few days later, on September 25, Tregaskis sought the general's permission to leave the island. The marine commander told the reporter that he had picked the right moment to do so. "They're putting in a shower for me in few days," Vandegrift confided to Tregaskis. "And when such luxuries come, the correspondent should go." There were a couple of reasons for the reporter's decision. Although he had been able to acquire fresh clothing from the quartermaster depot, he had less success replacing his last pair of serviceable shoes. When he tried to obtain a pair his size (14), he recalled, "the good quartermaster held up his hands in horror." Tregaskis had to wear a pair of rubber-soled tennis shoes, hardly the gear suitable for hiking through the dense jungle. He confided in a letter to his sister Madeline that he had always wanted to write a book about his experiences on Guadalcanal with the marines and had been making sure to take careful notes for such a purpose. "One potent reason for my leaving Guadalcanal when I did was that I wanted to get the book out and censored and into N.Y. [New York] before it cooled off," he wrote. Although he sent two radio messages to International News Service offices informing them of his plans to return and requesting a replacement, he heard nothing in return. Tregaskis decided to take a chance and leave. Once his book was completed, he planned on returning to Guadalcanal to resume covering the fighting.[24]

At least one of his colleagues, Miller, who had been on the island with Tregaskis from the start, knew of his planned book. The transports that had brought the Seventh Marines had also brought Miller's replacement from the United Press, Frank McCarthy. "I was never so glad to see anyone in a long time," Miller confided to his diary. "He [McCarthy] asked—foolishly— whether I wanted to stay on [in] the Solomons or leave." Miller vowed to Tregaskis and the other reporters on Guadalcanal that he was going to shave off his beard the minute he hit the deck of the ship scheduled to take him off the island. "We all cheered," Tregaskis reported, "for Miller's beard is one of the true horrors of Guadalcanal. It is almost as raggedy as my mustache." The UP reporter left Guadalcanal on board Rear Adm. Richmond Kelly Turner's flagship, the USS *McCawley*, along with the surviving remnants of the First Parachute Battalion, "a swell bunch," Miller noted, but "a bit jittery after what they went thru." Although Tregaskis had confided to him that he planned to write a book, Miller, who shaved off his beard the day after he left Guadalcanal, had no plans to do so, only wanting to make a record of what he had gone through for his own benefit, not for others.[25]

Tregaskis had to wrangle his own ride off the island. Planes out of Guadalcanal were "few and far between those days," so when a B-17 Flying Fortress flew in from its base at Espiritu Santo in the New Hebrides on September 25, he asked its pilot, Capt. Paul Payne of Des Moines, Iowa, if he could hitch a ride with him to Espiritu Santo, from where Tregaskis could start his long journey to Honolulu and begin to write his book. "Certainly, if you don't mind going by way of Bougainville," Payne told the reporter, as he and his rookie crew had to conduct a reconnaissance mission there the next day. It was a name that gave Tregaskis some pause, as Bougainville, the northernmost island of the Solomons, posed dangers to American aircraft. The mission called for Payne's lone B-17 from the 431st Squadron of the Eleventh Bomb Group to reconnoiter

Buin Harbor at the southern tip of Bougainville; follow the coastline to Buka Island, on which the Japanese had an airfield; and then wind its way down Bougainville's eastern coast to Kieta, where the enemy had built another airfield. All this was to be flown, Tregaskis pointed out, at an altitude of three to four thousand feet, "an extremely low altitude considering our vulnerability." Later reconnaissance flights by lone B-17s were usually made at altitudes of twenty thousand feet and above. As Payne later told the correspondent, "We just didn't know any better. We were fool lucky."[26]

Although Tregaskis outlined his exchange with Payne in *Guadalcanal Diary*, including his decision to fly on the mission as a passenger, he failed to include an unusual question posed to him by the pilot: Could the correspondent handle a .50-caliber machine gun? Although Tregaskis had no experience in handling such a weapon, he told Payne he could. The next morning, fueled by a breakfast consisting of a chocolate bar and wearing a knapsack filled with his notebooks and large, ledger-sized black leather diary (he preferred them because they were "hard to lose"), Tregaskis climbed into the bomber. The plane bounced down the runway, lifted off from Henderson Field, and headed over Tulagi Bay. After seven weeks on Guadalcanal with the marines, Tregaskis was finally on his way home. But before he could get to work on his manuscript, he would have to reckon with an enemy determined to end his life.[27]

10 GUADALCANAL DIARY

It was the shirtless navigator on the B-17 Flying Fortress, the tanned Lt. Clinton W. Benjamin of Noxan, Pennsylvania, who was too busy with his own duties at the time, who gave the ostensibly noncombatant passenger permission to fire. Seated in the cramped nose of the aircraft where Benjamin worked, correspondent Richard Tregaskis had noticed through the plexiglass a Japanese Zero floatplane stalking the American bomber. Flying just beyond the B-17's maximum machine-gun range, the enemy pilot had been shadowing the Fortress, giving its speed and altitude to Japanese warships cruising on the water far below. Benjamin told Tregaskis, "Go ahead," and he cleared the .50-caliber machine gun and fired a few rounds at the enemy. "The Zero was far out and I could see my tracers, like golden balls on a string, curving aft of the enemy plane," Tregaskis remembered. He corrected his aim and could see his tracers hit the Zero. The enemy pilot "heeled over and came straight toward me," the reporter said. "I could see his tracers coming toward me like smoky zips or dashes, a kind of aerial punctuation."[1]

The adrenaline rush of combat came after hours of tedium on the way to the target. After leaving Guadalcanal, the bomber, under the command of Capt. Paul Payne, had passed up the Slot, the stretches of water between the islands that made up the Solomons. Tregaskis passed the time by looking down on the "jungly islands that slipped under our wings. Time dragged." The first Japanese plane appeared as the bomber neared Bougainville. Listening in over the communication circuit, Tregaskis could hear an unidentified crewman report contact with an aircraft moving in the opposite direction, about two thousand feet overhead and to the right. "He was well out of range," said Tregaskis. "I got a glimpse of him; then he was gone to the rear, out of our vision." Suddenly, the tail gunner shouted that two Zeros were coming at them from behind, but, after a few seconds, he reported that they had turned away. The fighters were respectful of the "formidable B-17," Tregaskis noted, but he did begin to think about "our aloneness over enemy territory and the swarms of enemy planes which must be around." After another two Zeros came up from below but did not fire, Tregaskis, now on guard, spotted one of the enemy aircraft and opened fire. "The empties bounced out and clanged on the floor, and I remember the sharp smell of the burned powder," he recalled. "I also remember the feeling of tremendous exhilaration—and at the same time fear, of kicking myself for coming on this flight when I didn't have to. It seemed we were going to be shot down and not much chance of surviving this, because we were deep into Japanese territory."[2]

Others on the B-17 were also worried about what might happen if the plane crashed. Payne's copilot, Lt. James Norman Price, had just arrived in the Pacific. According to Price, Payne had let his previous copilot take his crew out several days before and they never returned. "When we got in there [Espiritu Santo] he latched onto my crew and I flew co-pilot for him for a while," Price noted. On their first mission, because the navigator was busy counting the ships in the harbor, the civilian correspondent, Tregaskis, had to man one of the plane's machine guns. Price worried that if the bomber had been shot down and they survived, the Japanese might learn that Tregaskis had operated one of the guns, would declare him a spy, and execute all the crew. The copilot remembered eight Zeros in all making attacks on his B-17. "They always come in nose to nose and they made several passes at us," Price recalled. "They made a lot of passes at us and why they didn't shoot us down I don't know."[3]

Although untrained, Tregaskis proved to be relentless when it came to keeping his gun chattering away at the Zero. He saw the enemy plane, in a three-quarter frontal pass, curve along the bomber's flank. As the Japanese pilot roared by, the other B-17 gunners brought their guns to bear, and "we all gave him plenty," noted Tregaskis. "One of us hit him in the engine and he went down. Naturally, I think it was my shooting that did it." The rear gunner reported that the floatplane had to make a forced landing on the water. Although other Zeros made additional passes at the bomber, Tregaskis noted that they seemed to do so in a "half-hearted" manner. The crew also had to endure antiaircraft fire from the ships below, with shell fragments thwacking against the bottom of the aircraft's fuselage and striking its right aileron. While all this was going on, Benjamin calmly counted the ships off the southern tip of Bougainville, reporting he saw twenty-seven. "We conducted the rest of our reconnaissance peacefully and ran into no more enemy aircraft or ships," Tregaskis recalled. At one point, the B-17 went as low as 350 feet trying to catch a glimpse of the airfield and harbor at Kieta, but it was no use, as the cloud cover was too thick. Tregaskis felt fortunate the bad weather intervened, because at such a low altitude "we would have been an easy shot for any Zero who happened to be wandering about in the vicinity." Hours later, the bomber landed safely at Espiritu Santo. Tregaskis remembered that he had "kicked himself" at first for risking his life on such a dangerous mission. He later changed his mind, recognizing that leaving Guadalcanal on a B-17, via Bougainville, seemed to be "highly appropriate when, as the marines would say, you considered how *rugged* our life had been on that f—— island."[4]

Tregaskis remained at the base at Espiritu Santo, code named Button, for only a short time. "Living there was primitive," he noted. "But compared to the night-and-day misery called Guadalcanal, it was a pleasant rest camp." There he began to shape the entries in his diary into a book. Eventually, Tregaskis flew on to Nouméa, New Caledonia, a French colony that had grown to become a major facility for supporting the fighting on Guadalcanal and also served as headquarters for Vice Adm. Robert L. Ghormley, commander of the South Pacific forces. Streams of military vehicles filled the streets "with their noise and motion," Tregaskis remembered. The Grand Hotel du Pacifique, formerly one of the top hotels on the island, had been taken over by army officers, and some of its rooms had been emptied of their comfortable iron beds and plumbing to serve as offices. An enterprising French woman, Tregaskis noted, had opened a sidewalk soda bar—labeled as "le sandwich du soldat"—and offered "limonade" for four francs (ten cents), sickly milkshakes for six francs (fifteen cents), and sardine sandwiches for eight francs (twenty cents). Dubbed the "juice" by soldiers, the soda stand offered none of the usual properties of an American soda fountain: no shiny syrup knobs, no marble counter, no racks of garish-colored magazines or cellophane-packaged crackers. Still, the proprietor had "caught the general idea at least," said Tregaskis, and had cannily hired a bevy of local beauties to tend the bar. "At all times of day, soldiers and a less number of sailors stood in line at the cashier's window, buying tickets, and lined the bar testing madame's delights and trying to make time with the sandwich jerkers," he recalled.[5]

Tregaskis had not expected to be on New Caledonia for long, as he wanted to return to Pearl Harbor to begin writing his Guadalcanal book. He had a rude awakening, however, when he came upon two associates eager to tell him about the "sluggishness and unpleasantness of life in this American base." One of the reporters went as far as to term the base the "world's a—— hole," with correspondents the "farthest people up the a——. The big shots around here treat us like poison." One of the biggest problems involved a rash of unnecessary paperwork Ghormley insisted upon, including orders permitting Tregaskis to continue his journey. "He signs them himself," one of the reporters told Tregaskis about the admiral. "He has to read them over first, too. Considering he has to read and sign practically every document, you're lucky it only takes a week or so to get your orders." In addition to checking in with American military officials for orders, Tregaskis had to complete forms with both the U.S. Army and U.S. Navy "pledging allegiance and agreeing to submit my copy for censorship." When he complained that he had already signed many of those same forms in Pearl Harbor, one of his informants replied that it did not matter, he would have to sign them all over again. The army also prohibited reporters from visiting airfields or hospitals, a regulation that tripped up Tregaskis when he tried to visit Col. Sam Griffith, a friend of his who had been shot in the arm on Guadalcanal and was recuperating in a Nouméa hospital. An army colonel refused permission for him to see his friend, "even though I promised I wanted to see him for personal reasons only," Tregaskis recalled.[6]

Getting to see Ghormley proved to be a problem. The admiral worked out of a converted merchant ship, the *Argonne*, anchored in Nouméa's harbor. On the ship, Ghormley, eventually replaced by the more aggressive Vice Adm. William F. "Bull" Halsey, had to contend with mountains of paperwork. "He worried about everything," the admiral's chief of staff said, "and I can't say that I blame him." To get out to the flagship, Tregaskis needed to hitch a ride on a boat that did not have a set schedule for such trips. "It might take all day to get out to the ship and back," he noted. If he made it to the *Argonne*, he had to check in with the flag secretary, a person often quite busy with paperwork and someone who possessed an uncertain temper and had to be handled with diplomacy. "Eventually one's petition for order would be taken to the admiral, and orders might result," Tregaskis said. Meanwhile, one of his fellow reporters warned him, "you have to wait in this a—hole."[7]

The rigmarole with orders and permissions seemed like a "slap in the face" to Tregaskis, especially considering his hazardous stay on Guadalcanal. On the island he had become used to something new in his life, men acting "without their masks, without posing; men being themselves and trying to accomplish things directly without delay, as they must in such situations of dire peril." Life at this advanced base, where the rulebook reigned supreme, came as a shock to him. A friend of his later described the situation at New Caledonia and other bases safe behind the lines as "not war, not peace," a description that Tregaskis found to be accurate the more he saw of such locales. Under the circumstances, since he badly wanted to get out of Nouméa and back to Pearl Harbor as soon as possible, Tregaskis realized there was little he could do "except go through the necessary forms and immerse myself in the prescribed reams of red tape."[8]

While waiting for his orders, Tregaskis secured living space in a one-room flat for a dollar per day from a French woman, Madam Rougon, and tried to settle down to do some writing. For days, however, he found himself out of sorts, with his vitality sapped by "a great desire to sit still, to just be quiet, to vegetate." Being yanked away from the unending danger of bombing and shelling was "a sudden and tremendous change," he reflected, as well as being a great letdown. "I wanted to stay where I did not have to move and where no one would speak or make any sound," he remembered. Talking to others who had similar experiences in the field, Tregaskis discovered that his reaction was "quite normal." Wandering around Nouméa did provide some diversion for the out-of-sorts correspondent, including a visit to a restaurant called the Circle Civile. He and his reporter friends enjoyed the numerous small courses of a French meal, accompanied by wine. "But the place was noisy with the conversation of crowds of officers," Tregaskis said. He found quieter entertainment with a French storekeeper and his wife, whom he was introduced to by a correspondent friend. The storekeeper invited Tregaskis into his home and regaled him with tales of hunting in New Caledonia. The host's daughter and her cousin were also on hand to dance with the visitors to "tunes careening from a staticky radio," and the storekeeper's wife played the piano and sang. "All these things were welcome novelties after a long spell in the battle area," Tregaskis said.[9]

After some time on Nouméa, the effects of his adventures in Guadalcanal began to fade, and Tregaskis returned to writing what became *Guadalcanal*

Diary, getting a "good bit of work" accomplished. He recalled that the writing went "fairly fast," but the memory of his time under fire on Guadalcanal, and the way it shaped his behavior, continued. "Even in Noumea, I found that my nervous system put me automatically in a state of alertness whenever lightning flashed in the sky or distant thunder rumbled," Tregaskis remembered. "These phenomena had become associated with gunfire, in my consciousness, and my instant impulse was to look for cover." He believed there was nothing "abnormal" about his reaction, as "one develops certain habits which fit any type of existence to which he is exposed, if he is exposed long enough, and it is just as natural for a man who has been living in a fighting zone to view thunder and lightning cautiously, as it is for a city dweller to look up and down before he crosses the street."[10]

Finally, Tregaskis's orders arrived and he made preparations for his journey to Pearl Harbor. He was anxious to get back as quickly as possible because he had heard a rumor (unfounded, as it turned out) that the U.S. Marine Corps was preparing to make a raid on Wake Island, the former American base captured by the Japanese early in the war. "I wanted to go along on the Wake jaunt, if there was actually to be one," he noted. When he left Noumea for the air base where he was to catch a U.S. Army B-24 Liberator long-range bomber that was to fly him to Honolulu, Tregaskis had only four dollars in his wallet. He had cabled the International News Service's New York office asking for additional funds, but, as he later discovered, the "cable had moved with the speed of a turtle, as most cables from the South Pacific did in those days, and the money had not been sent until just about the time I was leaving Noumea." (The needed funds finally arrived a month later.) He was able to borrow a money order for ten dollars, but found that nobody would cash it for him without, he joked, signed authorization from Secretary of War Henry Stimson or Secretary of the Navy Frank Knox. He saw himself being reduced to "becoming a beachcomber and being devoured by cannibals." Tregaskis landed in Honolulu with just fifty cents to his name.[11]

While flying on the B-24, Tregaskis continued to work, setting up an office in the bomber and typing away at his manuscript, actually getting about eight hours of work done on one leg of the flight. He also began to believe that air transportation would make great inroads as opposed to sea travel when the war finally ended, noting that it had originally taken him more than three weeks' sailing time to go from Honolulu to the South Pacific; now he had returned after just two days of flying time. "In the high sky we were missing all the discomfort of the sweltering days spent inching through the Equatorial regions," Tregaskis recalled. As the bomber stopped at bases along the way, he observed that the men at these Pacific way stations were reading recent American newspapers and magazines that had been brought from the United States by passing ferry pilots, while aboard the ships of the navy in the same area, or at the advanced naval bases, "a paper or magazine that was a mere six weeks or two months old was considered highly current."[12]

Once he arrived in Honolulu, Tregaskis "worked like a dog," spending all his leisure time typing away on his manuscript. The material he collected, which included his weeks with the marines on Guadalcanal, as well as notes he had made while covering the Doolittle Raid (details of which were still secret at the time), the Battle of the Coral Sea, and the Battle of Midway, caught the attention of U.S. Navy officials. They decided that the correspondent's black leather diary contained too much classified information for him to keep it in his possession. "They were afraid that a spy there (and there were spies in Hawaii) might steal or read it," Tregaskis recalled. He had to do his writing in the navy offices at Pearl Harbor, going there every morning, working under the censor's gaze, and watching as his diary was locked in a safe every night; he never got it back and could not find out what happened to it. "And as fast as I could write my manuscript, a naval intelligence officer took my efforts and hacked away with a pencil and a pair of scissors," Tregaskis reported. "That was the way it was with sharp-eyed military censorship in those days." Although a likeable fellow personally, the censor Tregaskis worked with was "stiff as a porcupine when it came to his official duties. He even chopped out a mention of the fact that the Japanese camps usually had a sweetish smell. He apparently felt that if they read my story the enemy might start using a deodorant as a kind of camouflage."[13]

On November 1 from Honolulu, Tregaskis cabled some exciting news to INS editor Barry Faris in New York. Using the telegram style of the day that packed in the greatest amount of information in the fewest possible words, Tregaskis wrote:

EYE WRITTEN CENSOR PASSED EIGHTY THOUSAND WORD
BOOK DEALING EXPERIENCES GUADALCANAL DIARY FORM
WRITTEN EXAMINUTEST NOTES MADE DAILY BEGINNING TWO
WEEKS BEFORE LANDING ABOARD TRANSPORT AND COVERING
FIRST GRUELLING SEVEN WEEKS ASHORE DURING WHICH EYE

WITNESSED PRINCIPAL LAND ACTIONS FROM FRONTEST LINES
ACCOMPANIED ALL EXPEDITIONS EYE FIRST CORRESPONDENT TO
LAND GUADALCANAL STAYED LONGEST PERIOD STOP WANT OFFER
YOU BOOK SERIALIZATION OR WHATEVER ELSE YOU WANT TO DO
WITH IT BUT I'D LIKE ROYALTIES CUT PROFITS STOP PLEASE WIRE
WHETHER WANT IT MOST CORDIAL REGARDS.
DICK TREGASKIS

Faris was quick to respond, wiring his reporter on November 2 asking him to immediately mail him the manuscript, pledging that the INS would find the best market for Tregaskis's work, including having it published as a book and serialized in magazines, and agreeing to split whatever profits might be made. That same day, Tregaskis airmailed his work to Faris. Ward Greene, head of King Features, which syndicated Tregaskis's articles to newspapers around the country, served as his agent. In what insiders called a first for the publishing industry, Greene made copies of Tregaskis's Guadalcanal manuscript and distributed them to nine publishing firms, asking for their best offers.[14]

With his manuscript completed, Tregaskis took the time to write his parents at their home in Elizabeth, New Jersey, about the project. Talking about his agreement with his employer, he noted that splitting the profits "may seem peculiar," but he pointed out that beyond that half, most of the money would go to the government in taxes (he also indicated that he would receive half the proceeds if the movie rights were sold to Hollywood). "So I won't be losing much, by letting INS take half," he wrote. Of course, there was always the possibility that his manuscript might not be picked up by a publisher, but he believed it would, as there "should be considerable interest in the topic at this time." If everything went well, Tregaskis wrote that he wanted to use his royalties to help pay off the mortgage on the family home at 153 Chilton Street, and maybe even help his parents buy a car, perhaps a 1941 or 1942 Pontiac. "Or maybe that's counting my chickens before they're hatched," he added. "I guess it is. Anyhow, here's hoping; and if nothing comes of the book, writing it has still been good experience." Tregaskis also made sure to send his parents souvenirs from Guadalcanal—half-shilling bills the Japanese had printed with the intention of using them in Australia and other English territory they expected to conquer and the collar tab of a Japanese naval lieutenant—and kept them updated about his condition, given his diabetes. "I am in pretty good health now," he reported. "I have been watching my diet as carefully as

I can, and my blood sugar is now 96; which is good; 80 to 120 is normal, and 100 is average."[15]

Tregaskis also related his hopes for success with his book to Madeline in a December 1942 letter. He admitted that his plans to pay off the family mortgage and purchase his parents a car might well be just a dream, but it was "a pleasant one at least. And now that the hard work of writing the book is done, I feel I can afford to dream a bit—and hope." Covering the war had started to become both "wearying and wearing to me," and he had thoughts of getting out of the Pacific for another theater of operation, or perhaps returning to the United States for a short time to see his family and wife, Marian, daydreaming of relaxing in one of the big easy chairs in his parents' living room and having dinner with them. "I also miss Marian, who I think is about as charming a person and fine a wife as a guy could hope to know," he added. It might be difficult to break away, however, as Tregaskis told his sister that action, and particularly any new variety of action, "gets to be like a drug. You feel let down without it and with it you feel a sort of unhealthy excitement." With the exhilaration came apprehension as, after all, people were shooting to inflict great bodily harm. "Everytime I get into a jam, I kick myself for exposing myself to getting killed," Tregaskis wrote. "But sometimes, there's a great excitement in the action; and it's interesting to look back on." He also found himself amazed that he was "getting interested in this damned war. I find myself thinking I'd hate to miss a big action or campaign or battle out here, even if the chance to get home should come up at the same time. There's something fascinating about this colossal chess game."[16]

Although Tregaskis had feared that publishers might have no interest in what he wrote, those fears were groundless. After reading the reporter's day-to-day account, Bennett Cerf of Random House saw the book's sales potential and snatched up the publishing rights. Although Tregaskis was a relative unknown, Cerf was not taking too big of a gamble with the book, as the American public hungered for any "I was there," first-person accounts about the war. As Richard Lingeman noted in his history of the American home front from 1941 to 1945, book sales were strong in spite of shortages of paper. "Total copy sales rose each year and each year broke an all-time record for the industry," Lingeman noted, and the Book of the Month Club, created in 1926 by Harry Scherman as a way to promote the best new books of the day, doubled its membership. Before accepting *Guadalcanal Diary*, Random House had just experienced popular success with another war-related publication,

Suez to Singapore (October 1942), a book by Cecil Brown. Brown had been a correspondent for NBC radio in the Far East who had been on the British battle cruiser HMS *Repulse* when it and the battleship HMS *Prince of Wales* were sunk by Japanese planes at Singapore early in the war. Deep in its vaults, the New York publishing house also had a book by Ted W. Lawson, one of the pilots who had flown on the still secret Doolittle Raid off of the USS *Hornet*, who wrote it in collaboration with another INS reporter, Robert Considine. (Random House finally received the all-clear from U.S. military officials to publish *Thirty Seconds over Tokyo* in June 1943 and issued a first printing of a hundred thousand copies.) Although the manuscript Tregaskis sent to the INS included a red stamp on each page indicating it had been passed by the U.S. Pacific Fleet's chief censor, Random House, eager to cooperate with the Office of Censorship in Washington, DC, sent the agency in early December a foundry proof (a proof pulled for a final check before printing plates were made) of *Guadalcanal Diary*, which included a postscript written by INS editors that had not yet been cleared by censors.[17]

On November 13, Cerf sent a telegram to a number of media outlets, including the *New York Times, New York Sun, New York Herald Tribune, New York World Telegram*, and the United Press, announcing that Random House had signed a contract with Tregaskis for *Guadalcanal Diary*, which the publisher called the "first eyewitness story of fighting" on the island. "The book will be rushed through for early January publication," Cerf wrote. "It is one of [the] most exciting stories I have ever read." Others shared Cerf's opinion. On November 18 the Book of the Month Club announced it had selected Tregaskis's book as its dual selection, along with Sir Ralph Norman Angell's *Let the People Know* (Angell had won the Nobel Peace Prize in 1933), for distribution to its 300,000 of members across the country in February 1943. Novelist and activist Dorothy Canfield, longtime member of the committee that selected what books were to be sent to BOMC members, noted that there were two reasons why Americans should read Tregaskis's factual, day-by-day account of the early fighting on Guadalcanal. The first was because it satisfied Americans' "intense desire to know in detail about the daily life of our service men in action." The second reason was that in his book Tregaskis "brings home to us by its matter-of-fact unarranged definiteness something we are—once more, all over again—in danger of forgetting: what war is." Canfield went on to note that the book seemed almost written to order for a public longing to learn more about the soldiers, aviators, or marines who had left their families far behind and gone off to war. "It is the long letter home we have longed for," she said of *Guadalcanal Diary*, describing it as an "authentic account of what daily happened under the eyes of the writer," who set down into print "what the men eat, what they talk about, what a sergeant-instructor tells his class during a lesson in mapreading; what strange tropical beast a pet dogs [*sic*] drags in from the jungle."[18]

Random House published *Guadalcanal Diary* on January 18, 1943, and Tregaskis's work made a steady climb up the bestseller charts, reaching, the publishing company's advertisements were quick to report, the number one position on lists compiled by the *New York Times* and *New York Herald Tribune*. Sales of the book, which cost $2.50, were boosted by positive reviews from critics across the country, who praised Tregaskis not for his literary flair but for his factual and honest reporting about what the marines faced in the Solomons. Fellow newspaperman Damon Runyon went as far as to compare Tregaskis to Stephen Crane, author of the classic war novel *The Red Badge of Courage*, when it came to "presenting a word picture of war that you can not only see but feel." Clifton Fadiman, book critic for the *New Yorker*, wrote that while the book was an "artless, rough diary," it did possess a "first-hand, on-the-spot quality" that atoned for its lack of "literary finish," as well as presenting a bracing quality about the fighting in the Pacific. "There is nothing in this book to confirm statements by starry-eyed vice admirals that one American can lick twenty Japs and that the war is as good as won," Fadiman wrote. In his review in the *New York Times*, John Chamberlain sketched for his readers how Tregaskis came to be with the marines on Guadalcanal, his interactions with the men, and what they faced from the enemy on the island. With his book, Tregaskis, wrote Chamberlain, had provided a "tonic for the war weary on the homefront." As a final thought, the critic pulled from *Guadalcanal Diary* an incident when a marine sergeant, hoping for mail from his loved ones, had instead received a bill from the BOMC. Chamberlain hoped that Scherman might find it in his heart to forgive the sergeant's debts. A reviewer for the *Infantry Journal*, the publication of the U.S. Infantry Association, praised Tregaskis for providing the essential facts a soldier would want to know about war, as it was "so rich in detail, so lacking in extra verbiage and nonessential passages that war itself is in it." The reviewer went as far as to rank Tregaskis's book "at the top among the war books" so far produced, noting it would also give Americans everywhere a "better notion of what land fighting in the South Seas is like than anything they've read before."[19]

Even before its official publication, officials at the INS and King Features were eager to help Random House promote its reporter's book. Greene offered promotional suggestions to Cerf, including pointing out that there were more than a hundred names of marines from every part of the country, and Tregaskis had supplied their home towns. "In the territory from which these fellows come there is at least one good newspaper," Greene wrote. "I think if separate stories are prepared about each man mentioned in the book, quoting from the book the story of his exploit, and if these stories were sent to the local papers every one would be glad to publish them." King Features also passed along to Random House requests for galley proofs or a copy of the book from a variety of Hollywood movie studios, including Paramount Pictures, Metro-Goldwyn-Mayer, and Columbia Pictures. Eventually, 20th Century Fox bought rights to film the book, releasing its film version in November 1943 with a cast that included William Bendix, Preston Foster, Lloyd Nolan, Anthony Quinn, and Richard Jaeckel. Most of the film was shot on location at Marine Corps Base Camp Pendleton in San Diego County, California, with numerous marines appearing as extras and a few having speaking roles.[20]

While his employer and publisher worked to promote his book and the public sealed its approval by buying copies, Tregaskis missed out on the hoopla involved in becoming a bestselling author; he had left Hawaii for a return to the action on Guadalcanal. On November 13, 1942, Greene wrote Cerf responding to a number of requests regarding *Guadalcanal Diary*'s publication, including providing photographs of and biographical material about Tregaskis. Although Cerf had sought an option from Tregaskis for any second book he wrote, Greene said he had cabled the correspondent the request and had received a response from Dick Haller, INS bureau chief in Hawaii. Haller had written Greene: "Tregaskis away indefinitely. Authorized me represent him re diary. Feel certain option next book acceptable. Forwarding him copy your radiogram fastest but delivery indefinite. Hope message reaches him within week when he probably have access direct communication with you." Greene theorized that Tregaskis was off on another assignment, possibly returning to Guadalcanal. Greene was correct; Tregaskis had left for another visit to the island, traveling on a battleship, the USS *Washington*, the flagship of Rear Adm. Willis Lee. "Along the line of bases leading to the Solomons, I found some people who felt sure that Guadalcanal would be lost," he recalled. "It seemed that the United States might not have enough strength, at this stage of the war, to support the amphibious landings in North Africa, the build-up of military might in England, and the Pacific operations too." Tregaskis, however, remained hopeful that American forces could "break the legend of Japanese invincibility" and take the first big step on the "bloody island-to-island ladder that led to Tokyo and victory." He wrote his parents that he expected to be in the Pacific for another six months or so but did not want them to be anxious about his safety, writing, "Among other things, I have learned a lot of tricks for keeping myself safe in dangerous places; so you musn't ever worry: I am getting to be quite a veteran bushwacker and sailor."[21]

11 OPERATION CLEANSLATE

Everything Richard Tregaskis observed as he scanned the wardroom on a steamy U.S. Navy transport near the Solomon Islands in February 1943 seemed like a recurring dream. A colonel stood at the end of the room, pointing occasionally to a map as he talked about what might face the officers gathered before him as they went into combat. The men listened closely as their superior droned on, paying close attention, no matter how dully he spoke, "because some day soon their lives might depend on the information he was giving out," Tregaskis noted. The correspondent listened as the colonel, Lester E. Brown of Cape Elizabeth, Maine, said that he wanted everyone involved in the landing to "become so familiar with this island that he will be able to draw a map of it." After all, the Japanese may "surprise us but the terrain is not going to."[1]

Six months earlier, a similar scene had played out as Tregaskis accompanied the U.S. Marine Corps' First Division as it prepared to storm ashore on Guadalcanal. He stayed to experience the tribulations of what seemed to be an ill-advised venture. Tregaskis remembered that "[t]hen, as now, the ship and group had been one of many ships and groups of fighting men all going to the same objective in great strength, bent on occupation." For his newest assignment on behalf of the International News Service, he was heading to a location not too far from where he had been with the marines. This time, however, Tregaskis would be following soldiers of the U.S. Army, accompanying the Forty-Third Infantry Division. The division was charged with occupying and holding the Russell Islands, a small archipelago approximately sixty miles west-northwest of Guadalcanal's Henderson Field, as part of a landing code named Operation Cleanslate. American military officials planned to eventually strike another target, New Georgia, and the capture of the two large islands in the Russells, Banika and Pavuvu, would provide the necessary space for supporting airfields and naval bases, on land best known for the Lever Brothers coconut plantation. Although the great mass of military movement seemed familiar to Tregaskis, there was "one great point of difference: we expected light opposition." There was a strong possibility there might not be any Japanese at the beaches where the approximately nine thousand members of the Forty-Third were poised to land. Quite a difference, Tregaskis recalled, from what he had expected on Guadalcanal, where he had heard intelligence officers estimate that the landing force might lose a quarter of its troops as casualties. He did expect that the enemy might fool everyone again, that instead of abandoning the Russells, the Japanese would appear in great numbers and offer the Americans "a good tough scrap."[2]

Tregaskis's mission with the army came after he had returned to Guadalcanal in December 1942, ferried to the Solomons on a fast battleship, the USS *Washington*. Shot through with battle casualties, malaria, and dysentery, the weary First Marine Division on Guadalcanal had been bolstered not only by the Second Marine Division, but also by army troops. "There were 50,000 American fighting men on the island—and 20,000 more of the 25th (Army) Division on the way," Tregaskis recalled. "There were enough troops so that early in December, about half of the famed Marine First Division, the First and Seventh Regiments, moved down the beach, climbed aboard transports and set sail for a rear area. They had been on the Canal for four months." The "gallant" marine general Alexander Vandegrift turned over command of forces on the island on December 9 to U.S. Army general Alexander "Sandy" Patch. Before Vandegrift left, he walked to the island's cemetery, called Flanders Field, to take, he remembered, his "farewell of the almost 700 officers and men of my command who died in this operation. I looked in silence on the rude crosses that bespoke valiant deeds by great men." (Japanese casualties during the six-month-long campaign had been estimated at nearly twenty thousand, most falling due to disease.) Those tired marines who were lucky enough to survive to be evacuated were barely able to climb the rope ladders dangling off the ships taking them away from their tropical nightmare. "They were dressed in frayed green dungarees or dirty khaki, stained with . . . sweat and muck," remembered Lt. Herbert Merillat, a marine public relations officer who served on the Canal. "Socks had become a luxury; many had long since rotted away." There was plenty of tough fighting to come, however, for the remaining forces. Visiting the western front on Guadalcanal via jeep late in December, Tregaskis came across a "hard-looking hombre with a bristly beard" who possessed the "almost haunted eyes" he found so characteristic in men who had been involved in hard fighting. The soldier told the correspondent that the Japanese were dug in behind heavily defended, well-prepared positions. "When we come in," the infantryman told Tregaskis, "they fight like hell. We take their positions, but it's a tedious job. We're knocking the b—— off, but it's a long, tough job."[3]

Tregaskis spent much of his time before the Russell Islands operation reporting about the grim new air war in the Solomons. He accompanied B-17 Flying Fortress crews from the Eleventh Bombardment Group on missions against Japanese airfields in the Solomons and beyond, which were being bolstered to provide air coverage for renewed attempts to retake Guadalcanal. He also had to contend with his newfound fame as the bestselling author of *Guadalcanal Diary*, tense negotiations with his employer about what he was worth to them in the future, and miscommunications and missed chances regarding his role in making a film from his book. He did have the satisfaction of being on Guadalcanal on February 9, when Patch's aides called correspondents to the general's headquarters and gave them a text of a radio message sent to Adm. William "Bull" Halsey: "Total and complete defeat of Japanese forces on Guadalcanal effected 1625 today." The Tokyo Express, the nickname Allied forces gave the Japanese navy ships that delivered supplies to the island and relentlessly bombarded American forces, Patch reported to the admiral, "no longer has terminus on Guadalcanal."[4]

By November 1942, with the availability of advanced Lockheed P-38 Lightning fighters, B-17 bombers could fly escorted from Henderson Field to hit Japanese airfields on the islands of New Georgia and Bougainville. These missions, Tregaskis noted, involved keeping the enemy airfield runways "pitted and useless." Bomber crews faced tough opposition from Japanese Zero floatplanes and from antiaircraft fire. On December 19 Tregaskis climbed aboard a four-engine B-17, taking up a position alongside the plane's navigator, Lt. Thomas P. Carter of Bossier City, Louisiana, who outlined the mission's primary objective as striking a group of supply ships in Buin harbor on the southern tip of Bougainville. The ships were apparently ferrying equipment to be used at the Kahli air base. "Bombing the ships would hinder the enemy's efforts to expand the base," Tregaskis recalled. If the weather was bad, the secondary target was Munda airport on New Georgia. Looking out the aircraft's windows, the correspondent could see silver, twin-engine P-38 fighters banking "against the towering white clouds ahead of and behind us" and the other B-17s in the formation swinging into position, with one on the right wing bobbing close enough that he could see "the row of small pink squares on the nose beneath the pilot's window—Rising Sun [Japanese] flags, each marking an enemy plane shot down; and a line of yellow stripes each marking a strike mission."[5]

As Tregaskis's B-17 neared Buin through rows of "tower-like white clouds," he heard over the intercom the plane's pilot, Capt. Walter E. Chambers of Birmingham, Alabama, order all gunners to man their positions. Meanwhile, the bombardier, Lt. Henry V. Myers of San Antonio, Texas, checked his Norden bombsight. "One felt the tension of the impending action," said Tregaskis. Carter attempted to break the tension by nodding his head toward Myers and telling the reporter that the bombardier was on the spot, as he had yet to miss, and if he did fail on this mission "we're going to ride [kid] the hell out of him. In fact, we're going to throw him overboard." Their conversation was interrupted, however, by a warning cry heard over the intercom: "Two Zeros on the right!" Looking in that direction, Tregaskis could see small dots of planes—the P-38 escorts and Zero floatplanes—milling crazily against the white of the clouds. "One dot curved toward us, came sweeping in from the right and forward," Tregaskis noted. "White smoke-lines of tracers darted from the wings toward us, and the enemy banked sharply and shot by under our right wing. The gray belly of the plane, turned toward us, was the single float. Our plane shook as our turrets fired, and bright lines of tracer zipped toward the foe. Then, swiftly, he was gone far astern."[6]

Despite the enemy's concentrated attack, Tregaskis's aircraft escaped any damage. As the B-17 closed in on Buin, however, the weather worsened and the bomber had to swing south toward its secondary target, Munda. "We droned on through the high mountains of cumulus clouds, which fortunately grew thinner as we moved south," Tregaskis recalled. "A curving arm of dark land appeared ahead of us. Lieutenant Carter pointed. 'Munda,' he said." The correspondent could see, as the plane neared the airfield, an orange light winking at it from the "dark mass of woods near the runway. Anti-aircraft fire. And then the orange bursts, each burst ringed with black smoke and debris: the bombs of the first flight falling." After Myers released his bombload, Tregaskis craned forward into the nose of his plane to see them hit, watching as the vivid orange flashes bubbled up "in a cluster in the woods, spread like a growing plague to the edge of the runway. Death down there; fragments flying. The noise of our engines drowned out the crack of our exploding missiles." Most of his plane's bombs had struck to the left of the enemy runway, wreaking havoc among the antiaircraft batteries. "Not much use putting 'em all on the runway," Myers explained to Tregaskis. "That job's been pretty well done already." With the B-17's mission completed, the correspondent checked on the rest of the crew and found the waist and ball-turret gunners taking a cigarette break. Corp. Wayne T. Gary of Toledo, Ohio, who occupied the cramped confines of the ball-turret position, told Tregaskis how he had hit the Japanese plane that had attacked them near Buin, watching as the Zero went down smoking.[7]

As the bomber swung along the northern shore of Guadalcanal on its way back to Henderson Field, it flew over beached Japanese transports and freighters. Word was passed that the crew was going to strafe the stranded hulks for practice. "The crew enjoyed swooping low and pouring the red balls of tracers into the abandoned hulks," said Tregaskis, who added that one of the gunners placed his shots right on the bridge of one of the ships. After landing, Tregaskis joined the crew as they checked in at operations headquarters, a dugout at the edge of the airfield. One of the pilots who had been part of the formation said he had a humorous story to share. "The joke was that anti-aircraft fire over Munda had knocked a five-inch hole in his wing, and done no damage except to knock out a little, and unimportant, strut," Tregaskis noted.[8]

Tregaskis remained with the heavy bombers for the next few days, flying other missions with various B-17 crews. On an attack against the Kahili airfield on Bougainville, he witnessed an unusual method for unsettling the enemy. In addition to high explosives, one of the bombers dropped cases of empty beer bottles. "Those bottles screech like bombs on the way down," Sgt. Randolph Colgin of Houston, Texas, the radio operator on the B-17 that dropped them, explained to Tregaskis. "They'll scare the hell out of the Japs." According to a history of the Eleventh Bombardment Group, intelligence reports indicated that for several days the Japanese avoided the places where the beer bottles had hit, fearing they had contained deadly chemicals. Tregaskis was particularly pleased when he learned that there were also night missions whose purpose was to not only damage Japanese installations, but also to keep the enemy awake and seeking shelter in their foxholes. "I was glad to see this; for often, I had sat on the ground, on the other end of the picture, and listened helplessly while

Japanese bombs rattled down from the sky," he said, remembering his dangerous days and nights on Guadalcanal. The correspondent also took pleasure on another mission in which B-17s hammered enemy shipping, comparing the attack to the "thrill of stalking game." Tregaskis was happy and showed no mercy thinking about the confusion that resulted from the bombing, with the Japanese on the ships running about "in fear of losing their lives, flattening themselves on the steel deck when the bombs hit. Yes, this was good medicine for the Jap. Such things as this might teach him civilized manners."[9]

As the last of the exhausted and starving Japanese troops evacuated Guadalcanal in early February 1943, Tregaskis prepared for another trip on board a naval task force, this one aimed at the Russell Islands, described by those who had visited there as a land of "rain, mud, and magnificent coconuts." Still, at least the island of Banika seemed an appropriate location for constructing the needed facilities to support future operations, as reports indicated that it had such positive attributes as "well-drained shore areas, deep water, protected harbors, and lack of malaria." As he had before, Tregaskis sailed with the master of amphibious warfare, Adm. Richmond K. Turner, commander of Task Force 61. Although Turner only expected limited opposition on the ground, he warned Tregaskis that the Japanese would do all they could to hit the Americans with numerous air raids once they had landed at the Russells and started setting up bases there. "Those b—— are going to react and do a lot of bombing here," Turner prophesied. "There's no doubt about that." The admiral also worried about a response by the Japanese navy against the limited forces at his disposal: destroyers, fast transports, minesweepers, and motor torpedo boats. Jack Rice, an Associated Press photographer who accompanied Tregaskis on the expedition, had the same fears as the admiral. Rice had experience being under enemy bombing and said he planned, once on solid ground, to dig a foxhole and "pull the top in after me." Maj. Gen. John H. Hester, the Forty-Third's commander, expressed confidence that his soldiers would be successful whatever opposition they faced. Although his troops had yet to experience combat, they had trained hard and appeared eager to get into action. Hester said about twenty-five men had broken out of the hospital when they heard the outfit was getting ready for the Russell offensive. "It cured 'em," the general informed Tregaskis. "There were a couple, though, who had appendicitis. It didn't do anything for THEM."[10]

Ambling about the deck of his ship before the February 21 landing, Tregaskis had the opportunity to compare the Forty-Third's soldiers to the marines he had come to know on Guadalcanal. In general, he noted, the soldiers were much more varied in appearance and age than the marines (one soldier from Pittsburgh was reputed to be forty-four years old), which he expected, as about half of the army troops were draftees (the marines had all been volunteers). An officer said that the men in the Forty-Third represented every state in the Union, but that most came from Maine, New Hampshire, Rhode Island, and Vermont, along with Mississippi and Georgia and Swedes from Minnesota. A former automobile mechanic from Mississippi told Tregaskis he thought that the outfit was glad to finally end its training and see some action, with most of the soldiers feeling as he did, that the job had to be done and the sooner it was, the sooner they all could return home to their families. "These people were not as wild or youthful or exuberant as the Marines," Tregaskis said. There was grousing from some involved in the operation, conceived by Turner and grudgingly approved by Halsey, who had told Turner, "go ahead, as some kind of action is better than none." One of the engineers, responsible for constructing the facilities on the Russells, complained to Tregaskis that those in charge "just put an X on the map and want us to build a base there. They never stop to think about terrain or anything like that." The correspondent attributed the nitpicking he heard to the usual "beefing that you find anywhere in normal military or naval circles." The army men passed the time shipboard in ways similar to what the marines had done on their way to Guadalcanal, Tregaskis remembered: playing cards, reading books and magazines, writing letters to loved ones, sharing photographs of their sweethearts, cleaning their weapons, and painstakingly reviewing their orders. Plans called for three simultaneous landings: on the north end of Pavuvu Island's Pepesala Bay (a task to be handled by the eight hundred men of the Third Marine Raider Battalion), on the east coast of Banika Island's Renard Sound, and on the southwest coast of Banika's Wernham Cove.[11]

Whatever tension there may have been about the impending action lessened when a reconnaissance team of six American and Australian officers that had explored the area before the February 21 invasion found no Japanese troops on any of the islands except for a dead fighter pilot lying beside his crashed Zero. On Bycee (also called Baisen) Island at the northern edge of the Russells the officers did find evidence of a recent large concentration of Japanese, estimating that anywhere from five hundred to one thousand had established a camp and started work on a base. "But now all the enemy were gone," Tregaskis reported. "The Japs had left large stores of supplies, including rifles, ammunition and medical items, behind them. They had evidently gone in a hurry, for even such items as packs and helmets were abandoned." Still, the Japanese did not let the operation go completely unchallenged. On the evening of February 17 a convoy of transports and escorting warships heading to the staging point for the invasion came under attack by a group of twelve to fourteen enemy torpedo planes. A naval officer who experienced the attack, Cdr. Charles O. Camp of Omaha, Nebraska, told Tregaskis that he could see one of the Japanese came right at his ship, and it seemed like a long time before the ship's gunners hit and destroyed the plane. "I found myself squeezing, saying to myself, 'I hope they hit him pretty soon.' Finally, he burst into flame and there was a splatter of fire when he hit the water." The other torpedo planes made their attack runs at intervals of about four or five minutes, Camp added. "Our destroyer screen would pick them up and shoot at them and then the transports would join in," the officer recalled. "It was like the Fourth of July. At one time there were five patches of flame on the water when the planes hit. As they struck the water in flames the planes looked like a mess of burning pieces. The ships kept turning to avoid the torpedoes and the attack was over in about 15 minutes. We had been unhit."[12]

In the days leading up to the February 21 landings, Hester and Turner were busy reviewing plans with their officers. Tregaskis recalled there were numerous last-minute changes and "an infinity of details" to be resolved. Turner's headquarters thronged with high-ranking army and navy officers: admirals, generals, colonels, and commanders. "That's the most gold braid I ever did see in one place," a soldier observed to Tregaskis. On the rainy night before the landing, soldiers had to jockey for space to sleep on deck. "The destroyers which formed a large part of our fleet had barely enough space below for their own crews," Tregaskis recalled. "And in the large troop-carrying lighters which spread around the destroyers and auxiliary transports like ducklings around their parents, there was no hope of cover. The boats were open to the weather." On the destroyer to which he was assigned, the correspondent noted that the troops had no shelter except for the scanty cover of torpedo tubes and gun mounts, and these spaces were crowded "by a fortunate few." Although reconnaissance had shown that there would probably not be any ground resistance in the Russells, some on board, he noted, were sure that before the morning was over "we would be bombed: that the Japs might tackle our ships as they were unloading their cargoes of men, and our landing boats as they were striking for the shore; or at least, that we would be intensively bombed after we had landed." Tregaskis overheard one of the soldiers holding forth to that effect in conversation with a circle of his friends and sailors. He asked them an unanswerable, it seemed, question about bombs being unleashed on them: "When you see the son of b—— comin' right at you, what the f—— you gonna do, where the f—— you gonna go?"[13]

No enemy projectiles fell on Tregaskis and the members of the Forty-Third the next morning. Because no Japanese had been unearthed, there was no need for a preliminary bombardment, and the ships' guns were silent. The soldiers had calm weather, which made for an orderly landing, except for, that is, the landing barge on which Tregaskis traveled. The unwieldy vessel experienced trouble at Wernham Cove at the southern end of Banika. "We had thought our boat would be one of the first ashore," Tregaskis remembered. "But we soon changed our minds: suddenly our craft thudded against a coral reef, and bumped its way solidly aground. The soldiers looked silently over the side, watching the schools of small, bright blue fish darting amongst the vari-colored coral formations." The correspondent noted that when one of the men asked their officer, Lt. Jackson S. King of Colusa, California, what they should do if the Japanese suddenly showed up, he offered a straightforward solution: "We'd just dive in and try to swim for shore." The craft's skipper, Bosun Charles T. Howard, directed a mass movement to the stern and port side and finally the weight shifted, the engine churned furiously, and the boat began to "shudder its way off the reef." The barge finally reached the beach, its ramp clanked down "like a medieval drawbridge, and our troops poured out," reported Tregaskis. All along the edge of a coconut grove he could see the "tangled impediments and bustling crowd of the typical landing. There were piles of blue, soggy barracks bags, rifles stacked and in piles, wooden boxes of small arms ammunition and the black cardboard cloverleaf cases of artillery shells in great dumps." At the water's edge he could see additional landing boats running ashore and disgorging their troops, as well as soldiers rolling loaded trucks down the ramps of huge landing barges. "Platoons and companies were forming up and setting out up the hill to reconnoiter neighboring woods," he said. All this would have made a perfect target for Japanese bombing, but the enemy "literally 'missed the boat,'" Tregaskis recalled. "Either they were intimidated or unaware of our operation."[14]

Wandering over to a nearby plantation house, Tregaskis met a coast watcher, Lt. Allan Campbell of Sydney, Australia, who sat calmly on the porch and looked out over the peaceful green lawn rimmed with frangipani trees and hibiscus bushes bearing crimson flowers. Campbell had been in the Russells for the past three months, reporting to U.S. headquarters by radio about Japanese ship and troop movements in the islands. "A dangerous job," said Tregaskis, who asked Campbell if he had had any close calls with the enemy. "Yes, they've been about," Campbell replied. He had seen the enemy on the other side of the island, but they had fled from the Russells the day after the Americans had mopped up on Guadalcanal. The Australian officer noted that the Japanese had counted on building an air base in the Russells and having another crack at dislodging U.S. forces from Guadalcanal. Another coast watcher joined the duo on the porch and asked Tregaskis if he would like a cup of tea. "It was an unexpectedly polite welcome to this island where we had expected a hot reception from Jap aircraft," the correspondent said. Later that afternoon, Tregaskis trudged for miles over a rough trail, stumbling constantly over coral extrusions, to reach the camp where he would be sleeping. He, Rice, and a handful of army officers struggled to erect a tent to shelter them for the evening, but they eventually succeeded. "Marvel of marvels," said Tregaskis, "we had folding cots too and did not have to sleep on the ground. Which was well because in the night the rain began to pour down and kept on pouring." Before they went to sleep, those staying in the tent made sure to pick out a nearby gully where they could seek shelter if, "as we expected," Tregaskis said, "the Jap bombers came over during the night. But they did not come."[15]

With the landings a success, Tregaskis spent the next few days, accompanied by Rice, plying the waters around the Russells, including checking in with the Third Marine Raider Battalion, which had been responsible for seizing Pavuvu Island. En route Tregaskis used his swimming prowess to investigate a downed Japanese Zero lying on a coral bank in shallow water about ten feet down. As everywhere else in the islands, the water was crystal clear, and he could see the plane's markings and the bullet holes in its wings as he peered down from his boat above. "I dived in and swam about the cockpit and around the tail of the of the plane. The cockpit was intact, untouched by bullets," he reported. Evidently the Zero had been struck in its engine or lubrication system and had made a forced landing, an observation Tregaskis later verified with occupants of a nearby village. According to their account, the Japanese aviator had survived, was captured by Australian coast watchers, and sent as a prisoner to the Americans on Guadalcanal. As he swam around the plane, Tregaskis could see that the instruments, machine guns, controls, and everything else exposed had been well covered with a mossy growth.[16]

Upon reaching Pavuvu, Tregaskis met with the men and officers of the Marine Raiders. Although they had discovered no traces of the enemy on Pavuvu, on the nearby Bycee Island they had uncovered the remnants of a Japanese camp. "There were shelter caves dug under [the] plantation house, there, and machine gun positions, more than 100 drums of fuel oil, and some foodstuffs," Tregaskis learned, along with medical supplies, machine-gun ammunition, and hand grenades. One of the unusual items they unearthed was a bottled, honey-tasting liquid. "It seemed like concentrated food to me," Lt. Murray Ehrlich of San Diego, California, said to the correspondent. "It's quite palatable when take[n] with something else and washed down with a hot drink. It tastes like mineral oil with a very sweet flavor." While his traveling companions left to check on the items left on Bycee, Tregaskis stayed behind with the raiders on Pavuvu to "work furiously" on a typewriter. "I was anxious to get some copy aboard ships which were leaving in the afternoon," he noted. Tregaskis's party had a pleasant return trip to Banika but had a rocky night. The camp was "full of disturbing shadows and misgivings," he recalled. "It seemed weird that the Japs had not yet attacked." Sentries were on edge and were quick to call out "Halt!" if they heard or saw any movement in the jungle. "We had an alert in the middle of the night, but no planes showed up," Tregaskis said. Rain, however, did appear, falling hard enough to flood the earthen floor of his tent.[17]

On the afternoon of February 25 it seemed as if the attack everyone had feared was finally happening. Two signalmen came running into Hester's headquarters clad only in trousers. They told everyone that their group had been fighting with a Japanese patrol in the jungle, and they had abandoned their position when they feared they might be surrounded. Officers scrambled to organize a platoon to send out, with the expectation, Tregaskis noted, that a pitched battle would be joined. The correspondent joined the soldiers as they marched off, with the remaining troops yelling at them "Give 'em hell boys!" as a farewell as they shoved off on a landing boat for the rescue mission. "We were ready, and had made the same grim mental adjustment for a fight which would have been necessary if we had actually run into one; but the Japs turned out to be phantoms," Tregaskis said. "We found, on landing, only a badly scared signal company and some croaking bullfrogs in the thick jungle; nary a Jap, as yet."[18]

Tregaskis discovered more newsworthy fare when he and Rice, on February 27, made a trip to see how progress was being made by the Seabees (the naval construction unit) on the new airfield. The correspondent and the photographer discovered the crews working savagely at the job of tearing down trees, "as if their very lives depended on speed—and perhaps, actually, this is the case," said Tregaskis. One of the men in charge of the project, Noel Woodward, told the reporter that the Seabees might as well rush the job, as they believed that the sooner they were finished, "the better for us. There's no reason why we can't beat the Japs to the punch, and with all this equipment, the work should really go fast." Tregaskis watched the "snorting bulldozers" uprooting the tall, slender trees, simultaneously pulling at them with lengths of chain until they cracked and dropped. "Down a long lane trees already felled lay like bowling alley pins," Tregaskis said, "as if a great fist had crushed its way into the coconut grove and leveled everything in its path. The men were working with dispatch, expertly, taking only a few seconds to knock down a tree." A navy corpsman standing by in case any first aid was needed spoke admiringly of the Seabees' work. "They don't waste time," the corpsman commented to Tregaskis. "You should have seen 'em yesterday; coconuts falling all around 'em, and trees comin' down, but they didn't care. Those guys ain't afraid of nothin'—except malaria; and you bet they take their atabrine [an antimalarial drug] every day." Having witnessed the work on the airfield, which made an obvious scar on the jungle from the air, Tregaskis expected a Japanese bombing raid that night, but, again, everything remained quiet. Rumors abounded that the Japanese were withdrawing from New Georgia (rumors that were unfounded). He did hear from reliable sources that enemy aircraft had bombed Henderson Field the same night. "That, it seems, should be good evidence that they have not withdrawn aircraft from the area," Tregaskis noted. "Nevertheless we are puzzled—and pleased—about the fact that we have not yet been attacked."[19]

The first enemy air raid did not hit the Russells until March 6. By that time, Tregaskis had left the islands, visiting New Zealand for a rest with another reporter, Gordon Walker of the *Christian Science Monitor*. Word had come to Tregaskis before the Russell Island invasion that his book, *Guadalcanal Diary*, had been successful, but he had yet to see any reviews. In correspondence with his parents, he wrote that he did read an advance notice in the *New York Times* review section for November 28, 1942, that his book was to be published sometime in January 1943. "I thought it appropriate that this notice, something I always looked forward to seeing, should accidentally be printed on my birthday," he wrote. Tregaskis also read an article reporting that King Features had sold the movie rights to his book to 20th Century Fox for $8,500. "I had no notification about that from my office—but suppose the reason is that the mail service out here has been very slow," he explained. Tregaskis's INS editor, Barry Faris, eventually visited him on a tour of the Pacific, bringing his correspondent letters from his parents, a copy of *Guadalcanal Diary*, and grudging permission, at first, to return to the United States on leave and possibly work on the script for the movie version of his book, a proposal that seemed fair to Tregaskis.[20]

Unfortunately, Tregaskis missed out on working on the screenplay for the film *Guadalcanal Diary*, a writing task he had wanted to attempt from the beginning of his writing career. He and Faris met a young marine officer who had only recently left the United States, where he had been an assistant director for 20th Century Fox. The officer said he knew the book well and that a script of it had been written before he left Hollywood in January. That initial script had been rejected by the studio, the officer added, and work had begun on another version by a different writer. All this, Tregaskis noted, seemed to be "a very interesting contradiction to what Faris had said." Later, Faris claimed that the young marine did not know what he was talking about. Things only got more muddled as the marine confided to Tregaskis that he had heard 20th Century Fox was prepared to pay the author $500 a week for six weeks to come and work on the script, but the INS office told the studio its correspondent was unavailable. Thinking about the situation, Tregaskis wrote to his parents that he could not blame his employer for wanting him to stay in the Pacific, but he did criticize the INS for "not telling me about it, fair and square."[21]

Faris and Tregaskis also battled over a two-year contract the INS wanted him to sign, giving him a salary of $100 per week for the first year, $125 per week for the second year, and requiring that all of his writings would be the property of King Features. "I said I wanted the contract to state specifically that I should split 50-50 any book or movie profits with the company," Tregaskis wrote, "and that the salary should be raised to a straight $150 [per week] all the way through." Faris did agree to the 50-50 split and offered to compromise on the salary, $125 a week the first year and $150 a week the second year. "I stuck out for the 150; since for the time being the name [his] is hot and I might as well capitalize on it," Tregaskis pointed out. The contract situation remained unsettled as Tregaskis left for New Zealand, but their disagreement did not seem to upset Faris, who wrote his reporter's parents that he "never found a correspondent better liked by the people he has associated with than Dick. All of the officers to whom I talked told me what a great fellow Dick is and how they liked to have him with them." The book's success did ease some of the frustration Tregaskis felt over missing out on being involved with the film version. He was happy to hear from his parents that money from his book had been able to provide them with "some of the things you need and want." Tregaskis reminded them that the money was "as much yours as mine" and if there was anything they needed all they had to do was ask.[22]

In late March 1943 Tregaskis and Walker flew to Wellington, New Zealand. Tregaskis later noted that it had been a "marvelous novelty... to see tidy houses in rows and city streets and groves of well-tended trees after the jungles of Guadalcanal." The reporters also experienced something that shocked them: cold weather. They bustled about the city trying to find warm clothes. The two men also made sure to sample what Wellington restaurants had to offer, dining on steak for breakfast, with sausage and eggs; steak again for lunch; and steak and eggs for dinner. "What a feast it was for us who had come from the land of Spam and Beans and Vienna sausages," Tregaskis wrote his parents. After three days in Wellington Tregaskis parted from Walker and flew north to Auckland. Once there, at an improvised nightclub called El Ray, he shared nearly all of a bottle of Scotch with a navigator from a B-17 he knew from the Solomons. Tregaskis found the New Zealanders quite friendly to visiting Americans, whom they credited with saving their country from a possible Japanese invasion. "A man approached me in the Wellington Post Office and said that he wanted to say that his people were grateful to the Americans," he wrote. "And when I was trying to buy a razor in a store, and not having much success, a New Zealander offered to bring me his; which he did; and then refused to take any money for it." Tregaskis's contract negotiations with the INS, however, remained at a standstill. The company had increased its offer for his weekly salary to what he had asked for, $150 a week for each year of the two-year contract. The news service was pressuring him, however, to sign his contract as soon as possible, as it wanted him to go to Australia to prepare to eventually fill in for one of its reporters in New Guinea. The reporter, Tregaskis explained to his parents, had "evidently packed up in disgust after being in the place for more than a year without relief, and [had] gone home. I'm afraid that if I go down there and fill in for this bird, I may be stuck for months."[23]

Tregaskis reconnected with Walker and in early April they flew to Nouméa, New Caledonia, the "Paris of the South Pacific," for more rest and a few baths. Even after their break in civilization, Tregaskis remembered that the two men still felt "punchy" and described both of them as "exhausted, dirty and miserable." Unfortunately, the mosquitoes in Nouméa proved to be ferocious adversaries that prevented them from getting any sleep at night, and the hot days, combined with plumbing problems that interfered with proper bathing, caused the correspondents to become so disgusted that they came to welcome any kind of change, no matter how violent it might be. They soon had their opportunity, as they received permission from Lt. Col. Robert H. Williams, commander of the First Marine Parachute Battalion, to participate in one of its practice jumps. The battalion, after hard and deadly action on Guadalcanal, had been sent to New Caledonia for rest and reorganization at a site near the Tontouta River that came to be known as Camp Kaiser, named for 2nd Lt. Walter W. Kaiser, killed in action at Gavutu. "Gordon and I thought a jump would be a novelty, and besides, I was tired of covering the war and I thought if anything went wrong, like, for instance, landing incorrectly and breaking a leg," Tregaskis recalled, "I would have a good excuse for going back to the U.S."[24]

The night before the jump, Tregaskis and Walker joined Williams in his quarters, a square, prefabricated house known as a Dallas hut, equipped with a wooden floor, board roof, and foldable screens to keep out the dreaded mosquitoes. Williams invited a few of his staff officers to meet the correspondents at a small party. "There were powerful refreshments, and after a few hours of drinking, most of the assembly were feeling no pain whatever," Tregaskis remembered. One of the officers, a gruff lieutenant colonel, was formally polite to the reporters but stressed to them that jumping out of a plane with a parachute was "a really dangerous affair unless you knew how to do it," and he related to them a "few gory incidents" in which paratroopers had their parachutes fail to open, a calamity that had proved fatal. The officer belligerently pronounced, "Tregaskis, I'll bet you two dollars you break your ass." Because the occasion was supposed to be jovial, Tregaskis laughed and accepted the challenge. Attempting to lessen the tension, Williams took Tregaskis to the hut's door. At the top were four front steps, and Williams, standing at the top and leaping off, demonstrated the proper method for landing. "Twice I jumped down the four steps, somersaulted at the bottom, and the second time the performance was said to be satisfactory," Tregaskis remembered. With Williams content with his pupil's progress, they went back to "the serious business of drinking," said Tregaskis. He noted when whiskey was available in New Caledonia in those days, "one made the most of it. I had seen servicemen pay as much as $125 for a quart of American rye."[25]

The next morning, Tregaskis and Walker lined up with the paratroopers at the airfield. Showing no signs of a hangover, the lieutenant colonel who had made the bet with Tregaskis reminded him that he had not forgotten about it, and he was determined to collect his money when the correspondent "broke my posterior this morning." Conditions were ideal for the jump, with gentle winds and sunny skies. On his plane, Tregaskis was second in line, jumping after his rival. As the aircraft took off and slowly gained altitude, Tregaskis recalled that his nerves were on edge. "The roar of the slipstream, the sounds of the big propellers and engines, and the rush of wind over the metal wings, were huge and frightening," he said. When ordered to stand up and snap his static line to a cable that ran the length of the plane's cabin, Tregaskis experienced a sinking feeling. He saw his nemesis jump through the open door and disappear to the aircraft's rear "like a sack of cement evaporating." Then it was the correspondent's turn. One of the paratroopers later kidded Tregaskis that he had to be kicked out of the plane, but the correspondent did not feel any blows, as he remembered being incapable of feeling anything but shock at that point. Once he was through the door and out of the plane and into the roaring wind, it only took a few seconds for Tregaskis to feel the "good hard jerk on the webbing straps around my shoulders. I didn't know exactly what had happened, but I knew my chute was opening, and I had held onto my emergency pack so that it didn't hit me in the nose."[26]

Grabbing his risers and looking up, Tregaskis could see that his parachute had opened without any snags, a sight he described as "a gracious and benign bloom that seemed to be suspending me dead-still in mid-air. I looked down and saw that the ground was miraculously keeping its distance." He could also see "puffs of white down" where other parachutists had landed safely. Tregaskis's problems came when he tried to land. The ground rushed up at him at a terrifying speed and he felt as if he was "falling with no chute at all." He kept his feet apart and bent his knees but still hit the ground with great force, conking himself on the back of the head so hard that he saw stars. Completing a backward somersault, he found himself lying slightly beaten up, but at least on the ground. "I had come in backwards and rolled over my least vulnerable part," he noted. One of the paratroopers helped him out of his harness, and Tregaskis stood up and saw Walker across the field. Walker, lighter in weight, had come down at a slower speed and managed to keep his footing when he hit the ground. As for the lieutenant colonel that had badgered Tregaskis, the correspondent could see him limping as he walked toward him, and "as he came closer, I could see that his nose was red and swollen, a real honker, as we used to say when we were kids. As he had climbed out of the plane, his emergency chute had biffed him in the nose; landing, he had smashed into a naoli tree." Even in his miserable condition, the officer laughed at his situation, proving, said Tregaskis, that he was "a good guy; so I didn't have the heart to ask him to pay the two dollars."[27]

Although Tregaskis's fantasy about being injured in the parachute drop leading to a trip home failed to come true, he finally received permission from the INS to return after more than a year overseas. His reporting work about Guadalcanal had been selected as the winner of the news service's annual George R. Holmes Memorial Trophy for 1942. Faris shared the news about the honor with Tregaskis's parents in an April 13 letter, a week before the official announcement was made at the American Newspapers Publishers' Association meeting in New York. "But more important," Faris wrote, "in cabling Dick the news I told him to come home immediately and to try, if possible, to get here by April 20th so that he could receive the award personally." Faris added that he had all the INS's people in the Pacific working on arranging transportation for Tregaskis. With the distances involved, however, Tregaskis could not be there to accept the award; his wife, Marian, picked it up for him. The correspondent did not make it back to New York until May 12. He did not stay there for long. By late June Tregaskis was in London, preparing to travel to the Mediterranean to cover the Allied invasion of Sicily, code named Operation Husky, and face a new enemy, the Germans. He traveled to Europe despite suffering from malaria, which he had contracted while in the Pacific. Tregaskis told no one about his illness except for his wife and Faris, dosing himself with atabrine and receiving additional treatment from army doctors in London. "Otherwise," he explained, "I probably wouldn't have been allowed to leave for the war zones." If Tregaskis had known what was to come, he might have decided to remain home while he healed.[28]

12 SICILY: GATEWAY TO A CONTINENT

The jeep crept through what seemed to be deserted streets on the outskirts of Messina, the last great prize sought by American and British troops on the island of Sicily as a successful conclusion to Operation Husky in mid-August 1943. The three men in the vehicle—Lt. Col. J. M. "Mad Jack" Churchill, commander of the British Number Two Commando outfit; the colonel's driver, Trooper Bill Holmes; and American war correspondent Richard Tregaskis—had broken away from the main body of the Fourth Armored Brigade headed toward Messina. Churchill had urged speed upon his driver, eager to reach the city to track down its mayor. "Be nice if we could sort of capture the city," he had said, with enthusiasm, to Tregaskis. The reporter did not share the commando's eagerness, telling him instead that it might be wise to show more concern for any mines or snipers left behind by the retreating German and Italian forces; after all, they were fully a half-hour ahead of the bulk of the British troops. Tregaskis's uneasiness did not disturb Churchill, who merely told Holmes to slow down a bit. Churchill did, however, pick up a submachine gun that had been lying on the vehicle's floor, ignoring, for the time, the sword and bagpipes he had stored away in the rear.[1]

Just hours before his drive with Churchill, Tregaskis had been part of an amphibious landing with Second Commando and the Fourth Armored Brigade at Cape D'Ali. The correspondent had stood on a cliff outside the town of Scaletta, just a few miles south of Messina, entranced by the sight of Italy appearing before him across the Strait of Messina. Peering through his binoculars, he could make out the white buildings in the town of Reggio and the gray alluvial fan of the Saint Agata River. "It was startling to realize that we were now so close to the mainland of Italy that we could see individual buildings and streets and rivers," he observed. His reverie was disturbed, however, by heavy German shelling that caused the ground to shake and filled the air with the sizzling sounds of shrapnel "zooming by like hornets on the prowl." It had made him skeptical, as he drove on with Holmes and Churchill, about tales he had heard about the enemy abandoning Sicily to Allied forces. Although Churchill had at last taken the precaution of putting on his helmet, Tregaskis, as they drove on, continued to feel "very conspicuous, sitting up in the high rear seat, unarmed, and looking into the empty windows of the myriad houses, each window seeming black and mysterious, like the eyesocket of a skull." One grenade tossed from a house could kill them all, Tregaskis realized. Miraculously, he noted, when they reached the last bridge before Messina, he could see no mines hidden in the pavement, no German shot at them, nor did the bridge explode underneath their wheels.[2]

Tregaskis's relief lasted only a moment, for after crossing the bridge his heart stopped when he spied something moving about in a nearby building, which had been wrecked by heavy shelling. He could see a face stirring in the darkness and came to realize it was an old Sicilian woman, her "gums barred in a snarl. It might have been a smile, but there was no mirth in it," Tregaskis recalled. "Only strange animal sounds, which could not have been words in any language, came from the toothless mouth." The first live person they had come across in Messina had been "shellshocked into insanity."[3]

The trio's splendid dash into Messina did not end as Churchill had hoped, as British forces had been beaten to the city hours earlier by their American allies. Tregaskis's adventure with the British commando put the finishing touches on a long journey that began in London and had included a stop in North Africa before finally reaching Sicily. He shared the rigors of the fighting on that island with American GIs of the First Infantry Division and Tommies of the British Eighth Army. Although Tregaskis had hopes of participating in an airborne drop on Rome, that potentially deadly mission was scrubbed. Instead, he hit the beaches of the Italian mainland near Salerno with members of the Eighty-Second Airborne Division and later dodged German fire with Col. William Darby's Rangers in the mountains outside of Venafro. In Sicily and Italy, as he had on Guadalcanal, Tregaskis saw troops getting hit on both sides of him, behind him, and in front of him, suffering terrible injuries. All the time he kept wondering when the odds might finally catch up with him, knowing he could diminish the chances of becoming a casualty by being "battle wise." He realized that there might be some reward in sticking his neck out, as "there might be a good story in it."[4]

Tregaskis also witnessed men suffering from battle fatigue due to the terrible conditions they experienced, and he understood, as he had in the Pacific, that "everybody, even the toughest, have a breaking point." Still, there were moments of humor among the bleakness of combat, including remarks from a First Division sergeant on Sicily who explained to the correspondent the technique for a successful bayonet charge: "You fire a helluva lot, yell like hell, throw a lot of grenades, and they take off—that's a bayonet charge." Tregaskis also came face to face with a new foe, the Germans. Confronting a bedraggled infantryman, a former machinist from Hanover and a veteran of the fighting in Russia, now captured in Sicily, Tregaskis had the opportunity to ask him the question that was on his mind and the minds of the American soldiers studying him: What was he fighting for? Tregaskis remembered the German looking down at his shoes and then, finally, looking up at his captors with tired eyes and answering: "'We're fighting for Adolf Hitler'—and then there was something slightly sardonic, but cautiously noncommittal, as he added, 'I guess.'"[5]

Early on during his time in England, Tregaskis believed he was in the perfect position to report on the long-anticipated invasion of western Europe, moving Allied soldiers and material across the English Channel to strike directly at the German troops occupying France. One of his first articles for the International News Service had him following American troops involved in large-scale amphibious training in collaboration with British commandos that also included tank destroyers, half-tracks, 75 mm guns, and artillery spotting aircraft. "Some of the landings in rough waters are dangerous," he told his readers, but the only "casualties," he reported, were two seasick soldiers. Tregaskis also traveled to an American air base to interview a bomber pilot with the Eighth Air Force, Lt. Col. Al Key of Meridian, Mississippi, who had flown missions over Germany and had previously battled with Japanese Zero fighters in the Pacific. German aircraft, such as the Messerschmitt Bf 109 and Focke-Wulf Fw 190 fighters, which doggedly pressed their attacks against American bombers, Key complained to the reporter, failed to "fall apart when you shoot at 'em as they should. . . . The opposition's much stiffer all along the line than it was in the Pacific." One consolation in flying in the European theater, Key added, was the vastly superior comfort when it came to living arrangements, at least for officers. "Here you go out to fight like hell for an hour and then come back and put on a dress coat for dinner," the pilot noted. "Down there in the Pacific, you lived war. When you got back to the field from a bombing mission, the Japs were always coming over, bombing and strafing. They didn't kid around. The food was a lot worse and half the time we didn't have enough to eat."[6]

The keenness American forces felt about a direct attack on western Europe was not initially shared by British military officials and political leaders, especially Prime Minister Winston Churchill. The British were wary of their allies, rookies at war in their minds, and fearful of the high casualties that could result in such a risky venture against a still-powerful foe. Instead, the British preferred continued operations in the Mediterranean, hitting at the "soft underbelly" of Adolf Hitler's "Fortress Europe," building on the success of the North African campaign that had ended in victory in May 1943. Concentrating operations in the Mediterranean also might give the Allies the opportunity to knock one of the Axis powers, Italy, out of the war, thus removing Italian divisions from the Balkans and Greece. Continued pressure also needed to be put on Axis forces to placate another ally, Russia, which had won a crucial victory against the Nazi invaders at Stalingrad earlier that year. The ten-thousand-square-mile island of Sicily seemed to be the prudent choice as the next target for Allied forces, and Operation Husky was approved at a conference in Casablanca, Morocco, by Churchill and President Franklin D. Roosevelt and their military advisers. Gen. Dwight D. Eisenhower served as the commander of the Allied Forces Headquarters, with British general Harold Alexander directing the Fifteenth Army Group: the U.S. Seventh Army under Gen. George S. Patton Jr. and the British Eighth Army under Gen. Bernard Montgomery. The approximately seven Allied divisions set to assault the island's southeastern coast in the early July amphibious operation faced off against between two to three hundred thousand Italian troops and approximately thirty thousand Germans. The main effort was to be expended in the British sector on Sicily's eastern side, seeking to capture the ports of Augusta and Catania, and continuing north to seize the strategic port of Messina, cutting off reinforcements and supplies from the Italian mainland. Patton felt frustrated by the Americans serving in a supporting role to Montgomery, complaining that it was what happened when "your Commander-in-Chief [Eisenhower] ceases to be an American and becomes an Ally."[7]

Lingering around the INS's bureau in London, Tregaskis and his colleagues began to doubt the chances of a landing in France by Allied forces anytime soon. Those doubts were laid out, as best they could be, given the military censorship imposed on the press, in a letter from INS London bureau chief Leo Dolan to J. C. Oestreicher, the news service's foreign editor in New York. Dolan said that as soon as Tregaskis had arrived in England he had taken him around to "meet some people who know the answers and on the basis of the answers he [Tregaskis] got added to the answers I already had Dick decided he wanted to get going and I think he is right. It just ain't in the woods here at the moment." Dolan even speculated that reporters were "being played for suckers in some quarters as part of the nerve war against the enemy," perhaps to deflect attention from planned incursions elsewhere. From various reports he had picked up in London, Tregaskis believed there would be an operation against either Sardinia or Sicily in the Mediterranean, and he did everything he could to be there for the invasion, arriving in Algiers from Morocco on July 9. He hurried to Allied headquarters and met with Pete Huss, the INS bureau manager, who led him to his room at the Aletti Hotel. Once there, Tregaskis learned that he was too late; the invasion of Sicily was set for the next day, which he should have realized by looking down from the room's balcony into the Bay of Algiers, where ten to twelve troop transports filled with soldiers were casting off. "And they're only reserves," Huss told him. "The main force left about a week ago." Noticing the reporter's crestfallen face, Huss grinned and said, "But you can still catch up. There'll be plenty of fighting left to cover."[8]

Huss's words proved to be prophetic. Tregaskis found plenty to write about by traveling to Tunis, the capital of Tunisia, where Eisenhower had established his headquarters. Tregaskis joined other correspondents at a press conference in which the general gave details about the invasion. "He is a good-looking man, with regular features, a balding crown, and notably pale blue eyes," he said of Eisenhower. "Most striking is his quick, agreeable manner. He seemed to sense the implication of every question quickly, and answered with concise phrases." Eisenhower expressed confidence that the action in Sicily would be over in a short time, perhaps two weeks, as the initial enemy resistance seemed insignificant and casualties were "far lighter than expected." In his article about the invasion, Tregaskis made sure to credit all the nationalities involved—Americans, British, and Canadians—and hinted at future operations. He noted that although Eisenhower described the invasion of Sicily as the "first stage in the liberation of the European continent," there was the possibility that it might not turn into the "big show" that might come in another theater. "There will be others," Eisenhower said, significantly, added Tregaskis. Possible actions cited by the correspondent included amphibious forces from England striking at Norway or across the English Channel into Holland or France, and troops in the Middle East spearheading an invasion of Greece or the Balkans, "a move that undoubtedly would affect Germany's current offensive in Russia quickly." Also, an early decision in Sicily could give the Allies control of vital airfields from which they could launch bombing raids against industrial targets in northern Italy and southern Germany. "No matter what other operations develop," Tregaskis added, "a quick victory in Sicily would virtually put Italy out of the war and might lead that nation to sue for a separate peace."[9]

Delayed in joining the forces fighting on Sicily, Tregaskis did all he could to arrange "at least a look at Sicily." Luckily, he tracked down Col. Elliott Roosevelt, the son of the president and commander of the Third Photographic Reconnaissance and Mapping Group, whose planes had made twenty-four flights over Sicily in one day alone. "He had flown with the most recent night photo reconnaissance himself in an A-20 [Havoc medium bomber], and would go over again tonight," Tregaskis recalled. "I asked him if I could go along and he consented." The correspondent took off shortly after midnight on July 15 with Roosevelt and Capt. George Humbrecht on a B-25 bomber, the same type of aircraft he had witnessed taking off from the USS *Hornet* in the Pacific for the Doolittle Raid. Flying over the part of Sicily where the hardest fighting was happening, Tregaskis could see through his field glasses "a remarkably symmetrical pattern of conical fires in a roughly shaped square on our right, at a distance of perhaps six miles. We could distinguish at least 14 separate blazes, all of which must have been of major magnitude." A short time later, Roosevelt, clad in his long-billed salmon fisherman's cap, poked at Tregaskis in the moonlight and shouted over the roar of the engines, "They're firing at us over there on the right." Tregaskis looked down and could see white flashes belching from the guns on the ground. "We were maneuvering violently, attempting to stay clear of the anti-aircraft fire," he reported. "As we passed over the U-shaped mass of fires, we saw a large orange explosion near by, and felt the lifting blast of the concussion. It might have been a bomb dropped on the ground by some plane we had failed to see, or perhaps a fresh fire in the munitions dump—if munitions dump it was." With dawn breaking, the plane returned to La Marsa Airfield in North Africa. "Not much of a show," Roosevelt said to Tregaskis after they had landed. "Come back again some time and we'll have another try." At least the correspondent had learned that the "President's son was not afraid to share danger with his men."[10]

On July 23 Tregaskis finally made it to the fighting on Sicily, setting foot in Licata, the harbor where the U.S. Forty-Fifth Infantry Division had originally landed nearly two weeks before. Traveling by truck, Tregaskis moved on to Palermo, the island's capital, captured by an impatient Patton, who was tired of merely protecting Montgomery's flank and was itching to be allowed to race ahead to Messina. From Palermo, Tregaskis decided to move on to hook up with troops from the First Infantry Division attempting to capture a road network near Nicosia. Arriving at the First Division's headquarters, established in a large stone building in an olive grove near Gangi, he heard a lieutenant colonel report that on the front beyond, the fighting with the Germans had been hand to hand, and the Germans had knocked out one of the American outposts that morning. "We counter-attacked. They attacked again this afternoon," the officer noted. "And we drove them off. It's been pretty bloody." The next morning, Tregaskis, before going off to join the men of the Second Battalion of the Sixteenth Infantry Regiment, had breakfast with an old friend he had met in the Pacific, John Hersey, a reporter for *Time* magazine. Hersey's book *Into the Valley*, about a failed attack by marines on Guadalcanal, had come out shortly after Tregaskis's *Guadalcanal Diary*. Dining on prunes, Spam fried in powdered-egg batter, hotcakes, and crisp biscuits, the two reporters were joined at their table by Brig. Gen. Theodore Roosevelt Jr., the eldest son of the late president Theodore Roosevelt and second in command of the First Division. He spoke enthusiastically about the upcoming attacks. "This is going to be one of those jolly nights when we go without sleep," Roosevelt said. According to Tregaskis, the general did not seem "at all disturbed by the thought." He briefed Tregaskis and Hersey about the impending action, which served as a good example of the exhausting slog experienced by many soldiers on the island's mountainsides. The Sixteenth and Eighteenth Regiments were to relieve the Twenty-Sixth Regiment, which had been bearing the brunt of the fighting for the past few days. "The 16th would push along the south side of the road from Gangi to Nicosia; and the 18th on the north side," Tregaskis noted. Hersey and Tregaskis hitched a ride with Roosevelt in his jeep for the drive to the Twenty-Sixth Regiment's command post, dining on Spam and cheese before proceeding on to the "stuffy little oblong tent" on a side of a mountain that served as the command post for the Sixteenth Regiment.[11]

The next morning, scrambling, slipping, and sliding over the craggy mountainside, Tregaskis and Hersey joined F Company, an outfit commanded by Lt. Melvin C. Groves of Lawrence, Kansas, for an attack on a mountain knoll known as Bald Head and the wooded ridge beyond. Along the way, the correspondents were pinned down for a time by German sniper fire while in the background they could hear the booming of the American artillery batteries. "[T]he sound echoed like summer thunder in the mountain caigs [*sic*]," wrote Tregaskis in his article about the action. "We heard shells passing overhead, singing peacefully, and then the loud crack, crack, crack, as they smashed into Bald Head Knoll beyond." German artillery responded in kind, wounding several Americans, hitting two soldiers just fifteen feet away from Tregaskis. "Then I, too, began to feel the increasing breathlessness, that almost unbearable tension of waiting for the next shell," he wrote. Tregaskis felt naked and helpless while seeking cover on the side of the hill, with "nothing to do but wait, no place to take shelter except in the stubby wheat." He could hear cries for "medics, medics!" similar to the desperate sounds he had heard on Guadalcanal, only there the shouts had been for a navy corpsman. Led by a buddy, a blinded soldier staggered by him, while Tregaskis could also hear another man "moaning for help in the grass of the hilltop as he had been hit in the stomach. Another carried off was only the wreckage of a body." In spite of the possible sniper fire that might await him, Hersey volunteered to help escort the wounded men to the rear, and he and two enlisted men led the "little column down the slope, and disappeared into the ravine," Tregaskis reported. Tregaskis was glad he had decided to go with Groves's company assault on its objective, as anything was better than waiting, helplessly, for the next enemy barrage.[12]

Groves offered no stirring, heroic words to urge his men into action. Instead, Tregaskis remembered him simply stating, "Wireman, get ready to go. Hook on there, boy, and let's have a good one." Tregaskis slung his map case, binoculars, and blanket roll over his shoulder and followed along as the company moved out through the wheat fields, the men stepping carefully over the slippery, sloping earth and coming under German rifle and machine-gun fire. "Then our artillery began to fire, laying torrents of shells on Bald Head Knoll and the ridge beyond, which took a terrific beating all day," he said. "We could see the clouds of smoke rising from the whole area, but as usual in an artillery barrage it was uncertain whether men were being killed or not." The Americans continued to move forward, all the time wondering whether the Germans were lying in wait, preparing to "set a devilish trap." Tregaskis's fears grew as he came upon a steep, rocky cliff covered with charred thorn bushes that he grabbed as he and the soldiers struggled up a steep incline, presenting, he thought, "perfect targets, but the enemy failed to fire." Reaching the top of the charred cliff side, the Americans discovered that the enemy had fled. Later, Tregaskis learned why the Germans had evacuated their position, as he could see that the ridge's burned earth was "sprinkled with shell and mortar fragments." Groves, Tregaskis recalled, allowed his soldiers only a few minutes to rest before reminding them to dig in for the night, a remark translated by a sergeant into the curt order: "You f——g eight balls get the f—— off this God-damn hill before I wrap this rifle barrel around your neck!" Looking down the slope the next morning, Tregaskis could see Nicosia and its neighboring town, Sperlinga. Climbing down the hill, the correspondent came across the battalion commander, Col. John Matthews, who ruefully pointed out to Tregaskis that other units were already making their way to Nicosia, "black dots against the winding white tape" of the road, Tregaskis observed. The colonel knew, however, that by seizing the knoll, Groves and his men had made Nicosia "practically untenable to the enemy and opened it to our troops." Watching the other soldiers moving into the town, one of Groves's men offered the comment, "Well, they've had a road to walk on, instead of these God-damn mountains."[13]

After his mountain adventure, Tregaskis returned to the public relations office camp on the north coast of Sicily, arriving on July 29. There he found a note from his INS employer telling him to divert his attention from American forces to the British Eighth Army and its attempt to capture Catania in the eastern portion of Sicily (the news service had no correspondent in that area). "The message, dated five days ago, urged that I transfer 'soonest,' which in cablese, means 'something you should have done long ago,'" Tregaskis noted. Reporters were under constant pressure from their superiors to provide a steady flow of copy updating the war's progress for curious readers on the home front. Ernie Pyle, the Scripps-Howard columnist who had won a measure of fame for his dispatches during the North Africa campaign and also covered the action in Sicily, remembered that although correspondents lived better than the average soldier they covered, their lives were "strangely consuming in that we did live primitively and at the same time had to delve into ourselves and do creative writing." Most of the good war correspondents Pyle knew "actually worked like slaves," constantly traveling "every few days," eating and sleeping

A young Richard Tregaskis and his sister Madeline relax in a garden near their home in Elizabeth, New Jersey. Richard Tregaskis Collection, American Heritage Center, University of Wyoming, Laramie, WY.

On the beach at Cape May in New Jersey, Tregaskis prepares for one of his lifelong pastimes, swimming. Richard Tregaskis Collection, American Heritage Center, University of Wyoming, Laramie, WY.

RIGHT Tregaskis's high-school graduation photograph. Richard Tregaskis Collection, American Heritage Center, University of Wyoming, Laramie, WY.

BELOW Tregaskis in uniform as a combat correspondent for the International News Service, circa 1942. Richard Tregaskis Collection, COLL/566, Archives Branch, Marine Corps History Division, Quantico, VA.

The USS *Hornet* launches U.S. Army Air Force B-25B Mitchell bombers from its flight deck at the start of the first American air raid on the Japanese home islands, April 18, 1942. Official U.S. Navy Photograph, now in the collections of the National Archives.

Commander in Chief Pacific Fleet Headquarters in Honolulu, Hawaii, Tregaskis (standing, at back, wearing black armband) talks with Waldo Drake, the chief of the Pacific Fleet's public relations office. Drake's assistant, Lt. Jim Bassett, sits immediately in front of Tregaskis. Richard Tregaskis Collection, COLL/566, Archives Branch, Marine Corps History Division, Quantico, VA.

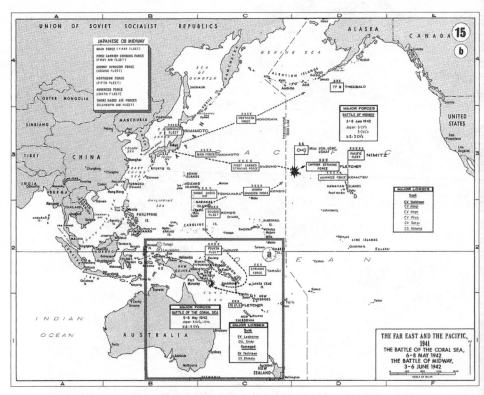

Map depicting the Battle of Coral Sea and the Battle
of Midway in May to June 1942. U.S. Military Academy.

Lt. Cdr. John C. Waldron, leader of Torpedo Squadron Eight on the USS *Hornet*. AV8 Collection 2 / Alamy Stock Photo.

Rear Adm. Richmond Kelly Turner (left) and Gen. Alexander Vandegrift go over details of the Guadalcanal operation on the flag bridge of USS *McCawley,* circa July–August 1942. Photograph from Department of the Navy collections in the U.S. National Archives.

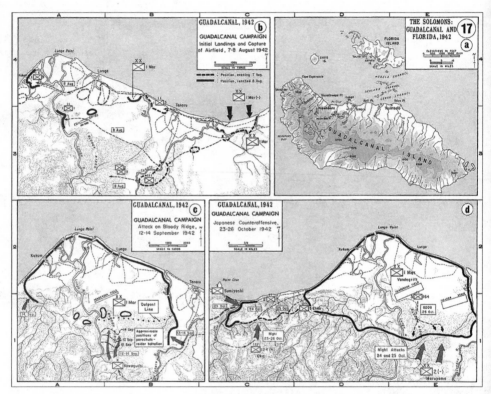

Maps detailing the initial landings on Guadalcanal, August 7–8, 1942;
the attack on Bloody Ridge, September 12–14, 1942; and the Japanese
counteroffensive, October 23–26, 1942. U.S. Military Academy.

ABOVE U.S. Marines rest in the field on Guadalcanal, circa August–September 1942. Most of the marines are armed with M1903 bolt-action rifles and carry M1905 bayonets. Official US Navy photograph, now in the collections of the National Archives.

LEFT Tregaskis talks with General Vandegrift on Guadalcanal. Notice the tennis shoes the correspondent was forced to wear near the end of his time on the island. PJF Military Collection / Alamy Stock Photo.

Tregaskis (left) shares a beer with INS editor Barry Faris (far right) and an unidentified officer somewhere in the Pacific after the correspondent had turned in the manuscript that became *Guadalcanal Diary*. Richard Tregaskis Collection, American Heritage Center, University of Wyoming, Laramie, WY.

On August 1, 1943, while in Palermo, Sicily, Tregaskis awoke to the sounds of a German bombing raid on Allied ships in the harbor. Here he examines a spent shell casing, possibly from antiaircraft guns protecting the city. Richard Tregaskis Collection, American Heritage Center, University of Wyoming, Laramie, WY.

Tregaskis interviews Gen. Mark Clark, commander of the Fifth Army, during the invasion of Italy, September–October 1943. The odd background was probably added by censors to mask the location. Richard Tregaskis Collection, COLL/566, Archives Branch, Marine Corps History Division, Quantico, VA.

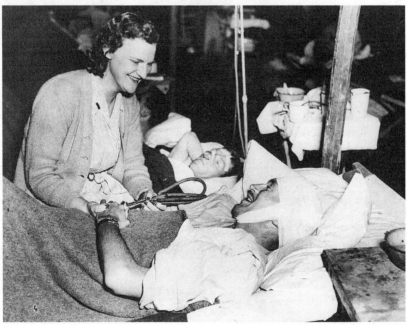

1st Lt. Martha Fliedner of Clinton, South Carolina, tends to a wounded and bandaged Tregaskis at the Thirty-Eighth Evacuation Field Hospital in Italy, November–December 1943. Richard Tregaskis Collection, COLL/566, Archives Branch, Marine Corps History Division, Quantico, VA.

ABOVE *Life* magazine photographer Margaret Bourke-White shares a meal with Tregaskis at a North Africa airport awaiting a plane that would ferry them to the United States, January 1944. Richard Tregaskis Collection, COLL/566, Archives Branch, Marine Corps History Division, Quantico, VA.

RIGHT Tregaskis signs copies of his bestselling *Guadalcanal Diary* during a February 1944 visit to Grumman Aircraft Engineering Corporation on Long Island, New York. His hair has not entirely grown back after his wounding in Italy. Richard Tregaskis Collection, COLL/566, Archives Branch, Marine Corps History Division, Quantico, VA.

LEFT Tregaskis interviews Lockheed P-38 Lightning pilots from the 367th Fighter Group, Thirty-Ninth Fighter Squadron, in France, summer 1944. Richard Tregaskis Collection, COLL/566, Archives Branch, Marine Corps History Division, Quantico, VA.

BELOW With notebook in hand, Tregaskis warily explores a town somewhere in Germany, fall 1944. Richard Tregaskis Collection, American Heritage Center, University of Wyoming, Laramie, WY.

Tregaskis jokes with three of the crewmen of Superfortress Number 688 on Guam. From left to right: Tregaskis, Raleigh Marr, Art Manning, and Ed Marchalonis. Richard Tregaskis Collection, COLL/566, Archives Branch, Marine Corps History Division, Quantico, VA

Ens. Paul R. Stephens of Topeka, Kansas, goes over details of a bombing mission against Japanese targets with Tregaskis in the ready room aboard the USS *Ticonderoga*, July 1945. Richard Tregaskis Collection, American Heritage Center, University of Wyoming, Laramie, WY.

Near Outpost Harry, Tregaskis visits with members of a Greek battalion in South Korea, fall 1953. Richard Tregaskis Collection, COLL/566, Archives Branch, Marine Corps History Division, Quantico, VA.

During his tour of South Vietnam to research his book *Vietnam Diary*, Tregaskis attempts to talk with some captured Viet Cong fighters. Richard Tregaskis Collection, American Heritage Center, University of Wyoming, Laramie, WY.

Richard and Moana Tregaskis pose for a photograph on the day of their wedding, September 12, 1963. Richard Tregaskis Collection, American Heritage Center, University of Wyoming, Laramie, WY.

In the summer of 1974 Moana Tregaskis donated memorabilia from her late husband's life to the U.S. Marine Corps Museum for an exhibit in the Correspondents Corner at the Pentagon. Moana (center) displays the helmet Tregaskis wore when he was wounded to (left) Jerry W. Friedheim, assistant secretary of defense for public affairs and (far right) Col. F. B. Nihart, deputy director of the Marine Corps Museum. Richard Tregaskis Collection, American Heritage Center, University of Wyoming, Laramie, WY.

outdoors, writing wherever and whenever they could find the time, and never catching up "on sleep, rest, cleanliness or anything else normal."[14]

Unfortunately, after Tregaskis drove into Palermo to make arrangements to join the British Eighth Army, he discovered it was not going to be easy in a city newly occupied by military forces. While waiting for his needed paperwork, Tregaskis joined other correspondents in grilling Eisenhower at a press conference about his earlier prediction that the operation could be over in a few weeks. The general kept his good humor, noting, "I'm a born optimist, and I can't change that. But obviously it will take a little longer than we thought." On August 1 Tregaskis went to the Palermo airfield and hitched a ride on a small Fairchild monoplane with two Royal Air Force officers flying to Cassibili near Syracuse on the British side of the island. The dusty airfield at Cassibili did not have any transportation available to take him to Syracuse until the next morning, so Tregaskis stayed the night and learned a bit about British soldiers. Eating a supper of beef stew with potatoes, tea, jam, and biscuits, the correspondent discovered that their favorite subjects of conversation matched that of their American allies: food, women, and mail from home. Later, before going to bed in a room in an old castle that served as headquarters, he asked the British Tommies who shared the quarters with him what they thought of their Americans allies. Tregaskis recalled that a voice in the dark answered in the "typical chopped, singsong English," commenting, "They 'ave more money than our chaps and take the girls about," but added that they also had "plenty of guts" when it came to combat.[15]

While covering the British drive to Messina, Tregaskis had a firsthand view of the havoc modern weapons could unleash on a civilian population. Moving from the port town of Catania toward the vital road junction of Randazzo, the correspondent entered Adrano, which he said looked "like a Flanders town of 1917," and he described the destruction as the "most appalling" he had seen while in Sicily. "There wasn't one building left untouched by bombs or shells and whole blocks were smeared across the ground as if by a colossal mason's trowel," he reported. The mountain town had undergone six Allied air raids aimed at dislodging German troops, as well as several bombardments that had culminated "in an earth shaking World War I style barrage of 180 guns" that had gone on for three and a half hours and had "ripped the sides from buildings, collapsed their tops and spattered every building liberally with shell fragments." At least the shelling had the desired effect, Tregaskis pointed out, of driving from Adrano the last enemy snipers, machine gunners, and mortar crews so that British forces were able to walk into town without opposition.[16]

During Adrano's ordeal, its population had taken to the surrounding hills, living in caves and other shelters, suffering few casualties from the high explosives but experiencing food shortages. Tregaskis visited the low caves in the volcanic rock where the Sicilians were living "on almonds and small amounts of bread," and he "even saw some of them eating kernels of wheat from stalks in the field. Hunger was mirrored in the faces staring at us through tortured eyes as we passed. Every being was an angular skeleton supporting ragged clothes, including the children—some of whom had no clothes at all." Along the road from Catania to Adrano through Santa Maria, Paterno, and Biancavilla, he saw that the villages were heavily damaged from bombing and shelling, but those who lived there still gave greetings to the approaching forces "with a genuine attempt at friendliness." The ultimate sign of openness occurred when the correspondent spied a refugee cart returning to Paterno. Atop a pile of chairs, tables, mattresses, and battered suitcases he saw a child toting an American flag larger than he was. "He was gripping it tightly—and the fact that the flag was upside down apparently did not detract from the sentiment," Tregaskis wrote.[17]

While covering the fighting on Sicily with both the American and British troops, Tregaskis and the other correspondents came to understand the importance of roads, which he described as the "arteries of transport lying in the stony body of the mountains. Vehicles, the nourishing blood and the strength of modern armies, must stay on the roads or be wrecked." Given this fact, the combat engineers (also known as sappers or pioneer troops), perhaps more than any other single outfit, had helped lead the way to victory. Tregaskis had witnessed the engineers blast detours in sheer rock, where the retreating enemy had "blown the roads behind him, or shoving bridges across demolition craters in an hour or two; or tenderly, but above all rapidly, fishing up mines from the roadbed so that our columns of vehicles might go ahead." The usual method of fighting on the island involved sending foot soldiers ahead on both sides of a road to flank the enemy. With heavy artillery support, the infantrymen would render enemy positions unsustainable, forcing their retreat, Tregaskis noted. "Then the main body of vehicles, trucks, half-tracks, tanks, self-propelled and truck-drawn artillery, would follow along the road, bringing supplies and firepower," he said. When they withdrew, the Germans would inevitably mine the roads and their shoulders, blow up bridges, and blast craters at the most precipitous turns; that was when the engineers got to work, and bulldozers became more important than tanks, Tregaskis pointed out. "Sometimes, when the terrain bordering on the roads seemed impossible, or where extra speed was desired, sappers and engineers mingled with the first parties of infantry and led the advance," he wrote. "I remember several times when I have seen the engineering troops serving as spearhead for an attack." On one occasion, on the road to capture Palermo, American engineers had even been able to capture what Tregaskis described as "a mess" of Italian prisoners.[18]

An engineering outfit that particularly caught Tregaskis's attention was one he saw at work on the coast road near San Stefano, on the way to Palermo. A mechanized column was halted when it came upon a crater in the road about a hundred feet across and fifty feet deep. Trucks stopped and men jumped out equipped with boxes full of explosives and shovels, he remembered. A captain cheerfully told him that they should be on their way in about a half-hour. Moments later, the correspondent heard a muffled explosion from ahead, and a part of the mountainside tumbled down onto the road. "The men with shovels quickly went to work leveling the irregular pile of gravel into a semblance of a road," Tregaskis reported. In just twenty minutes the engineers had done enough to allow the train of vehicles, which included artillery, to proceed. "That was typical of the speed with which the engineers worked," he noted.[19]

British sappers also served a valuable role in an operation Tregaskis joined, a mad dash to win the honor of capturing Messina. Hoping to beat Patton's troops into the city, Montgomery authorized an amphibious landing involving approximately four hundred troops, including a detachment from Number Two Commando, led by Churchill, and men and vehicles from the Fourth Armored Brigade, commanded by Brig. John Cecil Currie, fated to die in combat in Normandy, France. The task force, which included Sherman tanks, Priest self-propelled guns, artillery, and engineers, had been tasked with making its landing at Scaletta, about ten miles south of Messina, cutting off Highway 114 (the actual landings occurred about three to five miles north of the intended beach). Tregaskis heard about and received permission to accompany the operation, code named Operation Blackcock, along with Evelyn Montague of the *Manchester Guardian*. The correspondents secured berths on Currie's command ship, LCT (Landing Craft, Tank) 387, which set off from Catania's waterfront on August 15. Once on board, Tregaskis noticed tanks and scout cars jammed together in the ship's open hold and heard a briefing on the operation from a young lieutenant. Hearing about the plans, one of the soldiers noted that it sounded like "a damn bad show for Jerry. Hope he takes a lenient view of it." As the sailors tossed off the ship's bowline and the LCT slowly moved away from the dock, Tregaskis could see Currie waving his cap to the men still on the shore and heard soldiers begin to sing, with enthusiasm, "We're Shoving Right Off."[20]

After catching some sleep while sprawled on the hood of a scout car, Tregaskis awoke at about 2:00 a.m. on August 16 with his "mental alarm clock" telling him he had about an hour left before the landing. The correspondent shared a brief conversation with Currie, who asked him if he had been on one of these landings before. Responding that he had, Tregaskis quoted the officer as cheerfully noting, "Stimulating, isn't it?" To help pass the time, the correspondent went to the front of the LCT and spent a "pleasant hour" talking to three enlisted men manning a scout car that would serve as mobile headquarters when the force landed. The men—named Adlington, Fincham, and Bowles—were happy to chat with the American and even shared their civilian occupations: one was an automobile salesman, one an office boy in a stock brokerage firm, and one a store clerk.[21]

As his LCT reduced its speed and turned toward shore, Tregaskis witnessed a "terrific explosion," probably the work of the British commandos who had already landed. The ship proceeded with caution under the guidance of blinking green lights on the beach and grounded itself on the sand. "A small group of Commandos came down the beach, escorting a crowd of Italian prisoners," Tregaskis noted. "I talked to one of the Commandos, a captain, who told me that there had been only three British casualties in the landings; that the explosion had been caused by a Commando grenade which hit an enemy ammunition lorry on the bridge at the town, killing five or six Germans." High up on the hillside came another tremendous explosion, scattering rocks along the beach and bellowing smoke over the ship. "It's the wrong beach," Currie announced. "Tanks can't get up there."[22]

Tregaskis's LCT finally located the proper beach, coming under German fire as it landed and unloaded a column of men and machines from within. Unfortunately for the correspondent, the scout car he rode in became stuck in the gravelly sand and had to be pulled free by a nearby tank destroyer, all while under fire. The British mechanized column made its way to Scaletta, where Tregaskis transferred to a scout car driven for a forward observing officer, who directed his vehicle through the town. Sicilians shouted "*Viva Ingleterra!*" as they drove by. Eventually proceeding ahead on foot, Tregaskis had to dash for cover to avoid incoming shells, careful to skirt the charred remains of a British soldier, as well as several German casualties. Fire from a tank destroyer, augmented by a Sherman tank, quieted the enemy shelling enough for Tregaskis to hitch a ride to the Scaletta railroad station, where Currie had briefly established his headquarters. "Somehow, the Germans had discovered the location of the headquarters, and put a concentration of shells into it," he reported. "A blond private told us that 'about twenty' people had been killed or wounded." A Priest self-propelled gun had taken a hit, and although it did not look seriously damaged, Tregaskis quickly noticed that "the vehicle was spotted with wads of gore and smears of blood."

Catching up with Currie, Tregaskis learned that reconnaissance parties had been unsuccessful in establishing contact with the main body of the Eighth Army behind them, and the Germans had blown out the coast road in several places. Despite these difficulties, Currie remained undaunted, telling Tregaskis and Montague, "Our intention is to advance north and capture Messina." Churchill, the commando detachment's commanding officer, would lead the troops toward their objective, followed by the armored forces; Currie gave his permission for the journalists to accompany Churchill. A graduate of the Royal Military Academy Sandhurst, Churchill had been battle hardened in the early days of the war during the fierce fighting at the Dunkirk evacuation and a commando raid against the German-occupied harbor of Vaagsø in Norway, where he had guided his men ashore by playing "The March of the Cameron Men" on his bagpipes. He also possessed a unique view for modern warriors, believing that any officer "who goes into action without his sword is improperly dressed." As he dined on a mess kit containing soup, Churchill looked over at Tregaskis and advised him to obtain a British helmet for the mission, as some of his men might mistake him for a German if he wore his American headgear. Unfortunately for Tregaskis, the only British helmet available was a charred one formerly worn by a Tommy who had been burned to death. "The discomfort of wearing it," he noted, "was preferable to the prospect of being shot by a Commando."[23]

For the next several hours, Tregaskis shuttled between the different vehicles in the British caravan headed toward Messina. The vehicles were frequently halted by German shell fire and mines that blocked the roadway until they could be cleared by sappers, with Currie even lending a hand removing the rubble. In a broad valley north of the village of Tremestieri, the British column came upon a giant gap where a bridge had once been. "Our column halted, for the drop to the stream bed was too abrupt to be negotiated," Tregaskis remembered. He saw Churchill looking impatiently at his watch; it was 8:15 in the morning on August 17 and the colonel remained anxious that his troops beat the Americans into Messina. "Going to do a bit of reconnaissance," he announced, according to Tregaskis. The correspondent asked Churchill for permission to ride along, and the colonel told him to "jump aboard" his jeep. Although the correspondent kept worrying that at any moment German snipers would fire upon them or a squad of Nazi infantry would approach them from a side street and capture them, the small band made it safely into Messina. The first few civilians they came across ran away in fear, but finally a well-dressed man came upon them and indicated the Germans had left the city that morning; only a few snipers remained. The Sicilian, a doctor, said he was a friend of the mayor's and volunteered to guide the trio to him, sitting on the jeep's hood as they drove through the city's battered streets.[24]

Unfortunately, Churchill's dream of capturing the city was crushed when his small party saw an American soldier in the street. "Sure, we been in here two hours," said the soldier, Sgt. Pete Sumers of Sturgis, South Dakota. "The general took the mayor and the police chief back to headquarters." Tregaskis noted that there was at least some solace for the "energetic" Churchill, as he learned from the Italian doctor that about five hundred Germans had been evacuated from the city's southern beaches only an hour before Churchill's jeep had arrived. "The colonel, with his force of one driver and one correspondent, could not have arrived much sooner without being blown up or captured," Tregaskis recalled. Dropping off the doctor, Churchill, Tregaskis, and Holmes drove on through the city, looking for more Americans. They found them near a park, along with an unexpected participant in the celebration: Michael Chinigo, a colleague of Tregaskis from the International News Service, who had been covering the American Third Infantry Division and served as an intermediary in the city's surrender. Chinigo had walked ten miles to Messina, part of an original five-man patrol that also came upon more Americans trying to reach the city before the British. "At 6:10 a.m. we crossed the city limits and met the pathetic scene of a semi-dead city, with rubble-littered streets, gaping holes in the buildings and the razed harbor," Chinigo noted in his dispatch about Messina's surrender. Twenty minutes later, the patrol had found a building that housed both the Italian military command and the city's civilian officials. "Both groups agreed on unconditional surrender," he reported.[25]

The piazza at the city's center became the place where the Allied forces mingled. After talking with Chinigo, Tregaskis heard the roar and clattering of Currie's Sherman tanks arriving on the scene. "Commandos, smiling and shouting, sprawled over the exteriors of the tanks, and the little parade was made festive with many-colored flowers thrown by Sicilians," Tregaskis recalled. "Some of the dirty-faced soldiers clutched huge bunches of grapes." At about the same time that Currie had dismounted from his tank, an American staff car drove up bearing Patton, who got out and shook hands with Currie. "We got in about ten," Currie told the American general. "It was a jolly good race. I congratulate you." Although Patton later believed that Currie had been "quite sore that we had got there first," the British general, in a message sent after the Sicily campaign ended, seemed pleased with what his men had accomplished, writing, "We were a scratch force drawn from all quarters of the army, yet everyone worked together. The dash and determination shown by all ranks was beyond praise." Unfortunately for the Allied forces, while they had been preoccupied with the plaudits for taking Messina, the Germans and Italians had been able to evacuate more than a hundred thousand troops and ten thousand vehicles to the Italian mainland in an operation code named Lehrgang (Instruction Course).[26]

Capturing Messina also did not stop the fighting. Wandering about the battered city, Tregaskis could hear the booming of Allied artillery firing from somewhere in Messina. Looking out over the wrecks of boats in the waterfront and across the Strait of Messina, he saw "spouts of shellfire leaping from the water and into the sand on the shore of Italy. Some of the shells were falling into the buildings of the mainland. We had reached the gateway to the European continent." The enemy did not remain silent; they returned fire, and Tregaskis, who had been meditating about the closeness of Italy and Europe, was reminded "how dangerous that closeness could be." Shells started landing close by, and he scrambled to reach a nearby British scout car. As the vehicle's driver frantically attempted to start its engine, Tregaskis jumped onto the car's running board as it sped away. He soon realized he had seen the car before; it was the one manned by the enlisted men he had met on the LCT—Adlington, Fincham, and Bowles—who sped the correspondent to safety as two more shells exploded on the waterfront.[27]

13 "A GROTESQUE APPARITION"

Life magazine photographer Margaret Bourke-White had undergone a nerve-racking day in November 1943 near the front lines dodging enemy shells that whooshed into the surrounding hillsides and whistled over the roads in the Italian countryside about two hours outside of Naples. That evening she returned to the Thirty-Eighth Evacuation Hospital, set up near the hills bordering Cassino Valley, to continue her work photographing the heroic doctors and nurses who cared for the badly wounded American soldiers. One of the hospital workers expressed surprise at seeing her on her feet and walking, saying, "We expected to see you about now, but we thought they would be bringing you on a stretcher." Asking what he meant, Bourke-White learned that a well-known war correspondent had been brought in wounded to the field hospital just a few hours before.[1]

Curious who the journalist might be, Bourke-White went over to the new patient's bedside and discovered that it was her colleague, Richard Tregaskis, author of *Guadalcanal Diary*. Tregaskis had been brought in with a serious skull wound nearly identical to one she had previously witnessed and photographed, and the reporter had been operated on by the same doctor, Maj. William R. Pitts of Charlotte, North Carolina. Pitts had carefully removed approximately twelve bone fragments from Tregaskis's brain, driven in there by shrapnel that had penetrated the front of his helmet. Visiting Tregaskis, Bourke-White remembered that she had joked to the lanky International News Service reporter, "I suppose you don't have to be six foot six to reach up and stop a shell, but probably it helps." Hearing her remark, Pitts had chimed in to claim that the one thing that had helped Tregaskis most was that he had "a scalp like a bulldog—all corrugated. It made a sweet closing, sort of fell together." As for Tregaskis, robbed for a time of his speech and suffering from partial paralysis along the right side of his body, he could only remember that Bourke-White snapped some photographs of him lying in his cot, his head swaddled in white bandages. "She wanted me to smile and I tried several times, but the right side of my mouth resisted," he said. "Something like a grin resulted, but it felt lopsided, and the eyes were out of control."[2]

Just two months later, the journalists met again. They ran into each other at a North Africa airport awaiting a plane that would ferry them to the United States. Tregaskis had made a remarkable recovery from the wound he received on the afternoon of November 22 while observing U.S. Rangers battling German forces for control of the high ground on Mount Corno in the Venafro sector. Bourke-White noticed that instead of Tregaskis's head being covered in layers of white cloth, he now sported only a small bandage, about two inches across, protecting his head wound. She called Tregaskis "the bravest" among the group of battle-hardy correspondents she had known during the war. "Newspapermen are not compelled to go storming mountaintops with Rangers," Bourke-White said. "With Tregaskis, that inner desire to do truly firsthand reporting burned deep and clear." Feeling relieved at being alive, Tregaskis told the *Life* photographer that doctors had told him that once home he would have to have another operation to insert a metal plate in his head. "Maybe you'll autograph it for me," he said to Bourke-White. "What would be the use?" she joked. "Who is tall enough to read anything written on the top of your head?"[3]

Tregaskis's near-fatal wounding had capped an eventful two months of action covering the U.S. Fifth Army's September 9, 1943, landing near Salerno in Italy (Operation Avalanche), and subsequent attempts to capture Naples, a period in which he experienced elation and terror in equal measure. Tregaskis nervously waited at an airfield in Sicily with members of the Eighty-Second Airborne Division for a daring mission to capture Rome (canceled at the last minute), flew a practice mission in a Troop Carrier Command glider, sweated out a German attack that threatened to overwhelm a position held by American paratroopers in the hills near Altavilla, and endured a crowd of joyful Italians who mobbed his jeep when he and other correspondents had the honor of being among the first into Naples. That thrill was quickly followed by the brutal realities of war, including witnessing the ruined lives of Italian civilians. Accompanying American forces on the drive toward Teano, Tregaskis passed through the village of Pietramelara. "Entering the town we saw peasants in their rags," he reported, "some of them with bandages wrapped around their feet in place of shoes, standing in crowds looking blankly and helplessly at the piled hunks of broken stucco in the streets, the gaping insides of houses with wallpaper and furniture exposed like the tongue and larynx of an open throat." From one of the broken buildings, Tregaskis heard the voice of a woman screaming and wailing. As German shells rained down upon the town, the woman, described by the reporter as tall and emaciated and wearing a torn black dress, ran out of her shattered house and down the street, shouting hysterically, "How long will it go on! How long will it go on!" An American engineer, a bulldozer operator who had been sitting on a curb calmly eating the cheese from a K-ration, put down his food and commented, without excitement, to Tregaskis, "These Italians asked for it—now they're gett' it."[4]

Combat took its toll on those who did the fighting in a country that, as Scripps-Howard columnist Ernie Pyle observed, was "shockingly beautiful and just as shockingly hard to capture from the enemy." The seemingly endless series of hills and mountains, defended stubbornly by the Germans, translated into so many casualties that Tregaskis remembered medics, for the question "Place where injured" on the tags attached to wounded men, answered "hill." One day, seeking refuge after a full day of reporting from the front, Tregaskis spent the night at a medical unit in a church packed with wounded near the small town of Maiori. As *Life* photographer Robert Capa noted, the best place to "find food and a bed at the beginning of any invasion is always a hospital." Seeking a quiet place to rest, Tregaskis came across a young lieutenant from the 143rd Infantry Regiment he met before. He could see that the officer suffered from battle fatigue. "He looked lost," the correspondent recalled. "His eyes were sunken; his chin and neck jerked nervously in spasms, like a turtle's head poking out of his shell." The officer recognized Tregaskis and confided to him, "It's the God-damnedest feeling. I can't sleep, and I can't rest. I can't stop the jitters." In a nearby cot lay a soldier who had been shot in the neck, a wound that Tregaskis thought looked "rather innocent-looking." Medical staff tried to give the casualty oxygen, but to no avail. Tregaskis saw the oxygen inhalator's rubber bag inflate once, then saw it slacken and droop. A doctor came by to check on the soldier, looking under his eyelids and finding glassy eyes. As the patient's life faded away, the doctor turned away. "Well," he observed to Tregaskis, "that's the way it is."[5]

After the fall of Naples, Tregaskis could have avoided the grinding toil involved in following troops into action. He spent his time in early October and November writing dispatches about the efforts of American military-government officials to bring relief and re-establish normal life for the citizens of Naples. Tregaskis also reported on the country's political situation and the jockeying for power within the new Italian government following its surrender to the Allies. "But politics is not my field; I am a war correspondent," Tregaskis noted. The INS sent his colleague, Mike Chinigo, to report on Italian political matters, leaving him free to return to the war, something Tregaskis considered "not an unmixed blessing." He realized, however, that the attraction of covering combat acted almost like a drug. "After abstinence and the tedium of workday life, its attraction becomes more and more insistent. Perhaps the hazards of battle, perhaps the danger itself, stir the imagination and give transcendent meanings to things ordinarily taken for granted," Tregaskis noted. "The basic drama of men locked in a death struggle, with the stakes their own lives, offers a violent contrast to the routine conflicts in Naples."[6]

Preparing for the invasion of Italy while resting from his Sicilian labors in Algiers in late August 1943, Tregaskis had spent time making the necessary mental preparations for the coming ordeal. Lounging in the Hotel Aletti's sidewalk café overlooking the harbor, he had met Lt. Col. David Laux, chief of public relations for the Troop Carrier Command, the air transport group that had flown parachute troops into Sicily. Tregaskis had heard rumors that the command might play an important part in the Italian invasion, and Laux, although noncommittal, had indicated he would like for the correspondent to come along "in case anything happens." Pete Huss, the INS manager at Allied headquarters, later told Tregaskis that he had his choice, either jump into Italy with the Eighty-Second Airborne Division's 504th Parachute Infantry Regiment, or fly in with the glider-borne troops. Tregaskis, while scrounging for needed supplies at the public relations office—bedding roll, knapsack, mess kit, map case, and an air mattress, the "golden prize of every field soldier's possessions"—found a quiet room where he could sit and look down on the streets of Algiers and think about what was to come. "Always before a mission I try to calculate the odds," he recalled. "This is a dangerous job, no denying that. Airborne attacks always are. I figured my chances of getting killed or wounded would be three or four out of ten. I had the customary confidence that the worst could not happen to me; that chance would stay on the side." Across North Africa and in Sicily, Tregaskis noted that thousands of other men were also figuring out the probabilities of their survival. At least in his case, the correspondent added, he knew that the worse the conditions, the better chance he had to find an engrossing story to share with his readers.[7]

With the jump on Rome canceled, Tregaskis landed on the Italian shore with a small force of paratroopers in a landing craft on September 15. The next day, he learned just how precarious the operation had been in its first few days when he hopped in a jeep and drove down a dusty road on his way to the main highway running inland. While driving down the road, he was shocked to come upon four smashed German Mark IV tanks destroyed by American artillery fire less than a quarter mile from the beach. "The Germans had come that close to driving our forces out of Italy," Tregaskis noted. Stopping at the Fifth Army command post, Tregaskis joined other correspondents interviewing Lt. Gen. Mark Clark, the Fifth Army's commander, who attempted to rebut reports that his army was in bad shape. "Supplies and reinforcements are coming through well," Clark insisted. "We have our chins up, and we're keeping them up." The general's optimistic view of the situation was not shared by another officer at the headquarters, who informed Tregaskis that only three days before the Germans had come close to driving the Fifth Army into the sea and troops had been "ordered to hold on as independent units fending for themselves."[8]

To gain a better understanding of the situation, Tregaskis—joined by correspondents Seymour Korman of the *Chicago Tribune* and Reynolds Packard of the United Press—left Clark's headquarters to hook up with members of the 504th, who were moving up from Albanella for an attack on the town of Altavilla. "Boy, this certainly ain't like Sicily," Ray Justice, a sergeant from Huntington, West Virginia, commented to Tregaskis when he arrived at a hill on Albanella's outskirts. Tregaskis had no quarrel with the soldier's opinion. Unlike Sicily, he noted, the Germans seemed to have plenty of artillery to lob shells upon the advancing Americans. The enemy was skilled, heavily armed, and held the high ground, as well as possessing "aircraft strength almost as great as ours for a change." Through intense artillery and machine-gun fire, the paratroopers Tregaskis accompanied made it to their objective, a bare knoll edged with thick trees on a hill commanding Altavilla. Unfortunately, the patrol had only about sixty men to hold their position against the expected German counterattack. "Through the long hours of the night while the Germans continued to shell us, and toss machine gun fire, we waited for word from the rear," Tregaskis reported. "None came." Maj. Don Dunham had ordered two of his men, "all he could spare," the correspondent noted, down into the valley in an attempt to get through and bring back reinforcements. "We never heard from them," Tregaskis said.[9]

The paratroopers were hemmed in on three sides and shells were landing closer and closer to their positions. Tregaskis could also hear the short burps of firing from German Schmeisser submachine guns, a sound he registered in print as "brrdddt-t-t-t, brrdddt-t-t-t," with Americans guns responding with their slow rate of fire, "bap-bap-bap-bap-bap." Dunham had disappeared, hunting for a sniper threatening the American position. Trying to get some sleep, Tregaskis stretched out next to Korman on the stony, sloping ground, which seemed almost like a "luxurious couch" to the exhausted men. At about three in the morning, Tregaskis awoke when the major returned to tell him he had not been able to silence the sniper. "Things are not so good," Dunham said. "No support has come up. Somebody's got to get through and ask for help." Accompanied by Sgt. Henry Furst, Dunham decided to take the risk. He gave his map case and pistol to Korman for safekeeping, grabbed a Thompson submachine gun and two clips of ammunition, and shed his unneeded equipment. Dunham shook hands with Tregaskis and said good-bye in a way that caused the correspondent to believe that the major did not expect to return. Dunham and Furst slipped off into the night and into the dangerous valley below. "A few minutes later we heard bursts of machine-pistol fire, saw the sharp darting lights of tracer bullets amongst the black of the trees down there," Tregaskis reported. "Answering fires came from our weapons. We wondered if Don Dunham had got through."[10]

The major did not make it. While Tregaskis busied himself with digging a foxhole, Furst returned, and the correspondent could see that the sergeant's eyes had "the haunted, hunted look of a man who has been in mortal danger." Furst reported that he believed Dunham was dead, as he had heard "death-rattlin'" coming from the major's throat. That left only one officer, Col. Reuben Tucker, still available for action. Later, as Tregaskis continued to toil on his foxhole, a medic and Furst appeared and confirmed Dunham's demise. "The major's dead," the sergeant noted. "We went out and found him, and he's hit in the head, the neck and the chest." While safe behind the lines, Tregaskis learned that Dunham had been posthumously awarded a Distinguished Service Cross. Tregaskis wrote an article outlining the major's bravery, a piece published a month before Pyle's famous column from Italy about the death of another officer, Capt. Henry T. Waskow of Belton, Texas, a piece that appeared on the front pages of newspapers across the country. In Tregaskis's article, delayed from publication because of his own wounding, he recounted Dunham's death, writing:

> After that, I may say frankly, I forgot about Don Dunham: the shock of knowing he had died, faded in the strong and urgent light of the need that faced us: the fact that we were still cut off and almost helpless; that the Germans beginning at dawn would throw a tornado of artillery fire at us; and those men in camouflage suits that looked like awkward shapes of foliage would try to charge up the slopes leading to our hilltop; that tanks would be brought in to add to our torment; and that our colonel [Tucker], the only remaining officer who had not been killed or wounded but a man who lived for fighting, would hold us there till hell or relief came. These thoughts filled my mind then, and during the dawning, when the shells, tanks and charging Germans came as expected; during the day, when the shells came closer and closer; when there were bloody-bubbling wounds carved into layers of tissue by the score; when a nasty little tank came as expected and blasted away point blank; when, finally, through the squeak of sniper's bullets and the crash of shells some few of us got back to bring the word of need for reinforcements for those on the hill. Such experiences would stop the most confirmed philosopher from thinking.
>
> But after that ugly experience became a memory, we who had seen him go out to die thought of Don Dunham; and the steady, calm look of his eyes when he said "I'm going to try to get back." The mission he undertook had been a failure; but in his death he had been a success and a hero; no man who has that look in his eyes of knowing death and facing it willingly—can be other.[11]

Tregaskis faced quite a different challenge when, quite by accident, he and other journalists—Packard of UP, Noel Monks of the *London Daily Mail*, and Paul Green of *Stars and Stripes*—were among the first Allied forces to enter Naples. Tregaskis and his companions had started out from the village of Pontecagnano early in the morning of October 1 in a jeep driven by Pvt. Delmar Richardson of Fort Wayne, Indiana, a former dirt-track racer. They headed north over the coastal highway, passing through Salerno, Pompeii, and Torre Annunziata. The vehicle's progress was often slowed due to throngs of cheering Italians, who crowded the streets and pelted the jeep's occupants with flowers and fruit, all to the cries of "*Viva Ingleterra!*" that turned to "*Viva America!*" when they spied some of the reporters' American helmets. "We ducked to avoid the flowery and fruity missiles, except poor Delmar, who had to watch the road to avoid running over stray Italians. Bunches of grapes bounced off Delmar's helmet, and flowers and fruit littered the jeep," reported Tregaskis. "Suddenly Monks let out an oath. He had been hit in the eye by a package of figs." As they drove on, Packard remembered being suddenly aware that they were "alone in the heart of the immense city without an American or British soldier in sight." The crowds had thinned and Tregaskis began to worry about German snipers who might have stayed behind in some of the ruined buildings, as well as the possibility of enemy Teller mines buried in the road. Beyond the numerous windowless, smashed buildings, he could see the harbor in the distance. "The wreckage of broken cranes angled against the sky like awkward elbows," Tregaskis noted, "towering above remnants of sheds and storage houses. The once splendid water front had been blasted into a snarled mass of blackened girders."[12]

Keeping to the main road through the city, the correspondents finally reached the Naples railroad station, where they spotted a group of "ragged civilians" looking at them from a distance. The jeep halted, remembered Tregaskis, because he and the others wanted to ask the Italians if they knew if any Germans were still in the city or if any Allied troops had arrived. Before the reporters could ask their questions, their jeep was surrounded by a happy mob, some of whom had been able to bring out of hiding American and British flags, unfurling them with gusto for their liberators. "Men swarmed over our jeep, tried to grab us hysterically in their arms, tried to kiss our cheeks, and, when that failed, kissed our clothes," Tregaskis said. "I tried to push off three or four people who clawed at my shirt, and one man wanted to kiss my hand." Richardson was able to escape, avoiding the barricades of pavement stones heaped in the streets, but the correspondents ran into an even larger crowd in the Piazza Garibaldi, one large enough that Tregaskis worried that the jeep's springs would fail under the weight of those who attempted to clamber aboard. The reporters shoved the Italians off and Richardson again managed to escape. They permitted only a single Italian to stay with them, a man named Edward Capitelli, who had lived in the United States and spoke English. "You are the first troops in Naples," Capitelli told the correspondents. "I heard the rest are still in Portici. They haven't been here yet. Everything is quiet.

Most of the Germans left three days ago. We've been waiting for you. We're suffering." Thanking Capitelli for his assistance, Tregaskis and his colleagues left him and Naples and hurried to the rear to file their stories. As they drove toward Pontecagnano, they came across a British armored column and finally some American soldiers in trucks. After writing and filing their dispatches, the correspondents returned to Naples to spend the night, miraculously finding lodgings in one of the few hotels still standing, the Turistico.[13]

From the horror of combat and the jubilation of victory, Tregaskis turned his attention to the workday toil of the Allied Military Government, whose job it was to restore municipal services to the population of Naples. Before they left, the Germans had badly damaged the city's infrastructure, including its water supply and electrical grid. Tregaskis profiled the region's military governor, Col. Edgar E. Hume of the U.S. Army Medical Corps, who had reached the city the same day Allied troops arrived. Tregaskis learned that Hume was no stranger to Italy, as he had been in the country in charge of a relief expedition after a major earthquake and commanded American hospitals in the country during World War I. On his uniform Hume wore three rows of medals given him for his contributions by a grateful Italian government. "I'm at home here," he told Tregaskis. "A lot of these people very happily remembered me." Other AMG officials also had impressive backgrounds, including a former Los Angeles deputy chief of police, a former art museum curator from Kansas City, and a fire chief who had invented the fog nozzle. Because the Germans had confiscated "about half of the food and burned the rest," Hume said, the biggest problem was a food shortage. To distribute bread to the population, he worked to re-establish a normal flow of flour from the Apulia and Balabria Provinces. He also planned to use a system that had been successful when he served as the chief medical officer and commissioner for the Red Cross in Serbia after World War I. "We'll give the flour to a commissioner who will in turn sell it to the bakeries," Hume explained. "It will then be sold through the individual shops on a ration-card basis. . . . We'll dispense money through regular Italian relief channels, and the needy ones can do their own buying."[14]

Just a few days after talking with Hume, Tregaskis noticed that shops in the city were reopening and British and American soldiers had found their way into Naples hunting for souvenirs. "Shelves are well filled," he noted. "Canny Neapolitan shopkeepers must have buried or hidden most of their choice items." Among the rare goods, most unavailable in England or North Africa, were safety razors and blades, scissors, liquid shampoo, synthetic chocolate, and candied fruit bars. Cafés were well stocked with wine, fifty cents a bottle; good cognac, three or four dollars per bottle; and champagne, two dollars a bottle, while they lasted, Tregaskis reported. Clothing stores also had plenty of merchandise. "Attractive, full-bosomed Neapolitan girls, who have become affluent with mysterious suddenness, are thronging the streets, proudly exhibiting new sheer black stockings," Tregaskis said.[15]

In addition to GIs seeking keepsakes, Naples drew other visitors, including Tregaskis's boss, Barry Faris, INS editor in chief, who visited his star reporter on November 1, traveling to Italy from North Africa. Faris had an eventful day. It began early in the morning and included a visit to Prata, a village that had been the victim of a bombing by German demolition crews that had killed four civilians, prompting one villager to describe the one-time allies as "all animals"; a stop at the command post for the Second Battalion of the 168th Infantry Regiment, Thirty-Fourth Infantry Division; running for cover to avoid a strafing enemy fighter plane; and watching a bombing raid on Naples, a spectacle, said Faris, that rivaled "'The last days of Pompeii' in all its glory." Lt. Col. Ken Clark, a former Washington, DC, correspondent and chief of public relations for General Clark, had provided transportation for Faris and Tregaskis, who knew the driver, Richardson, from his earlier escapade in Naples. Also joining them were other reporters and a photographer, Jack Rice. "All seemed serene and quiet as we crept to the front through long lines of supply cars and various transport cars," reported Faris. "Richardson seemed to think he could get off to the front quickly and proceeded accordingly. Through the countryside which only a few days before had witnessed shellfire and bombings we proceeded in normal fashion. War seemed far away."[16]

Reaching the Second Battalion's command post, Faris and Tregaskis were being briefed by a colonel on where to go to see the most action when they heard whistles shrilling, the warning sounds for an air raid. The journalists raced for shelter in nearby foxholes. "Down the road not very far away we could see smoke rising from bombed sectors," noted Faris, who jumped into a shelter with Rice. "It was all over in a matter of minutes but it seemed much longer. War had come suddenly and unexpectedly, but as the others seemed unconcerned I tried to act the same." The party continued, reaching Fontegreca, a small village on the side of a valley that gave a commanding view into Venafro, which had been the scene of fierce fighting. Faris remembered that as the jeep they were in rounded the bend in a road, they came upon a fresh German cemetery. "There were 20 graves marked with the names and rank of the dead and a 21st unfinished grave," reported Faris. "It hadn't been half completed." As he peered into the graves, the INS editor could hear the artillery shells passing overhead on their way to "break up American concentrations behind us."[17]

Returning to Fifth Army headquarters, the journalists followed a column of empty trucks on their way to pick up supplies, which, as Tregaskis pointed out, "made a fine target for enemy strafing or bombing." The Germans did not pass up the opportunity. What Faris called "a sizable" force of enemy fighters and bombers appeared overhead. With the aid of his binoculars, Tregaskis counted twenty-four German aircraft. "Suddenly darts of golden tracer bullets spewed into the road, and a mass of little spurts of earth, like an inverted shower bath of fine dust columns, sprang up," he wrote. Amidst the din of American antiaircraft fire, he heard the "concentrated chorus of rattling machine guns and popping cannon, and realized that we were being strafed!" From the shelter of a protected slope, the newsman saw the white shape of a plane, probably a Focke-Wulf 190 fighter, screaming less than fifty feet overhead, speedily disappearing into the distance. Returning to his jeep, Tregaskis found Faris, "looking a little bedraggled" after having to dive into a clump of bushes to take cover. The editor had overshot his target and took a short plunge down the side of a small cliff. Safely back in Naples, Tregaskis invited Faris to go along on another trip to the front the next morning that would include five miles of hiking through the mountains. "I am declining," Faris declared.[18]

With Faris's departure, Tregaskis spent his time in Naples tracking down the latest news about the jockeying for power by a hodgepodge of Italian political parties and a purge by the AMG of pro-Fascists who had previously held governmental positions. Restless at being away from the front, on November 18 Tregaskis drove to Venafro. The vital sector was being held by a small group of the First Ranger Battalion, commanded by Lt. Col. William Darby, as well as members of the 509th Parachute Infantry Regiment. The rangers and paratroopers held the peaks of Mount Corno and Mount Croce, as well as the ridge that connected them, against the Germans. "The mountain mass, rising at the peaks of Corno and Croce to a height of more than 3,000 feet," Tregaskis noted, "commands the whole Venafro plain and also looks west toward Cassino." At the paratroopers' command post the correspondent ran into an old friend, Lt. Col. Bill Yarborough, who led the 509th. Yarborough's men had unearthed caches of food, blankets, mattresses, and warm clothing and had uncovered enemy dugouts measuring twenty or twenty-five feet across and seven feet deep. "It looks as if they're really dug in with the expectation of staying all winter," he said of the Germans. Yarborough invited Tregaskis to visit the mountain outposts with him, and the correspondent told him he would come back in a few days.[19]

On November 21 Tregaskis returned to the rangers' headquarters near the Venafro plain in time to witness an attack against German positions on Mount Corno. Peering at the slope leading to the top of the mountain, he could see flashes from American machine guns, and a few seconds later he heard the "slow-paced pap-pap-pap-pap-pap" sound they produced. An officer explained to him that if the Germans were able to capture the high ground of Mount Croce and Mount Corno, they would possess "a wonderful observation of the whole Venafro plain. Then they'll be able to blast hell out of all the artillery we have spread out down there." As darkness fell over the battlefield, Yarborough visited the rangers' post and told the correspondent that he and Capt. Edmund J. Tomasik, his executive officer, intended to visit the mountain outposts the next day. He invited the reporter to accompany them. "I accepted with alacrity," Tregaskis noted. He went with the paratroopers to their headquarters in an abandoned house on the banks of a stream that ran through Venafro. "We spread our blankets on the floor," Tregaskis remembered. "We joked about the vermin and the possibilities of being blown up at any minute. We talked about home and other pleasant places. . . . Then we heard the first shells coming." Fortunately, none of the deadly missiles made their way to where they were sheltering. "Waiting here on the floor was much more comfortable than lying in a ditch outside—and probably safer," he noted.[20]

After waking up the next morning, Tregaskis investigated the area and discovered that one of the German shells had landed only fifty feet from where he had been sleeping. Undeterred, he climbed into a jeep with Yarborough and Tomasik to gather material for an article about the rangers' efforts to hold their position on Mount Corno by using bangalore torpedoes to blast the Germans out of a cave they used to harass the American forces. The trio went as far as they could by jeep before finally stopping when they came up against "a virtually insurmountable slope," Tregaskis said. They left their vehicle and slowly made their way up a well-used, stony mule trail that led to Corno's summit. Looking down at the rocks underfoot, Tregaskis realized they were literally following a trail of blood. "This trail was the only negotiable route up the precipitous slope," he recalled. "Consequently, the wounded were bound to leave marks on the white rocks as they staggered or were carried down the winding path." Expecting to be fired upon, the men walked in single file, leaving plenty of room between them so that they would not all be wounded or killed by a single shellburst. They had some anxious moments when they could hear rocks tumbling ahead, but breathed easier when they realized it was only an American patrol. After a few miles of exhausting effort, they reached the American position and saw the rangers' commander, Darby, "grimy and disheveled." In spite of his unkempt appearance—a tear in his trousers exposed his long underwear—Darby, Tregaskis noted, spoke with his typical energy, telling the reporter, "Rough up here last night. The damn Krauts were giving us hell." Pointing to the top of the ridge, he added, "The sons of bitches were laying 'em right on there. Had to hang on so we wouldn't get blown off."[21]

Moving to an observation post higher up the mountain, Tregaskis watched through his binoculars a furious hand-grenade battle between the two forces and some excellent marksmanship by a ranger mortarman, whose shells landed close to the cave in which the Germans had dug in. He could see squirts of black smoke from exploding grenades, fires started by the mortar explosions, and a tremendous blast, probably the bangalore torpedoes going off. "Great fun, as long as we're dishing it out and not taking it," a ranger officer observed to the reporter. Rejoining his companions, Tregaskis started walking down the trail for the two-mile trip to their jeep, a journey he estimated should take about two and a half hours. "I felt a healthy fatigue," he said. "For the first time in several weeks, I had a bang-up eyewitness story of an action at a crucial sector of the front." He soon experienced something that gave him an even better story.[22]

Tregaskis spent a few moments talking to the rangers at their command post, telling Yarborough and Tomasik to go on ahead, as he "would catch up with them later." Reflecting on that day, Tregaskis realized that he had forgotten that the Germans had been shelling the trail daily, always at the same time. Hearing the approach of enemy fire, the correspondent, due to months of battlefield experience, instinctively threw himself to the ground seeking whatever cover he could find. It did not matter; shrapnel from the shell went through the front of his helmet and ripped through its side. "I knew I was hit right away. Sure I ducked. But not fast enough," Tregaskis later reported. He remembered experiencing rising and hovering for an instant. "In that measureless interval," Tregaskis recalled, "an orange mist came up quickly over my horizon, like a tropical sunrise, and set again, leaving me in the dark.

Then the curtain descended, gently." Regaining consciousness, he knew he had been badly wounded, but felt nothing. "Often I had seen badly wounded men—here and in the Pacific—and it had struck me that their lives had been filmed over by some barrier to the contortions of pain," he recalled. "That barrier was shock, the fortunate mercy of the wounded soldier. Now I knew that shock had dimmed my perceptions, just as I had seen other men cut off from pain by shock." Although his senses had been dulled, Tregaskis knew he had to make it to his feet and somehow find Yarborough and Tomasik if he had any hope of getting off the mountain before nightfall. After all, it would take eight men to carry him down "the virtually impassable slope to the nearest jeep trail, nearly a mile away," and, since he was alone, there seemed little chance of finding enough people to aid him. "The thought of self-preservation came strongly through my shock," Tregaskis remembered.[23]

In spite of the blood streaming down his face, the wounded correspondent, when he sat up, could see two men running by him in a crouch a few feet away. Tregaskis tried to call out for assistance, but his voice "rattled faintly like a broken gramophone, and I realized that the words didn't make sense. Surprised, I tried again and another time to make words: I had lost my power of speech." Hearing the approach of another shell, he automatically dropped to the ground, but the usually frightening sound of the shell and its explosion "were ghosts of themselves, almost comic," he recalled. A frightened soldier had sought cover among the rocks next to him, and Tregaskis tried to talk to him, fumbling over the words, trying to say, "Can you help me?" But he only managed to utter the question "Can help?" With other shells bursting down the slope, the spooked soldier could only respond, as he ran away, "I can't help you I'm too scared." Tregaskis realized that if he wanted to get off the mountain before dark, he had to get up and start walking. Writing about his experience, he noted:

> I saw my helmet lying on the ground, a hole like an open mouth in the front
> of it and another in the side. My glasses had miraculously been blown off
> but not broken. I put on my helmet and glasses unsteadily with my left arm
> because my right arm had been knocked out of action. It felt like a board
> by my side. I stood and began to stagger down the rocky trail. I dropped
> my helmet and stopped to pick it up and thought that it would be a good
> souvenir if I survived—probably that was the only extraneous thought I
> remember except that I felt my pockets to make sure I had my notes.

Then a shell was coming and I heard the same ragged distant whistling of the movement and the rattling, loose explosion. I was on the ground for a little time and then I found a medical soldier [medic] wrapping my head in a bandage and saw that he had stuck my right arm with a morphine surette but I was not aware of the prick of the needle. I picked up my right arm in my left hand and it felt like a foreign body and when I dropped it it fell inertly. Then the medic was gone and I became consciously alone and helpless.[24]

Enemy shells continued to fall around Tregaskis as he staggered down the rocky trail to safety, with one dropping so close that he believed he "could have touched it." The blast's effects towered over him "like a geyser, but I was not frightened but only startled by its proximity." As he walked on, a "red drapery of blood" ran down his face, his eyeglasses continually slipped down his nose, and he muttered to himself, attempting to talk clearly but producing only garbled words. "If anyone had been there to see me, I would have been a grotesque apparition," Tregaskis wrote. Seeking shelter, he found a cave a German had dug to escape the same sort of situation that faced the American. Tregaskis wondered if he would ever be able to catch up to his companions, knowing that if he failed, he probably would die, but "the mechanism of shock made the thought seem unimportant." He recalled being unconcerned about his predicament, likely an after-effect of the morphine he had received, combined with shock. "I seemed vastly good-natured and nothing seemed to disturb me—but the automatic force of my self-preservation seemed to be telling me what to do," Tregaskis recalled. As the shells faded in their intensity, he left the cave and continued to totter down the trail, stumbling over the rocks and falling automatically when he heard the approach of a shell. "Time did not seem to be moving fast or slowly; time seemed to be in neutral gear, but I knew that the distance I walked was long," he noted.[25]

Coming around the bend in the trail, Tregaskis finally saw Yarborough, who was bending over the body of an enlisted man whose arm had been blown off. Tomasik was also nearby; the two paratroopers had stopped to help care for the wounded soldier. The correspondent felt "a surge of pleasure at seeing them again, like a dog wagging his tail at the sight of some familiar person." At first, Yarborough started to wave at his tardy companion, but stopped when he saw Tregaskis's "bandaged head, the bloody glasses and red-stained shirt." Danger remained as the Germans continued to pound the trail with shellfire. Yarborough supported Tregaskis for the remainder of the half-hour journey to a command post in a peasant's house near the edge of a wooded area. The walk might have "seemed like a nightmare," remembered Tregaskis, who stumbled and fell several times in spite of Yarborough's help, if he had not been "shielded by the impervious barrier of shock. As it was, this was not a particularly unhappy dream."[26]

As he lay on the dirt floor of the house, awaiting transportation to an evacuation hospital, Tregaskis could see a line of soldiers standing by "with that certain fascinated, awed look written on their faces, as they stared at me, the badly wounded man. It was a novelty to me to be in place of the badly wounded man—and to know that those fascinated spectators felt more imagined pain that I did actually." After receiving sulfa tablets from Yarborough to help ward off possible infection and another shot of morphine from a medic, the correspondent stretched out in the back of a jeep for the ride to seek more advanced medical care. He continually sought reassurance that his notes and helmet were with him for the trip to the Thirty-Eighth Evacuation Field Hospital. "The air felt cool as we began to move down the steep mountain side," Tregaskis remembered. "A faint light hovered in the sky. It was late afternoon. The time must have been about four-thirty [p.m.], about two hours after I was hit." Once the jeep started off, Tregaskis lost consciousness.[27]

Staffed by members of the Mecklenburg County Medical Society and Charlotte Memorial Hospital from Charlotte, North Carolina, the Thirty-Eighth, veterans of the campaign in North Africa, had been receiving and treating a heavy flow of casualties from the fighting in the Italian hills that November, but none was as well known as Tregaskis. When the correspondent arrived at the hospital, Sgt. Clarence O. Kuester Jr., who was helping in the operating room at the time, remembered that "few people thought he'd make it." Major Pitts had already performed two brain operations before he started on Tregaskis at about two or three o'clock in the morning. "I remember when he came in he was virtually speechless," Pitts said. "Occasionally he could get a word or two out: he was semi-conscious, and his right arm was helpless and his right leg was weak. He was a diabetic and he was trying to get through to us that he was a diabetic. That was very important to know and he wanted us to know it, but it was very difficult for him to get through to us. Finally, though, he did." At the time, Pitts, described by one hospital staffer as "the best brain expert" he had ever seen, had no idea who he was operating on, seeing his patient as "just another man with a brain wound." It was only later, as other reporters came by to visit Tregaskis, that Pitts realized he had probably saved the life of the author of *Guadalcanal Diary*.[28]

For Tregaskis's four-hour-long operation, Pitts, as he often did on other patients with brain injuries, used local anesthesia, combined with a little morphine. "If you have a brain-injured patient," Pitts explained, "you want to test his state of consciousness, for that is your most important yardstick in knowing how he's getting along. If his state of consciousness diminishes, that's a bad sign." The correspondent remembered that the operating table seemed to be "a crude scaffolding of board," and he was placed in a semisitting position. Although the morphine had stupefied him, Tregaskis could still hear the doctor asking him questions from time to time, as well as "a crunching sound and a snapping of a bone as some sort of instrument gouged into my skull." As the operation continued, Tregaskis grew irritated, not at what the doctor was doing to his head, but due to having stiff legs from being tied down at the ankles (he had been given a blood and plasma transfusion through veins in his foot). Pitts noted that the German shell fragment "came in the front of his helmet and part of it hit his skull, part of it was embedded in his brain, and it had driven bone fragments into the brain, and another part of the shell fragment came out the back of his helmet." The scalp wound, called a "gutter wound" by Pitts, measured four or five inches long and an inch and a half wide, with the skull, the doctor said, "shattered over that distance and ten or twelve fragments of the bone had been driven into the brain. Part of the skull had been blown away, the brain was oozing out through the scalp wound." During the operation, Pitts removed shell fragments, the driven-in bone fragments, and the parts of the brain that had been damaged. "The bone was smoothed up and the scalp wound was closed," he added.[29]

The first few days of Tregaskis's recovery were "an agony of nausea," he remembered. He lay in a cot in Ward 13, housed in a tent with a dirt floor heated by a single pot-bellied stove. As he slept, his stomach always seemed to be "on the verge of revolt," and when he woke "it was always to retch." Although he had believed his surgery might improve his speech, Tregaskis was disappointed to learn that it had actually grown worse and his right side continued to be numb, making his arm and leg useless. "It was very embarrassing to try to say a few intelligent words and have something like 'boop' come out," he wrote. "I knew exactly what I was trying to say. My mind was completely clear. But my brain couldn't communicate the message to my speech organs." Unable to keep any solid food down, or even liquids, without vomiting, Tregaskis only began to feel better after receiving a glucose transfusion. He had plenty of company during his time at the hospital. In addition to Bourke-White's visit, such newspaper friends as Chinigo, Pyle, Clark Lee (an INS colleague who substituted for Tregaskis in the region), John Lardner, Bill Strand, and Red Knickerbocker stopped by to pay their respects; bring mail, which he could not read; and learn details about his wounding. When he was alone, Tregaskis brooded over his bleak future as "a writer with the self-expressive powers of an idiot, a war correspondent who couldn't talk or use his right arm or hand, or even ask intelligible questions." He was not the only patient who wondered what the future held for him. For those new arrivals to the hospital who could walk, they were given, he recalled, red corduroy robes with the white letters "M.D., USA" sewn on the pocket. The letters, the patients noted with black humor, stood for "Many Die, You Shall Also." Tregaskis might have cheered up a bit if he had been able to read a cable sent to him by INS founder William Randolph Hearst, who advised the reporter, "Please be a little more careful. Kindly report the war and don't fight all of it. Give Gen. Eisenhower a chance to do his stuff."[30]

Tregaskis continually pestered Pitts about how long it might take for him to fully recover. The doctor remained noncommittal, telling him that his recuperation could take as long as six months. Pitts laid out for Tregaskis what came next, including additional surgery to cover the hole in his skull (temporarily patched with scalp muscle) with a metal plate. One afternoon, however, Tregaskis awoke from a nap thinking he had dreamed that something was crawling over his hand. It was not a dream. He could feel "an electric tremor from my elbow to the tips of my fingers. It was as if something were prickling through all of the nerves, and the whole arm began to feel as if it were banging, like a door in the wind." After this incident, Tregaskis experienced additional feeling in his arm, he could see better, and could finally read his mail. Using a loaned copy of a *Pocket Book of Verse*, he practiced reading poetry "in an attempt to bring back my memory of the written word," as well as trying, badly, to entertain a night nurse he liked with a line from Lord Bryon, "She walks in beauty, like the night."[31]

As he improved, Tregaskis longed to be back in action, but because that appeared to be something that might take months, he began to get to know the other wounded soldiers in Ward 13. Most were officers designated by medical authorities as Class B or Class C, to be assigned, when recovered, to limited service or returned to the United States for additional therapy. Among those sharing the tent were Maj. Bill Hutchinson, a ranger who commanded a mortar section on Mount Corno, wounded in the foot by German shrapnel; Lt. Henry A. Pedicone, shot in the hip while sheltering in his artillery observation post during an enemy counterattack; and Capt. Stewart R. Dobbins of the Forty-Fifth Infantry Division, who had lost a finger on his left hand to a sniper's bullet. Tregaskis kept up the habit of engaging with his fellow patients during his stays in subsequent hospitals in Italy and North Africa. One of the correspondent's tent mates in North Africa, Lt. Richard M. Stone, remembered that he had "never seen anyone as intellectually curious" as Tregaskis. "Most of the officers here are glad to have a little rest," Stone noted, "but this big guy . . . is chafing under the restraint that keeps him from the various war fronts." He recalled that Tregaskis kept a typewriter under his cot and, when the doctors allowed it, spent his time "getting detailed information from the soldiers from beds nearby."[32]

Pyle visited Tregaskis on a couple of occasions at the Thirty-Eighth and noticed the improvement in his condition, reporting on his progress in his popular national column. When he first visited, Pyle noticed that Tregaskis could not control his speech, attempting, for example, to say "boat" and instead having a related word, "water," come out. "But he aways kept trying until the word he wanted came forth," Pyle reported. Doctors told him that while their other patients "usually lay and waited for time to do the healing, Dick worked at it," including repeatedly moving his arm to try "to get it back into action, and he read and talked as much as he could, making his mind practice." On his second visit, Pyle watched as a corporal in the medical corps came in hoping to get an autograph from Tregaskis on his copy of *Guadalcanal Diary*. Although uncertain if he was well enough to write his name, Tregaskis said he would try, and he worked at his signature for several minutes. When he was through, Tregaskis said to Pyle with pride, "Why, that looks better than the way I used to sign it." After the corporal left, Tregaskis added, "I always like to be asked to sign a book. It makes you feel important." Also, joking with the correspondents, a doctor pointed out that if Tregaskis had been short like Pyle (five feet eight inches instead of more than six feet five inches) he might have escaped injury. Tregaskis disagreed, with Pyle quoting him as saying that where he was the day he was wounded, with no cover available, even "'the tallest midget in the world would have got it.' He meant the shortest midget, but we understood."[33]

The greatest fear expressed by the wounded soldiers Tregaskis encountered involved the prospect, after being released, of being sent to a replacement depot, a "Repple Depple," and being reassigned to a new unit. A number of patients he knew told the correspondent they would desert and return to "their outfits at the front, go 'A.W.O. Loose,' rather than put up with the delay and inactivity of the Repple Depples," Tregaskis remembered. As they fretted about their futures—either returning to their old units or going home to the United States—wounded men were always interested in learning about the war's progress. But with radios scarce, patients, Tregaskis noted, had to depend on news bulletins "typed up and mimeographed by the hospital staff."[34]

On December 10 Tregaskis finally left the Thirty-Eighth, traveling by ambulance over rough roads toward what he later described as a "luxurious" general hospital outside of Naples. Doctors at the Naples hospital took skin from Tregaskis's thigh to create a "pinch graft" to speed the recovery of his scalp wound. He also discovered he could read better and now had the ability to write with a pencil. "The scrawl was practically illegible, and the act of writing was a great travail, but I succeeded in composing a few short notes to my family," he recalled. Tregaskis also began to walk on his own, at first a few steps, and eventually he could walk down a flight of stairs. Later, he had improved enough to write an account of his wounding and make daily notes about his time as a casualty. Finally cleared to return to the United States on January 14, 1944, Tregaskis, who arrived in New York by air ten days later, had seen in a North African tent hospital numerous mutilated Americans, including those who had lost legs and arms and others like him who had endured terrible brain trauma. Viewing these horrific injuries increased his vindictiveness toward the Germans. "My conception of war aims has become even more simplified than formerly: to crush the nations responsible for such suffering," Tregaskis observed.[35]

14 CHARLEMAGNE'S CITY

Peering through the flickering candlelight that offered the only illumination in a massive pillbox that helped make up part of the Siegfried Line near Palenberg, Germany, in the fall of 1944, reporter Richard Tregaskis could barely make out the mud-streaked faces of the American soldiers in their olive-drab uniforms who now occupied the bunkroom of their enemies. Tregaskis could hear German shells landing in the woods and U.S. artillery hammering at Nazi positions in preparation for the continued advance through the four-mile breach of the fortified belt that had stretched from near Kleve in the Netherlands to Lorrach on the Swiss border. Although tired and dirty, the GIs, among the first to break through the Siegfried barrier beyond the Wurm River in Holland, had to "take turns in the cold and mud outside to man the foxholes guarding the approaches to this pillbox because of the menace of a German counterattack," Tregaskis reported.[1]

The soldiers of the Thirtieth Infantry Division Tregaskis followed for the offensive into Third Reich territory had witnessed their buddies being cut down by artillery, mortars, and machine-gun fire. Looking out from their shelter, they could see a grim reminder of what the battle cost, the body of an American GI, the International News Service correspondent recalled, sprawled face down in the mud and grass. "His wet canvas leggin[g]s," Tregaskis noted, "stiff and inert, are sticking from under the raincoat thrown over his body." Also nearby, a dead German lay face up, his body uncovered. "Guns were banging outside—our guns—sending metallic echoes dinning through the pillbox," wrote Tregaskis. "There were a few score of crumping sounds coming from beyond the woods." The tired soldiers had endured much, but they saved their biggest complaints for faulty news reports that they had faced only "slight resistance" during the breakthrough, as well as a familiar complaint, Tregaskis pointed out, that the "slogging infantry deserved more credit—which undoubtedly is true."[2]

In his time covering combat, from the jungles of Guadalcanal to the mountains in Italy, Tregaskis had learned that as one progressed from headquarters behind the lines "down the ladder to the regiment, battalion and company, the war becomes more personal, even though there are only 'slight casualties.'" As he and the soldiers he gathered with in the pillbox knew, one of those casualties might well be a good buddy. That was also why the GIs were so eager to see their fallen comrades' names cited in newspaper stories. When Tregaskis tried to explain why he could not report on everyone, a private, Ralph L. De Roy of Pittsburgh, responded, "They deserve it, especially when they get letters like this." De Roy showed him a letter from a girl back home, dated two weeks prior, that read, "I hope you are well if you are in that little tussle going on in the vicinity of the Siegfried Line. How do you think you will like the Pacific after having experienced the European theater of operations?" Hearing what the girl had written, the soldiers yelled, "Put that in the paper!" Tregaskis obliged.[3]

Tregaskis had traveled far, both physically and emotionally, to ensure that those who sacrificed their bodies and lives to defeat Nazi Germany received the attention they believed they deserved. While American, British, and Canadian forces were hitting the Normandy beaches for the D-Day operation on June 6, 1944, Tregaskis was recovering from an operation conducted by army surgeons at Walter Reed General Hospital in Washington, DC. The procedure was aimed at repairing the hole in his skull created by fragments from the German mortar shell that had pierced his helmet in Italy. The procedure, which took place in late May, involved inserting a metal plate in the bone beneath Tregaskis's scalp. Researching what he described as an "amazing method of skull restoration," Tregaskis explained in an article he wrote about his experience that first the patient who is to have the "patching job" undergoes an electroencephalograph to chart the extent of any brain damage. As for the operation, he was "under local anesthesia, when I felt the cutting of the scalp as the bone was exposed; and then, the impact of the chisel and hammer. The surgeons were chiseling a ledge around the edge of the hole, so that the plate would fit in place. Once seated, the plate was fastened securely with small wedges of tantalum, just as a glazier fixes a piece of glass in its place." Talking with his doctors after the successful procedure, the journalist learned that the metal in his head was "a rare element, more like lead than silver in its atomic weight. It is pliable, relatively inert, and most important, it does not irritate human tissue, as silver and other metals do." Tantalum, however, could not do everything. Tregaskis had asked his doctors a question that he had been thinking over. "I wanted to know if the metal was bullet proof," Tregaskis recalled. "They said no."[4]

Before his procedure at Walter Reed, where he was awarded a Purple Heart by the government, Tregaskis had traveled with his wife, Marian, for a vacation in Florida. They stayed at the Driftwood, a resort hotel in Vero Beach. Although he still did not have full use of his right hand, Tregaskis took his voluminous notes with him so he could continue working on a new book describing his experiences in Sicily and Italy, especially his near-fatal wounding. "I am going to have to learn to work through dictation for a while," he said in an interview for his hometown newspaper, the *Elizabeth Journal*, adding that he had to do "an awful lot of x-ing out revising of the text afterward." Once he had a manuscript completed, Random House, the firm that had published *Guadalcanal Diary*, had committed to rush his work into print as soon as it could (*Invasion Diary* came out that summer). Marian kept Bennett Cerf, Random House publisher, up to date on her husband's progress, writing him that Tregaskis was working such long hours he would "need another vacation" when his work was done. By early April, as the couple prepared to return to New York, Tregaskis, according to his wife, had reached the homestretch on his manuscript. "He's gotten himself wounded and in the hospital all over again," Marian wrote Cerf. "After two months of this steady grind he'll surely be glad when the book is finished."[5]

Tregaskis had no illusions about what would be needed to finish the war in Europe and the Pacific. In his interview with the *Journal*, he had issued a warning to home-front civilians that the only way "to rid the world of its villainous gangsters is to be tougher than the toughest one of them." Tregaskis shared Col. William Darby's opinion that the United States could not achieve victory "by remote control," but had to take the enemy "close enough to shake hands with him, and then be able to walk up to him and knock him down." Given Tregaskis's view of the tough work to come for his country, he was shocked at what he observed while resting and writing in Florida: people paying $100 for neckties (with cats painted on them), gambling houses open at all hours, and visitors spending vast sums at nightclubs and hotels. It was just as bad when he returned to New York City, where he and his wife had an apartment. Theaters were sold out for weeks in advance, hotels were booked solid, and restaurants charged top dollar for their fare. "What has become of America? Don't they know there's a war on?" Tregaskis wondered. "Don't they know that boys are dying and being crippled and living in dirty-rain-soaked foxholes? Don't they know how close we came to having our cities bombed, our people killed, our children crippled and starved?" He lambasted civilians for complaining about food rationing, gasoline shortages, and crowded trains when "their own flesh and blood are suffering the agonies of hell" on their behalf.[6]

By late July 1944 Tregaskis had returned to action, reporting to the INS bureau manager in London, Joseph Kingsbury-Smith, with whom he got along well. Tregaskis wrote his parents that the "gang at the office has been very good, and all of my Army friends have gone out of their way to be friendly. Sticking at this foreign correspondent racket as long as I have does have its compensations." He had arrived at an opportune time. Since the successful D-Day landings, Allied forces had been stuck battling German defenders in the dense, centuries-old hedgerow country, or, as irritated GIs described the bocage terrain, "this goddamn country." The hedgerows provided perfect hiding places for the enemy, stalemating the advance before a July 25 massive bombing raid—Operation Cobra, involving more than 2,500 planes (fighters, medium bombers, and heavy bombers) dropping approximately five thousand tons of high explosives—helped to open the way for American forces. In his initial dispatch on his return to combat, Tregaskis had a perfect view of the death of a German panzer column, flying two hundred feet above the town of Gavray, France, in a small reconnaissance aircraft piloted by Staff Sgt. Bernard Brown of San Antonio, Texas. From the small plane, he could see the results of an attack by P-47 Thunderbolt fighter-bombers on a "closely packed flee-ing formation" that stretched for as long as four to five miles. "As we shuttle back and forth over Gavray, I can see about 250 vehicles—tanks, trucks and command cars—in flames," he reported. "This is only part of the destruction of German armored vehicles fleeing before the American advance south of Coutances."[7]

Back on the ground, Tregaskis joined the Third Armored Division and the First Infantry Division for the breakout beyond Mortain, which the correspondent described as "a blitzkrieg—American style." Looking down from a rise of ground on the seven-mile-wide escape route early in the morning,

Tregaskis had observed a platoon of enemy soldiers heading down a dirt road. "They thought they were in safe territory for their helmets were off and they were barely able to walk along," he recalled. "Suddenly they were blasted by our shellfire and their trucks were destroyed. A few minutes later a German motorcyclist rolled along the road and was potted." The action was so intense that the contending forces sometimes confused one another, usually to the detriment of the enemy. One night four enemy trucks pulled up in the moon-light alongside four American trucks and a jeep, "apparently thinking they were German," Tregaskis noted. "The German vehicles were destroyed and about twenty-five Germans killed or captured." The carnage pleased one American officer, who commented to the reporter that the enemy was "finally getting [a taste of] some of his medicine." Tregaskis also talked to a German prisoner, a clerk from a headquarters supply corps, who complained, "You Americans move too fast. There's no safe job in the German army any more."[8]

Reporting from what he described in his article as "a frontline town in France" in mid-August, Tregaskis came across a motley collection of the en-emy's infantry who had been overwhelmed by the speed of the American advance. These prisoners were not elite troops, but ill-equipped rookies forced, they proclaimed, to fight delaying actions at the point of a gun, sacrificing themselves so that Panzer, paratrooper, and Waffen-SS units could escape to fight again. Approaching three of the approximately two hundred Germans captured by the American unit he traveled with, Tregaskis first noticed that many were clad not in typical steel helmets, but soft, gray-visored caps. "All were anxious to please, and told how glad they were to be captured, principally because they were hungry," he reported. A thirty-five-year-old former factory worker, who had been replaced in his job in Germany by French prisoners so he could be free to fight, disgustedly told the correspondent that his company had not been issued rations for the previous five days, surviving by eating green apples and milking the French cows they encountered. "Five times on a two-week march from Germany, we had no hot food," the prisoner recalled. "Then we had to stay behind while SS troops going back left us nothing. We would have done nothing but a great big corporal . . . told me, 'we'll shoot you dead.' Those were his true words." Another prisoner verified the account, adding that every time he wanted to sit down and rest, he received threats of death from corporals, sergeants, and lieutenants. Lt. Col. Olinto Barsanti of Tonopah, Nevada, who led the unit that had battled with the Germans, did inform Tregaskis that the prisoners looked meek at the moment, but "they sure were giving us machine guns and mortars until we began throwing lots of lead in their direction—they didn't get meek until then."[9]

The prisoners Tregaskis talked to were lucky compared to some of their counterparts from the German Seventh Army desperate to escape the Allied armies—British, American, Canadian, and Polish—bearing down on them in the Argentan-Falaise sector. Near Chambois on August 22, Tregaskis came upon the shattered remnants of the enemy that had been hammered by artillery and air attacks while traveling on France's narrow, congested roads. Writing about what he witnessed, the correspondent noted that he had seen carnage before in the war, at Guadalcanal and elsewhere, but what he saw in France was far worse, so bad that GIs named the area Death Valley. "Everywhere—and I mean everywhere—there are bloated carcasses of men, horses and cattle," Tregaskis wrote. "Burned out tanks and trucks stand like tortured tombstones for unburied things. Ragged, shell-shocked, mumbling German soldiers wander through Death Valley, giving up—if there's enough reasoning left in them to know that surrender means surcease from their hell." Left behind were heaps of ammunition, food, vehicles, and clothing. American soldiers spent their time painting the "big white star insignia of U.S. forces on top of the captured equipment," noted Tregaskis, which to him represented a "symbolic end to an historic military job which this correspondent feels privileged to have witnessed." Gen. Dwight D. Eisenhower, Allied supreme commander, agreed with Tregaskis's assessment of the devastation he had witnessed. Surveying the area, Eisenhower remembered scenes that could have only been described by the Italian poet Dante. "It was literally possible," the general noted, "to walk for hundreds of yards at a time, stepping on nothing but dead and decaying flesh."[10]

American troops engaged in a profitable trade in German souvenirs with British forces in the area. According to Tregaskis, prized items included Luger and Walther pistols, German MP 40 submachine guns, and even horses. The reporter's jeep driver, Henry McDermott of Watertown, Massachusetts, surprised him one day by dumping a large load of German helmets in his lap. The haul included several "smart sponge-rubber German paratroopers' helmets." One of Tregaskis's colleagues, Paul Gallico of *Cosmopolitan* magazine, provided a moment of levity. Gallico had successfully bartered with a British soldier for a much-coveted Luger. After his cash transaction, he observed a red-faced Yorkshireman clattering by in a captured Tiger tank. Jokingly, the reporter called up to the soldier to ask how much he wanted for the monster vehicle. The Tommy climbed out and told the American, "Gaw! You can 'av th' bloody thing. Oi don't want un." Although Tregaskis believed the whole thing was a gag, Gallico later wrote that for him it had been the realization of one of his life's ambitions, namely, to "own a machine which some day I could slug it out with the tyrants and Tyrannosaurs of the road, truck drivers and trucks, on something like equal terms." The obstacles in getting his prize home, however, proved to be insurmountable.[11]

Traveling with the Third Armored Division, Tregaskis was impressed with the speed with which it struck at the Germans, but he also noted that such warfare could give "a man gray hairs, and possibly the worst scares of his life," as a correspondent often had to travel and cover the action out in the open in an unprotected jeep. It became normal for armored columns to be well in advance of infantry divisions. On one occasion, he recalled that the armored forces he rode with had been fifty miles ahead of the closest supporting infantry and were protected only by a small number of infantry riding in half-tracks. "Many times the Third Armored's tanks passed through a town and the Germans came back into the town behind the last vehicle," Tregaskis reported. "I remember one time when the jeep driver, two other correspondents and I became separated from the advancing column—an easy thing to do—and found ourselves in a German town, with several hundred German infantrymen and a few German tanks between us and the rest of our column." It also proved hard to tell what roads were safe as opposed to those "infested" by the enemy. This could prove deadly. The Third Armored's highly regarded commander, Maj. Gen. Maurice Rose, was killed in 1945 in a surprise encounter with a German tank unit while traveling in his jeep between one of his columns to another. Even those who manned supply trucks or served in headquarter companies were called upon from time to time to take up arms and fight off the enemy. One of the Third Armored's officers commented to Tregaskis, "It's getting so now that even the guys at headquarters have to carry hand grenades."[12]

With the breakout stalled for a bit as the Market Garden operation in Holland received priority for supplies, Tregaskis spent some time at the resort town of Spa, Belgium. While there, he heard news of a mission he had been trying to be a part of since his return to combat, hitching a ride on a "droop-snoot" Lockheed P-38 Lightning during a bombing mission into Germany. Although Tregaskis had nagged Gen. Elwood "Pete" Quesada, commander of the Ninth Tactical Air Force, about being allowed on a mission with the Lightning, which had the guns in its nose replaced by a transparent Plexiglas cap so a passenger could peer out, he had believed that the odds were about five to one against hearing anything more about his request. Surprised to hear his flight had been approved, Tregaskis ended up flying with Capt. Wayne G. McCarthy of the 367th Fighter Group, 39th Fighter Squadron, which was headquartered at the time at A-71 Clastres Airfield, south of Saint Quentin, France. The late September mission had the American planes attacking a rail line beyond the Moselle River in the German Rhineland. "If we were lucky, we might catch a freight train on the track," Tregaskis remembered. "Each aircraft had two thousand-pound bombs."[13]

As he climbed into McCarthy's P-38, Tregaskis, wearing a backpack parachute, noticed that the droop-snoot compartment in which he would travel had been equipped with a new, bright yellow cushion for him to sit on; an intercom system to communicate with McCarthy; and an instrument panel on which he could monitor the twin-engine fighter's airspeed, altitude, and other vital readings. The correspondent neglected, however, to check out one item he might need for the long mission, a relief tube if he needed to urinate. "Another item I should have checked, but didn't, was the oxygen system for me, the passenger. There wasn't any," Tregaskis noted. "But I didn't realize that until a much later and more critical juncture." Passing over the Moselle, Tregaskis caught sight of small villages and farms as they entered Germany. "Then everything was happening at once," he recalled. "We were at ten thousand feet, over railroad tracks like a set of silver threads over rolling hills. And we were diving, diving on the track, in a great roaring and whistling, with our nose down, and in the rush and scream, I saw that there was a toy freight train puffing below us on the metal band of the track."[14]

As McCarthy pulled up after releasing his bomb, Tregaskis's vision grayed over and he almost passed out from the g-force. As he strained to see where the plane's bombs had hit, the pilot informed him over the intercom that his bombs had failed to release and he had to make another attack, climbing up to twelve thousand feet and causing the correspondent to worry about his condition in the thin air. "Down we went again," Tregaskis reported. "It seemed to be straight down. I glimpsed the airspeed meter. It was reading around three hundred [miles per hour]. I gulped for air." Straining, he managed to glimpse out of his window in time to see an explosion on one of the train cars, which "slowly keeled over and fell off the track." As McCarthy zoomed up toward the clouds, Tregaskis heard through radio static that other planes in his flight report seeing "five bandits at angels eighteen, six o'clock." German Messerschmitt 109 fighters had joined the fray and were after the reporter's P-38, which had no machine guns due to the droop-snoot. McCarthy maneuvered his craft into a tight spiral to lose altitude to escape his attacker, causing his passenger to believe that his pilot had been shot and they were in danger of crashing. It also marked, Tregaskis believed, the first time during the war that a fighter aircraft carrying a reporter had been involved in a dogfight with the enemy.[15]

Relieved to hear from McCarthy that they were heading back to the American airfield, Tregaskis, after surviving another scare, a near hit by antiaircraft fire, began to worry about another problem: he needed to relieve himself. He proved unsuccessful at holding his bladder and realized "something vital had to be done. I looked at the magnificent, lemon-colored cushion which was my seat in the droop-snoot, and I felt creeping qualms of a schoolboy conscience. I hung on a few minutes more. Then I could hold on no more." After landing and struggling out of the nose compartment, Tregaskis remembered that McCarthy climbed out of the plane's cockpit and bounced over to ask what he thought of the mission. "I had to tell him the truth," Tregaskis noted. "'You scared the p– – out of me,' I said, 'and if you don't believe me, look at my cushion.'"[16]

Even while he barnstormed his way across France and Belgium and prepared himself for the push into Nazi Germany, Tregaskis, through letters with his parents in Elizabeth, New Jersey, tried to keep track of the critical and public reaction to his new book, *Invasion Diary*, in which, he noted, he had put everything he had available. "I was determined to get it out, or bust, and I guess I nearly did," Tregaskis wrote. "I feel that it's my big effort for the year. Everything else is extra." Before leaving the United States for Europe, Tregaskis had delivered a massive, six-hundred-page manuscript to Saxe Cummins, his editor at Random House. Although Cummins praised Tregaskis for being "scrupulously honest and uncompromisingly objective," he recommended that the manuscript be trimmed considerably and pointed out to his superiors a fatal flaw in this effort compared to Tregaskis's previous book, *Guadalcanal Diary*. Instead of providing vital information on a subject not many in the United States knew about, the new manuscript provided too much detail about "episodes in recent history [Sicily and Italy] which have been exploited by nearly every working correspondent," a point cited by some reviewers, who pointed out that most Americans' interest had moved on to the battle then raging in France. Despite Cummins' reservations, the book did appear on the *New York Times* bestseller lists for 1944, but it never reached the heights *Guadalcanal Diary* had reached. "It's been swell to get the clippings of the reviews, and subsequent news about standing on the best seller list," Tregaskis confided to his parents. "I'm glad the book's been there on the list, although after all the cautioning I've had from the Random House people, and the simple realization that the book isn't as hot news as the first, I don't expect too much. I do hope though, that it'll have a little more permanence, maybe a longer life and a longer continued sale. I hope."[17]

What set *Invasion Diary* apart from *Guadalcanal Diary* and other published personal accounts from other war correspondents was Tregaskis's recollections of his wounding in Italy. Random House realized this fact and emphasized it in its advertisements touting the book. One display advertisement from the publisher proclaimed that no other book "reveals so vividly the physical and psychological reactions of the wounded." In his review of *Invasion Diary* for the *New York Times*, Nash K. Burger complimented Tregaskis for writing about the Mediterranean theater "with the same skill and competence" he displayed with his Guadalcanal book, as well as for maintaining a good balance between the "achievements of small groups of fighting men, which is the frontline, and an over-all picture of the general plans and progress of the campaign." Burger noted that one of *Invasion Diary*'s best features was the author's firsthand account about the efforts to save the wounded by army doctors and nurses both in field hospitals and medical facilities behind the lines. Although Tregaskis's current book had less dramatic impact than *Guadalcanal Diary*, Burger noted it was simply because the "suspense inherent in the Guadalcanal operation was greater than that of Sicily and Italy.... At Guadalcanal the question was: Can we do it? At Sicily it was: How long will it take?" John Selby, a syndicated book reviewer, had an unusual complaint for the times, given that one of America's favorite war correspondents, Ernie Pyle, had partially made a name for himself by including the hometowns of the military men he mentioned, something Tregaskis had also done in both of his books. Selby groused that in *Invasion Diary* Tregaskis overdid "one of the hoariest of all newspaper maxims, which is the one about names selling papers. Names probably sell books, too, but in the over-all picture, nothing is gained by including hundreds of them."[18]

The typical authors' anxiety about reviews and sales faded away for Tregaskis as he immersed himself in the attempt by the First Infantry Division and Third Armored Division to capture the German city of Aachen. The correspondent had been particularly impressed with the speed of the Third Armored's tanks, half-tracks, and self-propelled artillery, as in just ten days they had driven across Belgium, crossing the Belgian-French border on September 2 and reaching Roetgen, Germany, a few miles southeast of Aachen, on the afternoon of

September 12. The division had averaged about twenty-five road miles per day. "Men and officers whipped themselves forward although fatigue dragged every motion," Tregaskis wrote in one dispatch. "They knew the war would end more quickly and with fewer casualties if they kept the enemy off balance." One corps commander admitted to the reporter that in its advance the division had "violated every known principle of the maintenance of armored vehicles and hoped they'd hold together. They did." The armored units had been ably supported by big P-47 Thunderbolt fighter-bombers, which acted "as a kind of winged artillery." While riding in one of the division's Sherman M-4 tanks, Tregaskis could listen in on the radio traffic between the armor on the ground and the planes in the air as they coordinated attacks on the Germans blocking the division's advance. He offered a sample of the radio traffic to his readers:

"You see that tank down there? It's shelling our men."
"Okay, I'll go down and take a look. I see him."
"Okay, then get him. That's got him."
"There's a lot more down there. There's four armored vehicles going down the road. We can get all of them."
"I just got another—that makes about 16, doesn't it."
"Maybe we can get some artillery on those babies."

The radio operator in Tregaskis's tank responded to the last message, passing it along with the proper coordinates. "Artillery picked it up in temp," he recalled, "and the whole woods ahead now are topped with a fat, far-spreading cloud of smoke and dust, and forward elements were moving again."[19]

Tregaskis remained with the Third Armored as its tank columns rolled into Roetgen, a border town approximately nine miles southeast of Aachen; it marked the first Nazi city captured by American troops. Those who had entered the city expected to be met with fear that would quickly turn into cold hostility. After just twenty-four hours, however, the tankers were astonished, noted Tregaskis, that several townspeople had smiles on their faces, displayed the "V for Victory" sign with their fingers, and gave them gifts of green apples. One soldier told the reporter, "Now that they know us they're beginning to cuss Hitler." Another member of the division said he had expected to see some "rough looking faces," but the enemy now seemed as happy to see them as the French had been. Capt. Jack Blinkhov of Mount Vernon, New York, a doctor who had established an aid station and spoke German, got to know the civilians who had remained in Roetgen and shared what he heard from them with Tregaskis. "One woman told me they are freer now that the Americans have come than they had been during the last 11 years," Blinkhov recalled. Everything he saw pointed to "terrific regimentation" throughout the population. As an example, Blinkhov said that a farmer had come to him seeking permission to kill one of his pigs. When the doctor laughed, not believing what he had heard, the farmer informed him that before the Americans came it had been "a capital offense to slaughter hogs without permission." One major reason the Germans in Roetgen seemed so happy to see the Americans, Blinkhov continued, was because their presence meant the end of air raids. "They have been living in big underground caves for three weeks," he added.[20]

As he continued traveling with American forces in northern Europe, Tregaskis began to realize that since his wounding in Italy, he had undergone quite a change in attitude. He had become quite sensitive to the dangers involved in covering combat, which made the sounds of battle "crushing and unbearable" to him, and he experienced "a succession of bad 'nerve shakes.'" He decided to test himself by plunging into covering the U.S. attempt to capture Aachen in early October. Originally, American commanders had hoped to bypass a direct attack on the city, instead having the First Infantry Division surround from the south, link up with the Thirtieth Infantry Division from the north, and convince the enemy to surrender without a fight. Of the approximately 165,000 civilians in Aachen, 145,000 had been evacuated, leaving only about 20,000 seeking shelter. Recent American and British bombing raids had also reduced many of the structures to rubble. Tregaskis described Aachen as a typical American city, that is, if it had "every house—every house—smashed to some degree by shellfire or bombs, with rubble, building stone, trolley-car wires clogging the street." Despite the damage, the German Führer, Adolf Hitler, refused to abandon a city that had been the birthplace of the emperor Charlemagne and had served as a critical symbol for the greatness of Germany, especially the Third Reich. Hitler ordered the approximately five thousand troops of the 246th Volksgrenadier Division to hold Aachen no matter what the cost in men and equipment.[21]

On October 10 Tregaskis waited a couple of hundred feet away from railroad tracks that marked the boundary between the suburb of Aachen-Forst and Aachen. Three U.S. soldiers—Lt. Cedric Lafley of Enosburg Falls, Vermont, a former teacher; Lt. William Boehme of New York City, who served as interpreter; and Pfc. Kenneth Kading of La Grange, Illinois, who carried a large white banner made out of pillow covers—prepared to embark on a dangerous assignment. They were taking an ultimatum to Oberstleutnant Maximilian Leyherr (later relieved by Col. Gerhard Wilck) warning him that he had until 10:55 a.m. to surrender his garrison or face sustained air, artillery, and ground attacks. "There is only one choice," the communique noted, "honorable and immediate surrender or complete destruction." Tregaskis noted that American guns hurled twelve thousand leaflets, printed in German, Polish, and Russian, into the city that repeated the message. When he and his comrades returned, Boehme recalled that none of the Germans they encountered seemed happy to see them. When they finally reached the enemy command post, delivered their message, and received a receipt in return, one of the German officers, a lieutenant, told them, "I can see you have good intentions and want to do the right thing. I will convey the message to the commandant through the proper channels."[22]

Lafley shared cigarettes with the soldiers who guided them back to American lines, and the GIs had to wait at one point "so that the Germans could take a drink of whiskey out of a bottle," Tregaskis reported. When the party reached the railroad tracks, Lafley did have to remind their guardians, "This is as far as you go." The Germans rejected the American offer, and after a couple of days of pounding by bombs from P-47 and P-38 aircraft and shelling from the artillery, grounds forces—two battalions of the Twenty-Sixth Infantry Regiment—assaulted Aachen on the morning of October 13. Lt. Col. Derrill M. Daniel, the Second Battalion's commander, noted that he and his men had come up with the slogan for the upcoming fight: "Knock 'em all down." After all, Daniel pointed out, Aachen's defenders would not be able to "deliver accurate fire with buildings falling about their ears." They had also determined to clear everyone out, civilians and soldiers, "from each building before passing to the next. We planned to search every room, every closet, every cellar, even manholes in the streets, to be absolutely certain that no German was left behind our front lines." It would be slow, he noted, but the "only alternative was to be subjected to sniping from our rear."[23]

For the advance, Tregaskis found himself with the infantry of Easy Company of the Second Battalion, which had pushed across the railroad tracks into the city's center at about 9:30 a.m. on October 13, throwing grenades to clear the path before them. The correspondent followed the company into Aachen at noon to the sounds of sniper bullets and small-arms fire as the GIs, supported by Sherman tanks, M10 tank destroyers, and antitank guns and resupplied with ammunition by M29 Weasel cargo carriers, engaged the

Germans. From his lookout inside a former school building, Tregaskis could see that the buildings in the vicinity all had their windows broken and many were "crushed in from the roof down." To him Aachen appeared as "a mass of burned, broken buildings, great craters—some of them so old the grass had grown back into them—and the streets glitter with broken glass that crunches and protests under the thick soles of advancing Americans." According to Capt. Ozell Smoot of Oklahoma City, Oklahoma, the commander of Easy Company, the initial opposition was "not as rough as we figured," adding that the Germans had not been resisting "as stubbornly as had been anticipated and were surrendering at every chance they got." The captain did warn that the Americans still had to "go through every damned building where snipers are hiding and dig 'em out." As he moved farther into Aachen, Tregaskis witnessed smoke billowing up from the city's center; it enveloped the Aachen cathedral's dome and spire and he could not determine if the historic monument had been hit, but noted that it "will be a wonder if it escapes all the destruction being hurled into the town."[24]

Among the prisoners taken in the factory district was the officer who had taken the surrender ultimatum and who had declared his men were determined to fight on to the death. A German lieutenant colonel, a veteran of eighteen years and decorated for bravery on the Russian front, had broken down in tears upon his capture, Tregaskis reported, because his military career had ended in such an ignoble manner. According to the reporter, the enemy officer had told his men before being taken prisoner, "I have led regiments and I have led battalions and I will be damned if I cannot lead a squad out of this mess." Later, Tregaskis spoke with about a dozen men and women, the "orphans of the war" who had stayed in Aachen, huddling in a dark basement, glad to be safe from the shellfire. One woman explained to the reporter that she and the others had tried to leave, but the trains had stopped running and they were afraid to travel by road due to American planes and artillery.[25]

The destruction only got worse and casualties mounted for Easy Company as it made its way farther into the city. Tregaskis learned that street fighting had much in common with the combat he had seen in the Pacific jungle. "In the civilized jungle which is a contested city or town, windows are bushes, houses are trees," he pointed out. "Every one of the thousands of windows, like every tropical bush or plant in the jungle, is a potential source of danger. And every house in a city, like every tree in the jungle, must be checked for enemy soldiers—probed by high explosive or an American foot soldier." The GIs blasted their way through the middle of a block of houses when they could, Tregaskis wrote, just as one would carve a path through a jungle's tangled growth with a machete. The agreed-upon technique involved blowing a hole through a wall large enough for a solider to walk through. "You see, when engaged in the war of the streets, you are supposed to stay out of the streets when you can; an anomaly when you consider it's called street fighting," he wrote. Streets, however, were dangerous to a soldier, as they were straight and relatively open. "A man walking down an avenue is a good target for a machine gunner or sniper sitting at any one of the hundreds or thousands of windows commanding the open stretch," said Tregaskis. Instead, he noted, squad leaders took their men through backyards and over fences and roofs; if they came up against a wall too high to climb, an officer would call for a bazooka team to blast it down.[26]

Tregaskis had an intimate view of what an infantry platoon went through in Aachen during a few days of fighting before Wilck finally capitulated on October 21. He attended a briefing one morning at a platoon headquarters in the tiled kitchen of a wrecked house, one of several such posts that day as the soldiers moved inexorably through the town. Lt. George Tragnitz gave some advice to his platoon: "I want you to clear out those basements even if you have to use a lot of thermite grenades. Give them a chance to come out. Yell down into the cellars and demand that if anybody is down there he must speak up. If you don't get an answer, throw the grenades in there." About fifteen minutes later, the platoon's squads began their push, which was signaled, Tregaskis recalled, by an intensification of noise, including the snap of M1 Garand rifles, the regular "tac-tac-tac" of Browning automatic rifles, and the louder explosions of bazooka shells and tank cannons. As a conscientious commander, Smoot circulated among his men, followed closely by Tregaskis, who joined him near the front lines. "Large guns were firing, swelling the clamor," the reporter wrote. "After another block, we saw two Sherman tanks squatting back to back in a little square. The muzzle of one of them was flashing out yellow fire, and the firing was filling the air around the tank with a mist of dust and smoke."[27]

One incident typified the bloody battle for the city for Tregaskis. As he crouched for cover with Smoot, two grimy soldiers hustled up carrying a badly wounded officer, the right side of his chest "an ugly blob of blood and red-soaked uniform 'Jesus . . . Jesus,' the wounded man mumbled." The correspondent noted that Smoot tended to the lieutenant, carefully cutting his torn clothing away from his gaping wound, feeding him sulfa tablets, offering "the tender, unprintable things that one brave man will say to another," and, now and again, shouting out profane words to someone to "bring up a stretcher, a jeep, a medic." The captain also had the presence of mind to notice that his men were bunching up, "as human beings instinctively will do in a time of danger," and yelled at them to spread out. A litter squad finally arrived and hoisted the wounded officer on their stretcher, promising him they had a "powerful" jeep ready to whisk him to the rear. As the aid men carried their burden away, the other soldiers returned to action, with Tregaskis noticing a machine gun firing to cover the soldiers' movement and a tank, "snorting and clanking like a pre-historic monster," pausing to fire five rounds at the house thirty feet away that had held the sniper. "Clouds of smoke, rosy with brick dust, ballooned out from the house's wall, smothering all sight of the place," Tregaskis wrote in his dispatch about the incident. "Then the tank went on about its day's business and when the smoked cleared there was no house, just more wreckage to add to the most-wrecked city I ever saw."[28]

Two days later, Tregaskis had a detailed view of another destructive phase of the fighting. He followed Tragnitz's platoon—veterans of the campaigns in North Africa and Sicily—on one of its bazooka team's "block-tunneling" missions. The correspondent had spent the night before with the first squad of the first platoon in the cellar of a German home, stopping first in the kitchen for a supper of scrambled eggs, a staple dish prepared for him by Pfc. Ed Gaetke from Saint Paul, Minnesota. One of the few advantages of fighting in Aachen was that soldiers discovered that kitchen larders were well stocked with such items as home-canned vegetables, hen and goose eggs, bread, cakes, and preserves. "Two or three members of the squad sat watching and whispering among the debris of the elaborate kitchen," Tregaskis remembered, "and periodically one of the men standing guard outside poked his head in and shushed us, reminding us that there were Germans on the other side of the street." The reporter and the squad retired to the basement, where the previous occupants had erected a makeshift shelter under arches of whitewashed bricks, equipped with three beds with sheets and blankets. From a tiny piece of paper, Sgt. Julius Oster, a veteran from Borough Park, Brooklyn, read the names of those taking successive three-hour watches. "They'd work in pairs: Kroll and Lawrence, Smith and Gaetke, Vereroni and Murphy, and so on," Tregaskis wrote. "The sergeant said that things would probably be O.K. for the night; if a Heinie patrol jumped us, there was another cellar room beyond this, with windows." The sergeant's statement had the reporter having visions of six to eight Americans attempting to find their way through the pitch dark and through the windows as enemy soldiers followed and shot at them. After a late night of sharing stories about "characters" who had been in the squad but had been killed, the men finally went to sleep, only to be awakened by enemy shells landing around the building, with "two landing practically on top of us," noted Tregaskis. He listened for the loud cries of a wounded man, but none came. "Everyone woke up, and after a pause somebody said something about being afraid the beer bottles upstairs would break," he wrote. "That released the tension."[29]

Early the next morning, Tregaskis followed the first squad of the first platoon through hallways, kitchens, two gardens, over an iron fence, over two garage roofs, through an alley, and through a school just to travel one block. On approaching a wall too high to surmount, a bazooka team knocked a hole through the wall so the GIs could push ahead. Although they had been able to outflank the streets, soldiers still had to investigate each house they had bypassed. Tragnitz's squads had developed a procedure for handling Aachen's buildings, Tregaskis wrote:

> The men moved fast, running most of the time, keeping under cover when possible, for they knew that they might run into enemy fire at any time, from any house. The technique was this: the G.I. would run up onto the front porch, place the muzzle of his rifle at the lock, blow off the lock, kick in the door, rushing in with the rifle at the ready; then you'd hear him yelling from inside as he presumably banged on every door and checked every room. I listened to one soldier bawling steadily, "Let's go! Come out, come out, you —— Heinies!"
>
> Occasionally, there'd be a blast or two inside the house, like a muffled cannon, as the men shot off locks or tossed grenades into suspicious rooms. First, however, they gave plenty of vocal warning to any possible civilians inside, in accordance with instructions.
>
> And once, in this line of houses, they did unearth civilians. There was a commotion, a blur of sobbing voices, and out came a short, fat, bespectacled German, a very scare[d] man wearing a tweed suit and stiff white collar, his stubby arms elevated in token of surrender. His sobbing *Frau* followed, her arms similarly raised. Desperate fear marked their faces, as if they expected to be shot. The German propaganda leaders had forecast that the Americans would be looters, beasts and rapists.

The worried fat man in the tweed suit trotted down the middle of the street, with an occasional apprehensive glance to the rear to see whether he was going to be murdered. He and his wife passed the corner where I was standing, and hurried half a block beyond; and then, when they found out they were not going to be shot, they stopped, carefully lowered their hands, and the man straightened his vest and reassumed his dignity.[30]

The strain of street fighting in Aachen took a toll on Tregaskis, who worked, as he wrote his parents, day and night. To satisfy his employers' call for stories about the battle, he had little time for anything else except for a walk in the evening before bed when the "sky isn't pouring rain." He had endeavored to keep pace with the other news services, organizations such as the Associated Press and United Press, each of which employed two men to tackle the assignment. "I'm alone and must watch news breaks night and day, on all fronts," he told his parents. Tregaskis had asked his editor, Barry Faris, to send someone to assist him so he could take a little time off or even return to the United States for a rest. "The office is very reluctant to let me go home," he noted, "but I can always just get up and go if I want to; that's one nice thing about not being in the Army. And perfectly proper, provided I give notice that I'm leaving."[31]

In addition to being overworked, Tregaskis had been shaken by a tragedy involving one of his colleagues, David Lardner, the son of the famous writer and humorist Ring Lardner. David had just been accredited to cover the war for the *New Yorker*; his brother, John, had been writing about the war for *Newsweek* for some time and had been with the first American troops sent to Australia. "More introverted than John, Dave was also a more skillful and unique writer," Tregaskis noted. On October 19 Lardner, Tregaskis, and Russell Hill of the *New York Herald Tribune* had gone up to the front; Tregaskis was set to stay in Aachen, while Lardner and Hill talked to him about the road back to Eupen, the site of First Army headquarters across the border in Belgium, where they were headed to write their stories. "I advised against following the main highway," Tregaskis recalled. "There were too many areas marked with engineers' tape, the route hadn't been demined. It was better to follow the more tedious, intricate back-road pattern which the tank columns of the Third Armored had taken." Lardner, Hill, and their driver, however, took a jeep down the main highway and on the way hit a German Teller mine on Aachen's outskirts. "Lardner sustained severe wounds from fragments, and, without regaining consciousness, died at 9:10 p.m. in a field hospital, five hours after the accident occurred," Tregaskis wrote in an article about the accident. The driver was also killed, while Hill suffered a broken right arm and a forehead laceration. "I should have been more insistent," Tregaskis later lamented.[32]

By November Tregaskis had returned to the United States, seized by a fever to write something about what he had gone through in Aachen. After seeing so many bloodbaths, he believed he had the right to "say what war seemed to mean to the infantrymen who fought in it." This time it would not be presented in a nonfiction, diary format, but in fiction through a character, named Capt. Paul Kreider, who fought a battle with fear in a city like Aachen that Tregaskis called Unterbach. Tregaskis found that writing fiction was like "working your way out onto the ice, trying this and that way to get to where you want to go, and hoping that your general plan and the place you think you are trying to get to are the right ones, and not some horrible suicidal mistake." After a couple of months of what he called "frenzied work," he produced the short novel *Stronger Than Fear*, which grew out of watching the men of the Twenty-Sixth Infantry Regiment and Captain Smoot. Tregaskis said he believed he had been able to strike closer to the heart of war than the previous books he had written, as his fiction touched on "the basic human values involved in war, aside from politics or patriotism. It was a strange paradox that in a way of life devoted to killing, maiming and destruction of the enemy, men could be kinder and more unselfish and self-sacrificing towards those on his own side than he had ever been before or probably ever would be if he survived the war."[33]

By May 1945 Tregaskis was not out promoting his soon-to-be released debut novel, but on his way to a familiar region—the Pacific—this time for a new employer, a national magazine that had been a mainstay in middle-class homes since the 1920s, the *Saturday Evening Post*. His task involved following the crew of a weapon—the B-29 Superfortress—meant to level Japan's ability to wage war in the Pacific and force the nation to surrender. While in Guam flying missions with a B-29 crew bombing the Japanese petroleum industry, Tregaskis finally received copies of *Stronger Than Fear*, which he had dedicated "to the valor of the infantry, the soldiers without armor who are the vanguard of every attack." Although the aviators he had grown to know had no experience in street fighting, the book, Tregaskis relayed to a friend at Random House, had convinced one of the pilots that "sweating out street fighting must be a lot like sweating out a bombardment mission. Which made me feel good, because I think there's a fundamental similarity in all kinds of fighting." Although some reviewers believed that the war correspondent should have stuck to nonfiction, some critics viewed the correspondent's venture into fiction a success, including Francis Hackett, whose piece in the *New York Times* Tregaskis believed was the "sharpest appreciation of everything I tried to say in the book." Of all the books on the war, Hackett wrote, Tregaskis's small, 144-page volume came nearest to making those on the home front feel why those who have returned from the fighting cannot seem to talk about what they experienced. "As a novel it is seemingly artless," noted Hackett. "But it has enough art to make you say, 'this is it,' and to bring the whole thing home to you." He went on to praise the novel as "grimly honest, but with beauty and consolation in it" as well. There would be much more grimness to follow as Tregaskis traveled the dangerous road seeking final victory.[34]

15 SUPERFORTRESS NUMBER 688

Shortly after midnight on June 30, 1945, as the B-29 Superfortress bomber Number 688 reached the initial point on its bomb run, Lt. Paul R. Ceman announced, "Number 4 is gone." Reporter Richard Tregaskis had been with the bright silver aircraft—the most advanced of its time—and its ten-man crew since it had left its Kansas training base for combat service with the 315th Bombardment Wing on Guam in the Pacific. He and the others jammed together in the cockpit craned their necks to see what might be wrong with the 2,200-horsepower Wright Cyclone engine on the outboard edge of the right wing. It appeared as if the engine had lost manifold pressure. "Looking out through the driving fog I could see no outward sign that it was out of commission: the big propeller seemed to be turning," Tregaskis remembered. Still, the cabin floor had begun to vibrate, so much so that the tail gunner had called over the intercom expressing alarm, reporting, "We're having quite a bit of trouble with vibration."[1]

The engine trouble occurred at an awkward time on the crew's approximately three thousand-mile roundtrip mission as one of thirty-six B-29s set to strike the Nippon Oil Company's refinery at Kudamatsu off the coast of Japan's Honshu Island. As the bomber closed in on its target, and Tregaskis and the others struggled to don their flak suits and parachutes and put on their oxygen masks, the aircraft was surrounded by "a tight ocean of 'soup' and a needle-like torrent of precipitation drummed against the bombardier's nose window," Tregaskis reported. Those in the plane's nose were keeping a sharp lookout for possible ice on the wings when the number four engine suffered what they later learned was a valve problem. Number 688's pilot, Capt. Bob "Pappy" Hain, a veteran of numerous missions over Europe in a B-17 Flying Fortress, remained unperturbed despite the glitches on this mission, only the crew's second against the Empire of Japan. Hain calmly commented about the vibration: "I don't feel anything excessive." The pilot remained confident, Tregaskis later noted, that the plane could reach the oil refinery and make it back to North Field on Guam, if need be, "with three or three and a half" engines.[2]

Hain's confidence in his plane and crew was rewarded, as the Superfortress made it to the target. "I unclipped my mask from my cumbersome oxygen bottle; it was too clumsy to permit movement and I wanted to see," Tregaskis wrote. "I half stood up, peering into the fog over the top of the bombardier's helmet. I saw flashes ahead; a blue flash stabbing through the mist, and next to it, a sudden rosy glow projected on the softness of the fog, to the left. These would be the bomb flashes of the B-29s ahead of us, and perhaps an oil explosion they had caused." Finally, the correspondent heard a report over the intercom, "bombs away!" As the B-29 plunged out of the fog and reached its top speed to avoid enemy antiaircraft fire and fighter planes sent to track it down, Hain, Tregaskis recalled, had a brief conversation with his precision-instrument operator, Lt. John Bond. "How'd it look?" Hain asked. "I think they [the bombs] were pretty close in," Bond responded.[3]

Unlike the crew of the Superfortress he flew with, who were rookies in the fight against the Japanese, the Pacific theater of operations was familiar territory to Tregaskis, the veteran of the Doolittle mission, the Battle of Midway, and the invasion of Guadalcanal. What was new for the war correspondent was the publication that was printing his stories. Instead of having his dispatches distributed to U.S. newspapers by the International News Service, Tregaskis's work appeared regularly in the pages of the *Saturday Evening Post*, owned and operated by the Curtis Publishing Company in Philadelphia, Pennsylvania. With a legacy stretching back to the days of Benjamin Franklin, the *Post* was a mainstay in middle-class American homes through the steady hand of its longtime editor, George Horace Lorimer, the son of a Boston minister. Millions of readers turned to the magazine each week for the artwork of Norman Rockwell, whose idealized drawings of American family life were featured on more than three hundred of the magazine's covers, as well as for short stories from such notable writers as F. Scott Fitzgerald, Sinclair Lewis, Ring Lardner, C. S. Forester, John P. Marquand, William Saroyan, and John Steinbeck. The

Post had hired Tregaskis to produce a new series, "Road to Tokyo," promising its subscribers that week by week they would share the dreams, heartaches, and heartbeats of the fighting men responsible for winning final victory over Japan. "Whether in the air, on sea or land he [Tregaskis] will live, eat, sleep, fight and sweat with them to bring you every week . . . the side of war you seldom read about," the magazine promised in advertisements touting its new feature. Tregaskis had been preparing himself physically for the grind of covering combat, walking ten miles and swimming an hour per day in a New York pool. When *Post* managing editor Robert Fuoss asked him if he really wanted to go to the Pacific, Tregaskis answered, "I don't want to, but I think I ought to go." His new situation offered him an opportunity to discover more about the "small personal conflicts which made up the bulk of a soldier's, sailor's or airman's life," Tregaskis later realized. "Even when he was in action, the dangerous moments were very few; the bulk of a man's life was concerned with his friends and enemies in his squad or squadron, his likes or dislikes of his superiors, his letters to and from home, his liberties or leaves, the local females he tried to make or decided not to try to make."[4]

For his "Road to Tokyo" series, Tregaskis not only accompanied a B-29 crew for five missions, but he also flew in combat on a Grumman TBM Avenger torpedo bomber stationed on the USS *Ticonderoga* and followed Gen. Douglas MacArthur's military government section to Tokyo at the war's end. It was not the first time Tregaskis had contributed to the *Post*, which praised him as "essentially a frontline reporter and one of the best." The magazine's February 24, 1945, issue included his detailed piece, titled "House to House and Room to Room," on the street fighting he had endured in Aachen with soldiers of the First Infantry Division. With victory in Europe obtained by Germany's surrender to the Allies on May 8, the *Post* intended to give Tregaskis free rein to report on what it hoped would be "human, intimate" tales of the men battling a nation, Japan, that had once haughtily proclaimed it was "looking forward to dictating peace in the United States in the White House at Washington."[5]

The veteran war correspondent started his journey in America's heartland, at a processing base in Herington, Kansas, meeting the veterans and rookies of the U.S. Army Air Forces he would fly with on bombing missions against Japan aboard one of the most complex machines ever devised to wage war, Boeing's B-29 Superfortress, an aircraft with thousands of miles of wires, fifty thousand separate parts, and a million rivets holding it all together. U.S. Army Air Forces general Henry A. "Hap" Arnold said that the idea for the long-range, four-engine bomber had been inspired by the early days of the war "when it appeared that England would go down to defeat, and there'd be no place where we might base our planes for future sorties against the Axis powers. Thus a much longer ranged bomber than any we then possessed would be essential to waging a victorious war."[6]

From the first, when he met the crew of Number 688 preparing to leave its Kansas training base for Mather Field in Sacramento, California, Tregaskis realized flying such a "huge but delicate machine" would be more complex than any other piece of military equipment he had ever encountered. (The B-29 was also the most expensive weapons project developed during the war, even outstripping the cost for the Manhattan Project that produced the atomic bomb.) "Even before starting engines," the correspondent noted, "I found the pilot must check on twenty-seven things, including the following: emergency-cabin press release (to let out oxygen from the air-conditioned cabins if something should go wrong with the pressurized machinery); hydraulic pressure, main and emergency; auxiliary power plant (to start engines); turbos (which provide high-altitude power and blow exhaust gases through a cooler to maintain cabin pressure); very-high-frequency radio set; emergency landing-gear release for the new-type tricycle landing gear." The checklists for the other crew members housed in the plane's nose were equally extensive, he added, and the details of each man's responsibilities were honed after months of training. Superfortress Number 688 was also part of a revised series—B-29Bs—that were stripped of all guns (except for the tail position) and sighting equipment to save weight. It also had on board the advanced AN/APQ Eagle radar unit that was ten times more efficient than previous models when it came to bombing navigation, giving its operator an enhanced view of the ground, even through thick fog. "You had to treat the B-29 like a baby, but if you did right by it, it would really perform," Tregaskis wrote.[7]

Initially, Tregaskis had hoped he could join an intact, veteran crew rotating from service in Europe. He learned, however, that air forces officials intended to reshuffle and retrain European crews, and, if he wanted to fly out to the Pacific with a "typical crew, then I would fly by B-29, and that I would find only one or two veterans of the European war in said crew, at the most—perhaps a bombardier or navigator who had flown with the 8th or 9th or 15th [Air Forces], and the rest would be men who had never seen combat before." Officials saw no reason for using the relatively light-load bombers used in Europe when a B-29 could carry five times as many bombs as a B-17 Flying

Fortress or a B-24 Liberator, and carry such a load, the reporter noted, with "very little more gasoline, at greater speed, and with far smaller total ground facilities required for maintenance."[8]

By luck, Tregaskis drew an experienced pilot, Hain, a native of Hollister, California, and his navigator, Lt. Dean Coleman, who both had flown fifty missions together with the Fifteenth Air Force, returning from one raid on Naples with sixty-five holes made by flak peppering their Fortress. Because of his combat record flying missions over Italy, Germany, and Austria, the thirty-year-old Hain, nicknamed "Pappy" by his crew for his advanced age and receding hairline, could have returned to his family's walnut farm. Asked by the correspondent why he decided to stick his neck out for another tour of duty, Hain said he had felt "kind of foolish, being hale and hearty, getting out now, with all the others gone. . . . And I mean gone for good." He also pointed out that the opposition in Japan would not match what he had faced in the skies over Europe when it came to enemy fighters and antiaircraft batteries. "It doesn't seem like there are many Jap fighters, and the flak isn't going to be the same as with the mediums (medium bombers) in Europe," Hain told Tregaskis. "We can get up to thirty thousand feet [in a B-29], and the flak isn't so thick up there." Coleman shared Hain's sense of duty but remained clear-eyed about the chance he took remaining in such a dangerous job. He pointed out to Tregaskis that out of the ninety-seven navigators in his original class, no more than thirty had survived their sorties over Europe; the odds looked grim for surviving the thirty-five missions over Japan that he needed for a ticket home.[9]

It took three weeks for the crew of Number 688 to fly from Kansas to California and on to Hawaii, Kwajalein Atoll in the Marshall Islands, and, finally, reach its home base on Guam in the Mariana Islands. "We could have done better by slow freight," one of the crew groused to the reporter. Tregaskis was reminded of a sign he had seen in some of the Air Transport Command terminals he had visited: "If you have plenty of time, travel by air." During his long journey, Tregaskis became well acquainted with the aircraft's officers and enlisted men. "But the crew of 688 is more than an average crew," he wrote. "It is a sort of microcosm in which one of the great historical facts of this war can be studied: the shift of gigantic military power from one theater of war, where the greatest enemy has been crushed, to the other side of the world, to smash into the ground the third and last of the gangster nations." In addition to the European veterans, Hain and Coleman, the crew consisted of Ceman, the young copilot; Bond, the precision-instruments operator; Flight Officer

Dominic "Moe" Martelli, the bombardier; Cpl. Paul Angelo, radio operator and the self-confessed Don Juan of the outfit; Cpl. Clarence Dawson, the hard-working engineer; Cpl. Raleigh Marr, the tail gunner; and Cpls. Art Manning and Ed Marchalonis, the gunners/observers. Although dedicated and professional, the crew could not help but think about the war finally ending. As the crew and Tregaskis, dusty and tired, waited for transportation to their barracks after landing at Mather Field, the correspondent said that the "feeling of being in a strange place, and heading for stranger and more forbidding ones," depressed them all. Ceman put the feeling into words when he said, "It looks like the last lap. I wish we were coming in, instead of going out." The copilot misread Tregaskis's sharp look at him as disapproval, and later went up to the reporter, showed him a photograph of his attractive wife, and noted she was the reason why he had said what he said.[10]

After ten long days of waiting at Mather Field—filled with briefings, paperwork, and postponements—Tregaskis and the crew finally flew on to Hawaii, staying there for four days. As an experienced visitor to the islands from earlier in the war, he had shared with his comrades that the evening air in Hawaii seemed like a "soft kiss on the cheek, that the place was really a land of a million flowers and rainbows, as it said in the song." Tregaskis praised the view from the Pali mountain pass, the feeling of swimming in the surf at Makapu'u beach, and dining on fresh pineapple and papaya. Unfortunately, Number 688 was a combat crew and had to get to its assignment, Guam, with a minimum of delay, so, Tregaskis noted, they saw "mostly the unpleasant, war-ridden parts of Hawaii on our short stay." They made sure to visit the post exchange to stock up on such essential items as shaving cream, soap, and candy bars, and were able to have lunch at one of the reporter's favorite haunts, Honolulu's Pacific Club, with fare far superior to the expected C-rations, pork loaf, and Vienna sausage waiting for them at other bases. They seemed to exist in a "sort of limbo between peace and war," Tregaskis recalled. By this time, Hain had opened sealed orders giving the name of the island, beyond Kwajalein, where the crew would be based for its missions against the Japanese homeland: Guam, recaptured from the Japanese by the U.S. Marine Corps in August 1944. In addition to housing airfields for the B-29s, the island served as the principal naval base in the Central Pacific west of Pearl Harbor. "All of the crew had learned about it previously, through the grapevine. But it was nice to know officially," Tregaskis noted.[11]

Once on Guam as part of the 315th Bombardment Wing's Sixteenth Bomb

Group, Fifteenth Bombardment Squadron, Number 688—designated as Crew Number 7 in the squadron—had to undergo additional training, including target study, aircraft and ship identification, instrument calibration, and air-sea rescue operations. Before tackling targets in Japan, they also had to make shakedown missions against enemy-held islands, including Rota, only sixty miles from Guam, and a June 16 mission against the garrison on Truk in the Caroline Islands. Tregaskis made a significant discovery while on one of these sorties: he found it nearly impossible to see the B-29's bombs hit from his position in the aircraft. He had to wedge himself into the very point of the plane's nose, next to the bombardier, with his "forehead pressed against the Plexiglas," in order to see an occasional bomb strike far behind the plane. Even the bombardier did well if he could see the explosions made by three or four of his bombs. "The B-29 certainly wasn't built for sight-seers," Tregaskis observed.[12]

In addition to honing the skills needed to fly such a complex machine, the officers and enlisted men of Number 688 did a considerable amount of manual labor constructing their living quarters set among banyan, bamboo, palm, and breadfruit trees near North Field. Tregaskis lent a hand as the officers conducted some "moonlight requisitioning" of wooden boards for the floors of their tents in which they slept before their metal Quonset huts were ready to occupy. The group's enterprising mess officer, 2nd Lt. Herbert R. Davis, had cultivated friendships with naval personnel and the Seabees, resulting in a dining hall that surpassed many of the same facilities Tregaskis had patronized at stateside air bases. With refrigeration available, Davis could offer roast beef, pork, and even steak on occasion. The special service officer also proved to be up to his job, offering recorded music over the speaker system at mealtimes and showing movies on a hillside open-air screen every night. Camp construction progressed so quickly that personnel could "watch the Quonset huts rising and taking shape as days, even as hours passed," Tregaskis wrote. An exchange of gifts helped procure materials outside the usual channels, a practice that became so widely known that Tregaskis heard some claim that if "you knew where to go on this island, you could receive the friendly gift of a Quonset hut, complete, in exchange for the friendly gift of eight quarts of whiskey."[13]

What *Post* readers did not learn from Tregaskis's reports were some of the more dramatic personal conflicts the crew of Number 688 had to face with one another and especially with their superior officers in the group and squadron. Reflecting on his time with the aviators, Tregaskis said there existed a "slight feeling of jealousy" between Hain and Ceman. The young copilot believed that the veteran flyer did not trust him to make takeoffs and landings and believed he was a better pilot. The two men were united, however, by difficulty with the squadron leader, Lt. Col. Richard W. Kline, a West Point graduate who was known as "the Grommet," because while other flyboys wore their caps without grommets, "giving them a shapeless, rakish contour," said Tregaskis, Kline kept his intact to comply with regulations. The correspondent recalled that some also resented Kline's insistence that those under his command stand muster at eight in the morning following twenty-four-hour missions against Japan, even though they did not have to fly that day. Hain believed that Kline and other noncombat veteran officers were too strict about enforcing petty regulations, what World War II veteran and scholar Paul Fussell termed "chickenshit," which he described as "behavior that makes military life worse than it need be: petty harassment of the weak by the strong; open scrimmage for power and authority and prestige; sadism thinly disguised as necessary discipline; a constant 'paying off of old scores'; and insistence on the letter rather than the spirit of ordinances." Kline, noted Tregaskis, believed that Hain and his supporters were "sloppy and didn't pay enough attention to discipline."[14]

These petty differences faded under the rigors of combat. For its first mission over Japan, Number 688 and other members of the Sixteenth Bomb Group were ordered to strike the Utsube River Oil Refinery near Yokkaichi on the evening of June 26–27. The mission was part of an effort by the American heavy bombers to cripple the Japanese petroleum industry, reducing the supplies of gasoline and lubricating oil to the enemy's air force. The morning of the mission, Ceman, who was in good spirits, visited Tregaskis and expressed frustration that some officers thought they might not return. "If they think they're going to die, why did they come over in the first place?" the copilot wondered. At the briefing, the wing's commanding officer, Gen. Frank A. Armstrong Jr., a veteran of the bombing campaign in Europe, told his men that they might have an easy trip or it could turn out to be "a stinker." Whatever happened, Armstrong said the crews had to have determination; "some call it guts. We don't turn back, whatever we suffer. We will make history tonight." Another officer warned them that the B-29s had the potential of facing 140 enemy fighters in the area, but they had one advantage, as they would be reaching the target on the heels of a daylight raid that had included approximately 400 bombers.[15]

Tregaskis and the crew of Number 688 reached their aircraft at 3:45 p.m., about an hour and a half before the scheduled takeoff. They had plenty of preflight work, including having Martelli, the bombardier, pull the pins on the bombs to leave them free for release. "While Moe sweated over the job amidst the rows of fat, brown, ugly projectiles in the big bomb bay, the others were occupied with equally important tasks," the correspondent wrote. While the crew set to work, a jeep pulled up to deliver two large metal boxes. "They would provide hot food, an experiment being tried out on two planes of our group," Tregaskis noted. The dinner menu included meatloaf, boiled potatoes, and canned carrots and peas. "We were one of the lucky planes—the rest had sandwiches," he wrote. Climbing aboard, the reporter took his place between Bond and Angelo in the plane's nose. Peering out of the plexiglass window, Tregaskis could see ahead of them the "long silver shapes of the 29's moving across the horizon, where the taxiway turned into the runway. Their tails, like the sails of sloops on the rim of the sea, inspired the reflection that we were a long way from the Larchmont [New York] regatta." As Number 688, weighing sixty-six tons with its bombload and gasoline, rolled down the runway for takeoff, Hain spotted in the distance a B-29 coming in for a landing on a field a few miles away. "Back from the daylight raid," the pilot said to Tregaskis. As the bomber leveled off, the crew listened to a radio news summary relayed from San Francisco to the nearby island of Saipan, with the announcer noting, "Our air attack on Japan continues with increased fury." Tregaskis thought to himself that the radio broadcaster viewed the B-29s as part of "a big war machine pouring death on Japan with continued ferocity. But here in the nose of No. 688 we were only six human beings passing a few hours of time before tonight's test. The fury of the attack, if any, would be concentrated in a few fleeting minutes over the target."[16]

Early in the mission, the crew kept themselves busy with, of all things, paperwork. Tregaskis watched as Ceman made notations on his weather report, which had to be filled out every hour with information about position, altitude, winds, and airspeed. "Looking around me in the nose," he reported, "I saw that almost everybody was occupied with some sort of form, all of them complicated." Although Hain had no form to worry about, he had plenty to do, including monitoring the plane's gas consumption and ensuring that the American installation on Iwo Jima knew of his aircraft's approach, as the machinery that ordinarily produced the necessary identification signals from the plane was out of order. Although on a mission that, if successful, would produce mayhem and destruction, Tregaskis was mesmerized by the sky's beauty. He could see the universe divided into level halves, under them "the deep purple of the terrestrial half, the level, dark undercast over which we were cruising; and above us, the lighter, indigo half of the upper sky." The bomber operated smoothly, feeling as steady, he recalled, as "if we were standing still. The engines were lulling us with their almost synchronous beat—a gentle rhum-rhum-m-m-rhum-m-bar-rum."[17]

When the B-29 reached the Nanpo Shoto group of islands, approximately five hundred miles from the coast of Japan, the crew and Tregaskis began the tedious routine of putting on what he called the "impediments of air combat," which included flak suits, parachutes, and oxygen masks (the crew could not pressurize its compartments in the high altitude because the plane's camera hatch was open to film the bombing). Tregaskis gave up wearing protective clothing to guard against any flak that might penetrate the plane, as he did not have enough room for the flak suit, parachute, oxygen tube, and himself in the cramped space he occupied. With the lights extinguished, Tregaskis could see in the gloom that Hain, Ceman, and Martelli appeared as "huge apelike shapes, not at all human. Their faces were transformed into muzzles by the rubber masks, and their flak suits gave them the hunched magnitude of gorillas." The correspondent's thoughts were interrupted by the harsh sound of an alarm bell warning about ice forming on the wings. Ceman used a signal lamp to see if there was any ice forming on the wings or propellers, but the fog was too thick. Hain remained unperturbed, noting that if the plane maintained its speed, they should be all right. Using the Eagle radar, Bond guided the B-29 over the target for a successful release of its bombload. "From below came a burst of orange fire that lit up the sky around and overhead—a fiery corona that hovered, then faded," Tregaskis reported. "And in the same moment the aircraft bounced sharply under our feet. I heard a sudden rattling sound; possibly hail, possibly antiaircraft fire."[18]

Once safely out to sea, the crew talked with one another about what they had observed while over the enemy refinery and took turns sleeping to overcome the exhaustion of their long, more than fourteen-hour mission. While Bond took over navigating, Coleman slumped over his charts, his glasses on his nose, mouth open, and snoring, Tregaskis noted, while Hain, with his red baseball cap pulled down over his eyes, also nodded off. The correspondent slept for a time, waking up to see the sun and hearing music from the radio station on Saipan. "Then we were turning into the sun," Tregaskis recalled. "We came in sharply, leveled out and swept smoothly down the runway, landing with hardly a jolt." Coleman noted that the veteran Hain had made a "very good landing for an old man after fourteen hours." As the aviators hauled their gear out of their aircraft, the ground crew found a hole from flak in Number 688's rear bomb bay door; it was the only plane in the group to be hit by enemy fire. Before he collapsed into his bunk at his quarters, exhausted from his experience, Tregaskis took time to compliment Hain for his intelligence, judgment, and luck, qualities that certainly helped to ensure a successful first mission for Number 688. Hain noted that he did not believe it was luck, but the grace of God, noting, seriously but not solemnly, "I think He kind of keeps an eye on us." All the crew slept until dinnertime and returned for more rest after they ate, pausing only long enough to shower and wash their dirty flying suits by hand. Tregaskis discovered that a mission on a B-29 was "a thick sandwich to chew, a twenty-four-hour slab of time, from briefing to landing, with plenty of work and worry all the way, but only a thin slice of excitement or fear in the center."[19]

As the B-29s pounded Japanese cities and industrial sites from bases on Guam, Tinian, and Saipan, naval aircraft from the U.S. Navy's Fast Carrier Task Force 38, under the command of Adm. John S. McCain Sr., ranged up and down the enemy's coast bombing and strafing any military target they could find in preparation for Operation Downfall, the invasion of Japan. From just fifteen miles offshore, battleships bombarded enemy factories at Kamaishi on the coast of Honshu Island. "However much propaganda a Japanese civilian will swallow," Adm. William "Bull" Halsey Jr. noted, "it must have been hard for him to digest the news that certain American warships had been sunk when he had just watch[ed] them blast his job from under him." During the third and fourth bombing missions Tregaskis made with Number 688, he heard radio broadcasts describing the naval activity off the Japanese coast. Also, at the briefings before their missions, the heavy bomber crews learned that they could expect little enemy fighter opposition because the American navy had been knocking out Japanese planes on the ground. Tregaskis very much wanted to observe the carrier action, so he wrangled a spot on one of the big *Essex*-class carriers, the USS *Ticonderoga*, which had been launched in February 1944. As he prepared to leave Guam, however, the correspondent already felt pangs of nostalgia for the time he had spent with Hain and his crew. While flying with them on their third mission, he jotted down in his notebook, "I'm fond of these guys—know all of them, now. It's going to be tough not to know how they are making out." At least he was able to stay long enough to see the crew settle well into its tour of duty, including seeing the enlisted men promoted to sergeant; learn that Bond's wife had given birth to a baby boy in Akron, Ohio; and share the pride that the crew had been cited for the air medal, signaling successful participation in five combat missions. He had faith, which was born out, that Crew Seven could take care of themselves and their aircraft. (The men of Number 688 completed eleven missions before the war's end.)[20]

Securing permission from navy authorities to make bombing missions with carrier planes over Japan, Tregaskis made it on board the *Ticonderoga* in time to be part of Torpedo Squadron 87's July 24 strike against ships of the Imperial Japanese Navy at the Kure Naval Arsenal on the island of Honshu. Spending time reviewing his notes in his hot cabin just under the flight deck, Tregaskis could hear a "Stravinskian concert of sound," including the "periodic, melancholy roaring of the planes taking off from the deck just over my head, one after another—the hornet-like drone of the fighters, the deeper toned bass of the dive-bombers and torpedo planes; rough blobs of sound strung like beads of an abacus on the background of the whirring of fans." He had observed a few changes in the naval air war since the last time he had been on a carrier. Some of the obvious changes included larger, more powerful aircraft; "mules," small tractors used to haul the planes around the flight deck, "replacing the muscular effort expended in the old days by deck crewmen who manhandled the planes into position"; and improvements in the ship's navigational techniques and radar equipment. Lt. Cdr. Walt Haas, an early navy ace now second in command of the ship's air group, also pointed out to the reporter that there was a basic change in the whole feeling of the war. "A lot less nerve-wracking now," Haas noted. In the early days, he added, U.S. forces were sometimes exceeded in numbers and skill by the enemy, but now the Americans overwhelmed the Japanese both in quantity and quality.[21]

The *Ticonderoga* was one of the carriers, along with the *Essex*, *Randolph*, *Monterey*, and *Bataan*, that made up Task Force 38.3, which also included the battleships *North Carolina* and *Alabama* and several screening destroyers. On his fourth day aboard the *Ticonderoga*, Tregaskis took his first flight, a warm-up to get the feeling of flying from a carrier, on board a Grumman TBM Avenger torpedo bomber, the largest of the carrier aircraft. It proved to be quite different from what he had experienced with the bomber crew in the Marianas. "I learned how small and relatively slow the carrier planes are; learned the feeling of insecurity that comes from operating from a moveable airfield, with only water, elsewhere, to land in," he recalled. He was surprised at the Avenger's small wingspan, as his eye had become accustomed to the bulk of the B-29. "But there was more than the small size in the feeling of this aircraft; there was a feeling of primitiveness and lightness compared to the refinement and solidity of the Superfort," Tregaskis recalled. "And I reflected particularly on the fact that we depended now on only one engine, not four." The limitations of carrier operations were severe, Tregaskis noted, especially regarding weight, power, and bombload.[22]

Lt. Cdr. Bill Miles, the skipper of the torpedo squadron, made sure the correspondent flew with a competent pilot, assigning him to his wingman, Ens. Paul R. Stephens of Topeka, Kansas, known as Steve to his friends on the ship. Tregaskis would be taking the place of one of the three-man crew; the enlisted man on board had to do double duty with both radio and gunnery. Aviation Radioman 3C Eugene Egumnoff, age twenty-one, from Vineland, New Jersey, joined Tregaskis on the Avenger, while its other usual crew member, Bob Pierpaoli, only nineteen, who had been in school before the war in Yuma, Arizona, flew with another Avenger pilot for the Kure attack. "He was always attentive in the premission briefings," Tregaskis said of Stephens, "sitting in one of the first few rows of the overstuffed airline chairs in the ready room where instruction sessions were held; always paying attention and making careful notes." The twenty-four-year-old pilot with thinning hair was so conscientious about his duties that he passed up participating in card games—practically the sole source of amusement among the young pilots—in favor of getting a good night's rest. The carrier's air group were "eager beavers," Tregaskis remembered. They were new to war, coming out from Hawaii three months before. Since then they had flown only a few missions, including practice strikes against Japanese bases in the Marshall Islands and supporting ground operations in the final stages of the Battle of Okinawa.[23]

Although Stephens was single-minded and determined when it came to combat, Tregaskis found him to be pleasant company off duty. The pilot possessed a "pleasant voice and modest way of speaking, with his head held rather low. He had a winning way of giving you all of his attention while you were talking; while he looked at you with level, wide-spaced light blue eyes. He also smiled easily—an ingenuous, sidewise smile." Before the war, Stephens had studied business at the University of Kansas and attended Colorado University and Washington University in Topeka. Newspaper articles about carrier operations intrigued him, especially one he had read about the tragic fate of the USS *Hornet*'s Torpedo Squadron 8 during the Battle of Midway, a story Tregaskis knew well. Some boys he knew from his hometown had become carrier pilots, including one of his friends, Steven Hall. Stephens earned his commission at Pensacola, Florida, on March 16, 1944, and went to Miami for specialized training in torpedo planes. In a strange coincidence, his instructor had been Lt. Cdr. George Gay Jr., the sole survivor of Squadron 8's Midway attack. Assigned to the *Ticonderoga*, Stephens's toughest mission up to the Kure raid had been one in support of the marines on Okinawa that involved low-level bombing from about four hundred feet into caves scattered along the side of a hill, he told Tregaskis. Although he did not anticipate pursuing a career in aviation after the war, Stephens told the reporter that he wanted to continue flying for fun, perhaps hiring a plane and taking off into the sky on weekends.[24]

Before launching from the *Ticonderoga*'s flight deck for his mission with Stephens and Egumnoff, Tregaskis remembered that the squadron had its main target changed three times. "Almost always, in my experience, there seem to be such last-minute changes in a military or naval operation; especially in a job as big as the one they were planning for us," he noted. Rumors abounded that the squadron would be attacking antiaircraft positions, then came reports that they would be hitting Japanese ships, but with torpedoes. The last mission sounded to Tregaskis like "a fairly efficient way to commit suicide; skimming in a slow-speed, cumbersome torpedo plane through a land-locked harbor with all the guns of Japan's great naval arsenal shooting at you." Gallows humor abounded among the pilots. When one, very young-looking ensign said he did not mind getting hit by enemy fire, but did not want to be shot down, one of his friends joked: "Hell, they [the Japanese] only cut your head off—that's a quick way to die." Finally, the squadron learned that it would be carrying four five-hundred-pound bombs instead of torpedoes and their target would be the battleship *Hyūga*, which had been adapted for use as an aircraft carrier with the addition of a flight deck to its stern. The enemy ship was berthed off the island of Nasake Shima, just outside the harbor, in shallow water. To Tregaskis, the changes meant that his chances for survival seemed far better than they had been just a few days before.[25]

The night before the Kure raid, as he had often done before participating in any attack, Tregaskis found his imagination filling in many of the possible outcomes. The squadron's safety officer, Lt. Algie Stuart Jr., visited the correspondent's cabin to regale him with unsettling stories about pilots who had been shot down, had ditched their planes in the Pacific, and were imprisoned by the Japanese. The two men agreed that fundamentally there were two possibilities facing a man making a flight the next morning: either he would be back aboard the carrier tomorrow afternoon, or he would not. Tregaskis thought about the risks he faced and went to sleep with surprising ease in his stuffy cabin. "But I woke up at regular intervals during the night, automatically, to check the luminous dial of my watch, to be sure I wasn't oversleeping," he recalled. He awoke at 5:00 a.m. and went to the wardroom for an early breakfast of eggs, bacon, oranges, apples, toast, and coffee. He found himself thinking as he ate, as he always did on such occasions: "The condemned man ate a hearty meal."[26]

Egumnoff, the crewman manning the radio and guns on Stephens's Avenger, suggested that he and Tregaskis go up on deck and get into their plane. They ducked through the carrier's low hatches, climbed onto the flight deck and into the morning sunlight, and, after some investigation among the close-packed aircraft, found the Avenger they had been assigned for their day's work. A few minutes later, Stephens arrived from the ready room and climbed into the pilot's cockpit. "He seemed harassed and serious," Tregaskis remembered, "apparently his usual mental attitude before a flight." The reporter swiveled, twisted, and shoved his elbows, knees, shoulders, and feet into the cramped position in the rear turret, where he would sit during the Avenger's approach to the target. When the plane began its descent before making its final dive on its target, Egumnoff would leave his radio position in the lower section (the bilge) and take Tregaskis's place in the turret in case any enemy fighters jumped them. "And as we lost altitude and ran in to drop our missles [*sic*] on the Hyuga, I'd climb up into the middle cockpit, whence a good view of the target and our drop on it, would be afforded," Tregaskis noted. He felt lucky that there was always a need for making such mechanical arrangements before an attack, as it "helped to keep one's imagination from working too hard."[27]

Danger could strike at any moment on a mission, as Tregaskis learned even before his Avenger had launched from the *Ticonderoga*. Because his turret faced aft, he could not watch the other planes taking off, but he could see the deck crewmen clad in bright-colored sweaters and helmets straining against the slipstreams to motion planes behind them into position. Tregaskis heard Stephens announce over the intercom: "A bomber just went in, off our right bow." Looking through the thick plate of bulletproof glass that protected the face of the rear gunner, he saw a number of the deck crewmen rush to look over the side of the carrier, as the wreckage of the crashed plane must have passed the ship's beam and sank. Suddenly, Tregaskis heard his Avenger's engine roaring full blast and the plane was rolling down the deck. "I braced against the headrest of the gunner's seat, saw the busy figures of the deck crews slide by, and in a second knew that we were off the deck, away from the ship," he remembered. "The floating island which had been our home and base became a ridiculous toy, with increasing distance—a model ploughing a white, high bow wave in the clear blue water." As his Avenger gained altitude, he could look out on a score of warships that were part of the task force, strung out to the horizon, as well as numerous dots of planes rising everywhere from the many carriers. The Avengers led the *Ticonderoga* air group, with the Helldiver dive-bombers and the Hellcat fighters ("our guardian angels," noted Tregaskis) that would escort them into the target falling in behind.[28]

Approaching Japan, Tregaskis could hear garbled voices in his headphones, with reports about American bombers making their runs. He heard something about enemy airfields being open and presenting themselves as good targets, and another voice, clearly stating, "I don't know what it is, but I hit it." Looking down he spied through a rift in the clouds a group of rock islands. Japan. Over the intercom came Egumnoff's tenor voice: "In about five minutes we can attack, Mr. Stephens. We're about nine minutes from our target." Passing over a large city, heading for the Inland Sea, Tregaskis imagined the panic below as the Japanese spotted the American planes and knew they were about to be attacked. "Once I had sat under Japanese bombers, on Guadalcanal, and watched them line up for a deliberate run in bright sunlight," Tregaskis noted. "The wheel had turned full circle, now. And I wrote, impetuously, in my notebook: They know by now they're under attack, by God." Switching positions with Egumnoff, the correspondent saw smoke rising from the surrounding rugged land, possibly from antiaircraft positions that had been hit. As Tregaskis's plane neared its target, bursts of flak smudged the sky around them, and he could see the "flashes of the guns on the ground, blinking like lights." A plane next to them discharged silvery sheets of some material from a side port, "strings of something like Christmas tree rain," he noted, which was chaff, thin pieces of aluminum scattered in the sky to confuse Japanese radar.[29]

As his Avenger flew through the spent bursts of antiaircraft fire, Tregaskis felt the aircraft diving, rushing headlong toward the water below, causing him to gasp for air as the g-forces built up. The experience was overwhelming. He later wrote:

I couldn't get enough air; my mouth reached out wide for air, as if I were shouting and couldn't shout, and the force of the dive pushed me forward until my forehead was pressed against the back of the pilot's headrest. Things were going too fast. I couldn't think. Were we under control? Was this right? Would I know if we were hit? Whatever we were going to get, whatever was going to happen, this was it. Then I saw the ship down there, the width and the great bulk, the gray color of it. It seemed smooth on top—the flight deck? The Hyuga? I saw a tall geyser of a bomb splash in the same instant, a tall column springing from the water, close to the ship. Beyond it, a shorter, smallish splash, a green geyser. I tried to shout and get air; couldn't. Our dive went on. Down and down. Too long? Was Steve alive? Had he been hit?

Then we were pulling out of our dive, turning sharply. I saw the enemy ship behind us over a wingtip; saw one, two, three, four bombs spring geysers, the green water, straddling the gray hull, sandwiching it. Violent single columns of water were striking around it, explosive fingers stabbing towards the sky. Another brace of four violent fingers, four bombs, smashed from the water around the ship, the innermost fingers striking her sharply at her edge, turning up smoke, churning the shallow water green and brown. They were braces of bombs from the planes of our squadron: four bombs for each plane. Another brace struck the water, one in the water, the second a blast of quick fire, a direct hit, that glared in the middle of the steel hull; the others, over, splashing on the other side. And then we had turned so far, and were jinking, vacillating, turning so sharply that I could see no more of the target.[30]

The squadron rendezvoused farther out into the bay for the return to the *Ticonderoga*. One by one, the Avengers, Helldivers, and Hellcats joined up, while Tregaskis nervously scanned the surrounding land masses and harbors straining to see if enemy fighters would appear seeking vengeance. Finally, after about fifteen minutes, the group set off for home, with the fighters weaving back and forth over the Avengers' tails to offer protection. Scrambling down into the bilge to talk to Egumnoff, Tregaskis heard him shout over the roar of the engine that he had seen a couple of "good hits" on the *Hyūga*. As they neared the *Ticonderoga*, the weather worsened. A low, gray rain squall grew so thick that "we lost sight of our ship each time we swung in a landing circle. I saw Steve slide his canopy back so that he could see better through the driving rain, felt the drops whipping through the small openings between his cockpit and mine," Tregaskis wrote. The Avenger circled the ship twice, finally making its approach on its third try and jolting to a stop. As they came even with the carrier's island structure, the correspondent saw the "sad, sunken form of a Helldiver which had crashed on deck," an obstacle that Stephens had just enough space to pass. Upon climbing out of his cockpit, Stephens, Tregaskis recalled, took a deep breath of air before commenting, "That was pretty rugged," squatting down to fondly pat the wet boards of the flight deck. "We wouldn't know the full story of the success or losses of our group until later when results were compiled, but at least we were certain of this: we, Steve, Gene and I, were home," noted a relieved Tregaskis.[31]

The July 24 strike at Kure cost Task Force 38 twenty-nine fighters and twenty-eight bombers, but it did produce solid results, including the sinking of the aircraft carrier *Amagi* and cruiser *Ōyodo*, as well as heavy damage to the battleship-carrier *Hyūga*. The *Ticonderoga*'s torpedo squadron, Tregaskis learned, had suffered light losses—only one plane and no people—on the morning mission. One of the Avenger pilots had to ditch his plane but steered his damaged craft into the water next to a destroyer, which snatched him from the water and had him back aboard the *Ticonderoga* in time for supper. The impressed pilot said the destroyer sailors had taken his wet clothes and those of his crewmen and had them laundered and dried before their transfer to the carrier. That evening, after supper, Lt. Bill Kummer, one of the ship's flight surgeons, passed out "medicinal" whiskey to the pilots, jigger by jigger, with ice and water. Tregaskis sat with Stephens, who declined the alcohol, saying he did not feel like it and, besides, he was scheduled to return to Kure the next day and wanted his head to be clear for the mission. Tregaskis decided not to accompany Stephens and Egumnoff, instead hoping to fly with them on a planned future sortie against airfields and other installations near Tokyo. After the *Ticonderoga* spent some time refueling and giving its crew a rest, the attack on the airfields was scrapped in favor of another go at Kure and the ships still afloat in the harbor; Tregaskis decided to remain behind.[32]

The *Ticonderoga* had lost pilots and crewmen on the mission. As he had noticed when he was on the USS *Hornet* for the Battle of Midway, those who survived appeared to react to the death of their colleagues with little or no emotion, adjusting "without noticeable effort, when suddenly there were empty chairs at the table," Tregaskis noted. Someone might comment about an absent aviator, saying he had been "a good guy," and there would be a moment of soberness, but then the conversation would return to "where it had been before, and if there was humor in the conversation, that was not sacrilegious or disrespectful." Deaths were expected in war and it was best, the correspondent pointed out, to "put the thing in the back of your mind, and not allow yourself to feel badly about it; at least, not to say so, for the sake of the morale of the others who were also still alive." That was what Tregaskis experienced with Cdr. Porter Maxwell, the fighter-bomber commander, whose plane had been hit by antiaircraft fire, went down out of control, and crashed. Haas informed the reporter of Maxwell's death, saying, "He was a fine pilot and one of the finest officers in the Navy. It's hard to live up to a man like him." Haas then looked away from Tregaskis, and nothing more was said.[33]

For the return mission to Kure on July 28, Stephens flew with his regular crew, Egumnoff and Pierpaoli. Tregaskis watched them prepare for the mission in the ready room, with Stephens working industriously over his plotting board, as usual, while the others gathered their flight gear. In the back of the room, the correspondent saw a group of radiomen/gunners kidding each other about the danger they faced, as they had just heard over the speaker system from the combat intelligence center that the task force's fighters, the first to reach the target, reported "plenty of bogies (enemy planes) in the air and some of them were being shot down." Hearing the report, one of the enlisted men shouted to another, "Hey, what are you chewin' gum so hard for?" while another covered his eyes with one hand, extended the other and pretended to grab and grip a machine gun, all the while grunting an imitation of the sound of rapid firing, "Bap-bap-bap-bap-bap." When word came over the speaker, "Pilots, man your planes," all the airmen in the room jumped from their seats and started to file out through the low exit door at the end of the ready room, heading for the flight deck. Tregaskis heard one of them shout, "Hit that boat!"[34]

At lunch the officer who usually sat across the table from Tregaskis told him he had heard that one of the torpedo bombers had spun in and crashed during the mission. The reporter asked what crew it had been, but the man said he did not know. After finishing his meal, Tregaskis wandered down to the torpedo squadron's ready room. Most of the squadron's members were being interrogated by the intelligence officer, Lt. Charlie Bartlett. Some had finished answering questions about the mission and were gathered in a pantry equipped with coffee, sandwiches, and ice cream. Tregaskis scanned their faces and could not find Stephens. "I wondered if he had been here, finished with his interrogation, and gone to his sack to rest," he recalled. Asking what had happened, Tregaskis learned from a shaken pilot, Lt. Dick Gale, that he had seen the Avenger with Stephens, Egumnoff, and Pierpaoli aboard crash into the sea. Apparently, while climbing through a thick overcast, both Stephens and Gale had lost their bearings, suffered vertigo, and fell into tight spins. Gale recovered from his spin; Stephens did not. After regaining control of his aircraft, Gale had seen Stephens, about two miles away, and watched as the other Avenger's wing started to disintegrate. "Then it broke off," Gale told Tregaskis. "The plane went straight in. I orbited the place and had my radioman look, but there were no survivors; only some smoke bombs and some dye marker. They must have broken loose when the plane broke up."[35]

Later that evening, Tregaskis sought solitude on the flight deck. His reverie was interrupted by one of the torpedo squadron's radiomen, who said to him that he wanted the correspondent to know how badly they all felt about Stephens's death. "Bob and Gene were good boys," Tregaskis responded. "It's a damn shame." But he realized that there were no words he could utter that would "really make it better," except that perhaps those who paid the ultimate price, by dying while engaged in combat overseas, became important, much more important to history than "any individual would normally be if he lived and died normally: and that furthermore, that they died as any man should, with honor." The deaths of Stephens, Egumnoff, and Pierpaoli came before they could hear the "Well done" plaudits from Admiral McCain for the task force's work at Kure. They were also not around to hear the shocking news of an advanced weapon of mass destruction dropped on the enemy by B-29s flown from the same island chain Tregaskis had visited. The first, nicknamed "Little Boy," was unleashed on Hiroshima on August 6 by a B-29 flown by Col. Paul Tibbets Jr. of the 509th Composite Group based on the island of Tinian. Three days later, a second atomic bomb hit the industrial city of Nagasaki. On August 15 the Japanese people heard over their radios a recording of Emperor Hirohito's speech announcing the nation's unconditional surrender. The end of the war came "as a breathless surprise to almost everyone," including himself, said Tregaskis, who left the *Ticonderoga* and wound up in Manila at the headquarters of Gen. Douglas MacArthur. Tregaskis was prepared to follow the skeleton staff of MacArthur's Military Government Section on its way to help manage the occupation of Japan. His focus would be on a small office on the fourth floor of Manila's shrapnel-pocked city hall. Inside were the people responsible for reshaping the conquered country "according to American democratic standards."[36]

16 "THE GLORIES OF PEACE"

The Douglas C-54 Skymaster transport plane emblazoned with special markings on its silver fuselage and "Bataan" printed on its nose glided in for a landing at Atsugi Airfield near Yokohama, Japan, on the afternoon of August 30, 1945. With his trademark corncob pipe clenched between his teeth and clad in aviator sunglasses, Gen. Douglas MacArthur climbed down a ramp wheeled up to the plane. As he ambled down the steps, the general was serenaded by a band and cheers from paratroopers from the Eleventh Airborne Division, the soldiers who had secured the airfield formerly held by Japanese kamikaze pilots determined to give their lives for their emperor. President Harry Truman had recently appointed MacArthur as supreme commander for the Allied powers, giving him the job of overseeing the occupation of the conquered country and directing him to "exercise your authority as you deem proper to carry out your mission." Shaking hands with Gen. Robert Eichelberger, head of the Eighth Army, MacArthur, as newspapermen and photographers (some American and many Japanese) swarmed around him, commented, "Well, Bob, it's been a long road from Melbourne to Tokyo, but as they say in the movies, this is the payoff." MacArthur also took time to compliment the band's performance, telling its leader that it had been "about the sweetest music I've ever heard."[1]

As MacArthur and his party, all unarmed at the general's orders, pushed on from the airfield to Yokohama in a motorcade along a road lined with thousands of Japanese soldiers providing security, more transport planes landed at Atsugi. One passenger, Richard Tregaskis, who had followed members of the Military Government Section from Manila in the Philippines to a muddy base in Okinawa and now on to Japan itself on behalf of the *Saturday Evening Post*, had trouble believing what was happening. "The nonchalance of this peaceful invasion seemed astounding," Tregaskis wrote. "I'd been flying with the B-29s on bombing runs, and on Admiral [William "Bull"] Halsey's torpedo planes, too recently to realize that the war was over, that all this could happen here." Although one of the passengers on his plane jokingly objected that he wanted to return to the United States, most were absorbed in sightseeing, sitting in "awed silence, now, straining to see everything," Tregaskis reported. As someone pointed out something on the ground to a man sitting next to him, others were quick to try to rush to see what it was. Tregaskis compared it to a "mass nerve response like the craning of necks at a football game or automobile race, when something exciting is happening." Two weeks ago the countryside would have been "spitting fire" at any American planes overhead, but today Tregaskis's plane landed without incident alongside aircraft bearing the Rising Sun emblem. Setting foot on the concrete taxiway with his tired companions, Tregaskis recalled something an enlisted man with the Military Government Section, Cpl. Vincent A. Livelli, a typist from Brooklyn, New York, had said to him in Manila: "Military government follows the glories of victory with the glories of peace."[2]

The speed and uncertainty of the end of the war in the Pacific had dampened any riotous celebrations in the Philippines. Tregaskis arrived at MacArthur's headquarters in Manila shortly after the Japanese news agency, Dōmei, had released a statement on August 10 from the Japanese Foreign Ministry announcing the country's capitulation. What followed, noted Tregaskis, was a period of hopeful waiting that soldiers called "the big sweat," which seemed to drag on for years. "Nobody was sure just when—or if—he should begin celebrating," he remembered. "It was like the first day of the double-headed V-E Day in New York; unsteady, uneasy, with people milling about and not knowing just what to do, not being sure, half waiting for the official handout on peace, half wanting to celebrate now." Peace had caught everyone off guard, just as had the start of the war for the Americans with Japan's surprise attack at Pearl Harbor nearly four years before.[3]

Although the moment did not seem climactic or clear-cut, it did provide inspiration for Lt. Col. Carl Erickson, the acting head of the Military Government Section (shortened to Milgov in Tregaskis's *Post* articles) at MacArthur's headquarters. Erickson, the executive officer for Brig. Gen. William E. Crist, who was hurrying back to the Pacific from a visit to Europe to review the occupation there, controlled a tiny staff: two other officers and five enlisted men, all of whom had been snatched away from the Philippines Civil Affairs Unit and assigned to the new section. "If Military Government had to be flown into Japan the next day, this tiny detachment, with whatever other officers could be gathered, borrowed or stolen from other outfits, would have to take over the entire job of administering the central government of Japan," Tregaskis reported.[4]

With the "air thick with plans" for just how to rule over occupied Japan, Tregaskis secured Erickson's permission to spend the next few weeks tracking the detachment's unsteady progress from Manila to Tokyo. Uncertainty and improvisation became key parts of the unit's existence as it waited for reinforcements; Erickson had been promised, Tregaskis wrote, that 230 men with specialized training were on their way from the United States, dispatched with "No. 1 air priority." In the meantime, those assigned to the section displayed remarkable skills at scrounging for needed supplies and office space for the new men. Livelli, who had told the correspondent that he had "never felt closer to history," found a Japanese phrase book produced for Filipinos during Japan's occupation of that country by one of the invaders' propaganda agencies. The only linguist during the detachment's early days, Livelli, who spoke French, Portuguese, Spanish, and Italian, in just a few days spent reviewing the phrase book had mastered some elementary Japanese language characters, including those that indicated "keep off," Tregaskis reported. Others on the staff, however, remained more interested in returning home than in participating in the grand adventure awaiting them in Japan. Like many who were still serving in the military, they anxiously tried to figure out where they stood in the "point system" instituted by the U.S. War Department to determine the order of demobilization. The more points they had amassed—for such items as time served, where they had served, decorations earned, and number of dependents—the sooner they could expect to be discharged to see their families again.[5]

Day by day, Tregaskis observed the Military Government Section grow with "the rapidity of a jungle plant in the monsoon season," taking up space in new offices in another wing of the building. Crist joined his new command, full of lessons he had learned from his European sojourn and determined to avoid the pitfalls he had observed. "It's inexcusable to make the same mistakes again," he told Tregaskis, especially since he and his men were on a twenty-four-hour notice for travel to Japan or other occupied zones, including Korea. The wall-board partitions that marked the boundaries of the detachment's office in Manila's city hall expanded as officers, most of them fresh from Civil Affairs Training schools in the United States, and rookie enlisted personnel joined the staff. It made for a colorful sight, said the reporter, who saw in the building a "motley ensemble of Navy and Army garb, a mixture of colors and patterns which indicated that the officers who would be supervising the government of Japan had been hastily gathered from many sources to be flung into the emergency situation."[6]

Tregaskis noticed a trend toward mollifying harsh American attitudes about the Japanese occupation. Instead of a strict military government along the lines of the one established in Germany, as had originally been projected, he saw a shift toward "indirect control," using the existing Japanese government bureaucracy to run the country, overseen, of course, by MacArthur as supreme commander. Crist gave similar welcoming remarks to all new members of his detachment, letting them know that their initial function would be advisory. "We want to avoid disrupting Japan too much," the general warned his troops. "Above all we must carry out orders. The commander is given tools. He is responsible for the results. We don't tell him how to use his tools. That's up to him. It's up to the commander to use you, or you, or you, or use me, as he sees fit." The "tools" that joined Crist's command were usually older-than-ordinary line officers, Tregaskis noted, and their "faces carried interesting marks of character, of developed individuality." They were men of so many specialties that Erickson, who had been told he would be remaining in Manila and not joining the section in Japan, referred to them humorously as "entomologists and anthropologists." Their specialties included public safety, finance, bank-ing, public health, public safety, public works, industry, and law. Those who had to stay in the Philippines were jealous of those selected for service in Ja-pan, remembered Tregaskis, who also would be traveling to the defeated foe's homeland. "We were envied not only for the chance to see the country with the first occupying forces; but also because the military government office in the City Hall was becoming almost mammoth; and like any expanding orga-nization," he said, "it was obscuring individuals in its expanding folds." One of the captains left behind lamented to the correspondent, "With colonels all around, what can a mere captain do?"[7]

Upon his appointment as supreme commander, MacArthur had been deter-mined to formulate his own policies and implement them through Emperor

Hirohito and the imperial government, running a conciliatory occupation. Unlike Germany, which had been divided into zones for the different Allied powers (United States, Great Britain, France, and the Soviet Union), the United States, despite Russia's late entry into the fight, controlled Japan except for token British and Australian troops stationed in Hiroshima. There was an Allied Council for Japan, which consisted of the United States, the Soviet Union, China, and the United Kingdom, meant to advise MacArthur, but the general ignored it, noting that as supreme commander he was the "sole executive authority for the Allied Powers in Japan." The general intended to use his unchallenged power to reform the country, to bring it "abreast of modern progressive thought and action" by eliminating its military power, punishing its war criminals, building a proper structure of representative government, modernizing its constitution, giving Japanese women the right to vote, releasing political prisoners, establishing a free press and labor movement, separating church from state, and liberalizing its education system. "It was true that we intended to destroy Japan as a militarist power. It was true that we intended to impose penalties for past wrongs," MacArthur recalled. "But we also felt that we could best accomplish our purpose by building a new kind of Japan, one that would give the Japanese people freedom and justice, and some kind of security." The principles he planned to follow during the occupation were the same ones, he added, "which our soldiers had fought for on the battlefield." MacArthur strove to turn Japan into "the world's greatest laboratory for an experiment in the liberation of a people from totalitarian military rule and for the liberalization of government from within."[8]

The Military Government Section's departure from Manila was "a masterpiece of hurry-up-and-wait," according to Tregaskis, with the U.S. Army playing its old game of ordering someone to be at a rendezvous location hours early "so as to allow plenty of time to get there yourself." The trip involved plenty of discomfort and misery, but the members of the Military Government Section he accompanied endured the hardships with good cheer. "I wouldn't miss this for the world," Livelli said as the group waited and waited for the flight to take off from Nichols Field in Manila. A dancer in civilian life, Livelli surprised Tregaskis by sharing that he would be filling his time reading James Joyce's *Finnegan's Wake*, as he was interested in the book "from a philological point of view." Another one of his companions related to Tregaskis that when he had first joined the army he used to complain quite a bit about its inefficiency. After being in the military for a time, however, he "decided they got things done somehow, so I decided they must be right. Now, I just take it." Another passenger, Lt. Melville Homfeld, was probably the most anxious among the group's members to reach their destination, the port city of Yokohama, south of Tokyo. When Homfeld entered the army, his wife had also volunteered to serve, joining the Red Cross. She had been assigned to the hospital ship USS *Benevolence*, which was supposedly anchored in Yokohama Harbor. "Homfeld was very vehement about wanting to see her again," Tregaskis reported. "In fact, when he talked about the possibility of finding her in Yokohama Harbor, he let out something like a cowboy whoop."[9]

After a miserable two days at a mosquito-plagued tent camp on Okinawa, Tregaskis set off for the last leg of his trip on a plush C-54E transport plane, equipped with comfortable reclining seats and an electric plate on which the passengers could brew cups of hot coffee. "All around us, on our flanks and ahead, silver specks of other C-54's, inward bound for Japan, dotted the sky," Tregaskis wrote. The passengers sat in "awed silence, straining to see everything" as the plane made its descent into Atsugi Airfield. After parking at the end of a long line of C-54s, Tregaskis and his companions climbed down to the tarmac and were met by an American paratrooper in a jeep, who radioed to seek transportation for their party. Unfortunately, the truck that arrived only took them as far as a barnlike wooden hangar a few yards away to play the army waiting game again. "It was fitting, after all, that we should end our journey to Japan as we had begun it—waiting," Tregaskis said.[10]

For the next two weeks, the members of MacArthur's Military Government Section moved slowly, establishing their offices in Yokohama's customhouse. Tregaskis helped to make signs for the various departments: General Aid, Secretary of Labor, Medical, Finance, Resources, and Public Safety, among others. The correspondent also joined Maj. Cecil Tilton, Crist's assistant, and Charles Thomas, a civilian financial adviser, on a trip to the city's main shopping district to purchase guidebooks and Japanese-English dictionaries. "We found no stores, only piles of rusty iron wreckage, many shacks made out of salvage, and one or two locked and bolted concrete buildings," said Tregaskis. Stopping for water for their dilapidated car at a Japanese garage, Tilton asked the proprietor where he could buy books, but discovered there were no bookstores in the city; the nearest ones were in Tokyo. Homfeld had better luck, making it to Yokohama Harbor, boarding the ship on which his wife served, and having a joyous reunion. Unfortunately, the days soon fell into a deadly dull routine of paperwork and more paperwork. While exciting events were happening elsewhere—the formal Japanese surrender on the USS *Missouri* in Tokyo Bay on September 2, for example—military government soldiers "worked long hours in the stuffy confines of their Yokohama customhouse office, from eight-thirty a.m. until eleven o'clock at night," Tregaskis recalled. "And because the high policy was to be cautious and to center responsibility only at the very top, most of the recommendations, instructions and plans prepared by Milgov had to be rewritten, redone." Orders for running the country, he noted, came from the supreme commander, MacArthur, directly to the emperor or his representatives, then through the Japanese government's or civil service's usual channels. "Our Milgov people were only to advise, check up and make reports," Tregaskis wrote.[11]

The military government staff did jump in to assist Lt. Gen. John R. Hodge's Twenty-Fourth Corps, which had been ordered to occupy the southern portion of the Korean peninsula, annexed by Japan in 1910. The occupiers were now gone, and because there were not enough trained men to take over and there was infighting among Korean nationalists seeking power, "real Military Government by outsiders—Americans—would have to be provided," Tregaskis wrote. Crist's section in Japan had to produce proclamations for Korea that then needed to be translated into Korean. That proved to be a problem, the correspondent noted, as the unit possessed a Japanese interpreter section, but it had no Korean translators. "However, men who could write Korean were discovered in the Psychological Warfare branch, and the job was done," Tregaskis wrote.[12]

Matters did not improve for the Military Government Section when it moved its operation from Yokohama to Tokyo along with MacArthur's headquarters, which established itself in a six-story insurance building that became known as the Dai Ichi (Number One) building. The military government staff rode on the "vertebra shattering road between Yokohama and Tokyo" to its new offices in a grimy building that was part of the Japanese Forestry Department. Instead of preparing to help govern the country, however, the officers and enlisted men Tregaskis had come to know were blindsided by a decision from MacArthur's headquarters (Order 170) creating the Economic and Scientific Section. This new department took over "not only some of the functions but even some of the personnel of the Military Government Section," he reported. "It seemed evident to many of the Milgov people that this would be only the first of a series of slices into the physical structure of its organization." One officer, whose name Tregaskis kept secret for fear his superiors might punish him for his honesty, said his unit had become "a hollow shell" and complained that those who had been trained for their jobs at a cost of thousands of dollars were now in limbo; it seemed as though the Military Government Section would be "liquidated," with the supreme commander exercising his authority through the Japanese government. MacArthur's statement that he expected to maintain only a skeleton military force, approximately 200,000 troops, only confirmed Tregaskis's belief that the occupation was "going to proceed on a cut-rate—for the Americans basis; that the policy of playing with the soft pedal was going to be continued indefinitely."[13]

Underlying Tregaskis's reporting on the situation was his own frustration at losing his ongoing access to a story he had been working on for the past few months, and in the process becoming close to several members of a unit that seemed to be vanishing before his eyes. Also, there were still bitter feelings among some Americans about the war and how severely Japan should be punished for what many saw as reprehensible conduct. In a Gallup poll taken during the later stage of the war, only 8 percent of Americans had favored rehabilitating and re-educating Japan (13 percent had agreed with the option "Kill all the Japanese people"). Tregaskis reflected some of that animosity against the enemy in his articles for the *Post*. Writing about the move from Yokohama to Tokyo, the reporter noted that enlisted men and junior officers from military government "had been assigned to dirty quarters in business buildings, with picayune sanitary facilities." This had caused "understandable growling," with the Americans wondering: "Who won the war, after all? Why aren't we in the best buildings in Tokyo?" Also, racial prejudice still marred relations between occupiers and the occupied. Tregaskis used the familiar war term "Japs" in his pieces, and in describing some of the Japanese awaiting the Americans arrival at Atsugi Airfield, he wrote, "A few of the little bandy-legged, dark-faced monkeys stood motionless watching us."[14]

To gain some insight into what the future might bring for military government, Tregaskis arranged interviews with two of MacArthur's top advisers: Brig. Gen. Bonner Fellers, the general's military secretary and head of the general headquarters' Psychological Warfare Section, and Gen. Richard K. Sutherland, MacArthur's chief of staff. Fellers, whose department's name had been changed "in line with the prevailing trend toward euphemism," Tregaskis noted, to Information Dissemination Section, said to the reporter that the Japanese government had been "100 per cent not only co-operative but subservient." Reminding Fellers that he had heard some people in the United

States had been critical of what they viewed as "too much softness" when it came to handling Japan, Fellers warned that if the Americans were too firm, the Japanese would view it as betraying agreements made before their unconditional surrender, including promises that the existing state structure would be maintained. There were also several liberal reformers in Japan who might be able to steer the country toward democracy. The liberals had been beaten down by the militarists who controlled the country in the past and needed to be encouraged to emerge and lead, noted Fellers, who had urged MacArthur against putting the emperor on trial as a war criminal. "The plan is practical," he told Tregaskis, "and we're going to let them do it."[15]

In his talk with Tregaskis, Sutherland confirmed that Crist's section would be dissolved and its functions absorbed by other departments, who would make reports to the supreme commander. "We'll do the same thing with Military Government people that we'll do with the (fighting) divisions—we'll release 'em," Sutherland told the reporter. "They were originally set up for a combat landing, like the divisions. They should be considered as divisions. We're using those who are needed and releasing the rest—and some of those being released are inevitably going to be high-powered people. It can't be helped." Tregaskis realized that MacArthur was sensitive to the call from many Americans, tired of war and its costs, for the government to send troops home and cut inductions into the armed services (the size of the U.S. military had been reduced throughout 1946, falling from 12 million to 1.5 million). In early 1946, wives of servicemen had organized "Bring Back Daddy" clubs to pressure Congress to speed up bringing their husbands home. Soldiers overseas had also organized protests lambasting plans by the War Department to slow demobilization. Tregaskis could not blame MacArthur "for a policy of expediency when the American people seemed to indicate they didn't want to follow through either—that they didn't want to send more boys and dollars to go out and police the world; at least, not until another war came along!"[16]

With the Military Government Section reduced in importance, Tregaskis ended his "Road to Tokyo" series for the *Post*, returning to the United States to report and write for the magazine for the first five months in 1946 about how veterans were handling their return to civilian life. Tregaskis, who had been covering the war for the past four years, had his own transition issues, including such simple problems as finding replacements for his size 14 military issue footwear. Like most men who had been discharged from the army, navy, or marines, Tregaskis was "glad to be alive at the end of the war, to have both arms, both legs, both eyes and both ears; to be reasonably sane; and, immediately, to be able to get something to eat, to be able to bathe in warm water, to sleep between clean sheets." Coming from Tokyo, which had been "thoroughly poor, starving and devastated," Tregaskis viewed his first port of call, San Francisco, as "a pleasant dream." He went on "an innocent orgy" of window shopping, haunting department stores, and making the circuit of hamburger stands, restaurants, and used-car emporiums. "It was a wonderful privilege," he noted, "to be alive in this country where everyone in the ragamuffin remainder of the world would like to live; where everyone, comparatively, is wealthy." With the passage of those first "dream-like days" and his return to his wife, Marian, and their apartment in New York, Tregaskis found that life was not as rosy as he had first thought. There were shortages in consumer goods, inadequate housing stock, and prices were rising. He began to "glory less and less in the material comforts Americans enjoy," and his sense of proportion began to revert to an American one, taking for granted such items as "a square meal, a clean suit of clothes, and a hot bath."[17]

Tregaskis visited a cross-section of returned veterans, including a bomber pilot he knew well, Bob "Pappy" Hain; a former actor and Coast Guardsman who had not seen combat trying to revive his Hollywood career, Jim Davis (best known today for his role as the Ewing family patriarch on the television series *Dallas*); a Medal of Honor recipient trying his hand as the owner of a gasoline and service station in Pittsburgh, Charles Kelly; the second-leading ace in the European theater now working in aviation, Bob Johnson; a U.S. Marine who received a Silver Star for gallantry at Iwo Jima, now a union auto worker in Detroit making up for lost time with a bevy of girlfriends, Jim Bradley; and a former lead bombardier with the Eighth Air Force who had destroyed German cities, now a student at Harvard looking to study how to plan cities, Chuck Zettek. Although most of the veterans seemed to be fitting in well, Tregaskis, unsurprisingly, found Hain, with whom he had flown five missions on a B-29 Superfortress, to be "stable, calm and content" with his return to life as a walnut and apricot farmer in San Benito County, California. "Pappy in peacetime was the same taciturn character I had known when he was wearing a captain's uniform," Tregaskis reported, noting he spoke about the attributes of his new puppy in the same matter-of-fact tone he used to warn his crew about an enemy fighter's approach. Hain seemed content to return to a life where, as his father pointed out, a man was his own boss "and you don't get fired or court-martialed."[18]

Tregaskis selected ex-Captain Zettek as a representative of the approximately eight million veterans who took advantage of benefits from the Servicemen's Readjustment Act of 1944, more commonly known as the GI Bill, to further their education at more than two thousand institutions of higher learning across the country. William F. Bender, Harvard's counselor for veterans, related to the reporter that Zettek and his desire to improve the world was something others returning from the war and now attending Harvard shared. "About two thirds, I would say, want to go into fields where there is an appeal of service to society and country—to public service, government, teaching, medicine, becoming a writer," Bender noted. In his application papers to Harvard, Zettek had remembered that as he had contributed his own share to destroying German cities from the air during his twenty-seven missions, he now wanted to learn how to restore them. "I have it in my dreams to build a city or at least so to lay plans in my lifetime that an orderly and organized plan will follow," Zettek wrote, adding that a properly planned city could "be the maker of men into 'good men'—education being the all inclusive rudiment." Zettek had big ideas for the future, but he balked at sharing them with anyone, even Tregaskis, telling him, "There's so much opposition. There's so much human resistance to dreams. But I'm not discouraged and I'm not pigheaded."[19]

From time to time, the war's grinding effect on the veterans broke through despite their best efforts to hide the horrors they had experienced. Bradley, the brash ex-marine who had several romantic adventures once he was home in Detroit, fought off his reconversion tensions by picking fights, "too many fights," he admitted to Tregaskis, and driving his cars and motorcycle at excessive speeds. Russell Chido, the owner of the East Side Recreation Center, where Bradley spent a lot of time playing snooker, noticed how the war had changed those of his customers who had fought. "When they lean over to make a shot under the lights, you can see the changes in their faces," Chido noted. "It takes about six months to get that certain spark back." Johnson, who had won a Distinguished Service Cross and five Distinguished Flying Crosses for his feats flying a P-47 Thunderbolt fighter, seemed to be adjusting well at his job for Republic Aviation, but there were, Tregaskis wrote, "stubborn currents subordinated in the distant impression of harmony." Johnson's wife, Barbara, became used to having her husband occasionally bolt upright in bed, shouting, "Go get him!" or "There he is!" while remembering his previous combat missions in the skies over Europe.[20]

Although Tregaskis continued to produce occasional articles for the *Post* through the early 1950s, including examinations of efforts in Washington, DC, to eliminate the U.S. Marine Corps and a profile of police officers' favorite television cop, Sergeant Joe Friday, as portrayed by Jack Webb in the long-running *Dragnet* program, he spent considerable time upon his return laboring over another book, his second novel. "When the war ended, there were millions like me who wondered about the overall meaning of war, and tried very hard to find a basic cause or causes, so it would not happen again," Tregaskis explained. "Like scores of other correspondents and thousands of others who saw and were affected by the war, I undertook to think out an answer and present it in a book." Through the story of an ordinary GI who is exposed by his wartime service to travel in many countries, Tregaskis attempted to prove through his work that the prescription for peace and happiness was democracy, "one vote for every man and woman, whatever color." His thesis became that if every adult had a vote, if everyone kept a sharp watch over those he or she elected, then "there would be no more wars and the greatest good would obtain for the greatest number." Unfortunately, several publishers turned down his manuscript, and he "began to wonder whether mine might be an inept novel and whether my political theory was sound."[21]

Tregaskis enjoyed a brief taste of the glamorous Hollywood life in 1946, working for 20th Century Fox to develop a script based on the 1945 historical novel *The Black Rose* by Thomas B. Costain. He was attracted, however, by an offer from *True: The Man's Magazine* for what he described as "a dream assignment that terrified me." In October 1947 he set out on a two-year, forty-five-thousand-mile round-the-world trip on assignment for *True* to write "the most exciting adventure stories" he could uncover in such locations as Australia, New Zealand, Java, Bali, Hong Kong, Singapore, China, India, Egypt, France, Switzerland, Holland, Denmark, Sweden, Germany, and England. "I would wander about, and look, and talk to ordinary, common people (through interpreters of course), and see what my reporter's eye and ear could tell me," he remembered, "and forget about trying to reach conclusions unless they were insistently evident in the facts." Before setting out for Australia, where he gathered material for a piece on American veterans who had decided to settle in that country, he joked to a reporter that his editor at *True*, Ken Purdy, a writer himself, hated him, noting "it must be rough for a writer to have to send another man on an assignment like this." Tregaskis retained the rights to his articles, and he used them to craft a book, published as *Seven Leagues to Paradise* (1951). Doubleday and Company, the book's publisher, publicized it as the author's trip "in search of the perfect place to live." Tregaskis saw his journey as a way to avoid the "standard nine-to-five business existence, the standard, narrow-gauge social life within one's own tiny hereditary clique." By doing so, Tregaskis also sought to discover "physical paradises on earth," and find out if they might work for him and others.[22]

On his travels Tregaskis interacted with a variety of families "caught in the jaws of tremendous social, economic and political forces," including a poor Chinese villager, Jong Yo-Sen, who endured in his small village of Chungli battles for control of the country between Chiang Kai-shek's nationalist forces and Mao Zedong's communists. Yo-Sen sought for his family's future such simple items as more clothing and food, but he also yearned for peace. In India Tregaskis stayed with Ramji Lal, a member of the untouchable caste, and explored his fight to escape the role set for him by his society (sweeper or sewer man) and rise to a job as a mechanic. Turmoil even followed Tregaskis when he visited Sweden, as he predicted that if a third world war broke out, the "Swedes would probably be among the first to feel the blast of an international conflict." With his experiences with aviators in the previous war, it seemed logical for him to write about one of the country's best jet pilots, Lt. Carl F. Schnell, whose squadron would be among the first to fight if war broke out. Tregaskis kidded the twenty-eight-year-old pilot that the first to fight usually did not fare well, using as examples the losses experienced by American forces at the battles of Midway and Guadalcanal. "Yes," Schnell responded seriously. "The others have to learn from the mistakes of the first."[23]

When his assignment for *True* ended, Tregaskis decided to move from New York with Marian to Southern California, settling in Newport Beach, south of Los Angeles. Living in New York had overwhelmed him, and he found himself increasingly annoyed by "the sheer crushing presence of so many hurrying people. And the annoyance grew into a kind of callous, selfish bad manners." He was drawn to Southern California, as many had been after the war, by its "mild climate, the sunshine and the openness of the country, the friendliness of the people, and the clean newness of the cities and towns." Tregaskis had also found a job he had been interested in pursuing since his days working for the Hearst newspapers in Boston: screenwriting. During his early days as a reporter, Tregaskis had regularly read *Time* magazine and the *New York Times* because he felt he should as a fledgling writer, but the features he had been most anxious to read in those two publications were in the movie and book sections. "I was anxious every week to see what was said of the latest books and movies, and of the two, I was always more interested in movies," he recalled. In those days he believed that if he could ever get to be a screenwriter, he would have reached "the pinnacle of achievement." Tregaskis planned to get to Hollywood by first making his mark as a newspaper feature writer, then moving to writing for magazines, from writing for magazines to writing books, and from writing books to creating screenplays. "It worked almost that way, although the war happened at the crucial time and I had to do it, with some luck, through writing about the war," he noted.[24]

For several months at the end of 1949 and the beginning of 1950, Tregaskis had been at odds about what to do with his career, wondering if it would be better for him as a writer to do movie work or "struggle on as a magazine scribe." He decided to see if he could get another job as a screenwriter, talking to some friends he had made in Hollywood and subscribing to the film trade paper, the *Hollywood Reporter*. While reading the *Reporter*, Marian came across the news that Warner Brothers planned on doing a World War II–related film titled "Breakthrough." Tregaskis's agent for his film work, George Lundy, arranged a meeting for his client with Jerry Wald, a hot producer at the time, who offered him a screenwriter's job. Tregaskis would work with a dramatist, John Rodell, on a different project than the one Marian had read about, crafting a love story about the Women's Army Corps set in Italy, an idea that the studio eventually developed into the 1951 film *Force of Arms*, starring William Holden and Nancy Olson. "I knew this would give me a good break into screen-writing, *if* I really wanted to make a life career in the movies," Tregaskis recalled. He initially decided to reject the job offer, worrying that film work was "so much a group enterprise" that it would be hard to make a movie a work of art, "except in the sense that a 1950 car, fresh off the assembly line, or any other product of a mass-production process, is a kind of art-object." In his freelance writing he had developed some independence, and although as a freelancer he was not a wealthy man, at least he had "self-respect that it's hard for movie writers to achieve." In the end, however, Warner Brothers talked him into taking the job, paying him $600 per week. As he confided to a friend, his position at the studio was precarious. "I can be fired on one day's notice, I never know how many more days or weeks it's going to last," Tregaskis wrote. "I am a peon and wage slave here at Warner's, but I realize I'm learning and it is good pay for an apprentice, so I don't feel too bad about the insecurity of tenure."[25]

Tregaskis continued to struggle with what to do with his writing career as he moved from studio to studio over the next several months. After completing the WAC story, Warner Brothers assigned him to work on a film about a subject he knew well, the exploits of Col. William Darby's Rangers. Tregaskis was supposed to produce a "treatment" of forty to fifty pages, and he worked with a former ranger captain, who served as a technical adviser. "After doing the job inside a two-week deadline, I was told I would be laid off for a couple of weeks until Washington [DC] approved the script," Tregaskis recalled. "Three weeks went by and no action." He moved on to 20th Century Fox to develop an idea from congresswoman Clare Boothe Luce about communism in central Europe, but that project was put on hold. As he juggled his screenwriting duties, Tregaskis received an offer in July 1950 from *Collier's* magazine to do a job he knew well: cover a war. Conflict had broken out the month before when troops from the communist People's Republic of Korea (North Korea) had moved south to invade the Republic of Korea (South Korea). The United Nations Security Council had condemned North Korea's aggression and recommended other nations offer military support to South Korea. The United States responded to assist South Korea, with President Harry Truman noting that if the communists were "permitted to force their way into the Republic of Korea without opposition from the free world, no small nation would have the courage to resist threats and aggression by stronger Communist neighbors." Although conflicted about his decision (he argued with himself "all day and night"), Tregaskis turned down the opportunity, mainly due to an old health issue, his diabetes. During World War II he had handled his condition by controlling his diet, but he had since gone on an insulin regimen and seemed to "have more difficulty keeping the thing under control," he wrote Louis Ruppel, *Collier's* editor. "It seemed wise to me to wrestle with the diabetes a bit longer before going out on a deal as rugged as the Korean war."[26]

Studios kept employing Tregaskis, a novice at the trade, because, he believed, he possessed a specialized knowledge about a subject they wanted to examine in their movies: war and the people involved in combat. "I figured the deal was that I was trading my knowledge of war for a chance to learn something about the art of writing screenplays; and I was lucky enough and tried hard enough to be able to arrange this," Tregaskis wrote in a letter to his mother. For example, Tregaskis produced the screenplay for Republic Pictures' 1951 release *The Wild Blue Yonder*, which focused on the B-29 Superfortress and bombing raids against Japan and starred such well-known character actors as Walter Brennan, Phil Harris, Harry Carey Jr., and Forrest Tucker. Republic must have been pleased with Tregaskis's work, since for his next project, *Fair*

Wind to Java (an adventure story set in the 1880s and based on the 1948 novel by Garland Roark), the studio sent him on a long trip to research the film in Southeast Asia. He traveled thirty-six thousand miles and visited Java, Borneo, Sumatra, Bali, Siam, Timor, and Singapore. Unfortunately, some of the actors involved in the production did not view the finished product fondly. Young actor Claude Jarman Jr., best known for his performance in 1946's *The Yearling*, called *Fair Wind to Java* "one of the worst films ever made. It was laughable." Jarman did enjoy working with the film's star, Fred MacMurray, who played an American sea captain searching for diamonds while menaced by pirates. Reminiscing about the experience, Jarman said that MacMurray often shook his head and asked him during the production, "Why am I in this movie?"[27]

Over time Tregaskis believed he had learned how to invent, develop, and write a screenplay, either from his own story or from an idea somebody else had created. He had begun to wonder, however, if screenwriting was a career he wanted to keep pursuing. There seemed to be no screenwriters in Hollywood that were satisfied with their work, Tregaskis confided to his mother. The only ones he came across that were content had been "those who are 'hyphens,' which out here means writer-directors, or writer-director-producers," he wrote. "These men have more control over their movies, and their movies are usually good because they retain the integrity and harmony of the creating personality. But the others, the simple writers, have too many other personalities to buck." A screenwriter's brainchild, Tregaskis noted, usually underwent dissection and alteration by producers, directors, front-office executives, actors, and actresses so much that it "comes out more like a hash than a self-respecting roast beef or turkey." Others had tried to warn him about this, including his friend MacKinlay Kantor, a former war correspondent and novelist, but Tregaskis said he had to experience it on his own. Perhaps, he reasoned, the "master artist" was the novelist, as he was the composer, conductor, and orchestra all in one. He thought about writing a family story, beginning in the 1920s and stretching through World War II and on into the nuclear age, "weaving three or four family stories into the narrative."[28]

Tregaskis's uncertainty about his writing career matched his uncertainty about his marriage, which ended in a divorce granted to Marian on May 18, 1953, in a Los Angeles courtroom. The couple had grown apart, and Marian had grown tired of her husband's constant travels. She bought two cats to help fight off her loneliness and complained that it was "as if I had no husband," as he spent all his time, when he was home, either reading, writing, walking, or swimming. Tregaskis, who did not contest the divorce, blamed the failure of his marriage on the instability caused by his often "migratory life." This instability might have motivated him to try to return to his old profession, war correspondent. In late 1952 he sent letters to the Associated Press and the *Chicago Daily News* syndicate that read, "Seems to me most Korean coverage lacking vividness and workaday detail humanity of Ernie Pyles world war two coverage and to lesser extent my own. How about letting me go Korea for following proved method of visiting all branches of service staying with each until familiar with people and available stories then writing feature mailers then moving on to another branch to soak up color and stories before writing another batch of mailers." Although no newspaper or news service accepted his offer, Tregaskis did make it to Korea, traveling there in the fall of 1953 with cameraman Wilson Kay Norton after an armistice agreement had been signed ending the fighting. They were tasked by the U.S. Information Agency to produce a documentary film titled, "The Faith We Hold," focusing on the United Nation forces who served there. Aided by a U.S. Signal Corps crew of eight men, Tregaskis visited troops from Ethiopia, Greece, Siam, the Philippines, Turkey, Great Britain, and Australia.[29]

Tregaskis had originally shared the opinion of many Americans who believed that because UN troops were fighting a limited war that could not be won in the traditional sense, the conflict was "stupid and senseless." But after visiting UN troops in the field, he saw that he had been "dead wrong. Because it was a UN-backed war, with troops from many smaller nations willingly contributing soldiers to keep the peace, he noted, it established a principle Tregaskis viewed as of colossal importance; "it was the first functioning of an international police force." Such a fact would not have struck him so forcefully if he had not been so close to the troops of the small nations involved. In particular, he pointed to the contributions of the Ethiopians and the Greeks; the Ethiopians had lost family members in the fight against Italian fascists from 1935 to 1940, so they had "an idealistic involvement in the plight of the Koreans," and the Greeks sympathized as well with a small country "attacked by massive Communist forces engineered from [the] outside."[30]

American newspapers, Tregaskis judged, had presented to the public "a cockeyed picture" of the conflict. Correspondents covering the war had been so anxious to service stateside papers with the names and street addresses of U.S. troops that they had rarely mentioned the contributions from other countries. Too many reporters, he alleged, were trying to be "bitter, cynical and disillusioned miniature [Ernest] Hemingways," using quotes from American soldiers along the lines of "I asked him what sense it all made and he said, 'None.'" It seemed to be unpopular in America to call the war "a police action," and at first Tregaskis had also believed it was a "silly name" until he realized that "as a police action it was the first time a war had proven anything. I could see that if we had been able to throw an international police force into Ethiopia or China in the Thirties, or the Sudetenland or Austria or the Rhineland, we might not have been afflicted with the last great catastrophe." He blamed MacArthur for pushing his forces beyond the Thirty-Eighth Parallel and bringing China into the war. "The Korean War has been a long, bloody and wearisome struggle," Tregaskis concluded, "and there have been blunders like MacArthur's. But it is good to see that others of the troops who fought on that front, if not the Americans, can see the logic of that long, limited struggle."[31]

Before jumping into his Korea assignment, Tregaskis took time in Japan to remarry, having a Shinto wedding with his bride, Walton Jeffords, an airline stewardess and former Miss South Carolina from Florence, South Carolina. The two had been introduced by one of Walton's friends and had bonded by a mutual love of swimming, meeting often at Zuma Beach near Malibu; both had to wait for divorces before they could wed. "The wedding ceremony, of course, was unusual," Tregaskis recalled. "We were purified by drinking cherry tea, by having birch wands wave over us, by the incantations of two small but very impressive priests." The couple also drank the traditional three cups of *sake*. Later, to ensure that the ceremony was legally binding, they had a second one under civil auspices. The night of his wedding, Tregaskis was awakened in his room at the Teito Hotel by a phone call from his film partner Norton, who was stuck at a military airport, Itazuke, and needed his help. "I did the best I could, and joined him a couple of days later in Korea," said Tregaskis, who added that he and Walton had a "hectic honeymoon" because he could see his new wife only occasionally when he returned to Tokyo from Korea.[32]

Upon his return to California from Korea, Tregaskis embarked on the "very uncertain" life of a freelance writer. Although he later always advised those who wanted to pursue a writing career that they should "get some other job and write on the side," he managed to be one of the rare few who made a living from what emerged from his typewriter. He traveled extensively to fulfill assignments for such publications as *Collier's*, *Nation's Business*, *Sports Illustrated*, *Argosy*, *True*, *National Geographic*, and *Reader's Digest*. A friend had suggested to him that if Walton learned photography, she could accompany him on his trips; she did. Over a two-year period, the couple traveled approximately eighty-six thousand miles, visiting Japan, Okinawa, Hong Kong, Taiwan (including the embattled nationalist islands of Quemoy and Matsu off the coast of China), the Philippines, and Thailand.[33]

Prompted by his experiences in Asia, Tregaskis began to think more about the battle of political philosophies—communism versus democracy—he had witnessed. He saw the people of what he termed "marginal nations" often wavering, wondering which side to support. These nations had to "be given a belief strong enough to risk their necks and die for," Tregaskis argued. "We were not spreading that kind of belief. Everywhere I could see that we Americans were being drubbed back and forward, up and down by the Communists in the battle of propaganda and public relations." In early 1962 he secured accreditation from the U.S. State Department for a four-month assignment to cover America's support on behalf of a country, Vietnam, engaged in the struggle between the two beliefs. While reporting on the clashes between American-backed South Vietnamese troops and communist insurgents from North Vietnam, Tregaskis also became involved in a different kind of conflict, a generational one with a new breed of combat correspondent.[34]

17 "SOMETHING DANGEROUS AND NEW, AND STRANGE"

At the age of twenty-eight, David Halberstam received a challenging assignment from his employer, the *New York Times*. In September 1962 he arrived to cover a civil war in a small Asian country named Vietnam. President John F. Kennedy's administration had decided to increase America's commitment to help South Vietnam fight off communist insurgents from the Liberation Army of South Vietnam, often referred to by the Americans as the Viet Cong or V-C, and Halberstam would be there to write about what happened. While in South Vietnam he also encountered one of his heroes, veteran journalist Richard Tregaskis, whose work from the frontlines of World War II Halberstam knew well. Tregaskis was in the country from October 1962 to January 1963 to research a book eventually published as *Vietnam Diary* (1963). He tried to obtain a "firsthand, eyewitness look at the strange, off-beat, new-style war in which we find ourselves engaged in the miserable little jungle country called Vietnam, which our nation's leaders have decided is pivotal and critical in our Asian struggle with Communism."[1]

The two journalists seemed to have much in common. Both were Harvard graduates (Halberstam class of 1955 and Tregaskis class of 1938) who had worked diligently at their craft and had seen war before, Tregaskis in the Pacific and Europe during World War II and Halberstam in the Republic of the Congo in Africa. They shared a respect for the approximately ten thousand American military personnel supporting South Vietnam, especially those young officers tasked with molding the Army of the Republic of Vietnam (simplified to

ARVN or Arvin in newspaper stories) into a professional fighting force against the guerrilla forces backed by North Vietnam. They also agreed with the Kennedy administration's commitment to resisting communism in Vietnam and shepherding its government toward democracy. Halberstam feared that "if the Vietnamese, who are perhaps the toughest people in Southeast Asia, fell to the Communists, the pressure on the other shaky new nations would be intolerable." He believed that just as America's commitment to South Korea in the early 1950s had discouraged "overt Communist border crossings ever since, an anti-Communist victory in Vietnam would serve to discourage so-called wars of liberation" in other countries in the region.[2]

Halberstam accompanied Tregaskis on a few assignments, including a trip along the Saigon River with the Vietnamese Junk Fleet (patrol boats searching for smugglers) and a resupply mission to U.S. Special Forces bases at the Montagnard villages of Ple Yit and Plei Mrong. "He was pleasant-spoken, well-educated, of good family background," Tregaskis noted of his colleague. "He very evidently yearned for adventure, he had a newsman's penchant for pursuing a story, attempting analysis of facts, and trying to achieve exclusive understanding or bring out news breaks. And, if the story were bad and it were being concealed by officialdom—which it always seemed to be—dragging it out in the open." Halberstam believed it was his job, and the responsibility of other journalists in Vietnam, to report on the news, positive or negative. "We were finding out stuff we didn't want to find out," he recalled. "We were going against our own grain. We wanted the Americans to win." Unfortunately, he came to understand that to U.S. officials in the country, including Ambassador Frederick Nolting and Gen. Paul Harkins, head of Military Assistance Command-Vietnam, it was vital that "the news be good, and they regarded any other interpretation as defeatist and irresponsible." Tregaskis must have heard the rosy scenarios outlined by the top officials in Vietnam, and Halberstam wanted him to talk to lower-ranking U.S. officers he trusted and knew would offer the visiting writer an accurate assessment of the war's lack of progress and problems with the American-backed government of President Ngo Dinh Diem. Halberstam decided to take the forty-five-year-old Tregaskis on a day-long excursion to review how the war was going in My Tho, south of Saigon in the critical Mekong Delta.[3]

In Halberstam's estimation his day with Tregaskis had gone well, as the veteran reporter had been well-informed about the severe challenges ahead, especially the ARVN's inadequacies in the field. But Tregaskis did not react to this information as Halberstam expected. Years later, Halberstam recounted that the older reporter had turned and said to him, "If I were doing what you are doing, I'd be ashamed of myself." Halberstam likened Tregaskis's comment to being slapped in the face, especially because he had a "reverence toward World War II people and Korean War people," noting that his father had been a medic in World War I and a combat surgeon in World War II. As for Tregaskis, he makes no mention of such an incident in his Vietnam book, nor did he directly disparage the young reporter's work anywhere in the volume. But in a review of Halberstam's 1965 book *The Making of a Quagmire* for the *Chicago Tribune*, Tregaskis quoted Nolting's description of the *Times* reporter: "He's always looking for the hole in the doughnut," which Tregaskis viewed as apt, considering Halberstam's "fundamental attitude in covering the Viet Nam war: that something must be wrong rather than right with it." Tregaskis also included a much harsher quote from an unnamed embassy official, calling Halberstam a "young punk who'd never seen a war before and thought it should always go well. He just didn't know about wars. It didn't seem to occur to him that in all our American wars in the past, we had to run a little short of absolute complete democracy for the sake of winning."[4]

As Halberstam pointed out, however, the senior U.S. officials in South Vietnam, who had been urging reporters to "get on the team," had lost their credibility with him and other journalists through their own mendacity. They continually lied to a group of tough, talented young reporters "whose friends are being killed, who have seen guys their own age killed, who are risking their lives themselves. Go and lie to them and then try to court-martial their sources. That will draw lines in the sand." Halberstam, who shared the Pulitzer Prize for international reporting in 1964 with the Associated Press's Malcolm W. Browne, pointed out that since mid-1962 some American military officers had turned to the handful of reporters in Saigon, using them as a conduit to air their complaints and skepticism to the public and government officials in Washington, DC. "The journalists kept showing up in the countryside," Halberstam recalled, "and it was only a matter of time before they saw how hollow the entire operation was, how many lies were being told, and how fraudulent the war was." Eventually he added, a "version of the war and the [Diem] regime, far more pessimistic, began to surface in the American press." Kennedy's aides remembered a time when the president, reading Halberstam's stories from Vietnam in the *Times*, exploded with frustration: "Why can I get this stuff from Halberstam when I can't get it from my own people?" Tregaskis maintained that top diplomats in Vietnam complained to him that the president gave "more attention to Halberstam's dispatches than to the reports of all his own people there."[5]

The uncharitable view Tregaskis held of Halberstam and the other young reporters based in Vietnam who questioned the official, optimistic view of events from top administration officials there seemed to be prompted by his experiences in combat during World War II; his unflinching belief to the end of his life in the need for the United States to respond forcefully to communist aggression, especially in Vietnam; and his continued admiration for the skill and bravery of U.S. troops in the field. The product of a generation accustomed to taking at face value what its government told them, Tregaskis believed that criticizing the war belittled the courage of the troops, while Halberstam saw pointing out errors in how the war was being run as helping the troops in the field. Tregaskis also believed that casualties and defeats on the battlefield were a small cost to pay to help stem the tide of communism from sweeping over South Vietnam and throughout Southeast Asia. Tregaskis remained committed to victory in Vietnam for the rest of his life, making regular visits to report on the war for the North American Newspaper Alliance. At one point he went so far as to suggest that U.S. officials should send an ultimatum to North Vietnamese leader Ho Chi Minh saying, "You come on down to our bargaining table at the place of our choice and settle this now, or there won't be any Hanoi. And Haiphong will be wiped off the map—and your rice crop will be flooded out." Although he believed the U.S. government could accomplish its task in Vietnam with conventional weapons, if such efforts failed, he called for the use of the deadliest weapon in the American military's arsenal, the atomic bomb. "It's a stupid war—because we're not using our strength," Tregaskis proclaimed. Although he doubted that the American government would ever resort to using nuclear weapons against North Vietnam, he told a reporter that doing so "might be more humane than letting the war go on and on."[6]

Since the end of World War II Tregaskis had grown increasingly concerned about the rise of communism and America's failure in countering its growth through a vigorous propaganda effort. He tried, but failed, to gain the attention of editors with a nonfiction story about "The War That Is, the Little Hot War Cycle which . . . was vexing us all over the world." Tregaskis even sent his essays to a variety of news services and told them they could publish them without charge, but he said his work was "too controversial" to be used.

He believed that the Chinese civil war, with the victory of Mao Zedong's revolutionary forces against Chiang Kai-shek's Western-backed nationalist government, had been the "Pearl Harbor" of what he called World War III. The cycle of small civil wars that had broken out in a variety of countries since that time, he reasoned, had all been laid out by Vladimir Lenin in the 1920s, with the Soviet Union spreading its political creed throughout the world and seeking to turn the nationalistic aspirations of newly independent nations into communism rather than democracy. "We have a Cabinet officer to handle our mail deliveries, but not one in charge of our international public relations," he complained to a reporter in 1961.[7]

Tregaskis juggled his worries about the world's political situation with a baser need: earning a living as a freelance writer. He continually searched for interesting and topical subjects to support his career, accumulating a large book collection he used for reference purposes for his work. "Books are tools to me," Tregaskis said, noting that 60 percent of the volumes on his bookshelves were reference works (at one time his personal library while living in California reached eight thousand books). He needed all the assistance he could find to succeed in what was a precarious profession. Tregaskis once explained to a reporter that he had heard that the Authors' League had determined that approximately two hundred Americans devoted themselves to writing full time, in addition to eight hundred film and television scribes. "Something like 25 of these free-lance writers get very high incomes," Tregaskis noted. "The average is something like $5,000." It took "immense courage," he argued, to stick to such an uncertain profession for any length of time. "There are always too many periods of famine and debt," Tregaskis reflected. "Given a minimum level of competence the main job of a writer is to buy time so that he can devote himself to projects which are important." The most stressful part of his career involved the large amount of time needed "for selling ideas, projects, books and scripts," he noted. Unfortunately, Tregaskis found that he spent 75 to 80 percent of his time selling himself to editors or promoting his work to the public. "One should have more time to *write*," he lamented. In addition to traveling around the world with his wife, Walton, for magazine assignments, Tregaskis paid his bills by writing episodes for a variety of late 1950s and early 1960s television series, including *Flight*; *Steve Canyon*; *Pepsi-Cola Playhouse*; *Behind Closed Doors*; *Combat!*; *Winston Churchill: The Valiant Years*; and *Blue Angel*.[8]

With his frequent travels to far-flung locales, Tregaskis decided in May 1961 to move with Walton from California to Honolulu, Hawaii, living in a house "on the palm-laced shore of Maunalua Bay on the island of Oahu." (Hawaii had been admitted to the union as the fiftieth state on August 21, 1959). Looking out onto his back yard, Tregaskis recalled that he could see the "sharp, dark peaks of the Koolau Range, where clouds drift over crags sharp as if cut from blue cardboard." Of special importance to Tregaskis, an avid swimmer, was the warm water of Hanauma Bay. "For anyone who likes to swim like I do, the water's too cold [in California]," he noted. "You can do no more swimming than in New York. You can't swim all year around. The water's colder than at Cape Cod, seriously." Hawaii also possessed all the qualities he sought for a place to live: a pleasant year-round climate, gorgeous scenery, and such amenities as "drinkable water and eatable food, books, restaurants, schools and hospitals, and good enough communications so that you can establish instant touch with the main stream of current history." Tregaskis told a Honolulu reporter that he and Walton had been looking for a house in Hawaii since 1957, but such a move would be costly for a freelancer who always had his income already allocated for bills. In April 1961, however, the author had the happy coincidence of having two of his books published at the same time, with the money for their paperback rights also in hand. Tregaskis found that the new state's climate and geography made it "one of the world's best places for just plain living, the most relaxed I have ever lived in."[9]

The two books that helped to finance Tregaskis's move to Hawaii were tied to the worldwide struggle between communism and democracy. From February 26, 1959, to August 15, 1960, Tregaskis followed the early development and flights of North American Aviation's X-15 rocket plane, designed to probe the outskirts of what Tregaskis described as "the Wild Black Yonder," the infinity of space. Tregaskis's book on the program, *X-15 Diary: The Story of America's First Space Ship*, was published during the space race between the Soviet Union and United States, with each country jockeying to earn the glory for putting the first man in space. The Soviets had struck first in this new endeavor, launching the artificial satellite *Sputnik* on October 4, 1957. Unfortunately, the United States had some early difficulties with its space effort. On December 6, 1957, before a host of reporters and a live television audience, an American Viking rocket rose only a few feet off its launching pad at Cape Canaveral, Florida, before disaster struck. The rocket broke apart and struck the ground with a roar that could be felt by scientists safe behind a blockhouse's two-foot-thick concrete wall and six inches of bulletproof glass. Not everything went wrong with Project Vanguard. The grapefruit-size satellite survived the explosion and landed in some nearby scrub grass, and its transmitters began to faithfully broadcast its radio signals. The sight and sound of the forlorn American scientific apparatus prompted columnist Dorothy Kilgallen to ask, "Why doesn't someone go out there, find it, and kill it?" On January 31, 1958, the United States finally managed to place an object in space with *Explorer 1* on board a Juno rocket.[10]

Using the diary format that had served him well with *Guadalcanal Diary* and *Invasion Diary*, Tregaskis presented a highly readable, behind-the-scenes account of the engineers, scientists, and pilots who worked together to make the X-15 program a success. Although Tregaskis seemed an unlikely chronicler of such a science-heavy project, he compared a space mission to a battle, as it could occur "only because of untold sagas of self-sacrifice and heroic devotion which preceded it and now make it possible." To prepare himself, he studied his subject, filling a five-foot shelf with approximately thirty books about space. He also meticulously traced the X-15's progress, roving throughout the country: the test site at Edwards Air Force Base in California's desert country, the place where Chuck Yeager had broken the sound barrier in the X-1 rocket plane; the Wright Air Development Center near Dayton, Ohio, where scientists had tested and trained those headed for space; Reaction Motors Inc. in Denville, New York, the security-conscious company building the XLR-99 engine that powered the X-15; the headquarters of the new space agency, the National Aeronautics and Space Administration in Washington, DC; and Cape Canaveral near Cocoa Beach, Florida, the testing site for the American missiles that would take astronauts into space. In his travels, Tregaskis experienced the "same excitement I had known when, as a war correspondent, I boarded a ship or plane heading for a beachhead where an unknown enemy waited, in one of the many armed conflicts which have plagued our times." He discovered that America's space campaign had "the same kind of dedicated, self-sacrificing, heroic men and women involved in it. But the dedication and sacrifice and heroism are for a nobler goal than war, the opening of a breath-taking new age of cosmic exploration."[11]

Years before Tom Wolfe's *The Right Stuff* (1979), the author's groundbreaking exploration of the fraternity of test pilots and NASA's selection of the original seven astronauts, Tregaskis introduced readers, with his book, to the tight-lipped, dedicated test pilots risking their lives in the dangerous upper reaches of the atmosphere. Scott Crossfield, who flew the first few shakedown flights for the advanced rocket plane, remembered Tregaskis "watching, questioning, probing into the smallest detail of our every step." But Tregaskis could never fully penetrate Crossfield's wall of imperturbability when it came to uncovering the test pilot's deeper feelings about risking his life in these dangerous machines. "I think that being a gentle and humane man he never fully understood that those traits were not in any way dominant in the flight-test population," Crossfield said of Tregaskis. But in talking to a scientist involved in testing rockets, Willard A. Knapp, Tregaskis did wrench from his subject a comment that he never forgot about the hazardous search for technological advancement. Knapp told him, "Like the turtle, science makes progress only with its neck out."[12]

As he researched and wrote his book on the X-15, Tregaskis also fiddled with another writing project. Since 1955 he had been intrigued about writing a novel featuring a public relations man working for an aircraft company who goes to the Korean War as a correspondent and is drawn into the ideological struggle. His story took a different shape when, later that year, he and Walton covered for *Collier's* the brief armed conflict between the communist Peoples Republic of China and the nationalist Republic of China on Taiwan for a group of islands in the Taiwan Strait, including spots on the map then known as Quemoy and Matsu. "I spent some time in Matilda Hospital in Hong Kong, and had a Russian-born nurse who had worked in Peking during the Korean War and had been sent to a Communist re-education center," Tregaskis noted, "and at last had escaped to Hong Kong. What she told me about her experiences in Communist China convinced me that the book should be set in China, not Korea." He reasoned that whatever he wrote about China could also be relevant to the turbulent events in unsettled nations such as Greece, the Congo, Laos, Kenya, Cuba, and Guatemala. "This was strong in my mind, and so, somewhere in the back, was this Valkyrie character," recalled Tregaskis, "this strong woman with absolute convictions, and the strength to fight through conflicting aspects and points of view, and the sick hurry of divided aims, the entangling complexities of machine-age life which make[s] it hard for us to look through and see what is central and true."[13]

At the same time he worked on *X-15 Diary*, Tregaskis rewrote parts of his novel about China, which reflected facets of his own life. The main character of *Last Plane to Shanghai*, Scott Osterman, is a cynical freelance writer of adventure stories whose wife in New York has drinking problems. In the summer of 1948 in Shanghai, Osterman meets Martha Shoop, a photographer facing her own marriage troubles, as her husband, an army captain, is growing rich by selling black-market military equipment to Chinese communists. Published by Bobbs-Merrill Company, the book met with a tepid response from most critics, who found the love story between Osterman and Shoop trite, but praised Tregaskis's knowledge about the Chinese civil war and the quality of his writing when it came to describing battle scenes. One reviewer, Ron Goben, pointed out that it had to be tough to be Richard Tregaskis. As the well-known author of *Guadalcanal Diary*, Tregaskis seemed to have no trouble getting his work published and had "a certain built-in reading public." The difficulty, however, Goben wrote, was that few books could measure up to his "wartime epic and the reader is likely to feel a letdown after a Tregaskis book that isn't as good as his best but that would be considered a good effort by many other writers. 'Last Plane to Shanghai' falls in this category."[14]

Unfavorable reviews like the ones he received for *Last Plane to Shanghai* made little impression on Tregaskis, he maintained. Over the years he had developed the same opinion about critics as had Ernest Hemingway and John Steinbeck: "very few of them are worth getting excited about." Discussing reviewers with Walton one day, Tregaskis recalled that critics were just like most people, they wanted "to get the work done with a minimum of effort so that they can have some fun." They sought to distinguish themselves, he added, by creating "some bright witticism about the book or saying something which sounds penetrating." Overall, however, Tregaskis expressed his pity for critics as being "frustrated" authors. "If they had the sheer unreasoning drive to be writers, they would be, but instead they end [up]. . . impotent on the fringes of creativity," Tregaskis concluded.[15]

During his writing career, Tregaskis had taken on different genres, including nonfiction and fiction. In spring 1961 he began research for a book on a subject he knew well but for an audience he had never written for before: children. He had been approached by his old publisher, Bennett Cerf of Random House, to write a volume on the World War II exploits of the new president, John F. Kennedy, whom Tregaskis had known at Harvard and with whom he had competed to fill a vacant spot (second backstroker) on the school's championship swim team. The two men's paths crossed again, tangentially, during the war. Tregaskis noted that when he had left the Pacific in 1943 after he had finished covering the invasion of the Russell Islands, he had returned to Hawaii aboard a U.S. Navy transport ship, the USS *Rochambeau*. "On her return voyage to Noumea, New Caledonia," Tregaskis recalled, "the ship brought Lieutenant (j.g. [junior grade]) Kennedy, assigned to PT Squadron Two in Tulagi, the island base about which I had written extensively in *Guadalcanal Diary*."[16]

Tregaskis's book about Kennedy was part of Random House's Landmark Books series. Cerf came up with the idea for the series in the summer of 1948 while vacationing with his family on Cape Cod after he could not find a book about the Pilgrims for his children to read. He recalled that it "struck me that there should be a series of books, each one on some great episode in American history," written for young readers. The renowned publisher came up with a list of the first ten titles for the series and determined "not to get authors of children's books, but the most important authors in the country" to write them. "I went from one author to another," Cerf noted, "and every one of them jumped at the chance." He insisted upon using authors known for reaching wide audiences and drawing upon proven writers, including a host of former war correspondents who had written for Random House before, such as Tregaskis, William Shirer, Quentin Reynolds, and Robert Considine. The hardback books were concise (under two hundred pages), inexpensive (under two dollars), and well illustrated when possible with maps and photographs. "The Landmark Books took off like a rocket," Cerf noted, "and as the series grew, more and more well-known writers were happy to participate."[17]

Tregaskis's book focused on one of the most famous incidents in Kennedy's life, the loss of the patrol torpedo boat he commanded, PT-109, on the evening of August 1, 1943, when it was sliced apart by a Japanese destroyer, the *Amagiri*, in the Blackett Strait south of Kolombangara in the Solomon Islands. Abandoning the wreckage of his boat, Kennedy led his surviving crew to an islet approximately three miles away, towing one of his men via a life-belt strap he clamped onto with his teeth. After an exhausting week-long struggle, Kennedy and his crew were rescued, in large part through the young officer's determination and courage, as well with key assistance provided by Solomon Island native scouts and an Australian coast watcher. Kennedy's story had been told before, by war correspondent John Hersey for *The New Yorker* and in a book for adults by Robert J. Donovan (*PT-109: John F. Kennedy in World War II*). For his children's book, Tregaskis secured cooperation from the White House through Kennedy's press secretary, Pierre Salinger, who sent him a letter he could use to show "any persons with whom you are dealing in the preparation of the book." Tregaskis did meet briefly with Kennedy, who informed Salinger, "Pierre, Dick beat me out for the Harvard Varsity Swim Team." In response, Tregaskis joked, "Sir, if I'd known you would be President, I would have let you win." Tregaskis produced a sixty-thousand-word manuscript that was cut by Random House's juvenile department editors to approximately twenty-eight thousand words. Tregaskis used most of the excised material for a Dell paperback version of his Landmark book, also published in 1962. Tregaskis believed his book to be superior to Donovan's, writing Cerf that his work offered readers "a feeling for the huge struggle in which Kennedy and his PTs were involved, and . . . an understanding of the emotional undercurrents of war which Donovan lacks."[18]

Controversy arose about Tregaskis's Kennedy book that pitted Random House and Dell Publishing Company versus the McGraw-Hill Book Company and Fawcett Publications. McGraw-Hill and Fawcett, which had paid $125,000 for paperback rights, sued Random House and Dell in a New York court seeking an injunction preventing them from publishing Tregaskis's book with the title *John F. Kennedy and PT-109*, claiming that it too closely resembled the title of the bestselling book by Donovan. A defiant Cerf argued that Kennedy's "heroic exploits . . . are matters which are in the public domain and may be freely written about and described by anyone." Although New York Supreme Court justice Abraham J. Gellinoff denied the injunction, ruling that the law did not "recognize a monopoly of the English language," and Random House used the *John F. Kennedy and PT-109* title for its Landmark book, Dell revised the title for the paperback version of Tregaskis's work to *John F. Kennedy: War Hero.* The lawsuit also provided well-known national humor columnist Art Buchwald with something to write about, as he joked that probably the only man who was in the South Pacific battle zone at the same time as Kennedy who had not yet published his recollections was Ichiro Kuichi, who was in New York making final preparations for the release of his manuscript, to be titled, "Destiny's Deckhand—The Autobiography of a Seaman on the Japanese Destroyer That Missed Ramming PT-109."[19]

The ups and downs of his freelance career were matched by the instability of his marriage to Walton. The problems between the couple came to a head during the summer of 1962, when Walton, according to Tregaskis, "gave unmistakable signs of wanting to set up her own separate life, business-wise, at least." Walton traveled on her own to American Samoa for two weeks on a magazine assignment and, during that time, she informed her husband, she had "been at peace" and free from the anxiety she had felt for some time during their marriage. "She perhaps should have known long before that a writer's life is always dramatic—i.e.: never free of turbulence and violent struggle, and besides, all writers including me are sons of bitches—but it was beginning to dawn on her," Tregaskis confided to one of his friends. In November, while Tregaskis was in Vietnam, Walton left Hawaii for a job in Samoa as editor of the country's press news and manager of its broadcasting station, WVUV. (Tregaskis later filed for a divorce and received it on July 25, 1963.)[20]

For his next project, Tregaskis decided to investigate a story that he believed had not received the attention it deserved: what American servicemen were doing in Vietnam and "how they got into their various kinds of derring-do." In doing a book about Vietnam, Tregaskis would be tackling a subject he had experience with. A veteran war correspondent, he had also written an article in 1957 on how the U.S. Marine Corps trained to conduct operations via helicopter from the U.S. Navy's first assault helicopter aircraft carrier, the USS *Thetis Bay*. The revamped former World War II escort carrier would serve, he wrote, as "Uncle Sam's answer to the bush-type wars the Russians seem to favor for Asia and the Mideast." During his time in Vietnam, Tregaskis flew on sixty helicopter assault missions on a variety of army and marine craft, including the two-rotor Piasecki H-21, known as the "flying banana" for its unique shape; the Sikorsky H-34 troop carrier; and the modern, turbine-powered Bell UH-1, commonly known as the Huey, which flew escort for the other transport helicopters. "The Hueys are wonderful to fly in," Tregaskis later wrote his mother. "They're like magic because they're quiet for helicopters and smooth. It's fun to sit up between the pilots where I did and look out those wide, tall front windows, with plenty of air coming in from the huge open side windows." He felt a "peculiar kind of power" because the Huey could move "magically any direction you want to go, or just sit still." Although not as advanced, the H-21 army choppers were fun to fly in as well, Tregaskis added, because, to make them less vulnerable to ground fire, they approached a target "right on the deck, at an altitude of fifteen or twenty feet, and lift up over obstacles like trees and houses.... It's quite a kick at those speeds, 90 or 95 miles an hour; a real roller coaster." Although he admitted to his mother that he had been shot at a few times, the firepower he encountered in Vietnam "was pretty desultory compared to the earlier times I've been targeted. Considering the number of engagements and operations the Americans are involved in, the casualties have been fantastically light." Tregaskis attributed the low losses to the guerrillas' shortages in weapons and manpower.[21]

The American advantage in air mobility, Tregaskis later learned, did not always translate into success on the battlefield. An American adviser with the ARVN Seventh Regiment in the Mekong Delta told him that fighting the VC could be frustrating. "You have to land right on top of them, or they disappear," he complained to Tregaskis. "The first 50 meters the guy's a VC. The second 50 meters, he's thrown his weapons away. By the time he's gone 200 meters, he's a peaceful farmer." An American colonel likened the problem to what happened with police in the United States, with "crooks and bank robbers among the civilian population. You've got to catch the people with the loot, or the tools of their trade."[22]

Tregaskis's 1962 visit was not the first time he had been in Vietnam. In 1948, as part of his world adventure trip for *True* magazine, he had stopped in what then was French Indochina during a time when French forces were fighting with Viet Minh guerrillas, an effort that saw the French defeated and the country split into North Vietnam under Ho Chi Minh and South Vietnam, eventually under Diem, its Roman Catholic president. Tregaskis also spent a few "unhappy" months in the new Vietnamese republic in 1957–1958 as it was "feeling its oats as a self-determined nation free of French colonial control," driving the length of the country in a jeep and discovering that it was "hardly a model tourist mecca." For his 1962 visit, Tregaskis discovered that going to war was quite different than it had been twenty years before, when he landed with the marines on Guadalcanal. "Then, it took weeks aboard transport ships to get our forces into position to attack the Japanese," he recalled, and the landing occurred on one day. Now, there was "no one big D-Day: every day is D-Day and the front is everywhere." Tregaskis realized there were no secure areas, and if someone was not careful, he could accidentally set off a bomb hidden in his closet or have one explode while relaxing with drinks at a bar.[23]

Because Tregaskis knew that the "most dramatic and exciting stories in war are found where the action and the danger are," he set out in Vietnam to gather information from the Americans doing the fighting. As he moved from unit to unit, from marines to the army and on to the special forces, the Green Berets, he lugged with him the "weighty impediments" a war correspondent going into combat needed: a haversack, air mattress, canteen, knives, camera equipment (he served as his own photographer), typewriter, extra shoes, large leather diary, pens, foot powder (to guard against fungus), spoon, can opener, insect repellent, toilet paper, and "no-go pills." Of all his equipment, the no-go pills were, Tregaskis recalled, essential, as viruses of all sorts were plentiful in Vietnam and "the kind of control no-go pills can give you is irreplaceable if you are going to be doing a lot of flying." He also experienced every night before a mission "sinister imaginings" about what might happen the next day, the way it must be, Tregaskis thought, when someone is headed into "something dangerous and new, and strange."[24]

Tregaskis began his research with the 163rd Marine Squadron at Danang, flying with the unit for his first helicopter assault. "They are a fine bunch, with the good morale and esprit which the Marines usually have," he wrote his mother, "and the pride in doing a good, thoroughgoing job of their military campaigning which they somehow manage no matter what the war." Before ferrying members of the ARVN's Tenth Ranger Battalion into action on October 15, Tregaskis loaded his 35 mm camera with fresh film and packed his camera, exposure meter, and extra canisters of film into his haversack. He also stowed away some emergency rations, filled his canteen with purified water, and clipped his sheath knife onto the belt of his new flying suit provided to him by the marines. On a future mission one of Tregaskis's army friends, Capt. Don Toth, provided him with a .45 automatic and a shoulder holster. "A VC with murder on his mind isn't going to ask questions before he shoots," Tregaskis noted. "It's much wiser to shoot first." He mentioned his reasoning to Toth, who agreed, noting, "Yeah, sometimes you have to do unto others as they would do unto you, but do it first."[25]

Tregaskis tried to assuage his mother's fears about his safety while admittedly putting himself, once again, in harm's way. He explained to her that the chances he took going into combat were "a lot less than when you drive your car onto the Los Angeles freeway system," and he and the marines took "fantastic precautions," including wearing body armor "so that if a stray bullet should fly around the chances are it would be deflected from any vital spot." He even copied a helicopter crewman's habit of sitting on his pair of armor pants to protect his vital body parts. But as Tregaskis later admitted in *Vietnam Diary*, he realized that as the marine H-34 helicopter approached the designated landing zone, the VC could be hiding in the foliage ready to fire at the fragile craft with anything from a "homemade popgun" to heavy machine guns or .57 mm recoilless rifles. Never quite knowing what might happen, Tregaskis found that in combat his senses "strained out like fragile antennae to anticipate any of the dire things that you knew *had* happened and could happen again at any moment." Even when missions were completed without any opposition from the enemy, he discovered that he suffered the same mental strain as if he had been fired upon. "In a way," Tregaskis reflected, "the uneventful flights were more harrowing than the donnybrooks, and much less satisfactory."[26]

As Tregaskis's helicopter, Number YP 80, prepared to land and dispatch the nine Vietnamese soldiers crammed inside its metal frame, he found his mind racing through "several hundred possibilities, all illustrated, most of the pictures dire and bloody." Tregaskis was comforted, however, by the professional attitude and quick thinking shown by the chopper's crew chief, LCpl. Roland Frech, whose father had been a German soldier, killed at Stalingrad. Spotting a potential target that Tregaskis had failed to spot, Frech, a naturalized American citizen, fired off a long burst from his M-14 rifle. After the mission, Tregaskis asked Frech about the incident, and the marine said he had spied three suspected guerrillas trying to hide near a creek. "I just thought I'd discourage 'em a little," Frech said of his sudden fusillade. "I don't think I hit 'em. You know, we were goin' too fast." One of the pilots did receive a minor wound from a VC rifle grenade through the leg of his flying suit, but his comrades kidded him that he had squeezed "the suit to get blood so he could get a Purple Heart," Tregaskis reported.[27]

Tregaskis could not resist testing every type of aircraft he could find in Vietnam. In addition to flying on the different models of helicopters, he wrangled a ride on a U.S. Air Force fighter, the navy version of the North American Aviation T-28 Trojan, a piston-engine craft used for counterinsurgency operations. Originally designed as a trainer, the T-28s had roughly the same engine as the one used on the marine helicopters, Tregaskis noted, but since the fighters were "so much lighter and built for maneuverability, they are very perky little aircraft." Tregaskis flew on a mission against suspected VC concentrations near Quang Ngai with a South Vietnamese pilot who had been trained in the United States, Lt. Ng Huy-Cuong. Although an American adviser, Lt. Col. Herbert R. Mann, also handled a T-28 for the mission, Tregaskis knew that the Vietnamese Air Force did not want "two Americans in one T-28. That would make operations seem excessively American." On his flight, Tregaskis realized what to him was a "shocking fact" about aerial warfare at that time in Vietnam. "Here, because ground opposition was light, compared to World War II or Korea," he recalled, "it was possible to make many more passes over an enemy target." In the other conflicts it had taken quite an effort on a pilot's part to penetrate enemy defenses and release his bombs without getting shot down. "And after dropping the bombs, you still had a long exit route, sometimes besieged by enemy fighters, before you could get home," he noted. "You certainly hadn't hung around long in the target area: it was too dangerous."[28]

On December 8 Tregaskis checked on how American advisers were progressing with South Vietnamese ground forces. He and Capt. Richard A. Jones, a "lean, hard bitten man whose uniform testified to his experience in the swamps," accompanied ARVN forces striking enemy forces in the Ca Mau peninsula in the southern tip of the country. Although a thorough professional at his job, Jones had been noncommittal when asked about the progress being made, telling the writer, "The only thing about this war is that you can't get two people to agree on anything." For the operation, Tregaskis tried to keep his mind from focusing on "macabre imaginings" by worrying about such practical matters as keeping his camera equipment, musette bag, and notes dry as he plunged into the muck with the troops. Before taking off, Jones, from Berkeley, California, acted like the "soul of energy," Tregaskis remembered, shouting directions to the fifty members of the ARVN's Eagle force ready to board the helicopters and "whirling his finger toward our pilots, ordering them to crank up and get airborne." For their part, the Vietnamese soldiers who crowded into the helicopter were fascinated by the writer's identification bracelet, his odd canteen, and the extreme size (14) of his rubber-soled shoes. "They seemed to be able, alert troops, with battle-worn gear and good arms and steel helmets, and a sureness that apparently came from many helicopter operations," he remembered. "This was fitting for an elite striking force used on sudden raids and flanking attacks against the VC's."[29]

After his helicopter settled into some tall marsh grass surrounding the landing zone, Tregaskis jumped out and found mud and water swallowing his legs above his knee (hip-deep on the shorter Vietnamese). "With every step I made the mud sucked at my feet, and each step was a resounding *plump* as I struggled to wrench my leg loose for the next forward movement," he reported. Tregaskis struggled to keep up with the troops, falling twice and all the while worrying about the possibility of VC opposition as they headed toward their objective, a nearby village suspected of harboring the guerrillas. Although no major action ensued, the Eagle force did come under fire, returned fire in kind, and captured four suspected insurgents. Tregaskis had been impressed by what he had seen, admiring the troops' tactics. "They kept a security screen out on both sides of the river, with well-spread riflemen scanning the fields for any further VC hostility," he noted. Jones and the ARVN officer leading the troops disagreed about where to be picked up for the return to base, with the Vietnamese lieutenant arguing for a route that might bring them into further contact with the enemy. Although Jones did not care for the commander's plan, he expressed grudging admiration for the officer's spirit. "At least he's eager, he wants to fight," Jones told Tregaskis. "You have to give him that."[30]

As he continued his travels throughout the country, Tregaskis discovered aspects of the war similar to what he had known in World War II, including a blasé attitude from some soldiers regarding their bravery and even some of the same jokes. Talking to Maj. Robert E. Runkle, the commanding officer of the Huey outfit at Tan Son Nhut airfield, Tregaskis learned that he was a combat veteran of the Korean War. When he asked Runkle about the decorations he had received, Runkle replied, "The Bronze Star, the Purple Heart, and scared." A pilot with the Ninety-Third Transportation Company had joked with Tregaskis that at his last outfit the mosquitos had been so fierce that they "would carry you off if you weren't looking." The writer recalled that such a jest had been around among the military as far back as Guadalcanal, where he had heard a story about two mosquitos buzzing outside of an antibug canopy. One mosquito said to the other, "I'll pick up the net and you drag him out." The other mosquito protested, noting, "No, don't do that, the big fellas'll take him away from us." There also existed the usual rivalry between the army and the marines. Before Tregaskis left the 163rd to fly with a helicopter unit stationed at Soc Trang, the marines warned him he would be taking his life in his hands by flying missions with the army. A marine said to him, "The Army guys try hard, they're pretty able people—but they have a half-ass airplane and half-ass maintenance, so naturally they have a half-ass operation."[31]

Despite the marines' barbed warnings, Tregaskis, as he had in the Pacific (Lt. Col. Merritt "Red Mike" Edson) and in Europe (Capt. Ozell Smoot) discovered in Vietnam a soldier he especially admired: Captain Toth, the level-headed officer with steady nerves who flew missions in H-21 helicopters in the embattled Mekong Delta. Discussing his experiences with the writer, Toth, from Pen Argyle, Pennsylvania, said that he and the other members of his unit toiled in obscurity when it came to attention from the American public: "The hell of it is, when you come back, they say, 'Where've you been?' And you say 'Vietnam,' and they say, 'Where's that? What state is it in?'" Tregaskis flew with Toth on combat sorties, drank with him in local bars, and depended on him as a guide for a disastrous battle in a village in the Mekong Delta named Ap Bac ("Northern Hamlet"), where five helicopters had been shot down and American advisers had been killed and wounded in early 1963. Tregaskis flew with Toth into the area to try to salvage some of the downed helicopters. Before leaving, Toth pointed to the H-21 he had earlier flown into the landing zone; it had two large holes in the tail and rear. "That's how I know the snipers were still at it this morning," Toth told Tregaskis.[32]

The battle proved disastrous for South Vietnamese forces, who were roundly defeated by the VC despite being supported by regular army forces, local militia, paratroopers, and infantry riding in M113 armored personnel carriers. One of the American helicopter pilots wounded in the action, Lt. Lewis Stone, described what he had experienced to Tregaskis as "about the worst engagement I was ever in." Other helicopter pilots and crewmen involved in the battle appeared to be "haunted by the specter of sudden death and injury," Tregaskis recalled. A crew chief, Specialist Charles Rowland of Junction City, Kansas, said that his helicopter had evacuated casualties into late in the evening. "I never saw so many damn dead Vietnamese in my life," Rowland said. "They were three deep all the way to the door." When Neil Sheehan of the United Press International wrote what Tregaskis termed an "excited and emotional story" that included information about ARVN artillery rounds falling short during the battle, Tregaskis protested that such critical news dispatches could do a lot of harm with the American public. (Sheehan also quoted an American military official describing the battle as a "miserable damn performance" by the South Vietnamese.) Tregaskis acknowledged that Ap Bac had been a setback, but the VC had suffered a similar defeat earlier at Phuoc Chau. "At Ap Bac, the VC, apparently a very well-disciplined and well-dug-in outfit did it to our side—but not quite as badly [as Phuoc Chau]," Tregaskis noted. "That's the way war goes, a bloody business any way you look at it."[33]

Tregaskis left Vietnam on January 11, 1963, returning to Hawaii to work on his manuscript, in which he planned once again on using a diary format. By the end of June he had completed a 180,000-word manuscript and sent it to his publisher, Holt, Rinehart and Winston, which released *Vietnam Diary* in November 1963. His professional and personal life got mixed up during the writing of the book, as he became captivated by his secretary, Moana (Maharam) Gilutin, who had been born in California and raised in Tahiti and had earned a doctorate in anthropology music folklore from Columbia University. The two had met when Moana's neighbor, who taught swimming at Gray's beach near the Halekulani Hotel, introduced her to the writer. The next day Tregaskis called her and asked if she would work for him. Tregaskis noted that on his Vietnam manuscript Moana had typed 1,400 pages (two drafts of 700 pages) in three months. In addition to being an excellent secretary and a good manager, she was praised by Tregaskis in a letter to his mother as "well-educated, intelligent, and mainly she has a big heart and is courteous and compassionate," comparing her favorably to his late sister Madeline. For her part, Moana liked Tregaskis because he was smart, fun, and always interesting. She later told a reporter that she estimated she typed more than a million words for the different revisions of what became *Vietnam Diary*, destined to become the second highest seller among Tregaskis's books (*Guadalcanal Diary* remained his top seller). Tregaskis and Moana, who became an accomplished photographer and war reporter in her own right, married on September 12, 1963. The couple had no children, with Tregaskis explaining, "Since I have diabetes, I would rather say that my children should be my books."[34]

Before leaving Vietnam, Tregaskis had made "elaborate plans" with Toth to spend time together in Hawaii after the captain's tour of duty ended. The commitment shown by Toth and the other Americans he met overseas had amazed Tregaskis. "They are many of them veterans of World War II and Korea," Tregaskis wrote his mother, "but they continue to extend themselves and risk their necks for no good reason I would guess, except that they think it is expected of them as Americans." He was deep into his manuscript when, on March 9, 1963, he received a letter from Maj. Allan Galfund, a public information officer who had aided him in Vietnam. Galfund informed him that a helicopter accident had taken the lives of several Americans Tregaskis had known, including his friends Toth, Stone, and Lt. Charlie Fitts. The tragic news stunned Tregaskis, who felt as if he had been "slugged—hard—and I couldn't shake the feeling." He tried to keep on working on his book but could not shake the feeling of injustice at the losses. Later, a thought came that made him feel better. He told Moana, "At least they died like men, like soldiers—doing their jobs well and bravely—for something bigger than they were. I hope that when I die, I can die as well, and that people will be able to say as much for me."[35]

EPILOGUE

Sunday, August 19, 1973

The approximately 150 people who gathered under an overcast sky on the beach at Waikiki late in the afternoon watched as the Reverend Abraham Akaka was joined in an outrigger canoe bedecked with leis by a woman who had taken off her long white dress to reveal an orange bikini beneath. Akaka, himself clad in a black bathing suit, had just finished praising the life of the person the crowd had come to honor, writer and journalist Richard Tregaskis, who had died four days before. "Brother Richard loved the sea and he loved his fellow man," Akaka sermonized. "He rode the waves of history and of private meditation. . . . To such a man, life is a journey full of wonder." As the mourners sang "Aloha Oe," volunteers pushed the canoe into the Pacific for its trip beyond the reef. The woman in the bikini, Tregaskis's widow, Moana, carried with her in the canoe an urn wrapped in white linen and covered in dozens of leis contributed by those attending the service. It contained her husband's ashes, which she scattered into the sea he had loved.[1]

Tregaskis, whose body had been found at 4:45 p.m. on August 15 floating face down by the shore off Ala Moana Beach Park, had been seen swimming alone earlier that afternoon. Although initial reports had questioned whether the fifty-six-year-old Tregaskis's diabetes might have been a contributing factor in his fatal accident, an autopsy later showed that he had suffered a heart attack and drowned. Tregaskis's friend and International News Service associate Bob Considine thought it appropriate that the former war correspondent's remains were returned to the "waters of an ocean [the Pacific] whose wars he knew so well, whose islands he helped immortalize" with his World War II dispatches and books. Long daily swims were part of Tregaskis's routine, and they offered him, Moana noted, "a breather before returning to the beat-up typewriter that machined his beautiful words." But always during the nearly ten years of their marriage, Moana had been on guard in case her husband's diabetes caused him any trouble. "He always tried so hard to keep [his] urine sugar low that he'd run out of gas (calories) at the most curious moments," she remembered. Moana became an expert at recognizing when Tregaskis might be in trouble, and if she saw any early signs she made sure to provide him needed sustenance, "even if I did have to jump up in the middle of a splendid dissertation to stuff some food down his throat." Tregaskis's medical condition, Moana noted, spurred him to seek greater and greater accomplishments in his career. "Never mind the enlarging, nearing cloud. Shove it away!" she said. "Produce." He went to war often, Moana added, yet fought a private battle all of his life, and "he never lost a battle. None." Her husband also stayed a good reporter to the end of his life because he never got blasé. "He never lost his curiosity and each man's story interested him," Moana noted. "I used to giggle watching him doing an interview so effortlessly that the poor clot never knew what was happening."[2]

The last few years of his life had been productive ones for Tregaskis, but he sometimes took chances that almost led to disaster. Moana noted that her husband "did not set back, give in or give up." In 1964 Tregaskis, accompanied by his wife, returned to South Vietnam to research articles for *Cosmopolitan* and the North American Newspaper Alliance, as well as a possible novel, which became the book *China Bomb* (1966). From South Vietnam, they traveled to India and into the Himalaya and Karakoram mountain ranges, the nearest border to the Peoples Republic of China's atomic testing ground in Sinkiang. "We carried his insulin kit and an odd assortment of food and drugs into the high cold mountains," Moana remembered. Unfortunately for Tregaskis, he injured his foot climbing in the mountains and later developed a bad blister while riding a horse. "The blister got infected and the Indians flew me out," Tregaskis said. Tregaskis was hospitalized in Srinagar in the Kashmir Valley, and medical officials at first did not know what to do. "The trouble was diagnosed as gangrene and they were afraid they would have a dead correspondent on their hands," he recalled. "When you have diabetes any kind of infection becomes tricky." Moana reported that her husband fell into a four-day diabetic coma and his foot turned black. Indian army doctors treated him with tetracycline until he was well enough to travel home, where it took him a year to fully recover, she noted.[3]

Tregaskis's injury did not slow him down for long. He revisited South Vietnam with Moana from 1967 to 1970, collecting material for what he hoped would be a second book about the war, which he tentatively titled "Vietnam Diary II." His wide range of other writing projects included publishing his first book of poetry, *Woman and the Sea* (1968); researching the life of Kamehameha the Great, the first ruler of the Kingdom of Hawaii (eventually published posthumously); traveling to India with his wife to investigate doing a biography of Mumtaz, the Lady of the Taj Mahal in Agra and wife of Emperor Shah Jahan; and producing a novel he called "Flame," which he described as "the best of all my books so far," a love story set in Hawaii. Tregaskis became comfortable working in divergent genres—biography, history, fiction, and poetry—noting that they involved different levels of reasoning and emotion, "like words and music." Tregaskis sometimes played music while he wrote fiction and nonfiction and felt "no conflicting effect. But poetry, and sometimes fiction, are allied to music and outside music might make discords in the alleged creative psyche."[4]

Tregaskis's travels took him and Moana all over the world, and in 1967 his wanderlust brought the couple to the Solomon Islands for the twenty-fifth anniversary of a battle and an island that had made Tregaskis famous: Guadalcanal. After the war the island had reverted to colonial control under the British Solomon Islands Protectorate with its capital at Honiara. Tregaskis's journey to the island to write an article for *Parade*, a Sunday magazine supplement distributed in hundreds of newspapers across the United States, was far faster and smoother than it had been for the INS correspondent a quarter-century before. The trip from Honolulu to Fiji took only six hours via a "luxurious" Boeing 707 operated by Qantas, Australia's airline. From Fiji, however, they returned to the South Pacific's traditional 130-mile-per-hour flights over long distances between overnight stops. From Nadi in the Fijis, they flew on a propeller-driven DeHavilland Heron to Vila in the New Hebrides and then on to Espiritu Santo for the final 632 miles to Guadalcanal and "its feverish creeping-crawling embrace," noted Tregaskis. His plane swooped over the familiar coconut groves and the old Henderson Field (unavailable at the time) before landing on Fighter Two, another airstrip used by the Americans.[5]

During World War II more than a half-million Americans had passed through Guadalcanal, from the initial attempt to wrest control of the island from the Japanese to its later role as a staging area for the push across the Pacific. On his visit Tregaskis uncovered only two other Americans, Alvin Blum and his wife, Gertrude. "They own the island's only motel, as well as a bakery, and small hand-labor plant for soda-pop and ice blocks," noted Tregaskis. Blum, like Tregaskis, came from Elizabeth, New Jersey, and served during the war as a medical aid, first reaching Guadalcanal in 1944 at a time when "the coastal part of the island was jammed with military material stacked as close as gold in Fort Knox: Seabee roads, divisions of artillery, bombs, ammo, fuel and earth-moving equipment, and of course and always, oceans of men moving to our fronts and back." Demobilized at war's end, Blum decided not to return home, but sought a new life in the South Pacific, ending up in Honiara, where many government buildings had been constructed by the American military, Tregaskis noted.[6]

As he visited former battlefields, Tregaskis remembered the marines who had fought there and one man whose story he had heard about but whom he had never met: Sgt. Maj. Jacob Vouza, a native scout. Tregaskis had heard Vouza's tale of bravery while at Gen. Alexander Vandegrift's headquarters after the Battle of the Tenaru. Learning about Tregaskis's return, Vouza, despite an injured leg, walked six miles from his village of Roroni to talk to the writer, meeting him at a wobbly suspension bridge. "Vouza's great military feat was that he never divulged our positions when he was captured by the Japanese and tortured for days," Tregaskis recalled. "Miraculously, he survived—and escaped—and later was awarded the Silver Star by General Vandegrift." When Tregaskis asked him why he had refused to talk when tortured, Vouza told him that Col. Edmond John Buckley, Vandegrift's intelligence officer, had promised him that the marines had come to drive out the Japanese and asked for his promise to be their friend. "That's very big promise for me," Vouza told Tregaskis. "So don't talk."[7]

Driving up an old Seabee road through tall, coarse kunai grass, Tregaskis made it up the steep slope that had been Edson's Ridge, named in honor of Col. Merritt "Red Mike" Edson, commander of the First Marine Raider Battalion. In September 1942 it had been the scene of hand-to-hand fighting between marine raiders and the Japanese. When Tregaskis visited in 1967, the "creeping, insatiable jungle growth looked as unaffected by man as anything in this near-equatorial environment of the South Pacific." He bent over, slashed the bushes apart, and could make out the shape of a former foxhole. Looking closer, Tregaskis saw scattered nearby spent .50-caliber slugs and an ammo clip covered in rust. "There were more of the same within a few feet, both kinds of foxholes, the large American sort and the small Japanese variety, and all kinds of rusting war material—mortar shells, grenades, sections of decaying jeep and truck," he remembered. It seemed to him as if every Guadalcanal battlefield was "an unclaimed and decaying museum of war souvenirs."

With the familiar jungle around him on the ridge, along with the oppressive heat and humidity weighing on him, Tregaskis's thoughts returned to the men who had fought there, including his friend Edson, "with the bristle of red-gray beard and three bulletholes through his Marine-green jacket, shouting ice-cool directions through the swirling fight." Tregaskis also remembered the heroics of Pfc. Ray Herndon, wounded and knowing he was about to die, asking his buddies to give him a .45 automatic and telling them, "You guys better move out. I'm done for anyhow. With that automatic, I can get three or four of the —— before I kick off." There were other words from the ridge that flashed through the reporter's mind, especially those said by Maj. Ken Bailey, who halted a pell-mell retreat by bellowing, "Fight! You want to live forever?" Although a bullet tore through his helmet, Bailey survived the fierce action on the ridge, but a few weeks later was killed during an operation near the Matanikau River.[8]

Roaming the other battle sites on the island—Hell Point, the Tenaru River, Tasimboko, Taivu, Point Cruz, and Mount Austin—the jungle appeared to be always the same, Tregaskis noted. Any swipe at the tangled green mass unearthed rusting war machinery, everything from airplane parts to spent ammunition, as well as the remnants of the men who fought there, including bleached-white skulls. No effort had been made to preserve the battlefields as memorials, as had been done with such sites as Valley Forge and Gettysburg. "Most strange, here where more than 52,000 Yanks and Japanese still lie buried in their ships in the depths of Iron Bottom Sound, there is no American or Japanese monument," Tregaskis noted. "Probably, this is because . . . Guadalcanal has always been too far from the corner drugstore and the police station. It must be that, because otherwise we continue to honor and cultivate our more civilized great battlefields of Europe and the memories of the thousands who died there." (On August 7, 1992, the Guadalcanal American Monument had its formal dedication at its Skyline Drive location overlooking Honiara.)[9]

To Tregaskis, on that visit to Guadalcanal in 1967, however, it did not matter if the jungle continued to engulf "the foxholes and shells and rusting guns and tanks, it doesn't matter if the jungle looks as savagely pristine as it did before—just so long as the same vigor, and guts, and bottomless springs of ingenuity, devotion, and humor continue to characterize our fighting men."[10]

ACKNOWLEDGMENTS

Each August thousands of high school graduates from the Hoosier State and around the country descend upon Bloomington to begin their college careers at Indiana University. That happy lot fell to me in 1978. As a journalism major, I attended many classes at Ernie Pyle Hall, a handsome limestone structure near the university's Union that housed the journalism department and the offices of the student newspaper, the *Indiana Daily Student*.

Climbing the steps to the building's second floor, I often noticed a display window that included a photograph of the famous World War II correspondent after whom the structure was named. Although I had heard of the Dana, Indiana, native, I knew little about the man or his career. In fact, before attending IU, if I thought of Pyle at all, the picture that flashed in my mind was not that of the newspaperman but the actor Burgess Meredith, who played him in the 1945 film *The Story of G.I. Joe*.

A hasty glance at Pyle's newspaper career left me less than impressed, typifying as it did, as the correspondent's biographer James Tobin has noted, a cheerleading style of "war journalism that fell out of favor during the Vietnam War and has not recovered since." Journalism students of my generation received their inspiration not from old-fashioned reporters such as Pyle but instead from such investigative journalists as the *Washington Post*'s Bob Woodward and Carl Bernstein, men whose work had helped bring down a president, and David Halberstam, who wrote so honestly and brilliantly about this country's early involvement in Vietnam.

Nobody is so pure of heart—and so self-righteous—as a freshman journalism student. I began to see the errors of my ways while working for the Indiana State Museum System, which at that time included Pyle's birthplace home in Dana as one of its state historic sites. While researching Pyle's life for a brochure about the site, I read several of his war columns and developed a deep respect for the man most World War II GIs regarded as "the soldier's friend." To the millions of Americans on the home front during the war, anxious for news of their loved ones, Pyle's column offered a foxhole view of the struggle as he reported on the life, and sometimes death, of the average combatant. Later, as part of my work for the Indiana Historical Society, I wrote a youth biography about the Hoosier hero of World War II for the IHS Press.

Writing about one war correspondent invariably, at least for me, led to investigating others, which led to my book on *Time* magazine reporter Robert L. Sherrod, *Dispatches from the Pacific: The World War II Reporting of Robert L. Sherrod*, published by Indiana University Press in 2017. Attempting to complete my war correspondent "trilogy," my attention turned to Richard Tregaskis, best known for his bestselling *Guadalcanal Diary*. Tregaskis intrigued me because of the wide scope of his travels during the war, from the Solomon Islands in the Pacific to the mountains of Sicily and Italy, from the rubble-lined streets of Aachen, Germany, to the skies over Japan inside the steel shell of a Boeing B-29B Superfortress. He accomplished all this while dealing with a serious medical condition, diabetes, that he kept secret. Also, what biographer can keep from researching and writing about a subject who shares his birthday?

Although my travels in no way matched those of Tregaskis during the war, I did range across the country, reviewing the correspondent's papers at the Howard Gotlieb Archival Research Center at Boston University, Boston, Massachusetts; the American Heritage Center at the University of Wyoming in Laramie, Wyoming; and the Archives Branch of the Marine Corps History Division at Quantico, Virginia. The dedicated staffs at all these institutions were helpful guides in my work. My trips to the archives would not have been possible without the support of the Marine Corps Heritage Foundation, which awarded me a grant for my research about Tregaskis's World War II experiences.

Several people assisted me in making this book possible. Tregaskis's widow, Moana Tregaskis McGlaughlin, responded to my questions via e-mail with information that helped me to better understand his writing life. My agent, Philip Turner, proved indefatigable in helping secure a publisher for my manuscript and offered helpful advice throughout the process. For editorial support, I relied upon the staff at the University of New Mexico Press, especially senior acquisitions editor Michael Millman. To make this manuscript accurate and readable, I turned to my friend and colleague Kathy Breen, who provided her editing expertise on what I wrote. As always, my most trusted companion throughout the publication process has been my wife, Megan McKee. Without her, I would be lost.

NOTES

Introduction

1. Richard Tregaskis, "My Most Inspiring Moment: Where Courage Begins," *Family Weekly*, June 7, 1964.

2. Alexander A. Vandegrift, *Once a Marine: The Memoirs of General A. A. Vandegrift, United States Marine Corps* (1964; New York: Ballantine Books, 1966), 17; Richard Tregaskis, "The War Starts," manuscript in Richard Tregaskis Collection, Howard Gotlieb Archival Research Center at Boston University, Boston, Massachusetts. Tregaskis and Miller were joined on Guadalcanal during the initial invasion by members of the first deployment of the Marine Corps Combat Correspondents program, 2nd Lt. Herbert Merillat and Sgt. James Hurlbut. See "Observations of 'the Canal,'" *Naval History Magazine* 26 (July 2012), https://www.usni.org/magazines/naval-history-magazine/2012/july/observations-canal/.

3. Moana Tregaskis, "Afterword," in *Guadalcanal Diary* (1943; New York: The Modern Library, 2000), 236; Bennett Cerf, "A Publisher's Note Book," *Tucson Daily Citizen*, January 4, 1943; Bennett Cerf, "Richard Tregaskis," in *The Book of the Month: Sixty Years of Books in American Life*, ed. Al Silverman (Boston: Little, Brown and Company, 1986), 65–67; Tregaskis to Paul R. Reynolds, September 22, 1966, Richard Tregaskis Collection, American Heritage Center, University of Wyoming, Laramie, Wyoming.

4. Sgt. Jack Folsie, "Sergeant Lauds Richard Tregaskis' Nose for News," *Lowell (MA) Sun*, December 16, 1943; "Tregaskis Aid Saves Wounded," *New York Journal American*, October 23, 1943.

5. Tregaskis, "My Most Inspiring Moment," 12; Bob Considine, "Peace at Last," *Lowell (MA) Sun*, August 22, 1973. Many articles written about Tregaskis during the war and after listed his height as six feet seven inches. According to his official correspondent's identification card, Number 95, issued by the War Department on March 9, 1942, Tregaskis stood six feet five inches tall, weighed 225 pounds, and had blue eyes and blonde hair. See identification card found in Tregaskis Collection, Gotlieb Archival Research Center.

6. Tregaskis, "My Most Inspiring Moment"; Richard Tregaskis, "House to House and Room to Room," *Saturday Evening Post*, February 24, 1945, 18. Paradoxically, for warfare labeled as street fighting, those engaged were advised to stay out of the streets when possible. "A man walking down an avenue is a good target for a machine gunner or sniper sitting at any one of the hundreds or thousands of windows commanding the open stretch," Tregaskis reported. Squad leaders took their men through backyards, over fences and roofs, and, when faced by a wall "too high to scale, you bring up your bazooka and have at it." Tregaskis, "House to House and Room to Room," 19.

7. Flint Whitlock, "Breaking Down the Door: WWII's Battle of Aachen," Warfare History Network, http://warfarehistorynetwork.com/daily/wwii/breaking-down-the-door-wwiis-battle-of-aachen/; Steven J. Zaloga, *The Siegfried Line, 1944–45: Battles on the German Frontier* (Oxford, UK: Osprey Publishing, 2007), 31; Tregaskis, "My Most Inspiring Moment," 12.

8. Richard Tregaskis, *Invasion Diary* (1944; Lincoln: University of Nebraska Press, 2004), 93; Tregaskis, "My Most Inspiring Moment," 12.

9. Richard Tregaskis, "Battle for Aachen Like Jungle Warfare; Snipers Hide in Houses Instead of Trees," *Coshocton (OH) Tribune*, October 15, 1944; Tregaskis, "My Most Inspiring Moment," 12.

10. Richard Tregaskis, *Vietnam Diary* (New York: Holt, Rinehart and Winston, 1963), 41.

11. Tregaskis, "My Most Inspiring Moment," 13.

12. Ibid.

13. Ibid.; Richard Tregaskis, *Stronger Than Fear* (New York: Random House, 1945).

14. Tregaskis, "My Most Inspiring Moment," 13.

15. Richard Tregaskis, "General Bradley Best of War," *Cedar Rapids Gazette*, April 29, 1945; Considine, "Peace at Last"; Folsie, "Sergeant Lauds Richard Tregaskis' Nose for News"; Richard Tregaskis, "How to Read the War News," Tregaskis Papers, American Heritage Center.

16. Tregaskis, "How to Read the War News."

17. Ernie Pyle, *Brave Men* (New York: Henry Holt and Company, 1944), 122;

Richard Tregaskis to Barry Faris, January 6, 1941, Tregaskis Collection, Gotlieb Center.

18. Michael W. Sweeney, *The Military and the Press: An Uneasy Truce* (Evanston, IL: Northwestern University Press, 2006), 107; U.S. War Department, Basic Field Manual, Regulations for Correspondents Accompanying U.S. Army Forces in the Field, January 21, 1942, in Tregaskis Collection, Gotlieb Center; James H. Madison, "Home Front, Battlefront, and the 'Good War,'" in Ray E. Boomhower, *"One Shot": The World War II Photography of John A. Bushemi* (Indianapolis: Indiana Historical Society Press, 2004), 14–15; Tregaskis, *Guadalcanal Diary*, 125, 129; Paul Fussell, "Thank God for the Atom Bomb" and "Postscript (1987) on Japanese Skulls," in *Thank God for the Atom Bomb and Other Essays* (New York: Summit Books, 1988), 24–27, 46–50.

19. Tregaskis, *Guadalcanal Diary*, 207; Richard Tregaskis, "Guadalcanal—Uncensored (From Here)"; Tregaskis to friend named Tom, March 5, 1954, Tregaskis Collection, Gotlieb Archival Research Center.

20. Fletcher Pratt, "How the Censors Rigged the News," *Harper's*, February 1946, 101; Sweeney, *Military and the Press*, 104.

21. Tregaskis, "How to Read the War News."

22. Ibid.

23. Richard Tregaskis, "Why We Cover Wars," 1966 article for the Overseas Press Club, Tregaskis Collection, Gotlieb Center; Ray Moseley, *Reporting War: How Foreign Correspondents Risked Capture, Torture and Death to Cover World War II* (New Haven, CT: Yale University Press, 2017), 3. An account of Post's death can be found in Steven Casey, *The War Beat, Europe: The American Media at War against Nazi Germany* (New York: Oxford University Press, 2017), 98–105.

24. Tregaskis, "Why We Cover Wars"; Robert Capa, *Slightly Out of Focus* (1947; New York: The Modern Library, 2001), 89–90. Details about the secret operation involving the Eighty-Second Airborne can be found in *Invasion Diary*, 92–108. Tregaskis discusses his parachute jump in "The Parachute Jump," in *Deadline Delayed: By Members of the Overseas Press Club of America* (New York: E. P. Dutton and Company, 1947), 244–50.

25. Tregaskis, "Why We Cover Wars."

Chapter One

1. Alexander Vandegrift, draft of foreword for an edition of *Guadalcanal Diary*, Richard Tregaskis Papers, 06346, American Heritage Center, University of Wyoming, Laramie, Wyoming.

2. Barry Faris to Richard Tregaskis, November 6, 1942, Tregaskis Papers, American Heritage Center.

3. Bennett Cerf, *At Random: The Reminiscences of Bennett Cerf* (New York: Random House, 1977), 162–63. *Guadalcanal Diary* was not the first book with a World War II theme that Random House published. The firm had success with war correspondent Cecil Brown's book *Suez to Singapore*, which included Brown's story of how the Japanese had sunk the British battleships *Prince of Wales* and *Repulse* at Singapore a few days after Pearl Harbor. Ibid., 162.

4. Cerf, *At Random*, 163; John Chamberlain, "Books of the Times," *New York Times*, January 21, 1943.

5. Clayton K. S. Chun, *The Doolittle Raid 1942: America's First Strike Back at Japan* (Oxford, UK: Osprey Publishing, 2006), 90; James M. Scott, *Target Tokyo: Jimmy Doolittle and the Raid That Avenged Pearl Harbor* (New York: W. W. Norton and Company, 2015), 319–20.

6. Richard Tregaskis, "The Bravest Men," unpublished autobiography, Tregaskis Papers, American Heritage Center (hereafter cited as "The Bravest Men").

7. Richard Tregaskis, series of articles about the Battle of Midway, in Tregaskis Papers, American Heritage Center.

8. "The Bravest Men."

9. Richard Tregaskis to Maude Tregaskis, January 15, 1951; Richard Tregaskis to Madeline Tregaskis, December 10, 1942, Tregaskis Papers, American Heritage Center.

10. Account of Richard Tregaskis's childhood prepared by Maude Tregaskis, Tregaskis Papers, American Heritage Center (hereafter cited as Maude Tregaskis account).

11. "The Bravest Men"; Maude Tregaskis account.

12. Harvard Club of New Jersey scholarship application and John Heine letter to Gerrish Newell, chairman of the Harvard Club of New Jersey, Tregaskis Papers, American Heritage Center. In addition to the club scholarship, Tregaskis received a $425 award from the Harvard Class of 1856. Ibid.

13. Arthur M. Schlesinger Jr., *A Life in the Twentieth Century: Innocent Beginnings, 1917–1950* (Boston: Houghton Mifflin Company, 2000), 108–10.

14. Theodore H. White, *In Search of History: A Personal Adventure* (New York: Harper and Row Publishers, 1978), 42–43. Conant was the first university official to "recognize that meatballs were Harvard men, too," said White, and "he set apart a ground floor room at Dudley Hall where we could bring our lunches in brown paper bags and eat at a table, or lounge in easy chairs between classes." Ibid., 43.

15. Richard Tregaskis autobiography for his application for Nieman Fellowship,

April 2, 1949, and Harvard grade reports in Tregaskis Papers, American Heritage Center.

16. Richard Tregaskis, notes for "JFK and PT-109," and Richard Tregaskis to Drew Pearson, June 30, 1961, Tregaskis Papers, American Heritage Center. The comments by Byrne about Tregaskis on the Harvard are from the 1938 Harvard Class Album.

17. Tregaskis article for *Reader's Digest* Humor on Campus, August 11, 1966, Tregaskis Papers, American Heritage Center.

18. Ibid.

19. Newspaper clippings in Tregaskis Papers, American Heritage Center.

20. "The Bravest Men."

21. "The Bravest Men"; Richard Tregaskis to Barry Faris, January 6, 1941, Tregaskis Papers, American Heritage Center.

22. Tregaskis autobiography for Nieman Fellowship, Tregaskis Papers, American Heritage Center.

23. Richard Tregaskis to Mike Meshekoff, April 7, 1954, and Richard Tregaskis to Barry Faris, January 6, 1941, Tregaskis Papers, American Heritage Center; Bob Considine, *It's All News to Me: A Reporter's Deposition* (New York: Meredith Press, 1967), 82–84.

24. Ronald H. Spector, *Eagle against the Sun: The American War with Japan* (New York: Free Press, 1985), 4–6, and William Manchester, *The Glory and the Dream: A Narrative History of America, 1932–1972* (New York: Bantam Books, 1975), 258–59.

25. Spector, *Eagle against the Sun*, 100–101, 106; Manchester, *The Glory and the Dream*, 263–64; Lee Kennett, *For the Duration: The United States Goes to War: Pearl Harbor–1942* (New York: Charles Scribner's Sons, 1985), 58.

26. "The Bravest Men."

27. Two prominent American specialists in diabetes, Frederick M. Allen and Elliott P. Joslin, had, from about 1915 until 1922, promoted severe calorie restrictions or "starvation" diets as the best treatment for the disease. "We literally starved the child and adult with the faint hope that something new in treatment would appear," said Joslin. "It was no fun to starve a child to let him live." See Allan Mazur, "Why Were 'Starvation Diets' Promoted for Diabetes in the Pre-Insulin Period?" *Nutrition Journal*, March 11, 2011, http://www.ncbi.nim.nih.gov/pmc/articles/PMC3062586/. For the development and distribution of insulin, see, James H. Madison, *Eli Lilly: A Life, 1885–1977* (1989; Indianapolis: Indiana Historical Society Press, 2006), 55–63. By the fall of 1923, Madison noted, approximately twenty-five thousand Americans were taking insulin, and newspapers included articles telling of diabetics "revived from the deathbeds by the wonder drug." Madison, *Eli Lilly*, 62. See also "The Bravest Men."

28. "The Bravest Men."

29. Ibid.

30. Ibid.

Chapter Two

1. "Martial Law in Hawaii," Densho Encyclopedia, https://encyclopedia
   .densho.org/Martial_law_in_Hawaii/; Harry N. Scheiber and Jane L. Scheiber, *Bayonets in Paradise: Martial Law in Hawaiʻi during World War II* (Honolulu: University of Hawaii Press, 2016), 55–75; Robert J. Casey, *Torpedo
   Junction: With the Pacific Fleet from Pearl Harbor to Midway* (Indianapolis,
   IN: Bobbs-Merrill Company, 1942), 39, 42.

2. Richard Tregaskis to Maude and Archibald Tregaskis, March 27, 1942, Richard Tregaskis Collection, Howard Gotlieb Archival Research Center at Boston University, Boston, Massachusetts.

3. Richard Tregaskis, "The Bravest Men," unpublished autobiography, Richard
   Tregaskis Papers, 06346, American Heritage Center, University of Wyoming,
   Laramie, Wyoming (hereafter cited as "The Bravest Men").

4. Ibid.

5. Ibid.

6. Ibid.

7. Ibid.

8. Ibid.

9. Ibid.

10. Ibid.

11. Ronald H. Spector, *Eagle against the Sun: The American War with Japan*
    (New York: Free Press, 1985), 145; "The Bravest Men."

12. Richard Tregaskis, "The War Starts," unfinished manuscript in Richard Tre-
    gaskis Collection, Gotlieb Archival Research Center; "The Bravest Men." Af-
    ter the war, Bassett used his experiences with the navy to write the bestselling
    novel, *Harm's Way* (1962), later used as the basis for the John Wayne film *In
    Harm's Way* (1965). See "California Newsman, Author Dies," *Lowell (MA)
    Sun*, September 27, 1978. Drake had a poor reputation with some correspon-
    dents, who accused him of playing favorites and being too harsh with their
    copy. Rumors abounded that he kept a "black book" filled with the names
    of correspondents who displeased him. See Elliot Carlson, *Stanley Johnston's
    Blunder: The Reporter Who Spilled the Secret behind the U.S. Navy's Victory
    at Midway* (Annapolis, MD: Naval Institute Press, 2017), 9–10; Robert B.
    Davies, *Baldwin of the Times: Hanson W. Baldwin, A Military Journalist's Life,
    1903–1991* (Annapolis, MD: Naval Institute Press, 2011), 137.

13. "The Bravest Men."

14. Ibid.; Carlson, *Stanley Johnston's Blunder*, 10. The navy restrictions on using a sailor's name, except for a few top officers, also frustrated the country's leading war correspondent, Ernie Pyle, when he decided to cover the war in the Pacific in 1945 after winning fame profiling the average infantryman in North Africa, Sicily, Italy, and France. "The rule had some basis in the early days out here when we were weak, but there is no justification for it now," Pyle wrote his wife, Jerry. Incensed at having the names of sailors and airmen he had talked to on the carrier USS *Cabot* removed from his stories, Pyle threatened to leave and concentrate his reporting efforts on Gen. Douglas MacArthur in the Philippines. The navy, fearing losing such good publicity from America's favorite columnist, caved and allowed him to use the names, but it did not mark an official change in policy. See James Tobin, *Ernie Pyle's War: America's Eyewitness to World War II* (New York: The Free Press, 1997), 233–34.

15. "The Bravest Men."

16. Ibid.

17. Ibid.

18. Ibid.

19. Ibid.

20. Richard Tregaskis, "Ace Reporter Who Accompanied U.S. Task Force Writes Graphic Account of Secret Mission to Tokyo," *Zanesville (OH) Signal*, April 26, 1943. In addition to the *Enterprise*, *Salt Lake City*, *Northampton*, and *Balch*, Halsey's task force included the destroyers *Benham*, *Ellet*, and *Fanning*, as well as the fleet oiler *Sabine*. See Bob Fish, "Additional Historic Information, The Doolittle Raid (*Hornet* CV-8)," USS *Hornet* Sea, Air & Space Museum, https://www.uss-hornet.org/wp-content/uploads/2017/11/Website-Extended-Info-Doolittle-Raid.pdf.

Chapter Three

1. James M. Scott, *Target Tokyo: Jimmy Doolittle and the Raid That Avenged Pearl Harbor* (New York: Norton and Company, 2015), 28–32; James H. Doolittle with Carroll V. Glines, *I Could Never Be So Lucky Again* (New York: Bantam Books, 1991), 1–2.

2. Lisle A. Rose, *The Ship That Held the Line: The USS* Hornet *and the First Year of the Pacific War* (Annapolis, MD: Naval Institute Press, 1995), 63; Scott, *Target Tokyo*, 149. In addition to the *Hornet*, Task Force 18 included the cruisers *Nashville* and *Vincennes*, fleet oiler *Cimarron*, and the destroyers *Gwin*, *Meredith*, *Grayson*, and *Monssen*. See Bob Fish, "Additional Historic Information, The Doolittle Raid (*Hornet* CV-8)," USS *Hornet* Sea, Air & Space

Museum, https://www.uss-hornet.org/wp-content/uploads/2017/11/Website-Extended-Info-Doolittle-Raid.pdf.

3. Rose, *Ship That Held the Line*, 52; Oscar Dodson, "The Doolittle Raid," Hornet Tales website, http://www.usshornetmuseum.org/StoriesOfHornet/the-doolittle-raid.

4. Richard Tregaskis, "The Bravest Men," unpublished autobiography, Richard Tregaskis Papers, 06346, American Heritage Center, University of Wyoming (hereafter cited as "The Bravest Men").

5. Richard Tregaskis, "Ace Reporter Who Accompanied U.S. Task Force Writes Graphic Account of Secret Mission to Tokyo," *Zanesville (OH) Signal*, April 26, 1943; "The Bravest Men."

6. "The Bravest Men."

7. Ibid.

8. Ibid.

9. Richard Tregaskis, "Shangri-La Diary," *San Antonio Light*, April 28, 1943. Tregaskis's news articles about the Doolittle Raid were not released for distribution to International News Service newspapers until a year after the mission. By that time, he was known for his bestselling book *Guadalcanal Diary*. Taking advantage of his fame, INS distributed his articles in installments under the title "Shangri-La Diary." When confronted with reports about the bombing of Tokyo in April 1942, President Franklin D. Roosevelt, keeping secret the name of the ship from which the bombers had launched, told reporters the mission had come from an American base on "Shangri-La," the mythical land from James Hilton's novel *Lost Horizon*.

10. Tregaskis, "Shangri-La Diary," *Fairfield (IA) Daily Ledger*, May 4, 1943.

11. Clayton K. S. Chun, *The Doolittle Raid 1942: America's First Strike Back at Japan* (Oxford, UK: Osprey Publishing, 2006), 45; Tregaskis, "Shangri-La Diary," *Fairfield Daily Ledger*, May 4, 1943. Spitkit, naval slang for any small vessel, came from the days when navy men chewed tobacco and used small wooden spittoons on their ships. See, Tregaskis, "Shangri-La Diary," *San Antonio Light*, April 30, 1943.

12. Tregaskis, "Shangri-La Diary," *Fairfield Daily Ledger*, May 4, 1943; Richard Tregaskis to Paul R. Reynolds, September 22, 1966, Tregaskis Papers, American Heritage Center; Doolittle and Glines, *I Could Never Be So Lucky Again*, 4; Chun, *Doolittle Raid*, 45, 49.

13. Tregaskis, "Shangri-La Diary," *San Antonio Light*, April 30, 1943.

14. Richard Tregaskis, "'I Saw The Planes Take Off for Tokio,'" *Lowell Sun*, April 21, 1943; Tregaskis, "Shangri-La Diary," *San Antonio Light*, April 30, 1943; James M. Scott, "The Navy Targets Tokyo," *Naval History* 29, no. 2 (April 2015). Unfortunately, the "Bat Out of Hell," after bombing Nagoya, had to

land in Japanese-occupied territory in China and its crew was captured, along with the men from another B-25, the "Green Hornet." The eight surviving crewmen from the planes were put on trial by the Japanese and found guilty of killing civilians, including women and children. Although all were sentenced to death, only 1st Lt. Dean Hallmark, pilot of the "Green Hornet"; 1st Lt. William G. Farrow, pilot of the "Bat Out of Hell"; and Sgt. Harold Spatz, gunner on the "Bat Out of Hell," were put to death on October 15, 1942. See Chun, *Doolittle Raid*, 85.

15. "Additional Historic Information, The Doolittle Raid (*Hornet* CV-8)"; Doolittle and Glines, *I Could Never Be So Lucky Again*, 11.

16. Richard Tregaskis, "Shangri-La Diary," *San Antonio Light*, May 1, 1943.

17. Ibid.

18. "The Bravest Men"; Tregaskis, "Shangri-La Diary," *San Antonio Light*, May 1, 1943.

19. "The Bravest Men." In his memoir of his time in the Pacific from shortly after Pearl Harbor to the Battle of Midway, *Chicago Daily News* reporter Robert J. Casey remembered a new correspondent in the theater, Tregaskis, stocking up with provisions before the Doolittle Raid. Instead of tins of sardines, however, Casey said Tregaskis had filled a box with "canned corned beef, canned salmon and, presumably, pemmican." See Robert J. Casey, *Torpedo Junction: With the Pacific Fleet from Pearl Harbor to Midway* (Indianapolis, IN: Bobbs-Merrill Company, 1942), 288.

20. "The Bravest Men."

21. "The Bravest Men"; Tregaskis, "Shangri-La Diary," *San Antonio Light*, May 1, 1943.

Chapter Four

1. Richard Tregaskis, "The Bravest Men," unpublished autobiography, Richard Tregaskis Papers, 06346, American Heritage Center, University of Wyoming, Laramie, Wyoming (hereafter cited as "The Bravest Men"). The *Hornet* had been the eighth aircraft carrier constructed by the U.S. Navy. The "C" in CV-8 stood for carrier, while the "V" represented the ship having on board heavier-than-air aircraft, as opposed to airships. See Lisle A. Rose, *The Ship That Held the Line: The USS* Hornet *and the First Year of the Pacific War* (Annapolis, MD: Naval Institute Press, 1995), 5.

2. "The Bravest Men"; Rose, *Ship That Held the Line*, 7; Richard Tregaskis diary while on the USS *Hornet*, Richard Tregaskis Collection, Howard Gotlieb Archival Research Center at Boston University (hereafter cited as *Hornet* Diary).

3. *Hornet* Diary; "The Bravest Men." After the war, Dodson, who retired from the navy as a rear admiral, served as president of the American Numismatic Association from 1957 to 1961 and was inducted into the association's Hall of Fame in 2000. See "League to Hear Admiral Dodson," *Grosse Pointe (MI) News*, May 19, 1960; "Oscar Henry Dodson," Newman Numismatic Portal, https://nnp.wustl.edu/library/PersonDetail/589/.

4. *Hornet* Diary; "The Bravest Men."

5. "The Bravest Men"; Alvin Kernan, *The Unknown Battle of Midway: The Destruction of the American Torpedo Squadrons* (New Haven, CT: Yale University Press, 2005), 54; Rose, *Ship That Held the Line*, 77, 83. Kernan, an aviation ordnanceman with Torpedo Squadron 6 on the *Enterprise* during Midway, noted that the "'Airedales' and ship's company rarely mixed. We were transient and they were not." See Kernan, *Unknown Battle of Midway*, 54.

6. "The Bravest Men."

7. Frederick Mears, *Carrier Combat* (New York: Ballantine Books, 1944), 33; Rose, *Ship That Held the Line*, 45.

8. See Ray E. Boomhower, *Fighter Pilot: The World War II Career of Alex Vraciu* (Indianapolis: Indiana Historical Society Press, 2010), 64; Mears, *Carrier Combat*, 35.

9. Boomhower, *Fighter Pilot*, 66–71; Mears, *Carrier Combat*, 43.

10. Mears, *Carrier Combat*, 35.

11. *Hornet* Diary.

12. "The Bravest Men"; Rose, *Ship That Held the Line*, 93; *Hornet* Diary.

13. "The Bravest Men"; *Hornet* Diary.

14. *Hornet* Diary.

15. Ibid. See also Samuel Eliot Morison, *History of United States Naval Operations in World War II*, vol. 4, *Coral Sea, Midway and Submarine Actions* (1949; Annapolis, MD: Naval Institute Press, 2010), 25–27. For the mission against the Japanese ships in Tulagi harbor, the *Yorktown* planes expended seventy-six 1,000-pound bombs, twenty-two torpedoes, 12,570 rounds of .50-caliber machine-gun bullets, and 70,095 rounds of .30-caliber machine-gun bullets. See *Combat Narratives: The Battle of the Coral Sea* (1943; Washington Navy Yard, DC: Naval History and Heritage Command, 2017), 8.

16. *Hornet* Diary; George Gay, *Sole Survivor: A Personal Story about the Battle of Midway* (1979; n.p.: Midway Publishers, 1986), 93–94.

17. Mears, *Carrier Combat*, 55–56; Recollections of Lieutenant George Gay, USNR, Archives, Naval History and Heritage Command, https://www.history.navy.mil/research/library/oral-histories/wwii/battle-of-midway/recollections-of-lieutenant-george-gay.html/.

18. *Hornet* Diary; Sidney L. James, "Torpedo Squadron 8," *Life*, August 31, 1942;

Robert J. Casey, *Torpedo Junction: With the Pacific Fleet from Pearl Harbor to Midway* (Indianapolis, IN: Bobbs-Merrill Company, 1942), 385.

19. "The Bravest Men"; Rose, *Ship That Held the Line*, 86–87.

20. *Hornet* Diary. For a description of the Devastator and its problems, and the difficulties with the Mark 13 torpedo, see Kernan, *Unknown Battle of Midway*, 30–33, 39–53, 62.

21. *Hornet* Diary; Morison, *Coral Sea, Midway and Submarine Actions*, 42, 63.

22. "The Bravest Men"; Rose, *Ship That Held the Line*, 94.

23. "The Bravest Men"; *Hornet* Diary.

24. "The Bravest Men."

25. *Hornet* Diary.

26. "The Bravest Men." For Admiral Nimitz's strategy regarding the planned Japanese operation against Nauru and Ocean islands, see John B. Lundstrom, *The First South Pacific Campaign: Pacific Fleet Strategy, December 1941–June 1942* (Annapolis, MD: Naval Institute Press, 1976), 156–59.

Chapter Five

1. Richard Tregaskis diary while on USS *Hornet*, Richard Tregaskis Collection, Howard Gotlieb Archival Research Center at Boston University (hereafter cited as *Hornet* Diary).

2. *Hornet* Diary.

3. Ibid.

4. Richard Tregaskis, "The Bravest Men," unpublished autobiography, Richard Tregaskis Papers, 06346, American Heritage Center, University of Wyoming, Laramie, Wyoming (hereafter cited as "The Bravest Men").

5. Craig L. Symonds, *The Battle of Midway* (New York: Oxford University Press, 2011), 185; Elliot Carlson, *Joe Rochefort's War: The Odyssey of the Codebreaker Who Outwitted Yamamoto at Midway* (2011; Annapolis, MD: Naval Institute Press, 2013), 334–36; Edwin T. Layton, Oral History Interview, National Museum of the Pacific War, http://digitalarchive.pacificwarmuseum.org/cdm/ref/collection/p16769coll1/id/2310/.

6. See Mark Stille, *Midway 1942: Turning Point in the Pacific* (Oxford, UK: Osprey Publishing, 2010), 34–36, 39–40; Chester B. Hearn, *Carriers in Combat: The Air War at Sea* (Mechanicsburg, PA: Stackpole Books, 2005), 88; Ronald H. Spector, *Eagle against the Sun: The American War With Japan* (New York: Free Press, 1985), 168–69; John B. Lundstrom, *The First South Pacific Campaign: Pacific Fleet Strategy, December 1941–June 1942* (Annapolis, MD: Naval Institute Press, 1976), 177.

7. Robert J. Mrazek, *A Dawn Like Thunder: The True Story of Torpedo Squadron Eight* (New York: Little, Brown and Company, 2008), 13; "The Bravest Men."

8. "The Bravest Men."

9. George Gay, *Sole Survivor: A Personal Story about the Battle of Midway* (1979; n.p.: Midway Publishers, 1986), 105–6; Frederick Mears, *Carrier Combat* (New York: Ballantine Books, 1944), 61.

10. Gay, *Sole Survivor*, 114–15; Recollections of Lieutenant George Gay, USNR, Archives, Naval History and Heritage Command, https://www.history.navy .mil/research/library/oral-histories/wwii/battle-of-midway/recollections-of-lieutenant-george-gay.html/.

11. "The Bravest Men."

12. Craig L. Symonds, "Mitscher and the Mystery of Midway," *Naval History Magazine* 26, no. 3, https://www.usni.org/magazines/naval-history-magazine /2012/may/mitscher-and-mystery-midway/; Theodore Taylor, *The Magnificent Mitscher* (1954; Annapolis, MD: Naval Institute Press, 1991), 136–37; "The Bravest Men."

13. "The Bravest Men."

14. Ibid.

15. Symonds, "Mitscher and the Mystery of Midway"; Symonds, *Battle of Midway*, 260–61.

16. Gay, *Sole Survivor*, 118–25, 170–71; Alvin B. Kernan, *The Unknown Battle of Midway: The Destruction of the American Torpedo Squadrons* (New Haven, CT: Yale University Press, 2005), 93. After the war, Gay noted that while some believed Waldron had been responsible for getting his squadron in trouble, he did not think so. "I know that if I had it all to do over again, even knowing that the odds were going to be like they were, knowing him like I did know him, I'd follow him again through exactly the same thing because I trusted him very well," said Gay. "We did things that he wanted us to do not because he was our boss, but because we felt that if we did the things he wanted us to do then it was the right thing to do. The Zeros that day just caught us off balance. We were at a disadvantage all the way around." See Recollections of Lieutenant George Gay.

17. "The Bravest Men"; Symonds, *Battle of Midway*, 287; Spector, *Eagle against the Sun*, 174; and Admiral John S. "Jimmie" Thach, "Flying into a Beehive: Fighting Three at Midway," *Naval History Magazine* 25, no. 3 (June 2007), https://www.usni.org/magazines/naval-history-magazine/2007/june/flying -beehive-fighting-three-midway/.

18. "The Bravest Men"; Symonds, *Battle of Midway*, 316–17.

19. "The Bravest Men"; Captain Marc Mitscher to The Chief of the Bureau of Ships, U.S.S. Hornet (CV-8) Report of Damage to Ship's Structure by

Machine Gun Fire, June 12, 1942, http://www.researcheratlarge.com/Ships/CV8/MidwayF4FDamageReport.html/.

20. "The Bravest Men"; Lisle A. Rose, *The Ship That Held the Line: The USS Hornet and the First Year of the Pacific War* (Annapolis, MD: Naval Institute Press, 1995), 139–40.
21. "The Bravest Men."
22. Ibid.
23. "The Bravest Men"; Symonds, *Battle of Midway*, 335.
24. "The Bravest Men."

Chapter Six

1. Richard Tregaskis, "The Bravest Men," unpublished autobiography, Richard Tregaskis Papers, 06346, American Heritage Center, University of Wyoming, Laramie, Wyoming (hereafter cited as "The Bravest Men").
2. "The Bravest Men"; George Gay, *Sole Survivor: A Personal Story about the Battle of Midway* (1979; n.p.: Midway Publishers, 1986), 138–39.
3. "The Bravest Men."
4. Ibid.
5. Richard Tregaskis diary while on USS *Hornet*, Richard Tregaskis Collection, Howard Gotlieb Archival Research Center, Boston University (hereafter cited as *Hornet* Diary).
6. "The Bravest Men."
7. Ibid. For details on the Marauder attack, see, Craig L. Symonds, *The Battle of Midway* (New York: Oxford University Press, 2011), 236.
8. "The Bravest Men."
9. Ibid.; John Costello, *The Pacific War* (New York: Rawson, Wade Publishers, 1981), 309.
10. "The Bravest Men."
11. "The Bravest Men"; Robert Trumball, "Big Bombers Won," *New York Times*, June 12, 1942; Ronald H. Spector, *Eagle against the Sun: The American War With Japan* (New York: Free Press, 1985), 177. See also Ian W. Toll, *The Conquering Tide: War in the Pacific Islands, 1942–1944* (New York: W. W. Norton and Company, 2015), 7.
12. "The Bravest Men"; Richard Tregaskis, "Eye Witness Tells How Carrier Based Planes Played Havoc with Jap Navy In Midway Fight," *Santa Ana (CA) Register*, June 23, 1942.
13. "The Bravest Men."
14. Ibid.
15. Ibid.

16. Ibid.

17. Richard Tregaskis, Guadalcanal notes, Tregaskis Collection, Gotlieb Archival Research Center; Barrett Tillman, *Enterprise: America's Fightingest Ship and the Men Who Helped Win World War II* (New York: Simon & Schuster, 2012), 91; Alexander A. Vandegrift, as told to Robert B. Asprey, *Once a Marine: The Memoirs of General A. A. Vandegrift, United States Marine Corps* (1964; New York: Ballantine Books, 1966), 18.

Chapter Seven

1. Richard Tregaskis, *Guadalcanal Diary* (1943; New York: Modern Library, 2000), 139–40.

2. Ibid., 141.

3. William Manchester, *Goodbye Darkness: A Memoir of the Pacific War* (Boston: Little, Brown and Company, 1979), 168; Herbert Christian Laing Merillat, *Guadalcanal Remembered* (New York: Dodd, Mead and Company, 1982), 36, 47, 71.

4. Richard Tregaskis, "What Really Happened at Guadalcanal," *Real: The Exciting Magazine for Men*, April–May 1958, 16–19.

5. Tregaskis, *Guadalcanal Diary*, 135, 160.

6. Ibid., 125, 129, 131; Peter Schrijvers, *The GI War against Japan: American Soldiers in Asia and the Pacific during World War II* (New York: New York University Press, 2002), 118, 120; Tregaskis, *Guadalcanal Diary*, 125, 131, 160; Gerald F. Linderman, *The World within War: America's Combat Experience in World War II* (New York: Free Press, 1997), 178.

7. Richard Tregaskis, "The Bravest Men," unpublished autobiography, Richard Tregaskis Papers, 06346, American Heritage Center, University of Wyoming, Laramie, Wyoming (hereafter cited as "The Bravest Men").

8. "The Bravest Men."

9. For the planning of the Guadalcanal campaign, see Mark Stille, *Guadalcanal 1942–43* (Oxford, UK: Osprey Publishing, 2015), 6–7, 11–12; Jeffrey R. Cox, *Morning Star, Midnight Sun: The Early Guadalcanal Campaign of World War II, August–October 1942* (Oxford, UK: Osprey Publishing, 2018), 42–49; Samuel Eliot Morison, *History of United States Naval Operations in World War II*, vol. 4, *Coral Sea, Midway and Submarines Actions, May 1942–August 1942* (1949; Annapolis, MD: Naval Institute Press, 2010), 245–63.

10. Alexander A. Vandegrift, as told to Robert B. Asprey, *Once a Marine: The Memoirs of General A. A. Vandegrift, United States Marine Corps* (1964; New York: Ballantine Books, 1966), 120; Merrill B. Twining, *No Bended Knee: The Battle for Guadalcanal* (New York: Presidio Press, 1996), Kindle edition, 54.

11. Alfred Campbell, *Mission to Guadalcanal* (n.p.: Uncommon Valor Press, 2015), 160, Kindle edition.

12. "The Bravest Men"; Tregaskis, *Guadalcanal Diary*, 7–9.

13. See, Ronald Spector, *Eagle against the Sun: The American War with Japan* (New York: Free Press, 1985), 191; Cox, *Morning Star, Midnight Sun*, 42–44; Vandegrift, *Once a Marine*, 120; Twining, *No Bended Knee*, 56–57. Some accounts have Turner reportedly confronting Fletcher after the conference and telling him about his decision to withdraw the carriers on the third day, "You son of a bitch, if you do that you are yellow." Fletcher adherents contend such a confrontation never took place. See James D. Hornfischer, *Neptune Inferno: The U.S. Navy at Guadalcanal* (New York: Bantam Books, 2011), 36. A defense of Fletcher's actions at Guadalcanal are ably presented in John B. Lundstrom's *Black Shoe Carrier Admiral: Frank Jack Fletcher at Coral Sea, Midway, and Guadalcanal* (Annapolis, MD: Naval Institute Press, 2006).

14. "The Bravest Men."

15. Ibid. Dirt was not the only problem the marines had to deal with on their transports. Many marines who sailed on the USS *John Ericsson* were sickened by rancid food, none of which, said one, was "fit to eat." See Cox, *Morning Star, Midnight Sun*, 38.

16. Tregaskis, *Guadalcanal Diary*, 10–11.

17. "The Bravest Men." Postbattle estimates had the actual number of Japanese at approximately 3,700 personnel on Guadalcanal, Tulagi, Guvutu, and Tanambogo, with only about 650 combat troops. See Stille, *Guadalcanal 1942–43*, 39.

18. Tregaskis, *Guadalcanal Diary*, 12, 14, 23.

19. Ibid., 14–15, 27.

20. "The Bravest Men"; Tregaskis, *Guadalcanal Diary*, 36; Memo from Leroy P. Hunt, August 3, 1942, in Richard Tregaskis Collection, Howard Gotlieb Archival Research Center at Boston University, Boston, Massachusetts (hereafter cited as Tregaskis Collection, Gotlieb Archival Research Center).

21. Tregaskis, *Guadalcanal Diary*, 28–30.

22. Tregaskis's unpublished notes regarding *Guadalcanal Diary*, November 14, 1965, Tregaskis Collection, Gotlieb Archival Research Center. Tregaskis noted that the diary summarized what had happened during each day on Guadalcanal, and he marked the key numbers of the notebooks in the diary. "The theory and practice was that I could get all the details I needed by referring to the notebook number 1, or 3, or 4 when and if I could later get to writing a book from my notes," he recalled. The notebooks included detailed information, and in comparing them with the final text of *Guadalcanal Diary*, Tregaskis noted that there were "20 or 40 or 50 facts in this kind of notebook for one which survives in to print." Ibid.

23. John Costello, *The Pacific War* (New York: Rawson, Wade Publishers, 1981), 322; "The Bravest Men."

24. Tregaskis, *Guadalcanal Diary*, 38, 40, 44.

25. Ibid., 48–50.

26. "The Bravest Men"; Vandegrift, *Once a Marine*, 127.

27. Tregaskis, *Guadalcanal Diary*, 53.

28. Ibid., 54–57.

29. Spector, *Eagle against the Sun*, 194–95; Jack Coggins, *The Campaign for Guadalcanal: A Battle That Made History* (Garden City, NY: Doubleday and Company, 1972), 41–42; Stille, *Guadalcanal 1942–43*, 45.

30. Vandegrift, *Once a Marine*, 131; Merillat, *Guadalcanal Remembered*, 77; "The Bravest Men"; Richard Tregaskis to Alexander Archer Vandegrift, May 22, 1959, Tregaskis Collection, American Heritage Center. Accounts differ on the number of rations available to the marines on Guadalcanal. See Richard B. Frank, *Guadalcanal: The Definitive Account of the Landmark Battle* (New York: Random House, 1990), 126–27, 673–74.

Chapter Eight

1. Richard Tregaskis, *Guadalcanal Diary* (1943; New York: Modern Library, 2000), 67–68; Richard Tregaskis, "Three Allied Boats Outrace Jap Submarine Off Coast of Solomons," *Greenfield (IN) Daily Reporter*, September 1, 1942. On August 12, 1942, Gen. Alexander Vandegrift had sent a message that the airfield on Guadalcanal was ready for operations. The Catalina that made the first landing on what became Henderson Field had been flown by Lt. William S. Sampson, the aide to Adm. John S. McCain Sr., Commander, Aircraft, South Pacific. See Robert Sherrod, *History of Marine Corps Aviation in World War II* (Washington, DC: Combat Forces Press, 1952), 77.

2. Tregaskis, "Three Allied Boats Outrace Jap Submarine Off Coast of Solomons."

3. Tregaskis, *Guadalcanal Diary*, 69–70.

4. Ibid., 82–83; Herbert Christian Laing Merillat, *Guadalcanal Remembered* (New York: Dodd, Mead and Company, 1982), 75.

5. Merillat, *Guadalcanal Remembered*, 71–72; Richard Tregaskis, "Guadalcanal—Uncensored (From Here)" manuscript, Richard Tregaskis Collection, Howard Gotlieb Archival Research Center at Boston University, Boston, Massachusetts. When *Time* magazine reporter John Hersey arrived on Guadalcanal in early October 1942, a marine officer gave him a pistol to take with him as he accompanied a combat mission. Hersey did not know that in his "untrained hands the gun was more a talisman than a weapon." Of course,

according to regulations issued by the U.S. War Department on January 21, 1942, war correspondents were forbidden from exercising command, being placed in positions of authority over military personnel, and bearing arms. For agreeing to follow such regulations, correspondents were "given the same privileges as commissioned officers in the matter of accommodations, transportation and messing facilities." See War Department, Basic Field Manual, Regulations for Correspondents Accompanying U.S. Army Forces in the Field, in Tregaskis Collection, Gotlieb Archival Research Center; John Hersey, *Into the Valley: Marines at Guadalcanal* (1943; Lincoln: University of Nebraska Press, 2002), xvi.

6. Tregaskis, *Guadalcanal Diary*, 144–46; Merrill B. Twining, *No Bended Knee: The Battle for Guadalcanal* (New York: Presidio Press, 1996), Kindle edition, 90.

7. Richard Tregaskis, "The Bravest Men," unpublished autobiography, Richard Tregaskis Papers, 06346, American Heritage Center, University of Wyoming, Laramie, Wyoming (hereafter cited as "The Bravest Men").

8. Alexander A. Vandegrift, as told to Robert B. Asprey, *Once a Marine: The Memoirs of General A. A. Vandegrift, United States Marine Corps* (1964; New York: Ballantine Books, 1966), 131, 134, 150.

9. Gen. Clifton B. Cates, oral history interview by Benis M. Frank, May 2, 1967, Historical Division, Headquarters, U.S. Marine Corps, Washington, D.C., https://www.usmcu.edu/Portals/218/Gen%20Clifton%20B_%20Cates.pdf/; Richard Tregaskis, "The War Starts," manuscript in Tregaskis Collection, Gotlieb Archival Research Center.

10. Tregaskis, *Guadalcanal Diary*, 86, 88; Vandegrift, *Once a Marine*, 150; J. W. Hurlbut, "Saga of a No. 1 War Correspondent," *New York Journal American*, May 29, 1943.

11. Stanley Coleman Jersey, *Hell's Islands: The Untold Story of Guadalcanal* (College Station: Texas A&M University Press, 2008), 186–87; Merillat, *Guadalcanal Remembered*, 69, 108; Twining, *No Bended Knee*, 90.

12. Merillat, *Guadalcanal Remembered*, 108, 118; Vandegrift, *Once a Marine*, 150; Richard Tregaskis to his parents, September 17, 1944, Tregaskis Collection, Gotlieb Archival Research Center.

13. Merillat, *Guadalcanal Remembered*, 108–9; Tregaskis, *Guadalcanal Diary*, 163–64, 192–93. Merillat noted that there was a split in the ranks among the correspondents, as Yarbrough, Durdin, and Kent were "vastly annoyed that Miller and Tregaskis had been on Guadalcanal from the beginning of the operation" and never missed an opportunity "to take a dig at them." See Merillat, *Guadalcanal Remembered*, 117.

14. Hurlbut, "Saga of a No. 1 War Correspondent"; Richard Tregaskis, "Tells

How Marines Dynamited Japs from Dugouts in Fierce Solomon Raids That Cost Enemy 2,000 Troops," *Mansfield (OH) News-Journal*, August 29, 1942.

15. Tregaskis, "Tells How Marines Dynamited Japs"; Martin "Whitey" Groft and Larry Alexander, *Bloody Ridge and Beyond: A World War II Marine's Memoirs of Edson's Raiders in the Pacific* (New York: Berkley Caliber, 2014), 60–61.

16. Tregaskis, "Tells How Marines Dynamited Japs"; Tregaskis, *Guadalcanal Diary*, 79–80.

17. Richard Tregaskis, "My Most Unforgettable Character—Red Mike Edson," undated, in Tregaskis Papers, American Heritage Center; Richard Tregaskis, "The Best Soldier I Ever Knew," *Saga Magazine*, February 1960, 17–19, 84–85.

18. Tregaskis, *Guadalcanal Diary*, 111, 221; "The Bravest Men"; Sherrod, *History of Marine Corps Aviation in World War II*, 79; Merillat, *Guadalcanal Remembered*, 93, 105.

19. Mark Stille, *Guadalcanal 1942–43* (Oxford, UK: Osprey Publishing, 2015), 46–47; "The Bravest Men"; Robert Leckie, *Challenge for the Pacific: Guadalcanal: The Turning Point of the War* (1965; New York: Bantam Books, 2010), 132; Jack Coggins, *The Campaign for Guadalcanal: A Battle That Made History* (Garden City, NY: Doubleday and Company, 1972), 59.

20. Tregaskis, *Guadalcanal Diary*, 112–17.

21. Richard Tregaskis, "News Man Sees 750 Japs Wiped Out by U.S. Marines," *Albuquerque Journal*, September 5, 1942; Tregaskis, *Guadalcanal Diary*, 127.

22. Stille, *Guadalcanal 1942–43*, 50; Vandegrift, *Once a Marine*, 142; Tregaskis, *Guadalcanal Diary*, 130–31, 134; Leckie, *Challenge for the Pacific*, 148, 153.

23. Richard Tregaskis, "Dear Mom: Johnny Marine Tells About 'Dull' Days on Guadalcanal," *Moline (IL) Daily Dispatch*, September 19, 1942.

24. Tregaskis, *Guadalcanal Diary*, 149–50.

25. Ibid., 152–53.

26. Joseph H. Alexander, *Edson's Raiders: The 1st Marine Raider Battalion in World War II* (Annapolis, MD: Naval Institute Press, 2001), 110; Tregaskis, *Guadalcanal Diary*, 165–66.

27. Alexander, *Edson's Raiders*, 111; Tregaskis, *Guadalcanal Diary*, 171–72.

28. Tregaskis, *Guadalcanal Diary*, 172–73; Richard Tregaskis, "Two Destroyers Put Up Struggle But Lose to Japs," *Greenfield (IN) Daily Reporter*, October 8, 1942.

29. Tregaskis, *Guadalcanal Diary*, 176–78.

Chapter Nine

1. Richard Tregaskis, *Guadalcanal Diary* (1943; New York: Modern Library, 2000), 181–82; Michael S. Smith, *Bloody Ridge: The Battle That Saved Guadalcanal* (Novato, CA: Presidio Press, 2000), 119–20.

2. Tregaskis, *Guadalcanal Diary*, 182; Joseph H. Alexander, *Edson's Raiders: The 1st Marine Raider Battalion in World War II* (Annapolis, MD: Naval Institute Press, 2001), 120; Samuel B. Griffith II, *The Battle for Guadalcanal* (1963; Annapolis, MD: Nautical and Aviation Publishing Company of America, 1979), 107; Marlin "Whitey" Groft and Larry Alexander, *Bloody Ridge and Beyond: A World War II Marine's Memoir of Edson's Raiders in the Pacific* (New York: Berkley Caliber, 2014), 83; Richard Tregaskis, "Writer Sees Marine Raiders in Surprise Move Against Japs," *Greenfield (IN) Daily Reporter*, September 26, 1942.

3. Tregaskis, "Writer Sees Marine Raiders in Surprise Move Against Japs"; Robert L. Sherrod, *Tarawa: The Story of a Battle* (1944; reprint, Fredericksburg, TX: Admiral Nimitz Foundation, 1999), 35.

4. Richard Tregaskis, "The Best Soldier I Ever Knew," *Saga Magazine*, February 1960, 17–19, 84–85; Stephen Mark Houseknecht, "The Elite of the Elites: The U.S. Marine Raider Battalions, 1942–1944: A Case Study in Elite Military Organizations" (master's thesis, Missouri State University, 2015). Tregaskis's honorary designation as an Edson's Raider came by Western Union telegram on August 7, 1954, signed by Col. John B. Sweeney, and can be found in Richard Tregaskis Collection, Howard Gotlieb Archival Research Center at Boston University, Boston, Massachusetts.

5. William Bruce Johnson, *The Pacific Campaign in World War II: From Pearl Harbor to Guadalcanal* (London: Routledge, 2006), 237; Alexander, *Edson's Raiders*, 118; Smith, *Bloody Ridge*, 157.

6. Tregaskis, *Guadalcanal Diary*, 183; Robert C. Miller, "Solomons Notes," *Amarillo (TX) Globe*, October 15, 1942; Richard Tregaskis, "Solomon Eyewitness: How Marine Commandos Landed and Took Japs," *Lowell (MA) Sun*, September 25, 1942.

7. Richard Tregaskis, "Japs Put Up Slight Resistance as Attack Is Complete Surprise," *Wichita (KS) Daily Times*, September 27, 1942; Tregaskis, *Guadalcanal Diary*, 185.

8. Tregaskis, "Japs Put Up Slight Resistance"; Miller, "Solomons Notes"; Tregaskis, *Guadalcanal Diary*, 187–88, 192.

9. Tregaskis, "Japs Put Up Slight Resistance"; Griffith, *Battle for Guadalcanal*, 109.

10. Tregaskis, "Japs Put Up Slight Resistance"; Miller, "Solomons Notes"; Smith, *Bloody Ridge*, 89. The practice of extracting gold teeth from the dead, and those barely hanging on to life, continued as the marines leapfrogged their way across the Pacific. During the invasion of Peleliu, marine mortar man Eugene B. Sledge noted that during a lull in battle some of his comrades stripped Japanese bodies looking for souvenirs. "This was a gruesome business, but Marines executed it in a most methodical manner," Sledge observed. "Helmet

headbands were checked for flags, packs and pockets were emptied, and gold teeth were extracted." Eugene B. Sledge, *With the Old Breed at Peleliu and Okinawa* (1981; New York: Oxford University Press, 1990), 118–20. See also Gerald F. Linderman, *The World within War: America's Combat Experience in World War II* (New York: The Free Press, 1997), 180–81.

11. Jon T. Hoffman, *Once a Legend: "Red Mike" Edson of the Marine Raiders* (Novato, CA: Presidio Press, 1994), 191; Alexander, *Edson's Raiders*, 132; Tregaskis, *Guadalcanal Diary*, 190; Tregaskis, "Japs Put Up Slight Resistance."

12. Tregaskis, *Guadalcanal Diary*, 190–91.

13. Griffith, *Battle for Guadalcanal*, 110, 112–13; George W. Smith, *The Do-or-Die Men: The 1st Marine Raider Battalion at Guadalcanal* (New York: Pocket Books, 2003), 220–21, 224.

14. Tregaskis, *Guadalcanal Diary*, 194–95; Alexander, *Edson's Raiders*, 142.

15. Tregaskis, *Guadalcanal Diary*, 198–99.

16. Griffith, *Battle for Guadalcanal*, 116–17; Herbert Christian Laing Merillat, *Guadalcanal Remembered* (New York: Dodd, Mead and Company, 1982), 122; Alexander A. Vandegrift, as told to Robert B. Asprey, *Once a Marine: The Memoirs of General A. A. Vandegrift, United States Marine Corps* (1964; New York: Ballantine Books, 1966), 154.

17. Tregaskis, *Guadalcanal Diary*, 202–3; Vandegrift, *Once a Marine*, 155; Richard Tregaskis, "Three-Pronged Japanese Assault Ends Disastrously in Solomons," *Port Arthur (TX) News*, October 13, 1942.

18. Griffith, *Battle for Guadalcanal*, 119–20; Smith, *Bloody Ridge*, 139–42, 151; Merillat, *Guadalcanal Remembered*, 123; Smith, *Do-or-Die Men*, 275; Herbert Christian Laing Merillat, *The Island: A History of the First Marine Division on Guadalcanal* (1944; Yardley, PA: Westholme Publishing, 2010), 99. The "do you want to live forever?" question was first posed by marine sergeant major Dan Daly at the Battle of Belleau Wood in World War I. Daly's full quote was, "Come on you son of a bitches, do you want to live forever?"

19. Tregaskis, "Three-Pronged Japanese Assault Ends Disastrously in Solomons"; Tregaskis, *Guadalcanal Diary*, 205–6, 209.

20. Houseknecht, "The Elite of the Elites," 119; Smith, *Bloody Ridge*, 147; Griffith, *Battle for Guadalcanal*, 122; Alexander, *Edson's Raiders*, 198.

21. Smith, *Bloody Ridge*, 148; Tregaskis, *Guadalcanal Diary*, 207–8.

22. Tregaskis, *Guadalcanal Diary*, 217–18.

23. Richard Tregaskis, "The Bravest Men," unpublished autobiography, Richard Tregaskis Papers, 06346, American Heritage Center, University of Wyoming, Laramie, Wyoming (hereafter cited as "The Bravest Men"); Smith, *Bloody Ridge*, 157.

24. Tregaskis, *Guadalcanal Diary*, 222, 231; Richard Tregaskis to Madeline Tregaskis, December 10, 1942, Tregaskis Papers, American Heritage Center.
25. Robert C. Miller diary, University of Nevada, Reno Special Collections, University of Nevada, Reno Knowledge Center, Reno, Nevada. As he left Guadalcanal, Miller said he felt odd leaving a place he had spent forty-two of "the most eventful days of my life." He experienced a pang in parting the island that was "mingled with a feeling of complete relief. The place looked so quiet and peaceful one would never suspect the horror that the place held or the deaths, suffering and destruction that had been wrought on the island." Ibid.
26. "The Bravest Men."
27. Tregaskis, *Guadalcanal Diary*, 225; Richard Tregaskis letter to Tom [no last name], March 5, 1954, Tregaskis Collection, Gotlieb Archival Research Center; Phil Mayer, "Tregaskis Was First on China Bomb," *Honolulu Star-Bulletin*, August 1, 1967.

Chapter Ten

1. Richard Tregaskis to Tom [no last name], March 5, 1954, Richard Tregaskis Collection, Howard Gotlieb Archival Research Center at Boston University, Boston, Massachusetts.
2. Richard Tregaskis, *Guadalcanal Diary* (1943; New York: Modern Library, 2000), 225–27; Tregaskis to Tom, March 5, 1954.
3. James Norman Price, interview with Floyd Cox, May 2, 2001, Center for Pacific War Studies, National Museum of the Pacific War, Admiral Nimitz Museum, Fredericksburg, Texas.
4. Tregaskis to Tom, March 5, 1954; Richard Tregaskis, "The Bravest Men," unpublished autobiography, Richard Tregaskis Papers, 06346, American Heritage Center, University of Wyoming, Laramie, Wyoming (hereafter cited as "The Bravest Men"); Tregaskis, *Guadalcanal Diary*, 228–29.
5. "The Bravest Men."
6. Ibid.
7. William Bruce Johnson, *The Pacific Campaign in World War II: From Pearl Harbor to Guadalcanal* (London: Routledge, 2006), 258–59; "The Bravest Men."
8. "The Bravest Men."
9. Ibid.
10. Ibid.; Richard Tregaskis to Archibald and Maude Tregaskis, November 7, 1942, Gotlieb Archival Research Center .
11. "The Bravest Men"; Tregaskis, *Guadalcanal Diary*, 231.
12. "The Bravest Men."

13. Ibid.; Phil Mayer, "Tregaskis Was First On China Bomb," *Honolulu Star-Bulletin*, August 1, 1967.

14. Richard Tregaskis, telegram to Barry Faris, November 1 and 2, 1942, and Faris telegram to Tregaskis, November 2, 1942, Random House Records, Rare Book and Manuscript Library, Columbia University, New York (hereafter cited as Random House Records). See also Bennett Cerf, *At Random: The Reminiscences of Bennett Cerf* (New York: Random House, 1977), 162–63.

15. Tregaskis to Archibald and Maude Tregaskis, November 7, 1942, Tregaskis Collection, Gotlieb Archival Research Center.

16. Richard Tregaskis to Madeline Tregaskis, December 10, 1942, Tregaskis Papers, American Heritage Center.

17. Cerf, *At Random*, 163; Al Silverman, ed., *The Book of the Month: Sixty Years of Books in American Life* (Boston: Little, Brown and Company, 1986), xiii; Richard Lingeman, *Don't You Know There's a War On? The American Home Front, 1941–1945* (1970; New York: Thunder Mouth's Press/Nation Books, 2003), 273; Saxe Cummins to N. R. Howard, December 3, 1942, Random House Records.

18. Bennett Cerf telegram, November 13, 1942, Random House Records; "'Diary' Chosen Book of Month," *Port Arthur (TX) News*, November 19, 1942; Dorothy Canfield, "War Correspondent Describes Fighting At Guadalcanal—Tells How Marines Landed and Took Over Jap Air Field," *Galveston (TX) Tribune*, January 22, 1943.

19. Damon Runyon column, *Endicott (NY) Daily Bulletin*, January 30, 1943; Clifton Fadiman book review, *The New Yorker*, January 23, 1943, in Richard Tregaskis Collection, COLL/566, Archives Branch, Marine Corps History Division, Quantico, Virginia; John Chamberlain, "Books of the Times," *New York Times*, January 21, 1943; *Guadalcanal Diary* review, *Infantry Journal*, February 1943, in Tregaskis Collection, Archives Branch, Marine Corps History Division.

20. Ward Greene to Bennett Cerf, November 19, 1942, Random House Records, and "Guadalcanal Diary," American Film Institute Catalog of Feature Films, https://catalog.afi.com/Catalog/moviedetails/462/.

21. Ward Greene to Bennett Cerf, November 13, 1942, Random House Records; Richard Tregaskis, "The War Starts," manuscript, Tregaskis Collection, Gotlieb Archival Research Center; Tregaskis letter to mother and father, November 29, 1942, Tregaskis Collection, Gotlieb Archival Research Center.

Chapter Eleven

1. Richard Tregaskis, dispatch on Russell Islands operation, Richard Tregaskis Collection, Howard Gotlieb Archival Research Center at Boston University, Boston, Massachusetts (hereafter cited as Tregaskis Collection, Gotlieb Archival Research Center).

2. Ibid. See also David L. Snead, "Obscure But Important: The United States and the Russell Islands in World War II," *Journal of America's Military Past* 29 (Spring/Summer 2003): 5–30.

3. Richard Tregaskis, "Victory" manuscript, Tregaskis Collection, Gotlieb Archival Research Center; Alexander A. Vandegrift, as told to Robert B. Asprey, *Once a Marine: The Memoirs of General A. A. Vandegrift, United States Marine Corps* (1964; New York: Ballantine Books, 1966), 203; Herbert Christian Laing Merillat, *Guadalcanal Remembered* (New York: Dodd, Mead and Company, 1982), 217; Richard Tregaskis, "Jap Attack to Regain Guadalcanal Forecast," *San Francisco Examiner*, January 7, 1943.

4. Tregaskis, "Victory" manuscript.

5. John Miller Jr., *Guadalcanal: The First Offensive* (1949; Washington, DC: Center of Military History, 1995), 173–74; Richard Tregaskis, dispatch, December 19, 1942, Tregaskis Collection, Gotlieb Archival Research Center.

6. Tregaskis, dispatch, December 19, 1942.

7. Ibid.

8. Ibid.

9. Richard Tregaskis, dispatch, December 20, Tregaskis Collection, Gotlieb Archival Research Center; *11th Bombardment Group (H): The Grey Geese* (Paducah, KY: Turner Publishing Company, 1996), Kindle edition, 713.

10. Snead, "Obscure but Important," 10; Tregaskis, dispatch on Russell Islands; George C. Dyer, *The Amphibians Came to Conquer: The Story of Admiral Richmond Kelly Turner* (Washington, DC: U.S. Department of the Navy, 1972), 460.

11. Tregaskis, dispatch on Russell Islands; Dyer, *Amphibians Came to Conquer*, 459, 468–70.

12. Tregaskis, dispatch on Russell Islands.

13. Ibid.

14. Tregaskis, dispatch on Russell Islands; Richard Tregaskis, "U.S. Occupies Russell Islands, 30 Miles North of Guadalcanal," *New York Herald Tribune*, May 4, 1943.

15. Tregaskis, dispatch on Russell Islands.

16. Ibid.

17. Ibid.

18. Ibid.

19. Ibid.

20. Richard Tregaskis to Mr. and Mrs. A. Tregaskis, January 23, 1943, and February 16, 1943, Tregaskis Collection, Gotlieb Archival Research Center.

21. Richard Tregaskis to Mr. and Mrs. A. Tregaskis, February 16, 1943.

22. Barry Faris to Mrs. Archibald Tregaskis, March 3, 1943, and Richard Tregaskis to Mr. and Mrs. A. Tregaskis, April 6, 1943, Tregaskis Collection, Gotlieb Archival Research Center. Later in his life, Tregaskis wrote to his agent at the time that one of the "most traumatic experiences" of his life had been when King Features sold the movie rights to *Guadalcanal Diary* for less than he thought it could, and that the 20th Century Fox film went on to gross millions of dollars at the box office. See Richard Tregaskis to Paul R. Reynolds, August 19, 1967, Richard Tregaskis Collection, American Heritage Center, University of Wyoming, Laramie, Wyoming.

23. Richard Tregaskis, *Seven Leagues to Paradise* (Garden City, NY: Doubleday and Company, 1951), 57–58; Richard Tregaskis to Mr. and Mrs. A. Tregaskis, March 27, 1943, and April 6, 1943, Tregaskis Collection, Gotlieb Archival Research Center.

24. Richard Tregaskis, "The Parachute Jump," in *Deadline Delayed, by Members of the Overseas Press Club of America* (New York: E. P. Dutton and Company, 1947), 244. For background on the First Marine Parachute Battalion, see Jon T. Hoffman, *Silk Chutes and Hard Fighting: U.S. Marine Corps Parachute Units in World War II* (Washington, DC: History and Museums Division, Headquarters, U.S. Marine Corps, 1999).

25. Tregaskis, "Parachute Jump," 245–56.

26. Ibid., 248–49.

27. Ibid., 249–50.

28. Barry Faris to Mrs. Archibald Tregaskis, April 13, 1943, Tregaskis Collection, Gotlieb Archival Research Center; "Tregaskis Awarded Holmes Reporting Trophy for 1942," *New York Journal-American*, April 20, 1942; "Tregaskis Back in U.S., Wants to Be Off Again," *Editor & Publisher*, January 29, 1944. The Holmes trophy was named in honor of the former manager of the INS's Washington, DC, bureau, and was voted on by a panel that included Neil H. Swanson, executive editor of the *Baltimore Sunpapers*; Kenneth MacDonald, managing editor of the *Des Moines Register and Tribune*; A. H. Kirchhofer, managing editor of the *Buffalo Evening News*; George W. Healy Jr., managing editor of the *New Orleans Times-Picayune*; and William Randolph Hearst Jr., publisher of the *New York Journal-American*. See "Tregaskis Awarded Holmes Reporting Trophy for 1942."

Chapter Twelve

1. Richard Tregaskis, *Invasion Diary* (1944; Lincoln: University of Nebraska Press, 2004), 86; Richard Tregaskis, "Lone Commando First in Messina," *Munster (IN) Times*, August 20, 1943.
2. Tregaskis, *Invasion Diary*, 80, 86–87.
3. Ibid., 87.
4. Richard Tregaskis, "The Bravest Men," unpublished autobiography, Tregaskis Papers, 06346, American Heritage Center, University of Wyoming, Laramie, Wyoming (hereafter cited as "The Bravest Men").
5. Tregaskis, *Invasion Diary*, 33, 93.
6. Richard Tregaskis, "'Amphibians' of Yanks Keen to Get Going," *Syracuse (NY) Herald Journal*, June 23, 1943; Richard Tregaskis, "Nazi Airmen Tougher Than Japs Key Says," *Syracuse (NY) Herald Journal*, June 22, 1943.
7. For the planning for Operation Husky, see Steven J. Zaloga, *Sicily 1943: The Debut of Allied Joint Operations* (Oxford, UK: Osprey Publishing, 2013), 6; John Keegan, *The Second World War* (New York: Viking, 1989), 316–19; Alan Axelrod, *Patton: A Biography* (New York: Palgrave Macmillan, 2006), 101–3.
8. Leo Dolan to J. C. Oestreicher, June 29, 1943, Richard Tregaskis Collection, COLL/566, Archives Branch, Marine Corps History Division, Quantico, Virginia; Tregaskis, *Invasion Diary*, 3–4.
9. Tregaskis, *Invasion Diary*, 4–5; Richard Tregaskis, "Gigantic Aerial Assault Precedes Allied Invasion," *New Castle (IN) News*, July 10, 1943.
10. Richard Tregaskis, "Col. Roosevelt Spurns Desk Job to Photograph Bomb Results in Sicily," *Saint Louis Star and Times*, July 16, 1943; Tregaskis, *Invasion Diary*, 5–8.
11. Tregaskis, *Invasion Diary*, 28–30.
12. Richard Tregaskis, "Snipers Worry Yanks, But They Grab Nicosia," *Greenfield (IN) Daily Reporter*, August 3, 1943; Tregaskis, *Invasion Diary*, 35–40.
13. Richard Tregaskis, "Yanks Face Mud and Bullets in Drive Toward Nicosia," *Saint Louis Star and Times*, August 4, 1943; Tregaskis, *Invasion Diary*, 46–49.
14. Tregaskis, *Invasion Diary*, 53; Ray Moseley, *Reporting War: How Foreign Correspondents Risked Capture, Torture and Death to Cover World War II* (New Haven, CT: Yale University Press, 2017), 201.
15. Tregaskis, *Invasion Diary*, 53–59.
16. Richard Tregaskis, "Yanks, British Near Junction," *San Francisco Examiner*, August 10, 1943.
17. Ibid.
18. Richard Tregaskis, "Sicily Campaign Called Battle of the Roads," *Richmond (IN) Palladium-Item*, September 3, 1943.

19. Ibid.

20. Christopher Chant, Codenames: Operations of World War 2, http://doen names/info/operation/blackcock-i/; Tregaskis, *Invasion Diary*, 74–75. Later, the same codename, Operation Blackcock, was used for an operation by the British Second Army in January 1945 to clear German forces near the Roer and Wurm Rivers. See Operation Blackcock, Commando Veterans Archive, http://www.commandoveterans.org/OperationBlackcock/.

21. Tregaskis, *Invasion Diary*, 76.

22. Ibid., 77.

23. Robert Barr Smith, "'Mad Jack' Churchill—A Rare Breed of Warrior," Warfare History Network, http://warefarehistorynetwork.com/2019/01/07/mad -jack-churchill-a-rare-breed-of-warrior/; Carlo D'Este, *Bitter Victory: The Battle for Sicily, 1943* (1988; New York: Harper Perennial, 2008), 518–19; Tregaskis, *Invasion Diary*, 82–83.

24. Tregaskis, *Invasion Diary*, 86–88.

25. Ibid., 88; Michael Chinigo, "How Messina Command Surrendered to Reporter," *Pittsburgh Sun-Telegram*, August 18, 1943.

26. Tregaskis, *Invasion Diary*, 89; Eric Ethier, "General George S. Patton's Race to Capture Messina," History Net, http://www.historynet.com/world-war-ii -general-george-s-patton-race-to-capture-messina.htm; Patrick Delaforce, *Monty's Marauders: Black Rat and Red Fox: 4th & 8th Independent Armoured Brigades in WW2* (Brighton, UK: Tom Donovan Publishing, 1997), 63; Zaloga, *Sicily 1943*, 80–81.

27. Tregaskis, *Invasion Diary*, 89–90.

Chapter Thirteen

1. Margaret Bourke-White, *"They Call It Purple Heart Valley": A Combat Chronicle of the War in Italy* (1944: Auckland: Pickle Partners Publishing, 2015), Kindle edition, 2338, 2349; LeGette Blythe, *38th Evac: The Story of the Men and Women Who Served in World War II with the 38th Evacuation Hospital in North Africa and Italy* (Charlotte, NC: Heritage Printers, 1966), 149.

2. Bourke-White, *"They Call It Purple Heart Valley,"* 2338; Richard Tregaskis, *Invasion Diary* (1944; Lincoln: University of Nebraska Press, 2004), 217.

3. Bourke-White, *"They Call It Purple Heart Valley,"* 2349.

4. Tregaskis, "Italian Town of Horror Is Sample of Their 'Answer,'" *Fort Worth (TX) Star-Telegram*, October 30, 1943; Tregaskis, *Invasion Diary*, 180–81. Tregaskis, in *Invasion Diary*, used a different quote from the bulldozer driver than the one he used in his original dispatch from the front. Instead of saying that the Italians had only got what was coming to them, the quote he used

in the book was gentler, as the soldier says, "Sometimes I feel kinda sorry for these poor bastards." See *Invasion Diary*, 181.

5. Ray E. Boomhower, *The Soldier's Friend: A Life of Ernie Pyle* (Indianapolis: Indiana Historical Society Press, 2006), 76; Robert Capa, *Slightly Out of Focus* (1947; New York: Modern Library, 2001), 91; Tregaskis, *Invasion Diary*, 139.

6. Tregaskis, *Invasion Diary*, 200–201.

7. Ibid., 92–93.

8. Ibid., 112–13.

9. Richard Tregaskis, "'Italy Will Be Tough': Tregaskis Depicts Yanks' Advance against Fierce Resistance," *Cedar Rapids (IA) Gazette*, September 20, 1943; Richard Tregaskis, "Creepy Details of an Advance," *Doylestown (PA) Daily Intelligencer*, September 23, 1943; Tregaskis, *Invasion Diary*, 120.

10. Tregaskis, "Creepy Details of an Advance"; Richard Tregaskis, "Tregaskis Tells of Major's Heroic Death," *Lowell (MA) Sun*, December 9, 1943; Tregaskis, *Invasion Diary*, 120–21. Tregaskis's dispatches about his troops did not go unnoticed by Maj. Gen. Matthew B. Ridgway, who commanded the Eighty-Second Airborne. In a November 15, 1943, letter to Barry Faris, INS editor, he noted that for weeks Tregaskis had been closely associated with his division. "Mr. Tregaskis, by reason of his professional competence, genial personality, and cheerful sharing of all dangers and hardships has come to be considered a member of the Division," wrote Ridgway. M. B. Ridgway to Barry Faris, November 15, 1943, Richard Tregaskis Collection, COLL/566, Archives Branch, Marine Corps History Division, Quantico, Virginia.

11. Tregaskis, "Tregaskis Tells of Major's Heroic Death." Waskow, commander of Company B of the 143rd Infantry Regiment, Thirty-Sixth Infantry Division, had been killed near San Pietro on December 14, 1943, while battling against German forces. Pyle's column, "The Death of Captain Waskow," appeared in American newspapers on January 10, 1944. See Boomhower, *Soldier's Friend*, 77–78.

12. Tregaskis, *Invasion Diary*, 149–50; Reynolds Packard, "First 4 Newsmen Ride into Naples in Hoosier's Jeep," *Indianapolis Star*, October 4, 1943; Richard Tregaskis, "Four Writers 'Take' Naples," *Port Arthur (TX) News*, October 3, 1943.

13. Packard, "First 4 Newsmen Ride into Naples in Hoosier's Jeep"; Tregaskis, *Invasion Diary*, 150–53. Always thinking of what might interest readers in the United States, the journalists in the jeep made sure to stop and obtain the names of the first American troops to enter Naples. Tregaskis reported that they were Lt. Ray Carey of Schuylerville, New York; Pvt. Ralph M. Wise of Chicago, Illinois; Pvt. Robert Miller of Chicago; and Pvt. Jack Sheriff of Detroit, Michigan. Tregaskis, *Invasion Diary*, 153–54.

14. Richard Tregaskis, "Food Shortage in Naples Most Serious Problem to Face Allied Military Government, Colonel Reports," *Port Arthur (TX) News*, October 8, 1943; Tregaskis, *Invasion Diary*, 159–60. See also "Major Edgar Erskine Hume," *Register of Kentucky State Historical Society* 19 (May 1921): 48–53, http://www.jstor.org/stable/23369552/.

15. Tregaskis, *Invasion Diary*, 161.

16. Barry Faris, "Front Line—Editor's Eye-View," *New York Mirror*, November 4, 1943, and Barry Faris, "Tregaskis Takes Faris on 'Cook's Tour' of Front," *Editor and Publisher*, November 6, 1943. See also, Tregaskis, *Invasion Diary*, 185–88.

17. Faris, "Tregaskis Takes Faris on 'Cook's Tour' of Front."

18. Tregaskis, *Invasion Diary*, 187–88; "Tregaskis Takes Faris on 'Cook's Tour' of Front."

19. Tregaskis, *Invasion Diary*, 193–97. After the war, Yarborough, who had a high opinion of Darby, added that mixing paratroopers and the rangers "was like mixing oil and water. Here we went in for the traditional esprit of the soldier based on the customs of the service, even in the shell holes. Every man shaved every day no matter what. Our people looked sharp. I required it and they took pride in the parachute uniform and the badge they had. Darby's guys looked like cutthroats. They looked like the sweepings of the bar rooms." See Kenneth Finlayson, "Lieutenant General William P. Yarborough," https://www.soc.mil/ARSOF_History/articles/pdf/v2n2_yarborough.pdf.

20. Tregaskis, *Invasion Diary*, 201–3.

21. Ibid., 204–5.

22. Richard Tregaskis, "War Writer, Seriously Hurt in Italy, Describes Sensations of Wounded Man," *Moline (IL) Daily Dispatch*, January 25, 1944; Tregaskis, *Invasion Diary*, 206–8.

23. Richard Tregaskis, draft of article about wounding, Richard Tregaskis Collection, Howard Gotlieb Archival Research Center at Boston University, Boston, Massachusetts; Tregaskis, *Invasion Diary*, 208–9; Michael Chinigo, "Wounded INS Correspondent Anxious To Be on 'Go Again,'" *Richmond (IN) Palladium-Item*, November 26, 1943.

24. Tregaskis, draft of article about wounding, Tregaskis Collection, Gotlieb Archival Research Center. See also Richard Tregaskis, "The Diary of a Wound," *Coronet* 16 (June 1944): 4–5.

25. "War Writer, Seriously Hurt in Italy, Describes Sensations of Wounded Man"; Tregaskis, draft of article about wounding, Tregaskis Collection, Gotlieb Archival Research Center; Tregaskis, *Invasion Diary*, 210–11.

26. Tregaskis, *Invasion Diary*, 211–12; Tregaskis, "Diary of a Wound," 5.

27. Tregaskis, draft of article about wounding; Tregaskis, *Invasion Diary*, 212–13.

28. Blythe, *38th Evac*, 148. See also Kenneth L. Dixon, "Dick Tregaskis Anxious to See More Action," *New York Journal*, December 8, 1943.
29. Tregaskis, *Invasion Diary*, 215; Blythe, *38th Evac*, 149.
30. Tregaskis, *Invasion Diary*, 216–20; "Tregaskis Back in U.S., Wants to Be Off Again," *Editor and Publisher*, January 29, 1944.
31. Tregaskis, *Invasion Diary*, 218–20, 223.
32. Tregaskis, *Invasion Diary*, 222–24; Richard Tregaskis, "Wounded News Writer Eager for More Action," *Newark (NJ) Star Ledger*, January 21, 1944.
33. Ernie Pyle, *Brave Men* (New York: Henry Holt and Company, 1944), 121.
34. Tregaskis, *Invasion Diary*, 239.
35. Ibid., 228–29, 234, 241.

Chapter Fourteen

1. Richard Tregaskis, "'Slight Resistance' Deadly, Writer Inside Nazi Pillbox Discovers," *Albuquerque Journal*, October 5, 1944; Charles D. MacDonald, *The Siegfried Line Campaign* (1963; Washington, DC: Center of Military History, United States Army, 1990), 29–30.
2. Tregaskis, "Slight Resistance."
3. Ibid.
4. Richard Tregaskis, "Tregaskis Skull 'Miracle' Told," *New York Journal-American*, June 13, 1944. The army doctors that worked on Tregaskis were Maj. Barnes Woodall, Lt. Col. Arthur Y. Hemberger, and Capt. Williams S. McCune. "Hemberger made and inserted the plate after Woodall and McCune performed the delicate bone surgery and the trepanning necessary to remove the bone fragments from the brain tissues," according to a newspaper report. See "Operate Again on Tregaskis," *New York Journal-American*, May 28, 1944.
5. "Gets Purple Heart," *Port Arthur (TX) News*, June 11, 1944; "Among the New Books," *Syracuse (NY) Herald American*, February 6, 1944; Marian Tregaskis to Bennett Cerf, March 16 and April 3, 1944, Random House Records, Rare Book and Manuscript Library, Columbia University, New York.
6. "Must Meet Foe Face to Face, Be Tougher, Says Tregaskis," *Elizabeth (NJ) Journal*, February 1, 1944; Erich Brandeis, "Correspondent Asks: What Has Become of America?" *Uniontown (PA) Morning Herald*, June 12, 1944.
7. Richard Tregaskis to Maude and Archibald Tregaskis, July 27, 1944, Richard Tregaskis Collection, Howard Gotlieb Archival Research Center at Boston University, Boston, Massachusetts; Martin Blumenson, *Breakout and Pursuit* (1961; Washington, DC: Center of Military History, United States Army, 1993), 11–12; John C. McManus, *The Americans at Normandy: The Summer of 1944—The American War from the Normandy Beaches to Falaise* (New York:

Forge, 2004), 175, 177, 281; Richard Tregaskis, "Tregaskis Sees Panzer Line Aflame," *Miami Herald*, July 30, 1944.

8. Richard Tregaskis, "U.S. Speed Too Much for Nazis," *Moline (IL) Daily Dispatch*, August 5, 1944.

9. Richard Tregaskis, "Guns 'Persuade' Nazis to Fight," *New York Journal-American*, August 17, 1944.

10. Richard Tregaskis, "Tregaskis Writes of Carnage in Argentan-Falaise Pocket," *Mattoon (IL) Daily Journal Gazette*, August 23, 1944; Dwight D. Eisenhower, *Crusade in Europe* (New York: Doubleday, 1948), 279.

11. Tregaskis, "Tregaskis Writes of Carnage in Argentan-Falaise Pocket"; Paul Gallico, "Dreams of Tiger Tanks Versus Road Trucks," *Indianapolis Star*, July 6, 1947.

12. Richard Tregaskis, "Tank Warfare Proves Most Nerve-Wracking," *San Francisco Examiner*, April 8, 1945. See also Dr. Ralph C. Greene, "The Triumph and Tragedy of Major General Maurice Rose," *Armor* 100 (March–April 1991): 21–29.

13. Richard Tregaskis, "Eleven Thousand Feet and No Place To Go," in *How I Got That Story, by Members of the Overseas Press Club of America*, ed. David Brown and W. Richard Bruner (New York: E. P. Dutton and Company, 1967), 156–57, and "367th Flight Group Newsletter," number 16, June 2019, https://fonfasite.files.wordpress.com/2019/06/newsletter-367th-fighter-group_issue16.pdf/.

14. Tregaskis, "Eleven Thousand Feet and No Place To Go," 158.

15. Ibid., 155, 160–61.

16. Ibid., 161–62.

17. Richard Tregaskis to Maude and Archibald Tregaskis, September 17 and September 26, 1944, Tregaskis Collection, Gotlieb Archival Research Center; Hildy Michelle Neel, "Let Us Now Praise Famous Men: A History of the American World War II Personal Narrative, 1942–1945" (PhD diss., College of William and Mary, 1998), 297–98. Tregaskis dedicated *Invasion Diary* to the memory of his "beloved" sister, Madeline, who had died on June 25, 1943. A statistician at Fort Monmouth, New Jersey, she had been discovered dead in her car in a closed garage. "Police said they believed she had taken her own life by inhaling carbon monoxide fumes from the motor of her car," according to a newspaper report. See "Madeline Tregaskis Found Dead in Car at Monmouth Beach," *Long Branch (NJ) Daily Record*, June 26, 1943.

18. *Invasion Diary* advertisement, *New York Times Book Review*, August 20, 1944; Nash K. Burger, "The Diarist Went to Italy," *New York Times*, August 20, 1944; John Selby, "'Invasion Diary' Good But Far too Many Names," *Saint Cloud (MN) Times*, August 22, 1944.

19. Richard Tregaskis, "U.S. Third Armored Division Led First Army in Dash Across France," *Port Arthur (TX) News*, October 3, 1944; Richard Tregaskis, "How Thunderbolts Work on Nazi Tanks," *New York Mirror*, September 11, 1944; Richard Tregaskis, "'Spearhead': Saga of the 3rd Armored," *Saga*, February 1963, https://www.3ad.com/history/wwll/feature.pages/saga.mag.1.htm/.

20. Richard Tregaskis, "Tregaskis Finds: Reich Civilians Welcome Yanks," *New York Journal-American*, September 14, 1944; Richard Tregaskis, "Beginning to Cuss Hitler for Oppression," *Hammond (IN) Times*, September 14, 1944; Robert W. Baumer, *Aachen: The U.S. Army's Battle for Charlemagne's City in World War II* (Mechanicsburg, PA: Stackpole Books, 2015), 1–3.

21. Richard Tregaskis, "My Most Inspiring Moment: Where Courage Begins," *Family Weekly*, June 7, 1964; Richard Tregaskis, "House to House and Room to Room," *Saturday Evening Post*, February 24, 1945, 18; John C. McManus, *Grunts: Inside the American Infantry Combat Experience, World War II through Iraq* (New York: NAL Caliber, 2010), 103–4.

22. Richard Tregaskis, "'Surrender or Die!': Dramatics of Aachen Ultimatum Today Told," *Newark (NJ) Star Ledger*, October 11, 1944; Steven J. Zaloga, *The Siegfried Line, 1944–45: Battles on the German Frontier* (Oxford, UK: Osprey Publishing, 2007), 44–45.

23. Baumer, *Aachen*, 276–77. In addition to artillery shells and bombs, American forces used an ingenious method to blast Aachen. Engineers from the 1106th Engineer Combat Group filled trolley cars with captured explosives and used a bulldozer to start them on their way down a hill into the city. The improvised car bombs, however, did little damage. See, McManus, *Grunts*, 110–11.

24. Richard Tregaskis, "Sniper Bullets Zing in Aachen," *Mansfield (OH) News Journal*, October 13, 1944; Zaloga, *Siegfried Line*, 40.

25. Tregaskis, "Yanks Find Aachen Groggy," *Newark (NJ) Star Ledger*, October 14, 1944.

26. Tregaskis, "House to House and Room to Room," 18–19.

27. Richard Tregaskis, "Battle for Aachen Like Jungle Warfare; Snipers Hide in Houses Instead of Trees," *Coshocton (OH) Tribune*, October 15, 1944; Tregaskis, "House to House and Room to Room," 19, 101.

28. Tregaskis, "House to House and Room to Room," 101.

29. Ibid., 102.

30. Ibid. For its efforts to capture Aachen from the Germans, the First Infantry Division received a Distinguished Unit Citation (today called the Presidential Unit Citation). See Peter R. Mansoor, *The GI Offensive in Europe: The Triumph of American Infantry Divisions, 1941–1945* (Lawrence: University Press of Kansas, 1999), 184.

31. Richard Tregaskis to Maude and Archibald Tregaskis, October 17, 1944, Tregaskis Collection, Gotlieb Archival Research Center.

32. Richard Tregaskis, "The Lure of the Front Is Like An Opiate," manuscript, January 18, 1966, Richard Tregaskis Papers, 06346, American Heritage Center, University of Wyoming, Laramie, Wyoming; Richard Tregaskis, "Another Son of Ring Lardner is Killed in Aachen," *Moline (IL) Dispatch*, October 23, 1944.

33. Richard Tregaskis, "Foreigners Are People Too: A Round the World Diary," memorandum; George Chaplin, "Love and War Give Life to Novel," *Honolulu Advertiser*, July 23, 1961; Richard Tregaskis, "Stronger Than Fear," manuscript, May 24, 1961, Tregaskis Papers, American Heritage Center.

34. Richard Tregaskis to Bob [?], August 25, 1945, Random House Records, Rare Book and Manuscript Library, Columbia University, New York, New York; Francis Hackett, "Books of the Times: K Rations and Thoughts of Home Fighting the Long Curve of Fear," *New York Times*, June 16, 1945.

Chapter Fifteen

1. Richard Tregaskis, "B-29," manuscript, Richard Tregaskis Papers, 06346, American Heritage Center, University of Wyoming, Laramie, Wyoming; Major Ralph L. Swann, "A Unit History of the 315th Bomb Wing, 1944–1946," Air Command and Staff College Air University, Maxwell Air Force Base, Alabama, https://apps.dtic.mil/dtic/tr/fulltext/u2/a168128.pdf.

2. Tregaskis, "B-29."

3. Ibid.

4. Theodore Peterson, *Magazines in the Twentieth Century* (Urbana: University of Illinois Press, 1964), 12–13, 188; "A New Kind of Magazine Feature," advertisement, *Dayton News*, August 16, 1945; "Richard Tregaskis Back to Cover War," *Honolulu Star-Bulletin*, May 31, 1945; "Keeping Posted: Tregaskis Has Got to Go," *Saturday Evening Post*, August 18, 1945, 4.

5. "A New Kind of Magazine Feature." Tregaskis wrote detailed reports about flying combat missions while aboard the USS *Ticonderoga*, but they were never published by the *Saturday Evening Post* as news of the atomic bombings of Hiroshima and Nagasaki, and the end of the war in the Pacific, overshadowed them. Instead, because of "public interest" in the subject, the magazine featured his articles on the military government team preparing for the occupation of Japan and indicated it would reserve his torpedo-plane experiences for the future. "Week by week," the *Post* told its readers, "he will write an intimate firsthand story of the problems encountered as American soldiers

undertook the prickly job of ruling the Japs." See Richard Tregaskis, "Road to Tokyo: Pay-Off over Japan," *Saturday Evening Post*, September 22, 1945, 20, 103.

6. Swann, "A Unit History of the 315th Bomb Wing," 2.

7. Richard Tregaskis, "Road to Tokyo: We of the B-29's Say Good-By," *Saturday Evening Post*, August 18, 1945, 87; Swann, "A Unit History of the 315th Bomb Wing," 38; Mark Lardas, *Japan 1944–45: LeMay's B-29 Strategic Bombing Campaign* (Oxford, UK: Osprey Publishing, 2019), Kindle edition, 92; Richard Tregaskis, "Letter from the Pacific (Road to Tokyo)," dispatch, number 1, Tregaskis Papers, American Heritage Center.

8. Tregaskis, "Road to Tokyo: We of the B-29's Say Good-By," 86.

9. Tregaskis, "Letter from the Pacific (Road to Tokyo)"; Richard Tregaskis, "Road to Tokyo: 'I Don't Intend to Ditch,'" *Saturday Evening Post*, August 25, 1945, 92.

10. Richard Tregaskis, "Road to Tokyo, Number 4," Tregaskis Papers, American Heritage Center; Tregaskis, "Road to Tokyo: We of the B-29's Say Good-By," 17, 88.

11. Richard Tregaskis, "Road to Tokyo: Disillusionment in Hawaii," *Saturday Evening Post*, September 1, 1945, 20; Richard Tregaskis, "Road to Tokyo Number 3," Tregaskis Papers, American Heritage Center.

12. Richard Tregaskis, "Road to Tokyo Number 5," Tregaskis Papers, American Heritage Center.

13. Richard Tregaskis, "Road to Tokyo: 'Fighters Right Close . . . at 7 o'Clock,'" *Saturday Evening Post*, September 14, 1945, 20, 102; Tregaskis, "Road to Tokyo Number 5."

14. Tregaskis, "B-29"; Paul Fussell, *Wartime: Understanding and Behavior in the Second World War* (New York: Oxford University Press, 1989), 80.

15. Tregaskis, "Road to Tokyo: Pay-Off over Japan," 20, 101; Documents of Sixteenth Bombardment Group, http://www.315bw.org/16bg_06_45.html/.

16. Tregaskis, "Road to Tokyo: Pay-Off over Japan," 20, 101.

17. Ibid., 101.

18. Ibid., 102.

19. Ibid., 103.

20. Chester G. Hearn, *Carriers in Combat: The Air War at Sea* (Mechanicsburg, PA: Stackpole Books, 2005), 226–27; Keith Wheeler, *Bombers over Japan* (1982; Alexandria, VA: Time-Life Books, 1998), 183; Tregaskis, "Road to Tokyo: Pay-Off over Japan," 103; Richard Tregaskis, "Road to Tokyo, Number 10," Tregaskis Papers, American Heritage Center.

21. Tregaskis, "Road to Tokyo, Number 10."

22. H. Paul Brehm, interview, Hyuga Strike Mission, *War Times Journal*, http://www.wtj.com/articles/brehm/hyuga.htm/; Tregaskis, "Road to Tokyo, Number 10."

23. Tregaskis, "Road to Tokyo, Number 10"; Richard Tregaskis, "Road to Tokyo, Number 11," Tregaskis Papers, American Heritage Center.

24. Richard Tregaskis, "Road to Tokyo, Number 13," Tregaskis Papers, American Heritage Center.

25. Tregaskis, "Road to Tokyo, Number 11"; Richard Tregaskis, "Road to Tokyo, Number 12," Tregaskis Papers, American Heritage Center.

26. Tregaskis, "Road to Tokyo, Number 12."

27. Ibid.

28. Ibid.

29. Ibid.

30. Ibid.

31. Ibid.

32. Barrett Tillman, *Whirlwind: The Air War against Japan, 1942–1945* (New York: Simon & Schuster, 2010), 214; Tregaskis, "Road to Tokyo, Number 13."

33. Tregaskis, "Road to Tokyo, Number 13."

34. Ibid.

35. Ibid.

36. Ibid.; Richard Tregaskis, "Road to Tokyo, Number 14," Tregaskis Papers, American Heritage Center; Richard Tregaskis, "Road to Tokyo: Peace Caught Us Napping," *Saturday Evening Post*, September 29, 1945, 20.

Chapter Sixteen

1. Charles A. Willoughby, editor in chief, *Reports of General MacArthur: MacArthur in Japan; The Occupation: Military Phase*, vol. 1: Supplement (1966; Washington, DC: Center of Military History, U.S. Army, 1994), 29–30; William Manchester, *American Caesar: Douglas MacArthur, 1880–1964* (1978; New York: Dell Publishing Company, 1979), 521; Seymour Morris Jr., *Supreme Commander: MacArthur's Triumph in Japan* (New York: HarperCollins, 2014), 10–11, 28–29. British prime minister Winston Churchill noted that "of all the amazing deeds in the war, I regarded General MacArthur's personal landing at Atsugi as the bravest of the lot." See Manchester, *American Caesar*, 520.

2. Richard Tregaskis, "Road to Tokyo: The Infantry Never Had It So Tough," *Saturday Evening Post*, October 13, 1945, 20, 108; Richard Tregaskis, "Third Milgov Dispatch," Richard Tregaskis Papers, 06346, American Heritage Center, University of Wyoming, Laramie, Wyoming.

3. Richard Tregaskis, "Road to Tokyo: Peace Caught Us Napping," *Saturday Evening Post*, September 29, 1945, 20.

4. Ibid.

5. Ibid., 121; Susan L. Carruthers, *The Good Occupation: American Soldiers and the Hazards of Peace* (Cambridge, MA: Harvard University Press, 2016), 195–96.

6. Tregaskis, "Road to Toyko: Peace Caught Us Napping," 122; Richard Tregaskis, "Road to Tokyo: We Soften the Peace," *Saturday Evening Post*, October 6, 1945, 20.

7. Tregaskis, "Road to Tokyo: We Soften the Peace," 105; Richard Tregaskis, "Second Milgov Dispatch," Tregaskis Papers, American Heritage Center.

8. Douglas MacArthur, *Reminiscences* (1964; Annapolis, MD: Naval Institute Press, 2001), 304–6; Morris, *Supreme Commander*, 64; John W. Dower, *Embracing Defeat: Japan in the Wake of World War II* (New York: W. W. Norton and Company, 1999), 73, 78; Manchester, *American Caesar*, 551.

9. Tregaskis, "Road to Tokyo: The Infantry Never Had It So Tough," 106–7.

10. Ibid., 108.

11. Richard Tregaskis, "Road to Tokyo: The Fine Hand of Mr. Suzuki," *Saturday Evening Post*, October 20, 1945, 18, 111–13.

12. Ibid., 114. See also Maj. R. R. Kroells, "On the Back of a Grasshopper: The XXIV Corps and the Korean Occupation," School of Advanced Military Studies, United States Army General Staff College, Leavenworth, Kansas, 2016, 15, 17.

13. Richard Tregaskis, "Road to Tokyo: Have We Given Japan Back to the Japs?" *Saturday Evening Post*, October 27, 1945, 20, 114.

14. Ibid., 20; Carruthers, *Good Occupation*, 5–6; Tregaskis, "The Infantry Never Had It So Tough," 108.

15. Tregaskis, "Road to Tokyo: Have We Given Japan Back to the Japs?" 116; Bonner Fellers, memorandum to the Supreme Commander, October 2, 1945, Bonner Fellers, http://www.bonnerfellers.com/uploads/B.Fellers_Memo_to _MacArthur_Oct_2_1945.pdf. Although Hirohito had offered to take sole responsibility "for every political and military decision made and action taken by my people in the conduct of [the] war" at a September 27, 1945, meeting with MacArthur, the general had already decided not to put the emperor on trial as a war criminal. See, Manchester, *American Caesar*, 577.

16. Tregaskis, "Road to Tokyo: Have We Given Japan Back to the Japs?" 116; Carruthers, *Good Occupation*, 191–95. See also Walter A. McDougall, *Promised Land, Crusader State: The American Encounter with the World Since 1776* (Boston: Houghton Mifflin Company, 1997), 162.

17. "Inside Information: Dick's Dogs (Size 14) Just Won't Reconvert," *Saturday*

Evening Post, February 2, 1946, Richard Tregaskis Collection, COLL/566, Archives Branch, Marine Corps History Division, Quantico, Virginia.

18. Richard Tregaskis, "Pappy Hain Comes Home," *Saturday Evening Post*, January 19, 1946, 20, 121. See also Richard Tregaskis, "Jim Davis Comes Home," *Saturday Evening Post*, February 9, 1946; "Commando Kelly, Businessman," *Saturday Evening Post*, March 2, 1946; "A Hot Pilot Cools Off," *Saturday Evening Post*, March 23, 1946; "Brash Young Man," *Saturday Evening Post*, April 13, 1946; and "The Bombardier Who Would Build Cities," *Saturday Evening Post*, May 4, 1946.

19. Tregaskis, "The Bombardier Who Would Build Cities," 21, 118; Glenn C. Altschuler and Stuart M. Blumin, *The GI Bill: A New Deal for Veterans* (New York: Oxford University Press, 2009), 7, 85. Zettek graduated magna cum laude from Harvard in 1949 and went on to earn a graduate degree in city planning from Harvard's Graduate School of Design. Before his death on June 17, 2011, he worked as planning director for the Worcester Housing Authority in Massachusetts, city planner for Lowell, and executive director of the Worcester Redevelopment Authority. See Charles Moran Zettek obituary, *Boston Globe*, July 3, 2011, and Mary Lena, "'Cities downtown areas are not dead': Zettek," *Lowell (MA) Sun*, May 24, 1974.

20. Tregaskis, "Brash Young Man," 117; Tregaskis, "A Hot Pilot Cools Off," 146.

21. Richard Tregaskis, "Foreigners Are People Too: A Round the World Diary," Tregaskis Papers, American Heritage Center.

22. Ibid.; "Correspondent Tregaskis Hits Hollywood Probe in Stop Here," *Honolulu Advertiser*, October 23, 1947; Richard Tregaskis, *Seven Leagues to Paradise* (Garden City, NY: Doubleday and Company, 1951), 3–4. Before leaving the country, Tregaskis criticized the probes started by the House Un-American Activities Committee to investigate alleged communist sympathizers in Hollywood. "I think this type of thing is a step toward Fascism," Tregaskis said. "It's unconstitutional, as far as I'm concerned, and I don't think any man should have the right to stand up and call a man a Communist because he doesn't like him." See, "Correspondent Tregaskis Hits Hollywood Probe in Stop Here."

23. Tregaskis, *Seven Leagues to Paradise*, 146–47, 159–68, 253–54.

24. Ibid., 260, 262–63; Richard Tregaskis to Maude Tregaskis, January 15, 1951, Tregaskis Papers, American Heritage Center.

25. Richard Tregaskis to unidentified recipient ["Dear Fellas"], February 6, 1950; Tregaskis to Mark [?], April 22, 1950, Tregaskis Papers, American Heritage Center.

26. Richard Tregaskis to Louis Ruppel, July 25, 1950; Harry S. Truman, *Memoirs of Harry S. Truman: Years of Trial and Hope* (1955; New York: Smithmark

Publishers, 1996), 333; Tregaskis to unidentified recipient ["Dear Kids"], August 3, 1950, Tregaskis Papers, American Heritage Center.

27. Richard Tregaskis to Maude Tregaskis, January 15, 1951, Tregaskis Papers, American Heritage Center; Tom and Jim Goldrup, *Growing Up on the Set: Interviews with 39 Former Child Actors of Classic Film and Television* (Jefferson, NC: McFarland and Company, 2002), 165.

28. Richard Tregaskis letters to Maude Tregaskis, August 3, 1950, and January 15, 1951, Tregaskis Papers, American Heritage Center.

29. Richard Tregaskis letter to Maude Tregaskis, August 29, 1950, Tregaskis Papers, American Heritage Center; "Wife Receives Divorce from Author Tregaskis," *Los Angeles Times*, May 19, 1953; "Six-Foot-Six Author, Cameraman Leave to Produce Korean Film," undated article from *Nippon Times* in Tregaskis Collection, COLL/566, Archives Branch, Marine Corps History Division; Richard Tregaskis bio, Tregaskis Papers, American Heritage Center.

30. Richard Tregaskis, "The First War That Made Sense," outline, Tregaskis Papers, American Heritage Center.

31. Ibid.

32. Richard Tregaskis, "Questions and Answers: Richard and Walton Tregaskis," January 18, 1956, Tregaskis Papers, American Heritage Center.

33. Tregaskis bio, Tregaskis Papers, American Heritage Center.

34. A. E. P. Wall, "Waikiki Diary: Richard Tregaskis, Author and War Correspondent, Battles Gangrene and the Pressure of a New Book," *Honolulu Advertiser*, December 20, 1964; George Chaplin, "Love and War Give Life to Novel," *Honolulu Advertiser*, July 23, 1961.

Chapter Seventeen

1. William Prochnau, *Once upon a Distant War: Young War Correspondents and the Early Vietnam Battles* (New York: Times Books, 1995), 265–66; Richard Tregaskis, *Vietnam Diary* (New York: Holt, Rinehart and Winston, 1963), 1.

2. Clarence R. Wyatt, *Paper Soldiers: The American Press and the Vietnam War* (New York: W. W. Norton and Company, 1993), 87; David Halberstam, *The Making of a Quagmire: America and Vietnam during the Kennedy Era* (1965; rev. ed., Lanham, MD: Rowman and Littlefield, 2008), 202.

3. Richard Tregaskis, draft of book review of David Halberstam's *The Making of a Quagmire*, April 25, 1965, Richard Tregaskis Papers, 06346, American Heritage Center, University of Wyoming, Laramie, Wyoming; "David Halberstam," in *Reporting America at War: An Oral History*, comp. Michelle Ferrari (New York: Hyperion, 2003), 117.

4. Ferrari, *Reporting America at War*, 120; Richard Tregaskis, "One Man's View of the Terrible War," *Chicago Tribune*, May 16, 1965.

5. Ferrari, *Reporting America at War*, 115; David Halberstam, *The Best and the Brightest* (New York: Random House, 1972), 205; Prochnau, *Once upon a Distant War*, 196; Tregaskis, draft of Halberstam book review.

6. Tregaskis, *Vietnam Diary*, 381; Richard Tregaskis, "Yes, War Still Makes Sense," *Boston Advertiser*, July 7, 1968; "'Order' Hanoi to Peace Table—Tregaskis," *Honolulu Advertiser*, July 11, 1968; Phil Mayer, "Tregaskis Was First on China Bomb," *Honolulu Star-Bulletin*, August 1, 1967. Marguerite Higgins, a veteran correspondent from World War II and Korea, also questioned Halberstam and the other young reporters, labeling them as "typewriter strategists" who always put the "accent on the negative." Higgins wrote that the communists, as they had in the 1950s with the French, were working to demoralize American public opinion, and there were "a great many Americans unwittingly serving North Vietnam's objective of undermining South Vietnam's will and stamina." See, Wyatt, *Paper Soldiers*, 120; A. J. Langguth, *Our Vietnam: The War, 1954–1975* (New York: Simon & Schuster, 2000), 243.

7. James Leveque, "Propaganda a Dull Weapon in U.S. Arsenal," *Honolulu Sun-Bulletin*, June 18, 1961; George Chaplin, "Love and War Give Life to Novel," *Honolulu Advertiser*, July 23, 1961. See also Richard Tregaskis, "'The Lure of the Front Is Like an Opiate," January 18, 1966, Tregaskis Papers, American Heritage Center.

8. "Richard Tregaskis," entry in *Something about the Author: Facts and Pictures about Contemporary Authors and Illustrators of Books for Young People*, vol. 3, ed. Anne Commire (Detroit, MI: Gale Research Company, 1972), 229–30; A. E. P. Wall, "Waikiki Diary: Richard Tregaskis, Author and War Correspondent, Battles Gangrene and the Pressures of a New Book," *Honolulu Advertiser*, December 20, 1964.

9. Spence Brady, "Pursuit of Paradise Ends at Last—Here," *Honolulu Advertiser*, May 28, 1961 Richard Tregaskis, "I Settle for Paradise," *Continental Magazine* 2 (March–April 1962): 1–3.

10. Richard Tregaskis, *X-15 Diary: The Story of America's First Space Ship* (1961; Lincoln: University of Nebraska Press, 2004), 15; Ray E. Boomhower, *Gus Grissom: The Lost Astronaut* (Indianapolis: Indiana Historical Society Press, 2004), 14–18.

11. Tregaskis, *X-15 Diary*, 12, 16, 92.

12. Ibid., 3, 157.

13. Chaplin, "Love and War Give Life to Novel."

14. Richard Tregaskis biography in Tregaskis Papers, American Heritage Center; Robert R. Kirsch, "Book Report: 'Last Plane to Shanghai' Exciting but Out

of Focus," *Los Angeles Times*, July 18, 1961; Ron Goben, "Books: Last Plane to Shanghai," *Honolulu Star-Bulletin*, April 16, 1961.

15. Richard Tregaskis to Maude Tregaskis, February 23, 1962, Tregaskis Papers, American Heritage Center.

16. See foreword, Richard Tregaskis, *John F. Kennedy: War Hero* (New York: Dell Publishing Company, 1962).

17. Bennett Cerf, *At Random: The Reminiscences of Bennett Cerf* (New York: Random House, 1977), 157–58. See also David Spear, "The Story of the Landmark Books," *Perspectives on History*, October 17, 2016, American Historical Association, http://historians.org/publications-and-directories/perspectives -on-history/october-2016/generation-past-the-story-of-the-landmark-books/.

18. Pierre Salinger to Richard Tregaskis, May 29, 1961, Tregaskis Papers, American Heritage Center; Moana Tregaskis, afterword, in Richard Tregaskis, *Guadal-canal Diary* (1943; New York: Modern Library, 2000), 238; Richard Tregaskis to Bennett Cerf, March 20, 1962, Tregaskis Papers, American Heritage Center. See also "Publishers Feud on JFK-PT Books," *Bridgeport (CT) Telegram*, January 25, 1962.

19. "Publisher Loses Move to Ban Book on JFK," *Pomona (CA) Progress-Bulletin*, February 9, 1962; "Publishers Feud on JFK-PT Books"; Art Buchwald, "The Very Last Book On PT-109 in Hand," *Detroit Free Press*, February 20, 1962.

20. Richard Tregaskis to Scott Wigle, August 28, 1963, Tregaskis Papers, American Heritage Center; "Samoan Editor," *Honolulu Star-Bulletin*, November 14, 1962. Tregaskis divorced Walton on the grounds of desertion. She had returned to Hawaii in June 1963 and did not contest the divorce. According to Tregaskis, Walton received in the divorce settlement half the mutual fund stock they jointly owned and some of the household goods. See Richard Tregaskis to Maude Tregaskis, July 2 and July 11, 1963, Tregaskis Papers, American Heritage Center.

21. Richard Tregaskis, "Helimarines: Troubleshooters of the Atom Age," *Parade* magazine supplement in *Jackson (MS) Clarion-Ledger*, November 24, 1957; Richard Tregaskis to Maude Tregaskis, November 25, 1962, Tregaskis Papers, American Heritage Center.

22. Tregaskis, *Vietnam Diary*, 155, 390.

23. Ibid., 2–3; Richard Tregaskis, "The Lure of the Front Is Like an Opiate," Tregaskis Papers, American Heritage Center.

24. Tregaskis biography, Tregaskis Papers, American Heritage Center; Tregaskis, *Vietnam Diary*, 147, 279.

25. Tregaskis, *Vietnam Diary*, 23, 279; Richard Tregaskis to Maude Tregaskis, October 25, 1962, Tregaskis Papers, American Heritage Center.

26. Tregaskis, *Vietnam Diary*, 34.

27. Tregaskis to Maude Tregaskis, October 25, 1962; Tregaskis, *Vietnam Diary*, 30, 33, and 34.
28. Tregaskis, *Vietnam Diary*, 138–39, 144.
29. Ibid., 165–66, 280–81, 287. See also Mark Moyar, *Triumph Forsaken: The Vietnam War, 1954–1965* (New York: Cambridge University Press, 2006), 178–79.
30. Tregaskis, *Vietnam Diary*, 281–82, 287, 290–91, 293.
31. Ibid., 147, 151, 306.
32. Ibid., 159, 161, 375–76. See also Malcolm W. Browne, *The New Face of War* (1965; Indianapolis, IN: Bobbs-Merrill Company, 1968), 19–20.
33. Tregaskis, *Vietnam Diary*, 376–78, 381. See also, Prochnau, *Once upon a Distant War*, 271; Neil Sheehan, "Vietnamese Ignored U.S. Battle Order," *Washington Post*, January 7, 1963.
34. Tregaskis to Maude Tregaskis, July 2 and August 29, 1963, Tregaskis Papers, American Heritage Center; Mayer, "Tregaskis Was First on China Bomb"; Lois Taylor, "Hawaii Diary: Hiking with the Indian Army," *Honolulu Star-Bulletin*, January 21, 1970; "Tregaskis-Gilutin Vows Said Thursday," *Honolulu Advertiser*, September 17, 1963; Tregaskis biography. See also Moana Tregaskis, e-mail to author, July 6, 2020.
35. Tregaskis, *Vietnam Diary*, 393–94.

Epilogue

1. Robert W. Bone, "Richard Tregaskis' Ashes Scattered Off Waikiki," *Honolulu Advertiser*, August 19, 1973; "Death Due to Heart Attack," *Honolulu Star-Bulletin*, September 12, 1973.
2. "Author, War Correspondent Tregaskis Dies," *Honolulu Star-Bulletin*, August 16, 1973; "Richard Tregaskis, Author, Dead at 56," *New York Times*, August 17, 1973; Bob Considine, "Peace at Last," *Lowell (MA) Sun*, August 22, 1973; Moana Tregaskis, "Death of a Soldier," *New Delhi Sunday Statesman*, November 11, 1973; Moana Tregaskis to Donald Klopfer, August 30, 1973, Richard Tregaskis Papers, 06346, American Heritage Center, University of Wyoming, Laramie, Wyoming.
3. Moana Tregaskis, "Death of a Soldier"; A. E. P. Wall, "Waikiki Diary: Richard Tregaskis, Author and War Correspondent, Battles Gangrene and the Pressures of a New Book," *Honolulu Advertiser*, December 20, 1964.
4. Richard Tregaskis biography, in Tregaskis Papers, American Heritage Center.
5. Richard Tregaskis, "Bright Ghosts of Guadalcanal," June 1, 1967, Tregaskis Papers, American Heritage Center. See also Richard Tregaskis, "A Name to Remember: Guadalcanal," *Parade* magazine supplement, *Detroit Free Press*, August 6, 1967.

6. Tregaskis, "Bright Ghosts of Guadalcanal."

7. Ibid. In addition to his Silver Star medal, Vouza received the George Medal for gallantry from the British and in 1979 was knighted by Queen Elizabeth II. Vouza died on March 15, 1984. See Al Hemingway, "Jacob Vouza's Defiant Stand during the Guadalcanal Campaign," Warfare History Network, https:// warfarehistorynetwork.com/2015/08/18/jacob-vouzas-defiant -stand-during-the-guadalcanal-campaign/.

8. Tregaskis, "Bright Ghosts of Guadalcanal."

9. Ibid. See also Chuck Thompson, *The 25 Best World War II Sites: Pacific Theater: The Ultimate Traveler's Guide to Battlefields, Monuments and Museums* (San Francisco: Greenline Publications, 2002), 112.

10. Tregaskis, "Bright Ghosts of Guadalcanal."

SELECTED
BIBLIOGRAPHY

Primary Sources

BOOKS

China Bomb. New York: Washburn, 1967.

Guadalcanal Diary. 1943; New York: Modern Library, 2000.

Invasion Diary. 1944; Lincoln: University of Nebraska Press, 2004.

John F. Kennedy and PT-109. New York: Random House, 1961. Republished as *John F. Kennedy: War Hero.* New York: Dell Publishing Company, 1962.

Last Plane to Shanghai. Indianapolis, IN: Bobbs-Merrill Company, 1961.

Seven Leagues to Paradise. Garden City, NY: Doubleday, 1951.

Stronger Than Fear. New York: Random House, 1945.

Southeast Asia, Building the Bases: The History of Construction in Southeast Asia. Washington, DC: U.S. Government Printing Office, 1973.

X-15 Diary: The Story of America's First Space Ship. 1961; Lincoln: University of Nebraska Press, 2004.

Vietnam Diary. New York: Holt, Rinehart and Winston, 1963.

The Warrior King: Hawaii's King Kamehameha the Great. New York: Macmillan, 1973.

Woman and the Sea: A Book of Poems. Los Angeles: Elysium, 1966.

COLLECTIONS

"Battle of the Ridge" and "Then I Got It." In *Reporting World War II: Part One: American Journalism 1938–1944*. New York: Library of America, 1995.

"Eleven Thousand Feet and No Place to Go." In *How I Got That Story, by Members of the Overseas Press Club of America*, edited by David Brown and W. Richard Bruner. New York: E. P. Dutton and Company, 1967.

"Guadalcanal Diary: Would I Change It Now?" In *I Can Tell It Now, by Members of the Overseas Press Club of America* edited by David Brown and W. Richard Bruner. New York: E. P. Dutton and Company, 1964.

Introduction, in *Combat: The War with Japan*, edited by Don Congdon. New York: Dell Publishing Company, 1962.

"The Parachute Jump." In *Deadline Delayed, by Members of the Overseas Press Club of America*. New York: E. P. Dutton and Company, 1947.

"Tregaskis Speaks for the Wounded." In *Typewriter Battalion: Dramatic Front-Line Dispatches from World War II*, edited by Jack Stenbuck. New York: Morrow, 1995.

"What It Means to Be Wounded." In *100 Best True Stories of World War II, with Thirty-Two Illustrations*. New York: Wise, 1945.

"Where Courage Begins." In *My Most Inspiring Moment: Encounters with Destiny Relived by Thirty-Eight Best-Selling Authors*, edited by Robert Fitzgibbon and Ernest V. Heyn. Garden City, NY: Doubleday and Company, 1965.

ARTICLES

"The Bombardier Who Would Build Cities." *Saturday Evening Post*, May 4, 1946.

"The Best Soldier I Ever Knew." *Saga*, February 1960.

"Brash Young Man." *Saturday Evening Post*, April 13, 1946.

"The Cities of America: Norfolk." *Saturday Evening Post*, July 9, 1949.

"Commando Kelly, Businessman." *Saturday Evening Post*, March 2, 1946.

"The Cops' Favorite Make-Believe Cop." *Saturday Evening Post*, September 26, 1953.

"Gabreski, Avenger of the Skies." *Saturday Evening Post*, December 13, 1952.

"Happiest Yank in England." *True*, November 1949.

"Helimarines: Troubleshooters of the Atom Age." *Parade*, November 24, 1957.

"A Hot Pilot Cools Off." *Saturday Evening Post*, March 23, 1946.

"House to House and Room to Room." *Saturday Evening Post*, February 24, 1945.

"Jim Davis Comes Home." *Saturday Evening Post*, February 9, 1946.

"The Marine Corps Fights for Its Life." *Saturday Evening Post*, February 5, 1949.

"Mr. Jong and the Fortunes of War." *True*, April 1949.

"My Most Inspiring Moment: Where Courage Begins." *Family Weekly*, June 7, 1964.

"Pappy Hain Comes Home." *Saturday Evening Post*, January 19, 1946.

"Pirates on the South China Sea." *True*, March 1949.

"Road to Tokyo: Disillusionment in Hawaii." *Saturday Evening Post*, September 1, 1945.

"Road to Tokyo: 'Fighters Right Close . . . at 7 o'Clock.'" *Saturday Evening Post*, September 14, 1945.

"Road to Tokyo: The Fine Hand of Mr. Suzuki." *Saturday Evening Post*, October 20, 1945.

"Road to Tokyo: 'Guam—This is It!'" *Saturday Evening Post*, September 8, 1945.

"Road to Tokyo: Have We Given Japan Back to the Japs?" *Saturday Evening Post*, October 27, 1945.

"Road to Tokyo: 'I Don't Intend to Ditch.'" *Saturday Evening Post*, August 25, 1945.

"Road to Tokyo: The Infantry Never Had It So Tough." *Saturday Evening Post*, October 13, 1945.

"Road to Tokyo: Pay-Off over Japan." *Saturday Evening Post*, September 22, 1945.

"Road to Tokyo: Peace Caught Us Napping." *Saturday Evening Post*, September 29, 1945.

"Road to Tokyo: We of the B-29's Say Good-By." *Saturday Evening Post*, August 18, 1945.

"Road to Tokyo: We Soften the Peace." *Saturday Evening Post*, October 6, 1945.

"Spearhead: Saga of the 3rd Armored." *Saga*, February 1963.

MANUSCRIPT COLLECTIONS

Random House Records. Rare Book and Manuscript Library, Columbia University, New York, New York.

Richard Tregaskis Collection, COLL/566. Archives Branch, Marine Corps History Division, Quantico, Virginia.

Richard Tregaskis Collection. Howard Gotlieb Archival Research Center at Boston University, Boston, Massachusetts.

Richard Tregaskis Papers, 06346. American Heritage Center, University of Wyoming, Laramie, Wyoming.

Robert C. Miller diary. University of Nevada, Reno Special Collections, University of Nevada, Reno Knowledge Center, Reno, Nevada.

Secondary Sources

ARTICLES AND DISSERTATIONS

Boomhower, Ray E. "A Slow Death: Norman H. Vandivier and the Battle of Midway." *Traces of Indiana and Midwestern History* 24 (Fall 2012): 14–25.

James, Sidney L. "Torpedo Squadron 8." *Life*, August 31, 1942.

Houseknecht, Stephen Mark. "The Elite of the Elites: The U.S. Marine Raider Battalions, 1942–1944: A Case Study in Elite Military Organizations." Master's thesis, Missouri State University, 2015.

Neel, Hildy Michelle. "Let Us Now Praise Famous Men: A History of the American World War II Personal Narrative, 1942–1945." PhD dissertation, College of William and Mary, 1998.

Pratt, Fletcher. "How the Censors Rigged the News." *Harper's*, February 1946.

Snead, David L. "Obscure but Important: The United States and the Russell Islands in World War II." *The Journal of America's Military Past* 29 (Spring/Summer 2003): 5–30.

BOOKS

Alexander, Joseph H. *Edson's Raiders: The 1st Marine Raider Battalion in World War II*. Annapolis, MD: Naval Institute Press, 2001.

Altschuler, Glenn C., and Stuart M. Blumin. *The GI Bill: A New Deal for Veterans*. New York: Oxford University Press, 2009.

Atkinson, Rick. *The Day of Battle: The War in Sicily and Italy, 1943–1944*. New York: Henry Holt and Company, 2007.

———. *The Guns at Last Light: The War in Western Europe, 1944–1945*. New York: Henry Holt and Company, 2013.

Axelrod, Alan. *Patton: A Biography*. New York: Palgrave Macmillan, 2006.

Barr, Niall. *Eisenhower's Armies: The American British Alliance during World War II*. New York: Pegasus Books, 2015.

Baumer, Robert W. *Aachen: The U.S. Army's Battle for Charlemagne's City during World War II*. Mechanicsburg, PA: Stackpole Books, 2015.

Black, Robert W. *The Ranger Force: Darby's Rangers in World War II*. Mechanicsburg, PA: Stackpole Books, 2009.

Blum, John Morton. *V Was for Victory: Politics and American Culture during World War II*. New York: Harcourt Brace Jovanovich, 1976.

Blumenson, Martin. *The Battle of the Generals: The Untold Story of the Falaise Pocket—The Campaign That Should Have Won World War II*. New York: William Morrow and Company, 1993.

———. *Breakout and Pursuit*. 1961; Washington, DC: Center of Military History, United States Army, 1993.

Blythe, LeGette. *38th Evac: The Story of the Men and Women Who Served in World War II with the 38th Evacuation Hospital in North Africa and Italy*. Charlotte, NC: Heritage Printers, 1966.

Boomhower, Ray E. *Dispatches from the Pacific: The World War II Reporting of Robert L. Sherrod*. Bloomington: Indiana University Press, 2017.

————. *Fighter Pilot: The World War II Career of Alex Vraciu*. Indianapolis: Indiana Historical Society Press, 2010.

————. *"One Shot": The World War II Photography of John A. Bushemi*. Indianapolis: Indiana Historical Society Press, 2004.

————. *The Soldier's Friend: A Life of Ernie Pyle*. Indianapolis: Indiana Historical Society Press, 2006.

Bourke-White, Margaret. *"They Call It Purple Heart Valley": A Combat Chronicle of the War in Italy*. 1944: Auckland: Pickle Partners Publishing, 2015.

Browne, Malcolm W. *The New Face of War*. 1965; Indianapolis, IN: Bobbs-Merrill Company, 1968.

Campbell, Alfred. *Mission to Guadalcanal*. N.p.: Uncommon Valor Press, 2015.

Capa, Robert. *Slightly Out of Focus*. 1947; New York: The Modern Library, 2001.

Carlson, Elliot. *Joe Rochefort's War: The Odyssey of the Codebreaker Who Outwitted Yamamoto at Midway*. 2011; Annapolis, MD: Naval Institute Press, 2013.

————. *Stanley Johnston's Blunder: The Reporter Who Spilled the Secret behind the U.S. Navy's Victory at Midway*. Annapolis, MD: Naval Institute Press, 2017.

Carruthers, Susan L. *The Good Occupation: American Soldiers and the Hazards of Peace*. Cambridge, MA: Harvard University Press, 2016.

Casey, Robert J. *Torpedo Junction: With the Pacific Fleet from Pearl Harbor to Midway*. Indianapolis, IN: Bobbs-Merrill Company, 1942.

Casey, Steven. *The War Beat, Europe: The American Media at War against Nazi Germany*. New York: Oxford University Press, 2017.

Cerf, Bennett. *At Random: The Reminiscences of Bennett Cerf*. New York: Random House, 1977.

Chun, Clayton K. S. *The Doolittle Raid 1942: America's First Strike Back at Japan*. Oxford, UK: Osprey Publishing, 2006.

Coggins, Jack. *The Campaign for Guadalcanal: A Battle That Made History*. Garden City, NY: Doubleday and Company, 1972.

Considine, Bob. *It's All News to Me: A Reporter's Deposition*. New York: Meredith Press, 1967.

Costello, John. *The Pacific War*. New York: Rawson, Wade Publishers, 1981.

Cox, Jeffrey R. *Morning Star, Midnight Sun: The Early Guadalcanal Campaign of World War II, August–October 1942*. Oxford, UK: Osprey Publishing, 2018.

Davies, Robert B. *Baldwin of the Times: Hanson W. Baldwin, A Military Journalist's Life, 1903–1991*. Annapolis, MD: Naval Institute Press, 2011.

Delaforce, Patrick. *Monty's Marauders: Black Rat and Red Fox: 4th & 8th Independent Armoured Brigades in WW2*. Brighton, UK: Tom Donovan Publishing, 1997.

D'Este, Carlo. *Bitter Victory: The Battle for Sicily, 1943*. 1988; New York: Harper Perennial 2008.

Doolittle, James H. with Carroll V. Glines. *I Could Never Be So Lucky Again*. New York: Bantam Books, 1991.

Dower, John W. *Embracing Defeat: Japan in the Wake of World War II*. New York: W. W. Norton and Company, 1999.

Dyer, George C. *The Amphibians Came to Conquer: The Story of Admiral Richmond Kelly Turner*. Washington, DC: U.S. Department of the Navy, 1972.

Eisenhower, Dwight D. *Crusade in Europe*. New York: Doubleday, 1948.

Ellis, John. *The Sharp End: The Fighting Man in World War II*. New York: Charles Scribner's Sons, 1980.

Feifer, George. *Tennozan: The Battle of Okinawa and the Atomic Bomb*. New York: Ticknor and Fields, 1992.

Ferrari, Michelle, comp. *Reporting America at War: An Oral History*. New York: Hyperion, 2003.

Ford, Ken. *Falaise 1944: Death of an Army*. Oxford, UK: Osprey Publishing, 2005.

Frank, Richard B. *Guadalcanal: The Definitive Account of the Landmark Battle*. New York: Random House, 1990.

Fussell, Paul. *Thank God for the Atom Bomb and Other Essays*. New York: Summit Books, 1988.

———. *Wartime: Understanding and Behavior in the Second World War*. New York: Oxford University Press, 1989.

Gay, George. *Sole Survivor: A Personal Story about the Battle of Midway*. 1979; N.p.: Midway Publishers, 1986.

Glass, Kenneth M., and Harold L. Buell, eds. *The Hornets and Their Heroic Men*. 1992; Hamilton, OH: American Printing and Lithographing Company, 1998.

Griffith, Samuel B. II. *The Battle for Guadalcanal*. 1963; Annapolis, MD: Nautical and Aviation Publishing Company of America, 1979.

Groft, Martin "Whitey," and Larry Alexander, *Bloody Ridge and Beyond: A World War II Marine's Memoirs of Edson's Raiders in the Pacific*. New York: Berkley Caliber, 2014.

Groh, Richard. *The Dynamite Gang: The 367th Fighter Group in World War II*. Fallbrook, CA: Aero Publishers, 1983.

Halberstam, David. *The Best and the Brightest*. New York: Random House, 1972.

———. *The Making of a Quagmire: America and Vietnam during the Kennedy Era*. 1965; rev. ed., Lanham, MD: Rowman and Littlefield, 2008.

Hearn, Chester B. *Carriers in Combat: The Air War at Sea*. Mechanicsburg, PA: Stackpole Books, 2005.

Hersey, John. *Into the Valley: Marines at Guadalcanal*. 1943; Lincoln: University of Nebraska Press, 2002.

Hoffman, Jon T. *Once a Legend: "Red Mike" Edson of the Marine Raiders*. Novato, CA: Presidio Press, 1994.

————. *Silk Chutes and Hard Fighting: U.S. Marine Corps Parachute Units in World War II*. Washington, DC: History and Museums Division, Headquarters, U.S. Marine Corps, 1999.

Hornfischer, James D. *Neptune Inferno: The U.S. Navy at Guadalcanal*. New York: Bantam Books, 2011.

Jeffries, John W. *Wartime America: The World War II Home Front*. Chicago: Ivan R. Dee, 1996.

Jersey, Stanley Coleman. *Hell's Islands: The Untold Story of Guadalcanal*. College Station: Texas A&M University Press, 2008.

Johnson, William Bruce. *The Pacific Campaign in World War II: From Pearl Harbor to Guadalcanal*. London: Routledge, 2006.

Keegan, John. *The Second World War*. New York: Viking, 1989.

Kennett, Lee. *For the Duration: The United States Goes to War: Pearl Harbor–1942*. New York: Charles Scribner's Sons, 1985.

Kernan, Alvin. *The Unknown Battle of Midway: The Destruction of the American Torpedo Squadrons*. New Haven, CT: Yale University Press, 2005.

Knightley, Phillip. *The First Casualty: From the Crimea to Vietnam; The War Correspondent as Hero, Propagandist, and Myth Maker*. New York: Harcourt Brace Jovanovich, 1975.

Langguth, A. J. *Our Vietnam: The War, 1954–1975*. New York: Simon & Schuster, 2000.

Lardas, Mark. *Japan 1944–45: LeMay's B-29 Strategic Bombing Campaign*. Oxford, UK: Osprey Publishing, 2019.

Leckie, Robert. *Challenge for the Pacific: Guadalcanal: The Turning Point of the War*. 1965; New York: Bantam Books, 2010.

Linderman, Gerald F. *The World within War: America's Combat Experience in World War II*. New York: Free Press, 1997.

Lingeman, Richard. *Don't You Know There's a War On? The American Home Front, 1941–1945*. 1970; New York: Thunder Mouth's Press/Nation Books, 2003.

Lundstrom, John B. *Black Shoe Carrier Admiral: Frank Jack Fletcher at Coral Sea, Midway, and Guadalcanal*. Annapolis, MD: Naval Institute Press, 2006.

————. *The First South Pacific Campaign: Pacific Fleet Strategy, December 1941–June 1942*. Annapolis, MD: Naval Institute Press, 1976.

MacArthur, Douglas. *Reminiscences*. 1964; Annapolis, MD: Naval Institute Press, 2001.

MacDonald, Charles D. *The Siegfried Line Campaign*. 1963; Washington, DC: Center of Military History, United States Army, 1990.

Madison, James H. *Eli Lilly: A Life, 1885–1977*. 1989; Indianapolis: Indiana Historical Society Press, 2006.

Manchester, William. *American Caesar: Douglas MacArthur, 1880–1964*. 1978; New York: Dell Publishing Company, 1979.

——— . *The Glory and the Dream: A Narrative History of America, 1932–1972*. New York: Bantam Books, 1975.

——— . *Goodbye Darkness: A Memoir of the Pacific War*. Boston: Little, Brown and Company, 1979.

Mander, Mary. *Pen and Sword: American War Correspondents, 1898–1975*. Urbana: University of Illinois Press, 2010.

Mansoor, Peter R. *The GI Offensive in Europe: The Triumph of American Infantry Divisions, 1941–1945*. Lawrence: University Press of Kansas, 1999.

Mathews, Joseph J. *Reporting the Wars*. Minneapolis: University of Minnesota Press, 1957.

May, Antoinette. *Witness to War: A Biography of Marguerite Higgins*. New York: Beaufort Books, 1983.

McDougall, Walter A. *Promised Land, Crusader State: The American Encounter with the World Since 1776*. Boston: Houghton Mifflin Company, 1997.

McManus, John C. *The Americans at Normandy: The Summer of 1944—The American War from the Normandy Beaches to Falaise*. New York: Forge, 2004.

——— . *Grunts: Inside the American Infantry Combat Experience, World War II through Iraq*. New York: NAL Caliber, 2010.

Mears, Frederick. *Carrier Combat*. New York: Ballantine Books, 1944.

Merillat, Herbert Christian Laing. *Guadalcanal Remembered*. New York: Dodd, Mead and Company, 1982.

——— . *The Island: A History of the First Marine Division on Guadalcanal*. 1944; Yardley, PA: Westholme Publishing, 2010.

Miller, John, Jr. *Guadalcanal: The First Offensive*. 1949; Washington, DC: Center of Military History, 1995.

Miller, Lee G. *The Story of Ernie Pyle*. New York: Viking Press, 1950.

Morison, Samuel Eliot. *History of United States Naval Operations in World War II*, vol. 4, *Coral Sea, Midway and Submarine Actions*. 1949; Annapolis, MD: Naval Institute Press, 2010.

Morris, Seymour, Jr. *Supreme Commander: MacArthur's Triumph in Japan*. New York: HarperCollins, 2014.

Mort, Terry. *Hemingway at War: Ernest Hemingway's Adventures as a World War II Correspondent*. New York: Pegasus Books, 2016.

Moseley, Ray. *Reporting War: How Foreign Correspondents Risked Capture, Torture and Death to Cover World War II*. New Haven, CT: Yale University Press, 2017.

Moyar, Mark. *Triumph Forsaken: The Vietnam War, 1954–1965*. New York: Cambridge University Press, 2006.

Mrazek, Robert J. *A Dawn Like Thunder: The True Story of Torpedo Squadron Eight.* New York: Little, Brown and Company, 2008.

Nijboer, Donald. *B-29 Superfortress vs Ki-44 "Tojo."* Oxford, UK: Osprey Publishing, 2017.

Nordyke, Phil. *All American All the Way: The Combat History of the 82nd Airborne Division in World War II.* Saint Paul, MN: Zenith Press, 2005.

Peterson, Theodore. *Magazines in the Twentieth Century.* Urbana: University of Illinois Press, 1964.

Prochnau, William. *Once upon a Distant War: Young War Correspondents and the Early Vietnam Battles.* New York: Times Books, 1995.

Pyle, Ernie. *Brave Men.* New York: Henry Holt and Company, 1944.

Rose, Lisle A. *The Ship That Held the Line: The USS* Hornet *and the First Year of the Pacific War.* Annapolis, MD: Naval Institute Press, 1995.

Scheiber, Harry N., and Jane Scheiber. *Bayonets in Paradise: Martial Law in Hawai'i during World War II.* Honolulu: University of Hawaii Press, 2016.

Schlesinger, Arthur M., Jr. *A Life in the Twentieth Century: Innocent Beginnings, 1917–1950.* Boston: Houghton Mifflin Company, 2000.

Schrijvers, Peter. *Crash of Ruin: American Combat Soldiers in Europe during World War II.* New York: New York University Press, 1998.

———. *The GI War against Japan: American Soldiers in Asia and the Pacific during World War II.* New York: New York University Press, 2002.

Scott, James M. *Target Tokyo: Jimmy Doolittle and the Raid That Avenged Pearl Harbor.* New York: W. W. Norton and Company, 2015.

Sherrod, Robert L. *History of Marine Corps Aviation in World War II.* Washington, DC: Combat Forces Press, 1952.

———. *Tarawa: The Story of a Battle.* 1944; reprint, Fredericksburg, TX: Admiral Nimitz Foundation, 1999.

Silverman, Al, ed. *The Book of the Month: Sixty Years of Books in American Life.* Boston: Little, Brown and Company, 1986.

Sledge, Eugene B. *With the Old Breed at Peleliu and Okinawa.* 1981; New York: Oxford University Press, 1990.

Smith, George W. *The Do-or-Die Men: The 1st Marine Raider Battalion at Guadalcanal.* New York: Pocket Books, 2003.

Smith, Michael S. *Bloody Ridge: The Battle That Saved Guadalcanal.* Novato, CA: Presidio Press, 2000.

Spector, Ronald H. *Eagle against the Sun: The American War with Japan.* New York: Free Press, 1985.

Stein, M. L. *Under Fire: The Story of American War Correspondents.* New York: Julian Messner, 1968.

Steinbeck, John. *Once There Was a War.* 1958; New York: Penguin Books, 2007.

Stille, Mark. *Guadalcanal 1942–43*. Oxford, UK: Osprey Publishing, 2015.

———. *Midway 1942: Turning Point in the Pacific*. Oxford, UK: Osprey Publishing, 2010.

Sweeney, Michael W. *The Military and the Press: An Uneasy Truce*. Evanston, IL: Northwestern University Press, 2006.

Symonds, Craig L. *The Battle of Midway*. New York: Oxford University Press, 2011.

Taylor, Theodore. *The Magnificent Mitscher*. 1954; Annapolis, MD: Naval Institute Press, 1991.

Tillman, Barrett. *Enterprise: America's Fightingest Ship and the Men Who Helped Win World War II*. New York: Simon & Schuster, 2012.

———. *Whirlwind: The Air War against Japan, 1942–1945*. New York: Simon & Schuster, 2010.

Tobin, James. *Ernie Pyle's War: America's Eyewitness to World War II*. New York: The Free Press, 1997.

Toll, Ian W. *The Conquering Tide: War in the Pacific Islands, 1942–1944*. New York: W. W. Norton and Company, 2015.

Treglown, Jeremy. *Mr. Straight Arrow: The Career of John Hersey, Author of* Hiroshima. New York: Farrar, Straus and Giroux, 2019.

Twining, Merrill B. *No Bended Knee: The Battle for Guadalcanal*. New York: Presidio Press, 1996.

Vandegrift, Alexander A., as told to Robert B. Asprey. *Once a Marine: The Memoirs of General A. A. Vandegrift, United States Marine Corps*. 1964; New York: Ballantine Books, 1966.

Voss, Frederick. *Reporting the War: The Journalistic Coverage of World War II*. Washington, DC: Smithsonian Institution Press for the National Portrait Gallery, 1994.

Wheelan, Joseph. *Midnight in the Pacific: Guadalcanal: The World War II Battle That Turned the Tide of War*. Boston: Da Capo Press, 2017.

Wheeler, Keith. *Bombers over Japan*. 1982; Alexandria, VA: Time-Life Books, 1998.

Whelan, Richard. *Robert Capa: A Biography*. New York: Knopf, 1985.

White, Theodore H. *In Search of History: A Personal Adventure*. New York: Harper and Row Publishers, 1978.

Whiting, Charles. *Bloody Aachen*. New York: Stein and Day, 1976.

Willoughby, Charles A., editor in chief. *Reports of General MacArthur: MacArthur in Japan; The Occupation: Military Phase*, vol. 1: Supplement. 1966; Washington, DC: Center of Military History, U.S. Army, 1994.

Wyatt, Clarence R. *Paper Soldiers: The American Press and the Vietnam War*. New York: W. W. Norton and Company, 1993.

Yeide, Harry. *The Longest Battle: September 1944 to February 1945: From Aachen to the Roer and Across*. Saint Paul, MN: Zenith Press, 2005.

Zaloga, Steven J. *Sicily 1943: The Debut of Allied Joint Operations*. Oxford, UK: Osprey Publishing, 2013.

————. *The Siegfried Line 1944–1945: Battles on the German Frontier*. Oxford, UK: Osprey Publishing, 2007.

INDEX